Welfare Economics and Antitrust Policy - Vol. I

Richard S. Markovits

Welfare Economics and Antitrust Policy - Vol. I

Economic, Moral, and Legal Concepts and Oligopolistic and Predatory Conduct

Springer

Richard S. Markovits
University of Texas School of Law
Austin, TX, USA

ISBN 978-3-030-79811-6 ISBN 978-3-030-79812-3 (eBook)
https://doi.org/10.1007/978-3-030-79812-3

This Springer imprint is published by the registered company Springer Nature Switzerland AG
The registered company address is: Gewerbestrasse 11, 6330 Cham, Switzerland

Preface

The vast majority of antitrust-policy analyses executed by economists and antitrust-law professors who are conversant with economics focus exclusively on the economic efficiency of various subsets of antitrust-law-coverable business-conduct and/or the economic efficiency of prohibiting subsets of such conduct. More recently, some younger American antitrust-law professors have argued that antitrust-policy analyses should pay considerable attention to what they claim are the undesirable effects that business-choices that increase seller-concentration have on the distribution of political power[1] and, derivatively, on the desirability of government decisions.[2]

This antitrust-policy study differs from its conventional counterparts in many ways. I will list here 15 of its most salient distinctive characteristics:

---

[1]Although these scholars have not articulated this objection in the following way, I would say that increases in seller concentration probably tend to disserve the instantiation of the liberal norm that all competent members of a society should possess "the same opportunity to influence" or have an "equal influence" on government decisions. I recognize that the expressions "the same opportunity" and "equal influence" require considerable elucidation. I also recognize that, regardless of the defensible way in which the just-referenced expressions are operationalized, the claim that increases in seller concentration disserve the instantiation of this liberal norm is vulnerable to a "countervailing power" critique that is connected to The General Theory of Second Best, which informs the protocol for economic-efficiency analysis that I claim is ex ante economically efficient (see the text that follows)—a critique that focuses on the fact that in a political regime that contains many individual features that would cause political influence to be maldistributed from a liberal perspective, one cannot assume that reducing one such "imperfection" (the greater ability of the owners of companies to exercise political influence by making contributions to political parties/campaigns/candidates and by participating in legislative, executive branch, and adjudicative decisionmaking processes) will tend to improve the relevant outcome. For a discussion of The General Theory of Second Best and the protocol for economic-efficiency analysis I think is ex ante economically efficient, see Chap. 8 infra and Markovits, R. 2020 pp. 1–34.

[2]As Chap. 2 will argue, in liberal-moral-rights-based societies (a category that I believe includes the USA, most Member Nations of the E.U., and many other countries throughout the world), choices can be morally desirable because they instantiate the liberal conception of justice or because they instantiate a morally-defensible conception of the moral good (when they are neither required by nor condemned by the liberal conception of justice).

(1) its economic-efficiency analyses recognize that antitrust policies affect the magnitudes of many categories of economic inefficiency and allocative costs that conventional antitrust-policy analyses ignore—inter alia, affect not only (A) the misallocation that is generated when goods in production are produced in economically-inefficient proportions but (B) the misallocation that results when too many resources are devoted to creating quality-or-variety-increasing (QV) investments in some areas of product-space relative to the amounts devoted to QV-investment creation in other areas of product-space, (C) the misallocation that results when too many resources are devoted to discovering production processes that might be used to produce the products produced in some areas of product-space relative to the amounts allocated to production-process research (PPR) that focuses on the production processes that could be used to produce the products produced in other areas of product-space, (D) the misallocation that results because of the proportions of the economy's resources that are devoted respectively to producing units of extant products (UO production), QV-investment creation, and PPR execution, (E) the misallocation caused by business-decisions about the advertizing and in-store promotion of their products, other aspects of the distribution of their products, and the pricing-techniques that businesses use to sell their products, and (F) the allocative transaction costs that businesses generate and the government generates when responding to business-conduct;
(2) its analyses of the impact that particular exemplars of particular types of business-conduct will have on the prices of the products that are produced in the area of product-space in which the conduct took place as well as on the equilibrium QV-investment or PPR quantities in that area of product-space are based on non-conventional analyses of the determinants of the intensity of price-competition and (QV and PPR) investment-competition;
(3) its analyses of the ability of antitrust-law-enforcement authorities to determine and prove that businesses have engaged in conduct all of whose exemplars the law prohibits or to determine and prove the illegality of particular exemplars of business conduct some of whose exemplars are illegal are based on non-conventional analyses of the determinants of the profitability of various sorts of oligopolistic and predatory conduct, of the determinants of the profits that mergers, acquisitions, and joint ventures can yield their participants in various ways, and of the functions that can be performed by the various surrogates for vertical integration;
(4) its analyses of the determinants of the profitability of the various surrogates for vertical integration firms can employ including the various techniques firms can use to price their products non-oligopolistically/non-predatorily are also non-conventional;
(5) its analyses of the impact that any exemplar of business-conduct will have on the magnitude of any category of economic inefficiency whose magnitude it

may affect take account of The General Theory of Second Best[3]—inter alia, take account of the different ways (different for each category of resource allocation) in which the economy's various Pareto imperfections interact to cause or not cause the profits yielded by exemplars of a relevant category of resource allocations to diverge from their economic efficiency;

(6) its analyses of the impact that antitrust-law-coverable business-conduct and government responses to such conduct have on allocative transaction costs take account of the fact that the interaction of the Pareto imperfections that actual economies contain will normally cause the conduct's impact on private transaction costs to diverge from its impact on allocative transaction costs (will normally "distort" the private-transaction-cost figure [in my judgment, will normally "deflate" that private figure—make it lower than the allocative figure with which it is associated]);

(7) its analyses of the economic efficiency of the various surrogates for vertical integration a firm can employ (including the non-oligopolistic/non-predatory techniques it can use to price its products) are also non-conventional;

(8) its normative evaluations of antitrust-law-coverable business-conduct and of the various responses government can make to such conduct recognize that economic efficiency is not an ultimate value and that, although a choice's economic efficiency is relevant to its desirability from the perspective of utilitarianism, a choice's being economically efficient is neither a necessary nor a sufficient condition for its increasing total utility;

(9) it points out that the members of, participants in, and governments of some societies ("moral-rights-based societies") engage in a bifurcated prescriptive-moral discourse in which a strong distinction is drawn between "the just" and "the moral good" and place a lexically-highest value on the instantiation of their respective conceptions of justice;

(10) it explains why I believe that that the U.S. and most Member Nations of the E. U. are liberal-moral-rights-based societies, delineates the abstract definition and extensions of liberalism, and defines the utilitarian and various non-utilitarian-egalitarian conceptions of the moral good to whose instantiation the members and participants of a liberal-moral-rights-based society may be committed that they are morally entitled to instantiate so long as the choice at issue is not required or forbidden by their society's commitment to a liberal conception of justice;

(11) it analyzes the liberal-moral-rights-violativeness or non-violativeness of the various types of antitrust-law-coverable business-conduct;

(12) it analyzes the impact of the various types of antitrust-law-coverable business-conduct on the instantiation of the utilitarian and non-utilitarian-egalitarian conceptions of the moral good;

---

[3]For the initial detailed mathematical illustration of this theory, see Lipsey and Lancaster 1956.

(13) it articulates the various tests of illegality promulgated by and delineates the categories of business-conduct covered by respectively U.S. antitrust law and E.U. competition law when these two bodies of law are interpreted correctly as a matter or law;

(14) it compares the tests of illegality promulgated by and conduct covered by these two bodies of law correctly interpreted as matters of law; and

(15) it analyzes how the differences between U.S. antitrust law and E.U. competition law as correctly interpreted as matters of law affects their respective "proneness" to prohibit economically-inefficient business-conduct, liberal-moral-rights-violative business-conduct, and business-conduct that disserves the instantiation of the utilitarian and various non-utilitarian-egalitarian conceptions of the moral good.

This book is Volume I of a two-volume study. The study has three parts. Volume I (this book) contains Part I (Chaps. 1–8) and the first two chapters of Part II (Chaps. 9 and 10). Volume II contains the last six chapters of Part II (Chaps. 11–16) and Part III (Chaps. 17 and 18). Part I (Chaps. 1–8) delineates the basic welfare-economics, competition-theory, moral, and legal concepts and analytic protocols I use to examine the impacts of the various types of antitrust-law-coverable business-conduct on economic efficiency, liberal moral rights, and the instantiation of different egalitarian conceptions of the moral good, to evaluate the various responses government can make to each such type of business-conduct, and to identify and assess the differences between U.S. antitrust law and E.U. competition law as written. Part II (Chaps. 9–16) analyzes the impacts of 8 related sets of business-conduct on economic efficiency, liberal moral rights, and the instantiation of various egalitarian conceptions of the moral good as well as the likely ability of government to increase economic efficiency, secure liberal moral rights, and instantiate different egalitarian conceptions of the moral good by prohibiting, permitting, or regulating such conduct. Part III identifies and assesses the differences between U.S. antitrust law and E.U. competition law as written. Chapter 17 describes and compares the tests of illegality promulgated by and the conduct and actor coverages of U.S. antitrust law and E.U. competition law as correctly interpreted as a matter of law. Chapter 18 examines the respects in which the differences between these two bodies of law affect their relative potentials to increase economic efficiency, secure liberal moral rights, and instantiate various egalitarian conceptions of the moral good.

I want to close this Preface with an admission and an explanation. Here is the admission. Some of the chapters of Parts II and III contain shortened versions of accounts of concepts and/or arguments already executed in Part I. I recognize that the repetition renders these chapters in Parts II and III less cost-effective for readers of the whole study. Now the explanation. The sales-reports of my two-volume study Economics and the Interpretation and Application of U.S. and E.U. Antitrust Law—Markovits, R. 2014a and 2014b—reveal that some of its readers electronically downloaded one or more chapters that deal with specific categories of conduct without downloading the chapters that contain discussions of basic concepts and analyses on which the applied chapters rely. Parts II and III repeat some of the material in Part I to render their chapters more comprehensible to readers who download them but not Part I.

Acknowledgements I thank the students, primarily in the USA and Germany, who participated in the courses and lecture-series I have given on U.S. antitrust law, E.U. competition law, economic-efficiency analysis, antitrust-policy analysis, and jurisprudence and constitutional law. I also thank the academic deans and masters-program coordinators, again primarily in the USA and Germany, who enabled me to teach courses and give lecture-series on these topics. Scholarship benefits when its author had the opportunity to explain the ideas it contains orally and to respond to probing questions.

Austin, USA — Richard S. Markovits

References

Lipsey, R., & Lancaster, K. (1956). The general theory of second best. *Review of Economic Studies*, 24, 11–32.

Markovits, R. (2006). Liberalism and tort law: On the content of the corrective-justice-securing tort law of a liberal, rights-based state. *Illinois Law Review*, 2006, 243–300.

Markovits, R. (2014a). *Economics and the interpretation and application of U.S. and E.U. antitrust law* Vol. I *Basic concepts and economics-based legal analyses of oligopolistic and predatory conduct*. Springer.

Markovits, R. (2014b). *Economics and the interpretation and application of U.S. and E.U. antitrust law* Vol. II *Economics-based legal analyses of mergers, vertical practices, and joint ventures*. Springer.

Markovits, R (2020). *Welfare economics and second-best theory: A distortion-analysis protocol for economic efficiency prediction*. Springer.

Contents

Part I
Introduction to Part I: Basic Concepts and Analytic Protocols

Part I contains 8 chapters. Chapter 1 articulates the equivalent-variation-in-wealth-oriented definition of "the impact of a choice on economic efficiency" that this study uses—the definition that I believe creates the variant of this concept that is most useful and that best conforms to professional and popular intuitive understanding.

Chapter 2 discusses the possible moral objectives of antitrust policy—distinguishes various positions that philosophers take on "the nature of" moral claims, identifies two categories of moral claims—claims about "the just" and claims about "the moral good," defines 5 moral categories of societies, describes 5 types of "foundationalist" arguments that purportedly can demonstrate that a particular concept of justice is objectively true and therefore universally applicable, explains two philosophically-informed empirical protocols for determining respectively the moral category in which a given society should be placed and the moral norm that any society of moral integrity is committed to instantiating in the service of the conception of justice or the moral good to which it is committed (and asserts that the USA and most Member Nations of the European Union are liberal-moral-rights-based societies of [admittedly-imperfect] moral integrity), provides an abstract definition of liberalism and an account of the extensions of that norm that are most relevant in the antitrust-policy-analysis context, defines various morally-defensible non-liberal egalitarian conceptions of the moral good to which members of liberal-moral-rights-based societies may subscribe (either individually or in combination).

Chapter 3 examines the tests of antitrust illegality that U.S. antitrust law and/or E.U. competition law promulgate and various other tests of illegality that could be applied to antitrust-law-coverable conduct. More specifically, Chap. 3 defines the specific-anticompetitive-intent, lessening-competition, distorting-competition, and "exploitative abuse of a dominant position" test of illegality, which are promulgated by U.S. antitrust law and/or E.U. competition law. Chapter 3 then defines various tests of antitrust legality that U.S. and E.U. law do not promulgate, though some of their tests of illegality may substantially overlap with individual members of this second set of tests of antirust illegality: (1)(A) an "economic inefficiency of covered conduct" test of illegality or (B) an "economic efficiency of prohibiting covered conduct" test of illegality, (2) a "seller-possession of economic power not acquired exclusively through 'skill, foresight, and industry'" test of illegality, (3)(A) a "liberal-moral-rights-violativeness of covered conduct" test of illegality or (B) a test of illegality under which covered conduct would be illegal if its prohibition would secure liberal moral rights, (4)(A) a test of illegality under which covered conduct would be prohibited if the conduct disserved the instantiation of a specific conception of the moral good or (B) a test of illegality under which covered conduct would be prohibited if its prohibition would secure the instantiation of a specified conception of the moral good, and (5)(A) a test of illegality under which covered conduct would be prohibited if it disserved a more concrete political/social objective (e.g., promoting understanding, friendliness, and empathy among the populations of different E.U. Member Nations or among their governments in part to prevent military conflicts between or among E.U. Member Nations).

Chapter 4 focuses on the concept of seller price-competition. More specifically, Chap. 4 considers the operational definition of the concept of "the intensity of price-competition in a given area of product-space," delineates the components of the gap between a seller's price(s) and its marginal cost(s), and executes a few preliminary analyses of the ways in which antitrust-law-coverable business conduct can affect the magnitudes of those components.

Chapter 5 focuses on investment-competition (both QV-investment competition and PPR competition). More specifically, Chap. 5 considers the operational definition of the concept of "the intensity of (QV-investment or PPR) investment-competition in any area of product-space," provides accounts of the intermediate determinants of the intensity of investment-competition in any area of product-space and the different ways in which those determinants interact to determine the intensity of such competition in different specified situations, and executes some preliminary analyses of the ways in which antitrust-law-coverable conduct can affect the intensity of investment-competition in any area of product-space.

Chapter 6 focuses on the concept of an "economic market." This concept is salient because U.S. antitrust law and E.U. competition law are market-oriented both in the sense that they frequently make the illegality of covered conduct depend on its relevant impact in one or more "markets" (say in "a line of commerce" or "in a line of commerce or a section of the country") and in the sense that (for the above reason) they have always been interpreted to require conclusions about the competitive impact of covered conduct or the motivation of the perpetrators of covered conduct to be generated from estimates of the pre-conduct or post-conduct magnitudes of market-aggregated parameters and/or the effects of the conduct on the magnitudes of those parameters (say, on the pre-conduct market share[s] of the perpetrator[s], on the effect of the conduct on the market shares of the perpetrator[s], on the share of market's sales/investment made/owned by its largest four or eight firms, on the effect of the conduct on that "concentration ratio," on the post-conduct HHI figure for a relevant market and the impact of the conduct whose legality is at issue on that HHI figure [where a defined market's HHI figure equals the sum of the squares of the market shares of the sellers in the defined market]). It should therefore be no surprise that U.S. and E.U. courts and U.S. and E.U. antitrust-law or competition-law enforcement-authorities have devoted much energy to analyzing how markets should be defined and defining "relevant" markets. Industrial Organization economists are no different. An enormous amount of economics scholarship has been devoted to the protocol that should be used to define markets. Originally, this literature focused on what I call "classical economic markets," whose definitions are supposed to satisfy "ideal-type" notions about the intensity of the "competitiveness" of all pairs of products placed in a given market, the "equality" of "the competitiveness" of all pairs of products placed in a given market, and the differences between "the competitiveness" of any pair of products placed in the same market and the "competitiveness" of any product placed in that market with any product not placed in that market. Since the mid-1950s, the economics literature and official documents—such as the U.S. Department of Justice and Federal Trade Commission Horizontal Merger Guidelines and the E.U. European Commission Horizontal Merger Guidelines—have focused on the correct (most-cost-effective) abstract definition of "antitrust markets" and the protocol that should be used to define so-called "antitrust markets"—markets whose definition's quality is to be judged by the contribution that the market definition makes to the "cost-effective" processing of the antitrust case in which it will be used. Chapter 6 not only defines the concepts of "a classical economic market" and "an antitrust market" but demonstrates that definitions of either type of market are inevitably arbitrary not just at their peripheries but comprehensively.

Chapter 7 focuses on the concepts of a firm's economic (market) power or (market) dominance. The concept of market power is relevant to this study because U.S. (federal) courts have held (1) that the legality of a seller's employing a tying agreement depends on whether it possessed market power over the tying good prior to engaging in the conduct in question (see Illinois Tool Works, Inc. v. Independent Ink, Inc. and, more generally, Markovits R. 2014 at pp. 389–393) and (2) that suits alleging that a defendant has monopolized or attempted to monopolize will be dismissed before further evidence is taken (that so-called summary judgments will be rendered in favor of the defendant) unless the State or private plaintiff has demonstrated that the defendant possessed market power in the market in which the allegedly-illegal conduct was perpetrated prior to or after (the holdings are unclear on this point) engaging in the allegedly-illegal conduct in question (see Hovenkamp 2005 at p. 151 for a discussion of this and related holdings). (The fact that these holdings are incorrect as a matter of law correctly interpreted is irrelevant to the point I am now making.) The concept of market "dominance" is relevant to this study because one source of E.U. competition law—Article 102 of the 2009 Treaty of Lisbon—promulgates tests of legality that apply to undertakings that occupy "a dominant position" in the area of product-space in which the relevant conduct took place. Three points or sets of related points about the concepts of market power and market dominance are salient: (1) even if the relevant area of product-space could be defined non-arbitrarily, the concept of a firm's "market power" or "dominant position" in that area of product-space is far more complex than those who invoke it recognize—depends not only on the firm's ability to secure supra-competitive prices but on its ability to obtain supra-normal profit-rates ("control" investment), both of which depend on the firm's monopoly power, its (natural and contrived—see below) oligopolistic power, and the monopoly and oligopoly power of its rivals; (2) there is no non-arbitrary way to decide (A) whether a firm's market power or dominant position depends solely on its power over price, its power over investment, its power over both price and investment, or if on both how on both and (B) whether the power over price or investment that is relevant to its economic power or dominance is its own monopoly power, its own oligopoly power, and/or (effects that are generated by) the monopoly and/or oligopoly power of its rivals; and (3) regardless of the operational definition one gives to "market power" or "market dominance," one cannot accurately infer a firm's market power or dominance from its market share.

Chapter 8 describes the protocol for economic-efficiency prediction or post-diction that this study employs—the protocol that I think responds ex ante economic efficiently to the central point of The General Theory of Second Best: since each individual Pareto imperfection that would individually cause economic inefficiency in an otherwise-Pareto-perfect economy will in general be as likely to counteract as to compound to any given extent the net misallocative tendency of the other Pareto imperfections the relevant economy contains, it is not ex ante economically efficient to predict the impact that a choice will have on economic efficiency by altering the Pareto-imperfectness of the economy in which it is made from whether it increases or decreases the Pareto-imperfectness of that economy. Chapter 8 describes the protocol for economic-efficiency prediction/post-diction that I think responds ex ante economic efficiently to this "mathematical reality." That protocol instructs the analyst (1) to take account of the impact that the choice whose economic efficiency is at issue will have (A) on all the categories of economic inefficiency whose magnitudes it may affect (including many that economists ignore), (B) on allocative transaction costs, and (C) if the choice in question is a government policy-choice, on the allocative transaction costs and misallocation the government will generate when financing the relevant intervention, (2) to base his or her prediction/post-diction of the impact that the choice under review will have on the magnitude of the misallocation that will be generated by economically-inefficient decisions to execute economically-inefficient resource allocations in a given category or not to execute economically-efficient resource allocations in that category inter alia on estimates of the impact of the choice on the magnitude of the difference between the profit-yield and economic efficiency of (on the magnitude of that "distortion" in the profits yielded by) the economics-marginal exemplars of the associated category of resource allocations and the impact of the choice under review on the amount of resources devoted to the resource allocations in question, and (3) to execute those and only those empirical or theoretical research-projects that are ex ante economically efficient.

References

Hovenkamp, H. (2005). *Antitrust*. Thomson West.

Illinois Tool Works, Inc. v. Independent Ink, Inc. 547 U.S. 28 (2006).

Markovits, R. (2014). *Economics and the interpretation and application of U.S. and E.U. antitrust law* Vol. II *Economics-based legal analyses of mergers, vertical practices, and joint ventures*. Springer.

Treaty of Libson Amending the Treaty on European Union and the Treaty Establishing the European Community, 2007 OJ C306 (December 13, 2007).

1 The Concept of "The Impact of a Choice (or Natural Event) on Economic Efficiency"

Although, as Sect. 2.4 will demonstrate, the impact of (antitrust-policy-coverable conduct)/(government responses to such conduct) on economic efficiency is less relevant to (the conduct's)/(the government responses') moral desirability than many suppose, such impacts are relevant to antitrust-policy analysis because (1) they are relevant to the conduct's/(government responses') impact on total utility and (2) many individuals' defensible moral evaluations of such conduct/ (government responses) depend at least in part on their impact on total utility. Even if conventional antitrust-policy analyses did not pay too much attention to the impact of non-government and government choices on economic efficiency, it would be appropriate to begin the study by carefully defining the concept of "the impact of a choice (or natural event) on economic efficiency."

1.1 The Criteria for Evaluating any Proposed Definition of "The Impact of a Choice on Economic Efficiency"

Two criteria should be used to evaluate definitions of such concepts as "the impact of a choice on economic efficiency": the conformity of the definition to professional and popular understanding and the ability of the concept as defined to contribute to the analyses in which it plays a role.

1.2 The "Correct" Definition of "The Impact of a Choice on Economic Efficiency"

In my judgment, the definition of "the impact of a choice on economic efficiency" that best fits the popular and professional understanding of this concept and creates the variant of this concept that can contribute most to the moral evaluation of

R. S. Markovits, *Welfare Economics and Antitrust Policy - Vol. I*,
https://doi.org/10.1007/978-3-030-79812-3_1

choices is a monetized definition that equates that impact with the difference between the equivalent-monetary (henceforth, equivalent-dollar) gains the choice confers on its beneficiaries (the winners) and the equivalent-dollar losses it imposes on its victims (the losers). In this formulation, a winner's equivalent-dollar gain equals the number of dollars that would have to be transferred to the winner to leave him (or her) as well-off as the choice would leave him if

1. he did not agree to the transfer,
2. he either was intrinsically indifferent to the substitution of the transfer for the choice in question or was unaware of the linkage between the transfer and the relevant choice's rejection,
3. his distributive attitude toward such transfers, non-parochial distributive preferences, or normative distributive commitments gave him no reason to prefer the transfer to the choice or vice versa, and
4. the financing of the transfer would not benefit or harm him indirectly by changing the conduct of others by altering their incomes and/or wealths (or by satisfying or dissatisfying his external preferences—i.e., his non-parochial preferences for or against specified others' obtaining resources or having opportunities).

Similarly, in this formulation, a loser's equivalent-dollar loss equals the number of dollars that would have to be withdrawn from him to leave him as poorly-off as the choice would leave him under the loser-counterparts of the four assumptions just delineated.

In essence, this definition of the impact of a choice on economic efficiency incorporates elaborated versions of what economists denominate the "equivalent-variation" as opposed to the "compensating-variation" operationalizations of, respectively, a choice's winners' equivalent-dollar gains and a choice's losers' equivalent-dollar losses: (1) it measures the winners' equivalent-dollar gains by the number of dollars that would have to be transferred to them (on appropriate assumptions) to make them as well-off as the choice would make them as opposed to by the number of dollars whose withdrawal from them (on appropriate assumptions) would leave them as well-off with the choice being made as they would have been had neither the withdrawal nor the choice been made, and (2) it measures the losers' equivalent-dollar losses by the number of dollars whose withdrawal from them would (on appropriate assumptions) leave them as poorly-off as the choice would leave them as opposed to by the number of dollars whose transfer to them would (on appropriate assumptions) leave them as well-off with the choice being made as they would have been had neither the transfer nor the choice been made.

I believe that the preceding definition of "the impact of a choice on economic efficiency" conforms to the intuitive understanding of this concept not only of economists but also of members of the policy-audience and the public in general. In brief, this definition does so because it conforms with the users' of this concept's implicit assumption that the relevant equivalent-dollar gains and losses are being calculated on realistic assumptions about who has won and lost and their wealths at the time at which the choice is made. Moreover, because my definition correctly measures the equivalent-dollar gains of a choice’s winners and the equivalent-dollar losses of the choice’s losers, it operationalizes the concept in the way that enables it to contribute most to the evaluation of choices from normative perspectives that deem relevant (even if indirectly) a choice’s equivalent-dollar impacts on its beneficiaries and victims.

I will now illustrate this second point. I begin by acknowledging that, regardless of whether the concept of “the impact of a choice on economic efficiency” is given a non-monetized definition according to which a choice is said to increase economic efficiency if and only if it makes some relevant creature better-off and no relevant creature worse-off[1] or a monetized definition according to which a choice is said to increase economic efficiency if and only if the equivalent-dollar gains it confers on its beneficiaries exceed the equivalent-dollar losses it imposes on its victims, increases in economic efficiency are not moral desiderata in themselves. Thus, a choice that makes somebody better-off and nobody worse-off may not be deemed morally desirable from various defensible moral perspectives that place a positive value on the resources’ and opportunities’ an individual has matching the moral quality of the creature’s conduct if the creature that is made better-off is a sadistic torturer/murderer (and those who would place a negative value on such a creature’s obtaining a benefit would not be aware that the choice would confer a gain on such an evil-doer). Moreover, the fact that a choice gave its beneficiaries an equivalent-dollar gain that exceeded the equivalent-dollar loss it imposed on its victims might not make the choice morally desirable from a utilitarian perspective if the average marginal utility to the choice’s winners of the equivalent-dollars the choice conferred on them were sufficiently lower than the average marginal utility to the choice’s losers of the equivalent-dollars the choice caused them to lose.

Still, from many normative perspectives, if “the impact of a choice on economic efficiency” is defined in the monetized sense that I claim is “correct,” the concept will make the greatest contribution it could make to the evaluation of the moral desirability of choices from a number of normative perspectives. Let me be more concrete. As Sect. 2.4 argues, the most desirable way from the perspective of utilitarianism to predict the impact of a choice on the total utility of all creatures whose utility counts is not to estimate directly the choice’s utility effects on individuals and then sum those utility effects but (1) to estimate the relevant equivalent-dollar gains and losses the choice would generate (and concomitantly the economic efficiency of the choice), (2) to identify the relevant winners and losers (in particular, the characteristics of the winners and losers that affect the marginal utility of money to them over the relevant ranges), (3) to estimate the average marginal utility to the choice’s winners and losers of the equivalent-dollars they respectively gained and lost, (4) to multiply the relevant equivalent-dollar gain and loss estimates by the associated average-marginal-utility estimates, and (5) to compare the two multiplicands. If the utilitarian-evaluation protocol I have just outlined (actually, a variant of that protocol that focuses on an appropriately-large random sample of any relevant choice’s winners and losers) is optimal from a utilitarian perspective, the definition of the economic-efficiency concept I have proposed will contribute more to utilitarian evaluations of choices than any alternative could do because my definition leads the evaluator to measure accurately any choice's winners' equivalent-dollar gains and any choice's losers' equivalent-dollar losses.[2]

Notes

1. This definition is called the Pareto-superior definition of a choice that increases economic efficiency. Correspondingly, choices that make at least one relevant creature worse-off and no such creature better-off are denominated Pareto-inferior choices. For a further discussion of these definitions, see Markovits (2008), pp. 48–51; (2020), p. 103.
2. For articulations and critiques of the other incorrect definitions of "the impact of a choice on economic efficiency" that economists have proposed and used (those implicit in the Kaldor–Hicks and Scitovsky tests for economic efficiency and the potentially Pareto-superior definition of that concept), see Markovits (2018), pp. 51–62; (2020), pp. 103–107.

References

Markovits, R. (2008). *Truth or economics: On the definition, prediction, and relevance of economic efficiency*. Yale University Press.

Markovits, R. (2020). *Welfare economics and second-best theory: A distortion-analysis protocol for economic-efficiency analysis*. Springer.

The Possible Moral Objectives of Antitrust Policy

2

To analyze the moral desirability of policies, one must understand how to execute moral analyses. This chapter provides brief accounts of basic moral concepts (such as "the just" [moral rights and moral duties] and "the moral good"), of different moral or purportedly-moral decision-criteria or normative positions (such as liberalism, utilitarianism, various non-utilitarian variants of egalitarianism, and libertarianism), of different moral categories of societies, of different types of conceptual arguments that some allege can demonstrate the "objective truth" of a particular conception of "the just" or "the moral good," of the philosophically-informed empirical protocols I believe it is correct to use to identify the moral category to which a particular society belongs, the conception of justice to which a particular "moral-rights-based society" is committed, and the conception of the moral good to whose instantiation a particular "moral-goal-based society" is committed, of different positions that different philosophers and economists have taken on the "intellectual status" of moral arguments and conclusions, of the moral defensibility of the libertarian conception of distributive justice, and of the moral relevance of a choice's impact on economic efficiency. This chapter is included to render more-comprehensible and more-criticizable both my claim that the U.S. and the Member Nations of the E.U. are liberal-moral-rights-based societies and my arguments about the moral desirability of various exemplars of antitrust-policy-coverable business conduct and of the various responses government can make to such conduct.

2.1 Philosophical Concepts and Positions: Some Contestable and Contested Accounts

Various philosophers and non-philosophers take different positions on the nature of claims about the just and the moral good (which they may or may not believe are distinguishable). Moral skeptics and emotivists believe that moral claims have no

R. S. Markovits, *Welfare Economics and Antitrust Policy - Vol. I*,
https://doi.org/10.1007/978-3-030-79812-3_2

substantive content (denotation) or communicate either nothing at all or nothing other than the claimant's strong emotional support for the communicated conclusion. (In my experience, most economists believe that any moral concept that cannot be concretized mechanically [say, deductively in something like a mathematical sense] has no substantive meaning.[1]) Moral relativists believe that moral claims have a distinctive justifying basis and communicate conclusions worthy of consideration—that there is, for example, a substantively-meaningful distinction among moral decision-criteria, immoral decision-criteria, and decision-criteria that have no moral salience—but believe that no morally-defensible moral-evaluation criterion (moral norm) is objectively superior to any other. Foundationalists (spelled with an upper case "F") believe that conceptual argument can demonstrate that a particular concept of the just (or perhaps of the moral good) is objectively true and universally applicable.

Since this study executes many "moral analyses" of various subsets of the categories of business conduct that could be covered by antitrust/competition policy (henceforth "antitrust policy") and of the various responses government can make to such conduct, it is appropriate to indicate at the outset the "ethics" positions that ground its moral analyses. First, I reject moral skepticism and emotivism. Second, I believe that some individuals and some societies draw a strong distinction between prescriptive-moral discourse about "the just" (about moral rights and duties) and prescriptive-moral discourse about "the moral good"—that is, about what choice would be most-morally-desirable in situations in which considerations of justice were not morally determinative and about what choice that was not moral-rights-violative would be most-morally-desirable. Third, I have not been persuaded that any conception of justice or the moral good is "objectively correct" and will proceed on the assumption that no concept of justice or the moral good can be shown to be "morally best." Fourth, with two elaborations that the fifth and sixth points in this list address, this study will adopt the standard moral-relativist position (1) that moral skeptics and emotivism are wrong—that prescriptive-moral analysis generates important conclusions that communicate more than the emotional fervor of those who subscribe to them—but (2) that no moral decision-criterion can be shown to be morally optimal. Fifth, this study supplements moral relativism (1) by claiming that not only individuals but societies can be committed to instantiating a particular conception of the just or the moral good and can fulfill that commitment sufficiently to merit being characterized as individuals or societies of moral integrity and (2) by delineating philosophically-informed empirical protocols (A) for determining whether given societies (or individuals) draw a strong distinction between prescriptive-moral discourse about the just and prescriptive-moral discourse about the moral good, (B) for identifying the conception of the just to which a society that has a justice-commitment is committed or the conception of the moral good to which a society that does not distinguish between the just and the moral good is committed, and (C) for assessing whether a society that might have a moral commitment fulfills that possible commitment sufficiently to deserve to be called a society of moral integrity. Sixth, this study proceeds on the assumption that the societies whose antitrust policies it is assessing are liberal-moral-rights-based societies of moral integrity—that is, (A) draw a strong distinction between discourse about the just and discourse about the moral good, (B) are committed to securing justice to the greatest extent possible, and (C) are committed to instantiating a liberal conception of justice whose abstract definition and antitrust-policy-relevant extensions the study articulates and applies. Seventh, this study explains that, unlike (say) the utilitarian conception of justice, the liberal conception of justice does not decide all moral issues—leaves room for some moral decisions to be grounded on a conception of the moral good—and discusses various conceptions of the moral good that can play a morally-legitimate role in the prescriptive-moral discourse of a liberal-moral-rights-based society (inter alia, some version of the utilitarian conception of the moral good and various non-utilitarian-egalitarian conceptions of the moral good [such as the equal-utility, equal-resource, and different variants of other sorts of equal-opportunity conceptions of the moral good]).

Some elaboration is required. I begin with an example that illustrates the distinction between discourse about moral rights and duties and discourse about the moral good. I should repeat at the outset that I am not claiming that the members and governments of all societies engage in a bifurcated prescriptive-moral discourse that draws this distinction, much less that such a bifurcated prescriptive-moral discourse is "a universal moral reality."

Assume that an individual has been hospitalized after being injured in an automobile accident. My claim is that at least in some societies two sorts of prescriptive-moral questions can be asked about someone's providing help to this accident victim. The first is whether the potential assistance-provider has a moral duty to provide such assistance (and concomitantly whether the victim has a moral right to the particular potential assistance-provider's help). In some societies that engage in the bifurcated moral-prescriptive discourse I am exemplifying (e.g., in the USA), the answer to this first sort of prescriptive-moral question depends on whether the possible assistance-provider has promised the assistance, on whether the possible assistance-provider has a relevant moral-duty-generating status relationship with the victim (e.g., is the victim's spouse, sibling, child, parent, other relative, friend, etc.), and on whether the possible assistance-provider is a culpable cause-in-fact of the victim's need for assistance. I believe that the fact that the members and governments of the USA consider the "facts" just listed to be sources of moral obligation manifests the USA's commitment to instantiating a liberal conception of justice, but that is a matter that will be considered later in this chapter. The point that is relevant at this juncture is that in moral-rights-based societies the conclusion that a possible assistance-provider has no moral duty to provide a victim with assistance leaves unresolved the issue whether it would be morally good for the possible assistance-provider to help the accident victim. The answer that any given individual of moral integrity should give to that question will depend on the conception of the moral good to which he or she is personally committed as well as on various facts that that conception of the moral good makes salient. In individual cases, some conceptions of the moral good will imply that it would be morally good for the potential assistance-provider to help the victim even if the potential assistance-provider has no moral duty to do so or that it would be morally good for the potential assistance-provider to decide this issue for himself or herself. Indeed, if the individual moral evaluator in question rejects his or her society's justice-commitment, he might conclude that it would not only disserve his conception of the moral good but be morally undesirable overall for the relevant potential assistance-provider to help the victim in question even if the evaluator's society's justice-commitment implies that the relevant potential assistance-provider has a moral duty to provide assistance.

To repeat again, I am not claiming that the bifurcated prescriptive-moral discourse just described and exemplified is "a universal moral reality." I am simply saying that such a bifurcated prescriptive-moral discourse is part of the empirical moral practice of some societies—namely, of societies that, in my terms, are moral-rights-based societies that are committed to instantiating a conception of justice (such as a liberal conception of justice—see below) whose instantiation leaves room for discourse about what I call the moral good (a moral desideratum whose defining attributes are to be determined [within the constraints of moral defensibility] by each of the relevant society's individual members for their respective selves and whose instantiation will at least sometimes favor choices that do not violate their society's justice-commitments).

The second concept that requires further elaboration is the concept of foundationalist arguments that purport to derive an objectively-true and therefore universally-applicable concept of justice. At least five categories of such conceptual arguments can be distinguished: (1) "foundationalist" arguments (spelled with a lower case "f") purport to derive such a concept of justice from the concept of "the moral"; (2) Kantian arguments purport to derive such a concept of justice from the concept of human freedom or what would be "rational" for a creature that can plan; (3) Aristotelian arguments purport to derive such a concept from the concept of human flourishing; (4) Natural Rights arguments purport to derive such a concept from the concept of human nature; and (5) Rawlsian arguments purport to derive such a concept from the combination of (A) what Rawls deems morally-appropriate disinterestedness, (B) various allegedly-universal (not culturally-dependent) facts about human society—including the facts of "political affairs," "the principles of economic theory," and "the basis of social organization," (C) "the laws of human psychology" (all of which he also assumes are not culturally dependent), such as the assumption that all human beings prefer more to less of the primary goods of liberty, opportunity, wealth, and authority, the "Aristotelian Principle" that human beings enjoy "the exercise of their realized capacities… [to an extent] that increases the more the capacity is realized or the greater its complexity," and the fact that "one of the main forms of the human good" is "the realization of self that comes from the skillful and devoted exercise of social duties," (D) the (obviously unrealistic) assumption that individuals feel no envy (which I admit may be better described not as an empirical psychological claim but as "the moral premise" that it is morally-wrong to allow envy to critically affect any choice), and (E) the (dubious) claim that it is "rational" to maximin (to make the choice with the best worst outcome).[2]

I have not been convinced by any such foundationalist argument, though I am open to being convinced and have an admittedly-self-serving suspicion that someone with more-philosophical knowledge and skill than I possess might be able to develop a foundationalist foundational argument for a liberal concept of justice, which Sect. 2.2 will describe.

My third elaboration relates to the five moral categories of society I believe are worth distinguishing. The first contains immoral societies—societies that systematically implement one or more decision-criteria whose use is immoral (regardless of whether they articulate their subscription to using the criterion or criteria in question). The second contains amoral societies. Two subsets of amoral societies can be distinguished: The first bases its decisions about the resources and opportunities individuals should have and the way in which individuals should act and be treated more generally on one or more criteria that have no more-salience—for example, on the amount of salt a relevant individual carries in his or her pockets; the second subcategory bases individual decisions of the above types on one or more criteria that are morally defensible but varies the criterion or criteria that are used from case to case on an ad hoc basis. The third moral category of society contains goal-based societies of moral integrity—societies that engage in a unimodal prescriptive-moral discourse that does not distinguish between discourse about the just and discourse about the moral good but are committed to instantiating a morally-defensible conception of the just or moral good and do instantiate that conception sufficiently (given the exonerating explicability of relevant non-fits—see below) to deserve to be called goal-based societies of moral integrity. I would place utilitarian societies in this category regardless of whether their governments and members reference "justice" and "moral rights and duties" because utilitarianism supports the moral desirability of a unimodal prescriptive-moral discourse—because utilitarian "justice" conclusions leave no room for non-utilitarian analyses of the moral good. The fourth moral category of society I distinguish contains moral-rights-based societies of moral integrity. Such societies (1) engage in a bifurcated prescriptive-moral discourse in which a strong distinction is drawn between discourse about the just and discourse about the moral good, (2) are committed to securing justice to the greatest extent possible—to sacrificing any amount of any conception of the moral good to secure even the smallest amount of additional moral-rights-related interests, and (3) conform their choices sufficiently to the conception of justice they are committed to instantiating given the exonerating explicability of relevant non-fits to deserve to be called societies of moral integrity. The fifth and final moral category of society contains "religiously-motivated societies." The members and governments of such societies base their moral decisions on religious texts and/or on the declarations of religious officials. But for one consideration, I would say that whether religiously-motivated societies deserve to be placed in one or the other of the preceding four moral categories depends exclusively on the moral character of the decision-criterion or decision-criteria on which the relevant sacred texts or authoritative religious officials base their conclusions or on whether the texts or officials are consistent in their use of decision-criteria. However, I do not think that the other consideration to which I just alluded can be ignored. Societies that are "religiously-motivated" in the sense in which I defined this expression either instruct those members that are not relevant religious officials to defer to religious officials when making moral choices or to base their moral choices on religious texts that they are instructed to interpret in a way that deprives them of their moral agency. If, as I believe, in this respect, all such societies are immoral—i.e., that it is immoral to instruct individuals to surrender their moral agency, such societies would deserve to be called immoral even if the authoritative religious texts commend morally-defensible choices or the authoritative religious officials announce morally-defensible conclusions.

My fourth elaboration relates to the protocol that should be used to determine the moral category in which a given society should be placed. It should be obvious that the general features of the protocol one should use to determine the moral category in which a particular society belongs are implicit in the various categories' definitions. Thus, to determine whether a society is a moral-rights-based society of moral integrity, one must examine its members' and governments' conduct to determine (1) whether they engage in a bifurcated prescriptive-moral discourse that draws a strong distinction between discourse about the just and discourse about the moral good, (2) place a lexically-highest value on securing justice, (3) make choices and have perceptions (see below) that are sufficiently consistent (see below) with the conclusion that they are committed to a particular conception of justice to justify the conclusion that the society is a moral-rights-based society of moral integrity that is committed to that conception of justice.

My fifth elaboration outlines the philosophically-informed empirical protocols that I believe should be used, respectively, to identify the moral norm that underlies the conception of justice that a particular society that one is assuming ad arguendo has a justice-commitment is committed to instantiating and to determine whether the society in question deserves to be called a moral-rights-based society of moral integrity—see below.[3] (I should add that perfectly-analogous protocols should be used, respectively, to identify the conception of the moral good that a particular society one is assuming ad arguendo is a moral-goal-based society is committed to instantiating and to determine whether that society deserves to be called a moral-goal-based society of moral integrity.)

The first of these protocols has two components. The first, "dimension of fit"-oriented component, examines the extent to which the conclusion that various possibly-justice-grounding "moral principles"—various "candidates" for a given society's justice-grounding "basic moral principle" title—fit the facts it should fit if the society really were committed to instantiating a conception of justice grounded on that moral principle and completely fulfilled its justice-commitments: (1) the moral-rights-claims and moral-rights-related legal-rights claims that were made and not made in the society in question, (2) the arguments that were made and not made in support of and against the moral-rights claims and moral-rights-related legal-rights claims that were made in the society in question by the disputants, by officials who decided the disputes, and by observers who commented on those disputes, (3) the conclusions that were reached about the correctness of the moral-rights claims and related legal-rights claims that were made both by the official decisionmakers who resolved the disputes and by observers, (4) how close the "cases" in question ("cases" enquoted because the relevant data extend to non-legal as well as legal disputes) were perceived to be both by any officials who decided them and by observers, (5) how certain the society's decisionmakers and observers were about the correct resolution of the claims in question (note that Items (4) and (5) in this list are different—one can be certain about the resolution of a close case that is correct if there is no doubt about the abstract definition of any relevant concept, the extensions of any relevant concept, the relative weights of relevant considerations, and any relevant facts), and (6) the extent to which the conduct of the members and governments of the society in question is consistent with the moral obligations and rights they would have if the relevant candidates for the society's basic-moral-principle title were in fact the moral norm that grounded the society's conception of justice.

The second component of this first philosophically-informed empirical protocol focuses on facts that can render non-fits not just explicable but on that account less-damaging to a basic-moral-principle candidate's candidacy: (1) perhaps most-problematically, the fact that the non-fit's winners were more-politically-powerful than its losers (a fact that is problematic because it undermines the conclusion that the society in question has moral integrity at the same time that it helps explain away the non-fit), (2) high conventional transaction costs or other types of transaction costs that may explain why parties whose moral rights have been violated did not make a claim, why parties whose moral rights were not violated did make a claim (attempted to "hold up" the target of the claim), why moral-rights violators did oppose claims against them, and/or why parties that did not violate their accuser's moral rights did not contest the claim made against them, (3) the fact that claimants, accused parties, official decisionmakers, and observers did not adequately consider the non-fitting conduct in which they engaged (e.g., that a moral-rights-violating legislative or enforcement decision was made in haste at a time of crisis), (4) the fact that the actor whose choice was non-fitting was not knowledgeable, intellectually sophisticated, and/or honest, (5) the possibility that the non-fit might be attributable to a conceptual error (e.g., to the conflation of the psychological, welfare, and entitlement senses of "interest" or "concern" or [don't laugh or even smirk: U.S. courts have made this mistake] to a belief that one cannot have a right to privacy in a publicly-owned facility), (6) the fact that the non-fit reflected empirical errors that relevant actors, decisionmakers, or observers made either innocently or in doubtful good faith (e.g., in the U.S., for many years, errors about the intellectual, physical, and moral capabilities of individuals of African descent and of women), and (7) the combination of the fact that the non-fitting choice was commended by a religious text or official that the actor believed that he or she was religiously obligated to follow and the mistaken belief that the alleged religious justification of the choice insulated it from moral scrutiny or condemnation. In any event, under the overall protocol, the moral norm that is associated with the smallest amount of non-fits discounted by their exonerating explicability and measured individually by the disservice they did to the candidate principle's instantiation is the winning candidate for the society's basic-moral-principle title.

The second protocol I want to delineate at this juncture is the protocol for determining whether the conduct and perceptions of the members and governments of a society that may be moral-rights-based or moral-goal-based society of moral integrity is sufficiently consistent with its purported commitments given the possible-partially-exonerating explicability of their failures to live up to their apparent commitments for the society to deserve to be characterized as a society of moral integrity. This second protocol has three components: (1) an analysis of how well the relevant facts must fit the conclusion that the society had the commitment it would be said to have if it had any commitment given the explicability of the non-fits for the society to deserve to be characterized as a society of moral integrity (an analysis about which I must admit I have little useful to contribute), (2) the previously-delineated analysis of the extent of the society's discounted-by-partially-exonerating-explicability non-fits relative to the moral norm to which it would be deemed to subscribe if it subscribed to any moral norm, and (3) a comparison of the society's discounted-fit performances with the discounted-fit performance standard for being a society of moral integrity.

2.2 The Liberal Conception of Justice and Antitrust-Policy Analysis

In my judgment, most countries that have antitrust or competition policies—for example, the USA, the member nations of the British Commonwealth, (most) member nations of the European Union—are not just moral-rights-based societies that fulfill their moral obligations sufficiently to deserve to be called moral-rights-based societies of moral integrity but are liberal-moral-rights-based societies of moral integrity. This judgment implies that, by these societies' own moral lights, the moral desirability of antitrust-policy-coverable conduct depends in part on whether it is liberal-moral-rights-violative, and the moral desirability of their respective governments' responses to such conduct depends in part on whether those responses instantiate the liberal conception of justice. Section 2.2's accounts of the liberal conception of justice and liberalism's antitrust-related implications are included for this reason.

In other publications (e.g., Markovits, R. 1998, 2006a, 2006b), I have provided both a detailed abstract account of the liberal conception of justice and detailed analyses of some of its concrete corollaries both for the moral obligations of members of liberal-moral-rights-based societies and for the moral obligations of the governments of such societies. I will limit myself here to providing a less-elaborate abstract account of the liberal conception of justice and an analysis of liberalism's antitrust-policy-relevant corollaries.

On my understanding, liberalism is a normative position that places a lexically-highest value on those creatures, that possess the neurological prerequisites for leading a life of moral integrity (on moral-rights bearers') having a meaningful opportunity to lead such lives and seizing that opportunity (1) by considering carefully the concrete corollaries (extensions) of liberalism, (2) by taking seriously the dialectical[4] task of developing their own conceptions of the moral good, and (3) by making choices that fulfill their liberal moral obligations and instantiate their respective personally-subscribed-to conceptions of the moral good.[5] Liberalism has concrete implications for the moral obligations both of the members of (and participants in—henceforth "members of") liberal-moral-rights-based societies and for such societies' governments. At the most-abstract level, liberalism implies that the moral-rights-bearing members of a liberal-moral-rights-based society have a basic moral obligation to treat each other with appropriate, equal respect and to show appropriate concern[6] for each other's "welfare" in part for their "utility" but pre-eminently for their having a meaningful opportunity to take their lives morally seriously. (I should acknowledge that the word "appropriate" needs to be operationalized and will be given some attention in the text that follows.) At the most-abstract level, liberalism implies that the governments of a liberal-moral-rights-based society are obligated to treat all moral-rights bearers for whom they are responsible with appropriate, equal respect and to show appropriate, *equal* concern for their "welfare."[7]

I will now address those more-concrete corollaries of liberalism (or of moral analysis more generally) that have implications for the liberal-moral-rights-violativeness of antitrust-policy-coverable business conduct and the antitrust-policy-related-moral obligations of the governments of a liberal-moral-rights-based society. I begin with one empirical assumption and one admittedly-contestable moral argument that bear on the moral obligations of members of liberal-moral-rights-based societies (and, derivatively, on the moral duties of the governments of such societies). The empirical assumption is that antitrust-policy-coverable conduct will never imperil any moral-rights bearer's ability to lead a life of moral integrity by killing such a moral-rights bearer, inflicting a neurological injury on a moral-rights bearer that deprives him or her of the intellectual capacity to act morally responsibly, or by imposing losses on a moral-rights bearer that are sufficiently devastating to deprive him or her of the psychological capacity to act morally responsibly.[8] In other words, I will assume that antitrust-policy-coverable business conduct inflicts what I have elsewhere called "mere-utility losses" on its losers.[9]

The second general point I want to make at this juncture relates to the metric for gains and losses that should be used to determine the liberal-moral-rights-violativeness of antitrust-policy-coverable conduct. Liberalism proclaims that when making choices that impose losses on others (see below) moral-rights bearers must give appropriate weight to the losses their decisions impose on others[10]—in particular, proclaims that choices that inflict losses on others in relevant ways are liberal-moral-rights-violative if the perpetrator would not have found the choice profitable or attractive if he or she had placed the same weight on each unit of loss the choice would impose on others as on each unit of gain it would confer on the actor. Obviously, this formulation leaves unspecified the nature of each loss-unit and each gain-unit whose relative total magnitudes determine the liberal-moral-rights-violativeness of the choice that generated them. One might think that—indeed, my use of the expression "mere-utility losses" seems to favor the conclusion that—the relevant desideratum is the util (a unit of utility). In fact, however, I think the relevant desideratum is a unit of equivalent-dollar loss or gain. I reach this conclusion not (1) because of the difficulty of mapping all affective states (ecstasy, pleasure, contentment, calmness, agitation, discontent, displeasure, pain, agony, etc.) into units of utility or disutility but (2) because the actor whose choice's liberal-moral-rights-violativeness is at issue is not (usually) a cause-in-fact or a fortiori a morally-responsible cause-in-fact of the interpersonal differences that could cause the liberal moral assessment of the actor's choice to depend on whether the losses and gains whose relative total magnitudes determine the liberal wrongfulness of the choice that generated them are to be measured in utils or equivalent-dollars. Let me be more specific. Three points are salient: (1) for a choice that should be predicted to yield the chooser and its other beneficiaries an equivalent-dollar gain that would be at least as large as the equivalent-dollar loss it should be predicted to impose on its losers to be predicted to yield the chooser and its other beneficiaries a prospective utility gain that was lower than the utility loss it should be predicted to impose on its losers, the average utility loss that would be associated with the equivalent-dollar losses the chooser should have predicted his or her choice would generate for the choice's losers must exceed the average utility gain that would be associated with the equivalent-dollar gains the chooser should have predicted his or her choice would generate for it and the choice's other beneficiaries sufficiently to offset or more-than-offset any positive difference between the equivalent-dollar gains the chooser should have predicted the choice to yield and the equivalent-dollar losses the chooser should have predicted its choice would impose on its losers; (2) the average utility loss that will be associated with the equivalent-dollar losses the chooser should have predicted its choice would generate will exceed the average utility gain associated with the equivalent-dollar gains the chooser should have predicted its choice would confer on it and the choice's other beneficiaries if (A) the choice's losers were less-well-off than the choice's winners pre-choice, as-well-off as the choice's winners pre-choice, or better-off than the choice's winners pre-choice by more than they were worse-off than the choice's winners post-choice and/or (B) the losers' (weighted-average marginal-utility-of-money function was higher than the chooser's weighted-average marginal-utility-of-money) function (ceteris paribus, the weighted-average losers gained more-utility from the desiderata money can buy than the choice's winners did where the relevant weights are proportionate to the individual losers' respective equivalent-dollar losses and individual winners' respective equivalent-dollar gains); and (3) the chooser is rarely if ever either a cause-in-fact or a fortiori a morally-responsible cause-in-fact of either of these possible differences between the choice's winners' and losers' wealth positions or "hedonistic dispositions."

I will now address in this order (1) the extensions of the liberal conception of justice that are most relevant to the liberal-moral-rights-violativeness of antitrust-policy-coverable conduct and (2) the four extensions of the liberal conception of justice that are most relevant to the antitrust-policy-related moral duties of the governments of a liberal-moral-rights-based society. In each instance, I will begin by discussing the extension in question and then analyze its antitrust-policy-coverable-conduct-related or antitrust-policy-related implications.

The first antitrust-policy-coverable-conduct-related extensions derive from the fact that liberalism draws a strong distinction between the moral duties that moral-rights bearers have (when acting in non-political capacities) to confer benefits on other moral-rights bearers and the moral duties they have (when acting in non-political capacities) to avoid conferring losses (in particular ways) on other moral-rights bearers. More specifically, although liberalism does imply that moral-rights bearers do sometimes have positive moral duties to confer benefits on others,[11] controlling for the equivalent-dollar cost to a moral-rights bearer of conferring a given equivalent-dollar gain or avoiding imposing the same equivalent-dollar loss on another moral-rights bearer and controlling as well for the difference between the associated equivalent-dollar effect of a choice on its prospective beneficiary and the chooser, liberalism is more-disposed to impose a negative duty on moral-rights bearers to avoid imposing equivalent-dollar losses on other moral-rights bearers than a positive duty on moral-rights bearers to confer equivalent-dollar gains on other moral-rights bearers. I base this conclusion on the "definitional fact" that liberalism places a lexically-highest value on moral-rights bearers' having a meaningful opportunity to lead lives of moral integrity and seizing that opportunity and on the following three, admittedly-contestable empirical psychological claims:

1. individuals are more likely to take their lives morally seriously if they perceive themselves to be the authors of their own lives;
2. individuals are less likely to perceive themselves to be the authors of their own lives the greater the extent to which their society's moral-rights positions and laws restrict their morally-legitimate and lawful "opportunity set"—the set of choices that is deemed morally legitimate and lawful for them to make; and
3. controlling for the magnitudes of the other components of the "costliness" of the positive and negative moral/legal duties in question, moral-rights positions and laws that impose, respectively, positive moral duties and positive legal duties on individuals (duties to benefit others) have a greater tendency to undermine their addressees' perceptions that they are the authors of their own lives than do moral-duty positions and laws that impose on individuals negative moral duties and negative legal duties (not to inflict losses on others).

This claimed extension of liberalism implies that firms have no liberal moral obligation to benefit their prospective and/or actual customers (or for that matter, their rivals). More concretely, it implies that (1) firm decisions to use complicated pricing-techniques that reduce the buyer surplus their customers secure without reducing the absolute attractiveness of the best offers against which the firm must compete are not liberal-moral-rights-violative and (2) firm decisions to make a more-profitable QV investment or to execute a more-profitable PPR project whose use will generate less buyer surplus rather than to create a less-profitable QV investment or to execute a less-profitable PPR project whose use will generate more buyer surplus are not liberal-moral-rights-violative, regardless of whether the choice that was made was more-economically-efficient or less-economically-efficient than the choice that was rejected.

The second extension of the liberal conception of justice that bears on the liberal-moral-rights-violativeness of antitrust-policy-coverable business conduct is its implication that conduct that is motivated by specific anticompetitive intent is liberal-moral-rights-violative in that it fails to show appropriate, equal respect and appropriate concern for the perpetrator' or perpetrators' actual and prospective customers, sometimes for the actual and prospective customers of the perpetrator's or the perpetrators' mutual rivals, and sometimes for one or more of the perpetrator's rivals or for one or more of the perpetrators' mutual rivals. In my terminology, conduct is motivated by its perpetrator's or perpetrators' "specific anticompetitive intent" if the perpetrator's or perpetrators' ex ante perception that the conduct was at least normally profitable was critically affected by its/their belief that it would or might reduce the absolute attractiveness of the best offers against which it or they would have to compete (by deterring a rival from competing, reducing the absolute proficiency of the rival's operations [e.g., by reducing the rival's access to credit, IP, or personnel], driving a rival out, deterring a rival investment, or bringing the rival "in-house" through a merger or acquisition) in one or more ways that would render the conduct profitable though it would be economically inefficient in an otherwise-Pareto-perfect economy. From the perspective of liberalism, four facts about conduct that manifests specific anticompetitive intent are salient:

1. the profitability of the conduct cannot be deemed to justicize it because, even if the perpetrator(s) (correctly) believe that some of the profits that the conduct will yield it/them are morally defensible, if, ex ante, one or more of the perpetrator(s) would not have perceived the conduct to be at least normally profitable unless it/they believed that the conduct would or might yield it/them profits in one or more ways that are not morally defensible (by reducing the absolute attractiveness of the most-attractive offers against which it/they would have to compete in one or more ways that would render the conduct profitable in an oPp economy despite the fact that it would be economically inefficient in such an economy): thus, the facts that the participants in a horizontal merger or acquisition believed ex ante (A) that it would be at least normally profitable and (B) that some of the operating profits it would yield them would be morally defensible (e.g., the profits it would yield them by creating a resulting firm that would operate more-allocative-proficiently than the participants would have operated as separate entities after the date of the M or A) would not justicize the (M or A) if one or more participants' ex ante perception that the M or A would be at least normally profitable was critically affected by its/their belief that the (M or A) would or might increase their profits by freeing them from each other's price-competition and/or reducing the amount of rival investments that would be operative in the relevant area of product-space;
2. the predatory exemplars of such conduct seek to give the perpetrator(s) a survival advantage not attributable to their organization's being more allocatively

efficient than their target's (such conduct constitutes unfair competition as opposed to competition on the merits);
3. conduct in this category (that has no efficiency justification) that is designed to worsen the objective competitive position of one or more rivals without driving them out by preventing them from operating proficiently (e.g., by blocking the entrance to a rival's store or making inherently-unprofitable purchases of personnel, IP rights, or raw materials the rival wants to hire/purchase) unfairly disadvantages the rival by placing it at a competitive disadvantage that it would not face absent the unjustifiable conduct in question; and
4. all conduct that is motivated by specific anticompetitive intent imposes equivalent-dollar losses on the actual and prospective customers of the perpetrator(s) and its (their) rivals that exceed the equivalent-dollar gains it confers on the perpetrator(s) in that, for example, any associated price-increases increase seller surplus by less than they decrease buyer surplus because price-increases reduce transaction surplus by reducing unit sales.

These facts imply that specific-anticompetitive-intent-motivated conduct (1) violates the liberal moral rights of any buyers on whom it imposes equivalent-dollar losses in that the perpetrator's or perpetrators' decisions to engage in such conduct yields it/them profits it/they cannot justify and manifests its/their placing less-weight on the average equivalent-dollar lost by the relevant buyers and rivals than on the average equivalent-dollar gained by the perpetrator(s) and (2) violates the liberal moral rights of any rival of the perpetrator(s) on whom it imposes an equivalent-dollar loss because (A) the profits the conduct yields its perpetrator(s) cannot be morally justified, (B) in many instances, the conduct constitutes unfair competition as opposed to competition on the merits, and (C) usually the profits the conduct yields its perpetrator(s) are lower than the equivalent-dollar loss the conduct imposes on relevant buyers and rivals all tolled.

The third extension of liberalism that relates to the liberal-moral-rights-violativness of antitrust-policy-coverable conduct could be described as a variant of the second in that it also focuses on conduct that is motivated by specific anticompetitive intent. Liberalism implies that a firm's decision to place one or more of its rivals at an undeserved competitive disadvantage by making false claims about its own product, by explicitly denigrating the target rival's product, or by joining with some rivals through a trade association or conceivably by using disinformation or bribes to induce the government to promulgate safety or quality standards that imply incorrectly that the target rival's product is less-safe or less-good for some other reason than it actually is is liberal-moral-rights-violative for the same reasons that other variants of conduct that are motivated by specific anticompetitive intent are liberal-moral-rights-violative. I have distinguished this implication of liberalism from its immediate predecessor because this variant of specific-anticompetitive-intent-motivated conduct succeeds by reducing the buyer-perceived absolute attractiveness as opposed to the objective absolute attractiveness of the offers against which the perpetrator(s) will have to compete.

I turn now to the four extensions of liberalism that have most relevance to the antitrust-policy-related duties of the governments of any liberal-moral-rights-based society. All four derive from the "fact" that the governments of any moral-rights-based society (whether liberal or non-liberal) are morally obligated to secure the moral rights of its members (and participants) to the greatest extent that it can. Two of these extensions are actually extensions of the generic concept of justice whose concrete implications depend on the relevant moral-rights-based society's being a liberal-moral-rights-based society, and two of these extensions are more specifically related to liberalism.

The first extension in this category derives from the fact that the governments of any moral-rights-based society are morally obligated to secure the moral rights of those for whom it is responsible to the greatest extent possible. The antitrust-policy-related corollary of this claim is that the governments of moral-rights-based societies are morally obligated (1) to respond to the antitrust-policy-coverable conduct of non-government actors in the way that maximizes the extent to which the moral rights of those for whom it is responsible are secured and (2) not to engage in moral-rights-violating antitrust-policy-coverable conduct itself. When the society in question is a liberal-moral-rights-based society, these obligations focus on the liberal moral rights of those for whom the relevant governments are responsible. Two elaborations are required.

First, to fulfill its obligation to secure the liberal moral rights of those for whom it is responsible to the greatest extent possible, the governments of a liberal-moral-rights-based society must adjust their antitrust-policy-implementation protocol to take morally-appropriate account of the liberal moral rights of its society's members not to be forced to testify against themselves, not to have confessions coerced from them, to be found liable in a civil case only if liability has been established by a preponderance of evidence, to be found guilty in a criminal case only if guilt had been established "beyond a reasonable doubt,"[12] not to have "costs" imposed on them if found liable/guilty (damage-awards, civil fines, custodial sentences, non-custodial restrictions) that are more burdensome than the conduct in question was morally wrongful (say, to increase deterrence), etc. Second, if the relevant society's material and human resources and knowledge-base do not suffice to enable its governments to secure all of what would otherwise be the liberal moral rights of all those moral-rights bearers for whom they are responsible, the governments' duty is to secure the relevant individuals' liberal moral rights to the greatest extent possible (to maximize the extent to which the relevant moral-rights-bearers' moral-rights-related interests are secured when it cannot secure all of what might be called their "prima facie liberal mora rights"). More concretely, this extension of the liberal conception of justice implies that the governments of a liberal-moral-rights-based society have a moral duty to prohibit all antitrust-policy-coverable conduct that "directly" (see below) violates the liberal moral rights of the actual and possible customers of the perpetrator(s), of the actual and possible customers of the perpetrator's or perpetrators' rivals, and/or of the rivals of the perpetrator(s)—more specifically, to prohibit all conduct that is motivated by specific anticompetitive intent including acts of unfair competition that are designed to induce potential buyers to undervalue the products/services of one or more of the perpetrator's or perpetrators' rivals relative to the value of the perpetrator's or perpetrators' products/services[13]—and to enforce such prohibitions to the greatest extent it can without violating its basic obligation to maximize the extent to which the liberal-moral-rights-related interests of those for whom it is morally responsible are secured.

The second antitrust-policy-related extension of the concept of justice or the liberal conception of justice is that the governments of a (liberal) moral-rights-based society are morally obligated to provide victims of (liberal-)moral-rights-violating antitrust-policy-coverable business conduct with an appropriate opportunity to obtain legal redress from the violators of their relevant moral rights by making the wrong civilly actionable and making justice appropriately available to such victims by holding down court-fees, providing legal aid, and providing evidence and other sorts of assistance when appropriate.

The third antitrust-policy-related extension of the concept of justice or the liberal conception of justice I want to discuss is an extension of liberalism. In my judgment, liberalism implies inter alia that governments of any liberal-moral-rights-based society have a moral obligation to insure that all creatures for whom they are morally responsible who possess the neurological prerequisites for taking their lives morally seriously receive the material wherewithal (nutrition, clothing, housing, health care), psychological nurturing, formal education, opportunities to form and participate in intimate relationships, privacy protection, exposure to alternative moral systems, religions, and lifestyles, etc., that contribute significantly to their having a meaningful opportunity to take their lives morally seriously. Some antitrust-policy-coverable conduct may inflict equivalent-dollar losses on some of its losers that critically reduce their opportunity to lead a life of moral integrity. Although liberalism does not imply that such conduct is liberal-moral-rights-violative on that account since liberalism does not imply that non-government actors have a generic moral obligation when performing non-political roles to provide others with material wherewithal that will critically affect their opportunity to lead a life of moral integrity, it does imply that the governments of a liberal-moral-rights-based society have a moral obligation to prevent any moral-rights bearer for whom they are responsible from suffering a life-of-moral-integrity-imperiling diminution of his or her material wherewithal probably by transferring resources to individuals who have suffered such losses.

The fourth antitrust-policy-related extension of the concept of justice or the liberal conception of justice I want to discuss is also an extension of the liberal conception of justice (though it might be an extension of various other [say, utilitarian, equal-utility-egalitarian, or equal-resource-egalitarian] conceptions of justice as well). In my judgment, the liberal right of individuals to be treated by their governments with appropriate, equal respect and concern entails a moral right to participate equally in the society's electoral processes and government-decisionmaking processes and a moral right to have one's parochial interests and morally-defensible moral-good positions have an influence on governmental decisions that gives them a weight that is proportionate to the percentage of the members of the society in question that shares them. (I recognize that these claims require substantial additional specification.) Unless the governments of a given society do something to prevent this outcome, some antitrust-policy-coverable conduct will disserve these liberal-moral-rights-related interests of the members of a liberal-moral-rights-based society by concentrating the seller-side of a particular area of product-space and thereby enabling its sellers to exercise undue influence on government decisionmaking by helping them to reduce and/or overcome the collective-action problem that would otherwise prevent them from making collectively the amount of expenditures on political parties/campaigns/candidates and legislative/administrative/adjudicative government-decisionmaking-process participation that would be in their collective interest to make. (I recognize the possibility that any related increase in one set of sellers' political influence may not disserve this interest of the members of a liberal-moral-rights-based society because different sets of sellers' efforts to secure inappropriately favorable government decisions may counteract each other. However, I believe that—although the just-referenced possibility may be salient in individual instances—across all "cases" the power that sellers exercise because the seller-sides of their area of product-space are concentrated produces illiberal outcomes and violates liberal participation and influence rights.) Once more, governments could prevent this outcome directly by prohibiting the business conduct in question and/or indirectly (and, I suspect, preferably) by placing limits on corporate electoral and government-decisionmaking-process expenditures, by prohibiting elected and non-elected government officials from accepting emoluments when in government service or working for those who were affected by the decisions they made when in government service after they leave government service, by improving the hiring standards/training/salaries of government "workers," by requiring government decisionmakiers to provide reasoned justification for their decisions, etc.[14]

2.3 Conceptions of the Moral Good and the "Moral Goodness" of Various Categories of Antitrust-Policy-Coverable Conduct and Antitrust Policies

The members of a liberal-moral-rights-based society can individually subscribe to any of a large number of morally-defensible conceptions of the moral good (which can also be the conception of the moral good that a moral-goal-based society of moral integrity is committed to instantiating). This section delineates a number of morally-defensible conceptions of the moral good, explains why I find morally indefensible one variant of the conception of the moral good that values the resources and opportunities' that individuals receive appropriately matching the "moral worthiness" of their conduct—the distributive component of the libertarian variant of this conception, and investigates the implications of the preceding analyses for the "moral goodness" of various categories of antitrust-policy-coverable business conduct and the "moral goodness" of various antitrust policies.

2.3.1 Some Morally-Defensible Conceptions of the Moral Good

At least two utilitarian conceptions of the moral good[15] and a number of non-utilitarian-egalitarian conceptions of the moral good are (or may be) morally defensible. To start, utilitarian conceptions of the moral good would be morally defensible if one could measure all affective experiences (ecstasy, happiness, pleasure, contentment, boredom, discontent, pain, unhappiness, anger, agony, etc.) by units of utility or disutility (by utils). According to the first utilitarian conception of the moral good or moral desirability—the classical-utilitarian conception, the "moral goodness" of a non-government or government choice (or of a natural event) should be measured exclusively by its impact on the total utility of all creatures whose utility counts. According to the second, more-modern utilitarian conception of the moral good, the moral goodness of a choice or the moral desirability of a natural event should be measured exclusively by its impact on the average utility of all creatures whose utility counts. These two conceptions of utilitarianism must be distinguished because they may yield critically-different moral-good conclusions in cases in which the choice or natural event in question alters the number of creatures who satisfy the criterion or criteria for a creature's utility's counting morally. To be complete, both these variants of utilitarianism must specify and morally justify their conclusion about the attributes that a creature must possess for its utility to count: I am disposed to believe that in a utilitarian goal-based society, the qualifying attributes for any creature's utility to count in a moral-good assessment is its possessing the capacity to experience utility and disutility, and I see no reason why that conclusion should also not apply when the utilitarian assessment plays the more limited role it plays in the prescriptive-moral-discourse of liberal-moral-rights-based societies where the attribute a creature must have to be moral-rights-bearing—that is, to possess moral-rights-related interests that count in the determination of whether a choice is liberal-moral-rights-violative or is mandated by the society's commitment to a liberal conception of justice—is possessing the neurological prerequisites for leading a life of moral integrity.[16] However, for simplicity, this study will proceed on the conventional assumption that the variant of utilitarian analysis that is in play takes account of those and only those utility effects that are experienced by moral-rights bearers.

Utilitarianism can be characterized as an egalitarian conception of the moral good because it gives equal weight to each unit of utility or disutility, regardless of the identity of the morally-relevant creature that experiences it. A large number of non-utilitarian-egalitarian conceptions of the moral good are also morally defensible: egalitarian conceptions that value all relevant creatures' (1) experiencing the same amount of utility, (2) being allocated the same amount of resources measured by their allocative cost, or, more morally contestably, (3) having the same opportunity to develop and/or exercise some specific skill whose development and/or exercise the subset of egalitarians in question particularly values. (Note that the set of equal-opportunity conceptions of the moral good does not include liberalism since liberalism places a lexically-higher value on relevant creatures' having a meaningful as opposed to an equal opportunity to lead a life of moral integrity. I acknowledge, however, that liberalism does imply that all relevant creatures should have an equal opportunity to participate in electoral and government-decisionmaking processes and to influence government outcomes.) Obviously, a full account of these different non-utilitarian-egalitarian conceptions of the moral good must include an operational specification of the inequality-metric each uses.

A third general family of conceptions of the moral good that may be morally defensible contains conceptions that value relevant creatures' having resources and opportunities that match the moral merit of their conduct. This family of moral-good conceptions includes the version of retributivism that values punishing wrongdoers because respect for their moral agency implies that they should be sanctioned for their wrongdoing (not because it would give their victims or other observers pleasure to see the wrongdoers have negative experiences or because it would deter future wrongdoing). I hasten to add that the members of this family of conceptions of the distributive moral good includes not only positions that favor punishing morally-bad conduct but also positions that favor rewarding morally-good conduct where the moral goodness and moral badness of conduct may depend not only on whether it violates or fulfills (liberal) moral obligations but also on whether it serves or disserves the instantiation of a (morally-defensible) conception of the moral good. Obviously, a complete account of any such "matching rewards to conduct-related desert" conception of the moral good would have to specify the "non-match" metric its proponents deem morally desirable to use.

Finally, I should point out that it is morally-defensible for individuals to subscribe to a "mixed" conception of the moral good according to which two or more of the morally-defensible desiderata just listed play a role. In fact, I am certain that many members of liberal-moral-rights-based societies subscribe to such a mixed conception of the moral good—for example, value both total utility and the equality of utility.[17]

2.3.2 One Conception of the Distributive Moral Good That I Think Is Morally Indefensible: The Libertarian Conception of the Distributive Moral Good

I focus on the libertarian conception of distributive justice because many Americans appear to subscribe to it—that is, appear to believe that it would be morally good (or that justice requires) that individuals receive resources whose allocative cost equal "the dollar value of what they produced."[18] I do not find this moral claim defensible, but before explaining why, I want to point out two ambiguities in the concept "the dollar value of what they produced." First, one must specify whether the relevant dollar value is (1) the dollar value of the relevant labor to the worker's employer (or the profits the individual's efforts yield the "employer" if he or she is an entrepreneur, is self-employed in the market, or does non-market labor) or (2) the allocative value of the individual's efforts—the net equivalent-dollar gain those efforts yielded all those affected. Even if one assumes that the relevant figure relates to what might be called[19] the marginal product of the worker in question (as I think the Lockean position from which this strain of libertarianism derives implies one should)—i.e., to the dollar value generated by the last person who performed the relevant individual's work as proficiently and assiduously as he did, the (total) "marginal revenue product" of the last worker will equal his or her (total) marginal allocative product only rarely and fortuitously (only if the economy is Pareto-perfect [see Chap. 8]) or the extant Pareto imperfections perfectly counteract each other's individual tendencies to cause marginal revenue product to diverge from marginal allocative product—in my terminology, to "distort" marginal revenue product). Second, one must determine whether the dollar value of an individual's "production" should be defined to refer to the "marginal revenue product" or "marginal allocative product" of all the labor performed by the last individual to perform his work as skillfully and assiduously as he did or to the average "marginal revenue product" or average "marginal allocative product" of all the workers who performed his category of labor as proficiently and assiduously as he did. To see why this distinction matters, assume that all relevant doctors are equally skilled and assidious and supply an equally-valuable type of medical services and that all relevant sanitation workers are equally skilled and assidious and perform an equally-valuable type of labor and note that although the "marginal revenue product and marginal allocative product" of the last doctor are, respectively, almost certainly much higher than the "marginal revenue product and marginal allocative product" of the last sanitation worker, I suspect that the "average revenue product and average allocative product" of the average sanitation worker are higher than their counterparts for the average doctor. (The members of industrialized, urban societies would be very sick indeed if sanitation workers did not dispose of their garbage.) I mention this second ambiguity despite the fact that the Lockean origin of libertarianism favors a reading of this libertarian norm that focuses on "the product" of the last rather than the average worker in any category (since it claims that each individual is entitled to keep whatever he or she contributed to [added to] the relevant society's output) because the initial response of the vast majority of self-styled libertarians to whom I have raised this issue was that the relevant referent was the "product" of the average as opposed to the marginal worker in any relevant set of relevantly-identical workers. (I wrote "initial" because many of these interlocutors changed their minds when I used the doctor/sanitation-worker example to illustrate the salience of this issue.)

I will now offer a moral critique of the variant of the libertarian position that claims that (ignoring any complication introduced by gifts, bequests, and lucky findings) it is just or morally good for individuals to be allocated resources whose allocative cost equals their respective contributions to their society's total allocative products. For this libertarian conception of distributive justice or the distributive moral good to be morally defensible, individuals must be morally responsible for their contribution to the allocative value of their society's output (including leisure). Even if one rejects determinism and agrees that individuals' productivity is partially attributable to choices they made for which they are morally responsible (in some cases, for which they deserve moral credit), there can be no doubt that a high percentage of interpersonal differences in such productivity is attributable to factors over which the relevant individuals had no control: their genetic endowments, the nutrition they received in utero, the material, intellectual, and emotional support they were given in their infancy, the family and neighborhood in which they grew up, the formal education that was available to them, the "utility" preferences of potential consumers of the products and services they could create or produce, the wealths and incomes of potential buyers of the products and services they could create or produce, the errors that potential buyers of their labor or the goods they could create or produce would make when buying those goods, the externalities generated by the creation, production, and consumption of the goods they could create or produce, the availability of complements to the products and services they could create or produce, the number of individuals who had the knowledge and skills needed to perform their category of labor, the other sorts of labor their potential competitors could perform and the facts that determine the market value of the alternative labor their competitors could perform, and so on and so forth. Even if one grants that individuals are partly morally responsible for their respective allocative products, the percentage of inter-individual differences in individual allocative products that is attributable to factors over which the relevant individuals had no or little control seems to me to be clearly too high for the variant of the libertarian conception of distributive justice or the distributive moral good on which I am now focusing to be morally defensible.

2.4 The Moral Relevance of the Economic Efficiency of Antitrust-Policy-Coverable Business Conduct and the Economic Efficiency of Particular Antitrust Policies: Some Preliminary Comments

This section's analyses are preliminary because to be thorough one would have to take account of the conclusions that subsequent chapters will generate about (1) the determinants of the economic efficiency, liberal-moral-rights-violativeness, and impact on the instantiation of various conceptions of the moral good of the various categories of antitrust-policy-coverable business conduct and (2) the determinants of various antitrust policies' impacts on economic efficiency, liberal moral rights, and the instantiation of different conceptions of the moral good. This section's preliminary analyses will proceed on four assumptions or sets of related assumptions. The first set is that (1) the profits yielded by conduct that increases/decreases the amount of resources devoted to creating new product variants, new distributive outlets, and/or additional capacity and inventory (devoted to creating what I call quality-or-variety-increasing [QV] investments) in the area of product-space in which it is practiced will tend to be inflated/deflated on that account, (2) the profits yielded by conduct that increases/decreases the amount of resources devoted to producing units of existing products (to increasing unit output [UO]) with known production processes will tend to be deflated/inflated on that account, and (3) the profits yielded by conduct that increases/decreases the amount of resources devoted to executing production-process research (PPR) in the area of product-space in which it is practiced will tend to be deflated/inflated on this account. These assumptions reflect (1) theoretical/empirical analyses that Sect. 8.4 will summarize that favor the conclusion that QV-investment creation is more profitable than economically efficient while UO production and PPR execution are less profitable than economically efficient, (2) empirical assumptions about the magnitudes of the "percentage-profit-distortions [inflations and deflations]" in question where a relevant percentage-profit distortion is defined to equal (100%) *times* (the ratio of the difference between the relevant profit-figure and the relevant economic-efficiency figure] to [the profit-figure in question]), and (3) empirical assumptions about (A) the percentages of the resources devoted to the production of relevant units of existing products (to relevant UO production) that are withdrawn, respectively, from QV-investment creation and use on the one hand and PPR execution on the other hand, (B) the percentages of the resources devoted to PPR execution that are withdrawn, respectively, from QV-investment creation and use on the one hand and UO production on the other, and (C) the percentages of the resources that are devoted to the creation and use of QV investments that are withdrawn, respectively, from the production of existing products and the execution of PPR projects (see Chap. 8 and Markovits, R. 2020).

The second assumption is a related pair of assumptions: (1) in virtually all cases, the weighted-average beneficiary of any profitable business-conduct that manifests the specific anticompetitive intent of its perpetrator(s) or "lessens competition" in the sense of imposing a net equivalent-dollar loss on the actual and possible customers of the perpetrator(s) and the perpetrator's or perpetrators' rivals by reducing the absolute attractiveness of the best offers they, respectively, receive from any "inferior" (worse-than-privately-best-placed) supplier (primarily the shareholders of the perpetrator[s] but also its/their managers and employees and sometimes its/their creditors and in some instances individuals who have the same connection to one or more rivals to the perpetrator[s]) will be better-off materially than the weighted-average losers of such business conduct (usually the actual and potential customers of the perpetrator[s] and their product-rivals and sometimes the shareholders/creditors/managers/employees of product-rivals of the perpetrator[s]), and (2) in virtually all cases, the number of beneficiaries of any profitable business-conduct whose poverty is eliminated or significantly reduced by the conduct will be lower than the number of losers from the conduct who will be impoverished or whose poverty will be significantly increased by the conduct.

The third assumption is that (for reasons that Sect. 8.5 will explain) business conduct or government policies that increase/decrease poverty and material inequality will tend to decrease/increase economic efficiency on this account.

The fourth assumption (actually, pair of assumptions) is that (1) business conduct or antitrust policies that increase/decrease the concentration of the seller-side of any area of product-space will tend to increase the expenditures that the relevant sellers collectively make on political parties/campaigns/candidates and government-decisionmaking-process participation (by reducing or helping the relevant sellers overcome the collective-action obstacles to their making the amount of such expenditures that is in their collective interest to make) and (2) increases in seller expenditures of these kinds will tend to cause government to make choices that are less-economically efficient, more-liberal-moral-rights-violative, and less-instantiative of any morally-defensible conception of the moral good as well as disserving the liberal-moral-rights-related interest of all members of a liberal-moral-rights-based society to participate equally in electoral politics and government-decisionmaking processes and have their parochial interests and moral-good positions have an equal influence on government decisions.

2.4.1 The Relationships Between the Economic Efficiency of any Antitrust-Policy-Coverable Business Conduct and Its Liberal-Moral-Rights-Violativeness and the Relationship Between the Economic Efficiency of any Antitrust Policy and Its Serving or Disserving the Instantiation of the Liberal Conception of Justice

At this juncture, I will restrict myself to making three comments about the relationship between the economic efficiency of antitrust-policy-coverable business conduct and the conduct's liberal-moral-rights-violativeness. First, the overwhelming majority of conduct that is liberal-moral-rights-violative because it was motivated by specific anticompetitive intent will be economically inefficient because it was inherently unprofitable, because it will tend to cause economic inefficiency by increasing the incidence of poverty and increasing material inequality, and because its tendency to yield its perpetrator(s) profits by concentrating the seller-side of the area of product-space in which it takes place will be associated with its decreasing economic efficiency by increasing the expenditures the relevant sellers make on political parties/campaigns/candidates and government-decisionmaking-process participation. Second, a few exemplars of conduct that is liberal-moral-rights-violative because it is motivated by specific anticompetitive intent may be economically efficient because (1)(A) it reduces equilibrium QV investment in the area of product-space in which it is practiced (because it reduces equilibrium QV investment more by reducing QV-investment competition than it increases equilibrium QV investment by increasing the prices that are charged at various relevant QV-investment quantities by decreasing price-competition) and (B) the associated increase in economic efficiency exceeds the decrease in economic efficiency the conduct generates in other ways or (2)(A) it increases equilibrium PPR in the area of product-space in which it is practiced (because it increases equilibrium PPR by raising the prices that are charged for the production processes that would be discovered when total PPR reached various relevant quantities in the relevant area of product-space and perhaps by creating a firm that can execute one or more more-profitable PPR investments than the participants could have executed as separate entities or that any non-participant could have executed by more than it decreases equilibrium PPR by reducing the intensity of PPR-investment competition in the relevant area of product-space) and (B) the associated increase in economic efficiency exceeds the decrease in economic efficiency the conduct generates in other ways. Third, much antitrust-policy-coverable business conduct that is not liberal-moral-rights-violative (e.g., the use of complicated pricing-techniques to convert into seller surplus what would otherwise be buyer surplus or decisions to make investments that are less-economically-efficient but more-profitable because their use generates less-buyer surplus) is economically inefficient.

At this juncture, I will restrict myself to making five comments about the relationship between the economic efficiency of antitrust policies and their instantiating the liberal conception of justice. First, given the allocative cost of devising and implementing an antitrust policy that declares particular conduct illegal, it will sometimes not be economically efficient to effectively prohibit antitrust-policy-coverable business conduct that is liberal-moral-rights-violative even when that conduct is economically inefficient. Second, the governments of a liberal-moral-rights-based society are morally obligated to secure the liberal moral rights of the society's members by deterring liberal-moral-rights-violative antitrust-policy-coverable business conduct whenever they can do so in a way that increases the extent to which the society's members' liberal-moral-rights-related interests are secured even when it is economically inefficient for the relevant governments to do so. Third and relatedly, the governments of a liberal-moral-rights-based society are prohibited from preventing liberal-moral-rights-violative antitrust-policy-coverable business conduct by using evidence-collecting techniques, evidentiary-burden rules, and/or sanctions whose use sacrifices weightier liberal-moral-rights-related interests than they secure. Fourth, the governments of a liberal-moral-rights-based society are morally obligated to give victims of liberal-moral-right-violative antitrust-policy-coverable business conduct appropriate opportunities to obtain legal redress regardless of whether it is economically efficient for them to do so. Fifth, it will sometimes be economically efficient and liberal-moral-rights-non-violative for the governments of a liberal-moral-rights-based society to more-or-less-effectively prohibit antitrust-policy-coverable business conduct that is economically inefficient even though the conduct is not liberal-moral-rights-violative.

2.4.2 The Relationship Between the Economic Efficiency of any Antitrust-Policy-Coverable Business Conduct and Its Serving or Disserving the Utilitarian, the Various Non-Utilitarian-Egalitarian, the Various Mixed Utilitarian-and-Non-Utilitarian-Egalitarian, and the Libertarian Distributive-Good Conceptions of the Moral Good and the Relationship Between the Economic Efficiency of an Antitrust Policy and Its Serving or Disserving any Such Conception of the Moral Good

2.4.2.1 The Relationships When the Relevant Conception of the Moral Good is the Total-Utility-Focused Utilitarian Conception

One could, of course, analyze whether a particular exemplar of antitrust-policy-coverable business conduct or a particular antitrust-policy decision served or disserved the instantiation of the total-utility-focused variant of the utilitarian conception of the moral good without estimating the economic efficiency of the conduct or policy decision in question. In particular, one could do so by identifying all or (better yet from the utilitarian perspective) an appropriately-large random samples of the conduct's (antitrust policy's) winners and losers, estimating each covered individual's util gain or loss, and summing the figures in question. However, in practice, I suspect it will be more-morally-desirable from this utilitarian perspective to estimate the impact of such business conduct or antitrust policies in a more-circuitous way in which economic-efficiency estimates or something related to them play an important role. In particular, I suspect that the utilitarian conception of the moral good will be best served by estimating total-utility impacts by (1) estimating the equivalent-dollar gains and losses the non-government conduct or antitrust policy conferred on an appropriately-large, random sample of its winners and losers, (2) estimating the average utility gain associated with the equivalent-dollars won and the average utility loss associated with the equivalent-dollars lost, (3) multiplying the equivalent-dollar-gain estimate by the average-utility-of-the-equivalent-dollars-gained estimate and multiplying the equivalent-dollar-loss estimate by the average-utility-of-the-equivalent-dollars-lost estimate, and (4) comparing the two multiplicands. I suspect that from the perspective of the total-utility-oriented utilitarian conception of the moral good it will be best to derive the average utility estimates in question by combining estimates of the pre-conduct/policy and post-conduct/policy income/wealth positions of the identified winners and losers with estimates of the function that relates the marginal utility of money for members of the society in question to their income/wealth positions. Obviously, this account implies that the economic efficiency of non-government conduct or a government policy is neither a necessary nor a sufficient condition for its increasing total utility. Business conduct/(antitrust policies) that are economically inefficient will increase total utility if the average marginal utility of their winners' equivalent-dollar gains is sufficiently higher than the average marginal utility of their losers' equivalent-dollar losses—for example, if the winners were sufficiently poorer than the losers both pre-conduct/policy and post-conduct/policy.[20] And again, (business conduct)/(antitrust policies) that are economically efficient will decrease total utility if the average marginal utility of their winners' equivalent-dollar gains is sufficiently lower than the average marginal utility of their losers' equivalent-dollar losses. Moreover, although some economists have argued that this variant of utilitarianism will always be well-served by economically-efficient choices because any undesirable distributive impact such choices have from this utilitarian perspective (because the average marginal utility of money to the winners is sufficiently lower than the average marginal utility of money to the losers) can be overcome by combining the original choice with an appropriate redistributive policy, this argument will not avail when the necessary redistributive policy is not politically available or when it would be (from a utilitarian perspective) prohibitively economically inefficient (for allocative-transaction-cost and/or distorting-incentive-effects reasons).

I will now make five general claims about the impact of antitrust-policy-coverable conduct on total utility. First, virtually all business conduct that is motivated by specific anticompetitive intent will decrease total utility because it will not only decrease economic efficiency but will also generate a distributive impact that is undesirable from the utilitarian perspective by yielding equivalent-dollar gains whose average utility is lower than the average utility of the equivalent-dollar losses it yields (by increasing material inequality). Second many of the rare exemplars of specific-anticompetitive-intent-motivated business conduct that increase economic efficiency will decrease total utility because they will increase material inequality. Third, most business conduct that imposes equivalent-dollar losses on the actual and potential customers of its perpetrator(s) and the actual and potential customers of its/their product-rivals will decrease total utility because most such conduct is economically inefficient and virtually all such conduct has a distributive impact that is undesirable from the utilitarian perspective. Fourth, most business conduct that yields its perpetrator profits by enabling the perpetrator to convert potential buyer surplus into seller surplus decreases total utility because it is economically inefficient and has an undesirable distributive impact from the perspective of utilitarianism even though such conduct is (usually) not motivated by specific anticompetitive intent and does not lessen competition by imposing an equivalent-dollar loss on the relevant buyers by reducing the absolute attractiveness of the best offers they, respectively, receive from "privately-inferior" (worse-than-privately-best-placed) suppliers.[21]

I will close this section by making two related claims about the effect of antitrust policies on total utility. First, the impact that antitrust policies have on total utility depends not only on the economic efficiency and distributive impact of the conduct they deter but also on the economic efficiency and distributive impact of the decisions that are made to finance the formulation and execution of the relevant antitrust policy, on the allocative cost and distributive impact of the government's, defendants', and private plaintiffs' participation in any related prosecutions and civil litigation, and on the allocative cost and distributive impact of determining and implementing the damage-awards, civil fines, incarcerative sentences, and non-incarcerative sentences the policy's execution entails. Second, the preceding point implies that antitrust policies that prevent business conduct that would reduce total utility may reduce total utility (though any such assessment must take account of the specific-deterrent and general-deterrent effects of any effort to implement antitrust prohibitions).

2.4.2.2 The Relationships When the Relevant Conception of the Moral Good Is a Non-Utilitarian-Egalitarian Conception of the Moral Good

Particular exemplars of any antitrust-policy-coverable business conduct will serve/disserve the instantiation of the equal-utility, equal-resource, and other equal-opportunity conceptions of the moral good if they increase/decrease material equality.[22] Regardless of how the subscribers to any such non-utilitarian-egalitarian conception of the moral good operationalize (respectively) the notion of "the equality of the distribution of utility, the equality of the distribution of resources, and the equality of the distribution of any unrelated positively-valued opportunity (and concomitantly of the relevant distribution of material resources), the economic efficiency of antitrust-policy-coverable business conduct will have no "direct connection" to its serving or disserving the instantiation of any of these conceptions of the moral good, though I acknowledge that Sect. 8.5's argument that choices that increase/decrease poverty and/or material inequality will tend to increase/decrease economic inefficiency on that account favors the existence of a positive correlation between the economic efficiency of a choice and its instantiation of these non-utilitarian-egalitarian conceptions of the moral good. Footnote 21's claim that several categories of antitrust-policy-coverable conduct that decrease economic efficiency (the use of fancy pricing-techniques, horizontal price-fixing, predation, and horizontal mergers and acquisitions that are economically inefficient) also increase material inequality provide a non-causative reason for believing that antitrust-policy-coverable conduct that is economically inefficient will also disserve the instantiation of non-utilitarian-egalitarian conceptions of the moral good. However, footnote 21's claim that many horizontal mergers and acquisitions that increase economic efficiency will increase material inequality (and the fact that this latter conclusion also applies to some conglomerate mergers, many joint ventures, and many decisions of firms to engage in internal growth cut) in the opposite direction. Hopefully, Part II will place readers in a better position to assess the relevant correlation.

I will close this section by making three obvious points that affect the relationship between the economic efficiency of an antitrust policy and its serving or disserving the instantiation of any of these non-utilitarian-egalitarian conceptions of the moral good: (1) An antitrust policy's economic efficiency depends not only on the economic inefficiency or efficiency of any business conduct it deters and the economic efficiency or inefficiency of any conduct it elicits but also on the economic-efficiency effects of its financing, the allocative transaction costs generated by its formulation and any investigative, "bargaining," and litigative efforts made to implement it, the allocative cost of collecting the damage-awards and civil fines its implementation involves, and the allocative cost of the prison sentences and non-custodial restrictions its implementation involves, (2) an antitrust policy's impact on material equality depends not only on the distributive impact of the business conduct it deters and elicits but also on the distributive impact of its financing, of the investigative, bargaining, and litigative efforts it entails, of the damage-awards and fines it causes to be paid, and of the custodial sentences and non-custodial restrictions with which its implementation is associated, (3) point (2) in this list complicates the analysis of whether particular antitrust policies serve or disserve the instantiation of any non-utilitarian-egalitarian conception of the moral good, and (4) points (1) and (2) complicate the analysis of the correlation between the economic efficiency of antitrust policies and their serving or disserving the instantiation of any of these non-utilitarian-egalitarian conceptions of the moral good.

2.4.2.3 The Relationships When the Relevant Conception of the Moral Good Is a Mixed Conception in Which Two or More of the Previously-Referenced, Morally-Defensible Pure Conceptions of the Moral Good Play a Role

The analysis of Sects. 2.4.2.1 and 2.4.2.2 applies mutatis mutandis when the relevant conception of the moral good is a mixed conception of a type the heading of this section references.

2.4.2.4 The Relationships When the Relevant Conception of the Moral Good Is the Libertarian Conception of the Distributive Moral Good (or the Libertarian Conception of Distributive Justice)

If I ignore ad arguendo the libertarian position on the "moral goodness" or "justness" of individuals' keeping what they found through luck and/or what they received through gift or bequest, libertarianism claims that it is morally good or just for each individual to be allocated resources whose allocative cost equals the allocative value of his or her contribution to the allocative value of their society's output. The issue with which this section is concerned then is: What is the relationship between the economic efficiency of antitrust-policy-coverable business conduct or antitrust policies and the extent to which the relevant society's distribution of income comports with this libertarian view?[23]

I will start by articulating a mathematical relationship that some might think bears on this issue, explaining why those who subscribe to this position think that this mathematical relationship has great significance for the connection between the economic efficiency of antitrust-policy-coverable business conduct or antitrust policies and their effects on the instantiation of the libertarian conception of the distributive good or of distributive justice, and then explain why the mathematical relationship in question is less significant in the current context than some might suppose. At least if (for simplicity) I assume that workers are either hired to do the amount of work they do or not hired at all, if all the Pareto-optimal conditions are fulfilled, (1) economic efficiency will be maximized, (2) each worker will be paid his or her marginal allocative product, and (3) each saver will receive compensation for saving equal to the marginal allocative product of his or her decision to save. This relationship does imply that (antitrust-policy-coverable business conduct)/(antitrust policies) that increase economic efficiency by eliminating the only Pareto imperfections in the relevant economy may increase the extent to which the libertarian distributive "norm" is instantiated and cannot decrease the extent to which that "norm" is instantiated because it implies that the conduct/policy in question will create a situation in which this libertarian "norm" is perfectly instantiated in circumstances in which it may or may not have been perfectly instantiated absent the conduct policy in question (given that the Pareto imperfections the conduct/policy removed may have perfectly counteracted their respective tendencies to yield in an otherwise-Pareto-perfect economy distributions of income that are suboptimal from a libertarian perspective). However, this relationship does not imply that (antitrust-policy-coverable conduct)/(an antitrust policy) (that is engaged in)/(that is implemented) in an economy that contains some misallocation before the conduct took place or the policy was implemented that (increase economic efficiency without eliminating all economic inefficiency)/(that decrease economic efficiency) will on that account, respectively, serve/disserve the instantiation of the libertarian distributive "norm" because, in economies that will contain some Pareto imperfections after the conduct/policy in question is (engaged in)/implemented, economically-efficient conduct/policies (1) are as likely (put crudely) to confer equivalent-dollar gains on parties who were originally allocated resources (or money to buy resources) whose allocative cost exceeded those parties' allocative products as to confer equivalent-dollar gains on parties who were originally allocated resources whose allocative cost was lower than their allocative products and (2) are as likely (put crudely) to impose equivalent-dollar losses on parties who originally were allocated (or could buy) too few resources from the libertarian perspective as to impose equivalent-dollar losses on parties who originally were allocated too many resources (or received too much money to buy resources) from the libertarian perspective.

I do not want to devote the space here to execute the relevant analyses. Those analyses would take account of (1) Chap. 8's conclusions that the combined effect of the various Pareto imperfections all contemporary economies contain is to cause (A) the net wage of workers who perform unit-output-producing and production-process-research-executing labor to be lower than their marginal allocative products, (B) the net wage of workers who perform quality-or-variety-investment-creating labor to exceed their marginal allocative products, (C) the profits yielded by the (creation of) quality-or-variety-increasing investments to exceed their contribution to economic efficiency, and (D) the profits yielded by the execution of production-process-research projects to be lower than their contribution to economic efficiency, (2) whether the relevant perpetrators produced goods created by quality-or-variety-increasing investments or discovered production processes, (3) whether the conduct in question conferred equivalent-dollar gains or imposed equivalent-dollar losses on its perpetrator's or perpetrators' product-rivals, (4) the percentages of the buyers the conduct affected who performed respectively unit-output-producing, quality-or-variety-investment-creating, or production-process-research-executing labor, (5) the impact that the conduct in question would have on the relationship between various workers' net wages and marginal allocative products and various investors' profits and the economic efficiency of their investments by altering the intensity of price-competition and investment-competition in the areas of product-space in which the relevant conduct is practiced, and (6) the economic efficiency of the conduct in question, which is relevant not only because the issue is the relationship between the economic efficiency of conduct and the desirability of its distributive impact from a libertarian perspective but also because it affects not only the equivalent-dollar gains and libertarian "entitlements" of the perpetrators but also the conduct's impact on relevant consumers. I will simply assert that most economically-inefficient antitrust-policy-coverable business conduct will have a distributive impact that is undesirable from a libertarian perspective, but I suspect that quite a high percentage of economically-efficient antitrust-policy-coverable business conduct (e.g., horizontal mergers or acquisitions that increase their participants' organizational allocative efficiency—see Chap. 11) will have distributive impacts that libertarianism deems undesirable (because they will reduce the price-competition and investment-competition their participants wage against each other and on that account confer equivalent-dollar gains on participants–shareholders, who on the weighted-average were allocated too many resources originally from the perspective of libertarianism, and impose equivalent-dollar losses on the actual and possible customers of the participants, who on the weighted-average were allocated too few resources originally from the perspective of libertarianism).

Perhaps I should have restricted myself to stating that the analysis of the relationship between the economic efficiency of antitrust-policy-coverable business conduct or antitrust policies and the desirability of their distributive impact from a libertarian perspective is complicated, and the actual relationship is complex. I state that now.

2.5 Conclusion

Historically, the antitrust-policy analyses that have been executed by Industrial Organization economists and by academic lawyers who have significant knowledge of economics have focused almost exclusively on the economic efficiency of the business conduct they addressed or the economic efficiency of prohibiting the conduct in question. Even if these experts' economic-efficiency analyses were correct, this focus would be unfortunate because economic efficiency is not a value in itself and the economic efficiency of business conduct or an antitrust policy has less bearing on its moral desirability—on its justness or its instantiation of the various conceptions of the moral good that are morally defensible—than many of these scholars appear to believe. This chapter prepares the way for Part II's policy analyses by explaining inter alia the liberal conception of justice, the concept of a liberal-moral-rights-based society, why I believe that most nations that have antitrust policies are liberal-moral-rights-based societies, the various conceptions of the moral good that can play an important role in the moral assessment of antitrust-policy-coverable business conduct and antitrust policies in liberal-moral-rights-based societies, and the relationship between on the one hand the economic efficiency of any antitrust-policy-coverable business conduct or antitrust policy and on the other hand that conduct's or policy's instantiation both of the liberal conception of justice and of the morally-defensible conceptions of the moral good to which individual members of a liberal-moral-rights-based society may subscribe—two variants of utilitarianism, equal-utility egalitarianism, equal-resource egalitarianism, different variants of other sorts of equal-opportunity egalitarianism, and mixed conceptions of the moral good that value two or more of the individual desiderata on which the non-mixed egalitarian conceptions of the moral good exclusively focus.

Notes

1. See, for example, Kaplow and Shavell (2001), pp. 1006–1019.
2. See Rawls (1971), pp. 62, 84, 92, 137, 143, 152–157, 426, and 530. For a detailed critique of Rawls' argument, see Markovits (1998), pp.109–134.
3. For a more-complete account of these protocols, see Markovits (1998), pp. 23–34.
4. "Dialectical" because the choices that individuals make to instantiate any conception of the moral good to which they subscribe may lead them to have experiences or to obtain insights that cause them to change their conceptions of the moral good.
5. I do not mean to imply that—to lead a life of moral integrity—an individual must think through his (or her) conception of the moral good in the self-conscious, carefully-considered way in which intellectuals might be disposed to do so: One can also come to subscribe to and be guided by a conception of the moral good intuitively without articulating the conception that grounds one's choices.
6. Liberalism does not imply that moral-rights bearers have a moral duty to show appropriate *equal* concern for the welfare of all other moral-rights bearers. More specifically, liberalism recognizes the rightfulness of moral-rights bearers' acting in ways that manifests their being more concerned with the welfare of intimates (family members, friends, individuals with whom they have love relationships) than with the welfare of others. Liberalism has this implication because it values and seeks to promote intimate relationships not just for the pleasure or satisfaction such relationships yield their participants but primarily because (1) liberalism values most-highly moral-rights bearers' leading lives of moral integrity and (2) participation in intimate relationships disposes the participants to take their lives morally seriously by leading them to consider and discuss with each other how they should treat each other and how they have treated each other and by creating situations in which the participants must make morally-salient choices.

7. Liberalism implies that the governments of any liberal-moral-rights-based society have a moral obligation to manifest appropriate, equal concern for all moral-rights bearers for whom they are responsible because governments have no intimate-relationship-related justification for favoring one moral-rights bearer over another.
8. Two related points are salient. First, liberalism implies that conduct that is life-of-moral-integrity-imperiling because it may inflict a life-of-moral-integrity-imperiling injury on a moral-rights bearer is liberal-moral-rights-violative unless ex ante the perpetrator should have believed that its choice would not disserve the "objective" of giving moral-rights bearers a meaningful opportunity to take their lives morally seriously all tolled. Thus, a pharmaceutical manufacturer's decision to produce additional units of one of its medicines would not be liberal-moral-rights-violative despite the fact that the production would generate pollutants that would cause some victims to contract a fatal cancer if the manufacturer could prove (for example) that (1) the only way it could reduce the cancer (or other relevant illnesses or injuries) its production caused would be to reduce its unit output and (2) any reduction in its unit output it could effectuate would cost at least as many lives (given the efficacy of the pills in question) as it would save. Second, although it is possible that antitrust-policy-coverable conduct could preclude one or more moral-rights bearers from having a meaningful opportunity to take their lives morally seriously by imposing straightforward material losses on them (by impoverishing them), this reality would not in my judgment render the relevant conduct liberal-moral-rights-violative because on my understanding liberalism does not impose a moral duty on moral-rights bearers when acting in their non-political capacities to provide any other moral-rights bearers (with whom the relevant actor does not have an intimate relationship—see note 6 supra) with the material wherewithal that critically affects the latter individual's opportunity to take his or her life morally seriously. Of course, the previous conclusion is compatible with the conclusions that (1) the moral-rights-bearing members of a liberal-moral-rights-based society have a liberal moral obligation to support their government's assuring that all moral-rights bearers for whom it is responsible have the material wherewithal, psychological nurturing, formal education, and experiences that significantly contribute to their opportunity to take their lives morally seriously and (2) the governments of a liberal-moral-rights-based society have a moral duty to assume that all the moral-rights bearers for whom they are responsible have a meaningful opportunity to take their lives morally seriously.
9. The expression "mere-utility losses" is not intended to suggest that the losses in question are small: Antitrust-policy-coverable conduct can inflict substantial non-life-of-moral-integrity-imperiling equivalent-dollar losses on individual losers. In saying that the losses are "mere-utility" losses, I mean to indicate solely that the losses are not life-of-moral-integrity-imperiling (except in the unusual case in which they deprive the loser of the material wherewithal to take his or her life morally seriously).

10. The text that follows will explain why liberalism distinguishes between choices that impose losses on others and choices that fail to confer gains on others.
11. Inter alia, liberalism imposes (1) duties to rescue when the potential rescuee faces a significant risk of suffering a life-of-moral-integrity-imperiling loss and the potential rescuer is "best-placed" (an enquoted phrase that requires considerable elucidation) to reduce that risk significantly by making a rescue-attempt that does not create a significant probability that the rescue-attempter will suffer a substantial injury, (2) duties to fulfill gift-promises when circumstances have not changed in a way that the promisee should recognize relieve the promisor of what would otherwise have been his/her obligation (which will usually not be the case when the promisee has relied on the promise and the promisor was aware of or should have anticipated the reliance and may not be the case more generally, given the "psychological cost" of receiving a promise and having that promise broken), (3) duties to give help to intimates when they have significant needs that may or may not be life-of-moral-integrity-imperiling, (4) duties that parties to contracts that involve relationships that are lengthier than those entailed in immediate exchanges to respond to contingencies the contract did not explicitly anticipate in the way that maximizes the joint equivalent-dollar interest of the contracting parties (see Markovits, D. 2004), (5) duties of sellers to devote an appropriate amount of resources to providing prospective buyers with accurate information about the sellers' products'/services' attributes and repair and maintenance costs and (perhaps) to correct associated errors that they know prospective buyers are making, and perhaps (6) political duties to secure and support governments that fulfill the government's liberal moral duties. I should add that liberalism also implies that rescuees have an obligation to compensate their rescuers for the rescuers' rescue-efforts that the government may have an obligation to provide such compensation to rescue-attempters if the rescuee cannot do so, and that—when one or more contract-participants have responded to an unanticipated contingency in the way liberalism implies they are morally obligated to respond—liberalism implies that the parties have a moral obligation to make cross-payments to restore the division of the net contract gain or contract loss that the parties anticipated when they did not take account of the unanticipated contingency.
12. I have enquoted this expression because its denotation is ambiguous. Some experts believe that it refers to the number that a trier-of-fact must assign to the probability of guilt to find a defendant guilty, some believe that it instructs the trier-of-fact to find a defendant guilty only if he or she cannot provide a reason for doubting the defendant's guilt, and some believe that it refers to some hard-to-specify combination of the preceding two "possibilities."
13. The text reflects the fact that business conduct (e.g., pricing-technique choices and choices among competing investments) that reduce the buyer surplus of the relevant firm's customers (say) below some percentage of the transaction surplus the firm's transactions generate (or, indeed, that eliminate such buyer surplus altogether) are not on that account either generically unjust or

liberal-moral-rights-violative. Chapter 17 will discuss the "exploitative abuse of a dominant position" test of illegality that some experts claim Article 102 of the 2009 Treaty of Lisbon should be interpreted to promulgate (in addition to "the exclusionary abuse of a dominant position" test of illegality Article 102 clearly does promulgate). This test of illegality could be rendered judicially cognizable (if one ignores the inevitable arbitrariness of any operationalization of the concept of "a dominant position") by interpreting "exploitation" to refer to the reduction of the relevant buyers' share of the transaction surplus generated by a specified set of transactions below some stated percentage. However, such a test of illegality does not instantiate the liberal conception of justice by preventing firms from violating the liberal moral rights of their customers. I should point out that both U.S. antitrust law and E.U. competition law do prohibit most exemplars of antitrust-policy-coverable conduct that are liberal-moral-rights-violative. Thus, as Chap. 17 indicates, (1) Sections 1 and 2 of the Sherman Act prohibit all conduct that manifests its perpetrator's or perpetrators' specific anticompetitive intent aside from natural-oligopolistic conduct, unsuccessful attempts to enter into contracts in restraint of trade, and specific-anticompetitive-intent-motivated efforts to secure government decisions in ways that do not violate norms of fair play, (2) Section 5 of the Federal Trade Commission Act prohibits "unfair methods of competition," (3) Article 101 of the 2009 Treaty of Lisbon prohibits agreements, concerted behavior, and trade-association conduct (but not single-firm conduct) that is undertaken with the object of preventing or restricting competition or that has the effect of distorting competition, and (4) Article 102 prohibits any individual firm's exclusionary abuse of its dominant position (or by a legally-dubious interpretation, a set of rivals' exclusionary abuse of their collectively-dominant position [whatever that means]).

14. Many features of a State's electoral systems and government-decisionmaking processes not referenced in the text also affect whether the relevant society's members' liberal-moral-rights-related interests in electoral/governmental-decisionmaking-processes participation and influence are secured: inter alia, (1) whether electoral districts are single-member or multiple-member, (2) whether electoral districts are gerrymandered, (3) the qualifications for voting-eligibility (whether felons are disqualified, whether literacy is an eligibility-requirement, whether poll taxes are levied), (4) the difficulty of voting (the number and placement of polling places, the length of time they are open, whether, when, and how absentee ballots can be cast), (5) how individual elections are decided (on a plurality basis with voters indicating only their most-preferred candidate, on a majority basis with run-off elections between the leading two candidates being held if no candidate obtained a majority in the first election, or on a majority basis through a system in which voters rank the candidates and if no candidate is ranked first by a majority of voters the votes of voters who ranked first the candidate who received the fewest votes are reallocated to those voters' respective second-preferred candidate and, if that vote-reallocation does not result in any candidate's having a majority, the votes of voters whose most-preferred candidate came second-to-last are reallocated to

the candidate they preferred second or third if their second-preferred candidate received the lowest voter total and the votes of those voters who preferred first the candidate with the lowest vote total and preferred second the candidate with the second-lowest vote total are reallocated to the candidate they preferred third and so on and so forth), (5) if elections are run on a nationwide or statewide basis, whether there is proportional representation or proportional representation for all parties whose vote exceeds some required minimum percentage of all votes cast, (6) whether eligible voters are legally obligated to vote, (7) whether the majority party in the legislature can condition a bill's coming to the floor on the bill's receiving majority support from the members of the majority party, etc.

15. I acknowledge but will hereinafter ignore the fact that most utilitarians consider utilitarianism to be a conception of justice (indeed, to be the objectively-correct and therefore universally-applicable concept of justice).
16. I believe that "candidates" for the title of being "the criterion a given moral-rights-based society is committed to using to assess the moral-rights-bearing status of a creature" should be assessed through a protocol that takes three considerations into account: (1) how well does the moral-status-determining-criterion candidate fit the conduct and perceptions of the society's members and governments that relate to the moral-rights-bearing status of various creatures, (2) to what extent is the damage to the candidacy of each candidate done by the non-fits with which it is associated reduced by the (partially-)exonerating explicability of those non-fits, and (3) how well do the various candidates for the relevant society's "moral-rights-bearing-status-determining-criterion" title fit the relevant society's conclusions about the substantive moral rights its moral-rights bearers possess. In my judgment, the relevant societal facts that a candidate for a society's moral-rights-bearing-status-determining-criterion title should ideally fit would include facts that relate to the moral-rights-bearing status of fetuses at various stages of development, children who are not yet morally responsible, members of "the human species" that have neurological disabilities that render them morally irresponsible, members of "the human species" that have the neurological prerequisites for taking their lives morally seriously but are currently asleep, unconscious, or in a reversible coma, members of "the human species" that once had the neurological prerequisites for taking their lives morally seriously but no longer do so (as a result of injury or neurological deterioration), men, women, Caucasians, non-Caucasians, (if one assures ad arguendo that the concept of race is operationalizable), Christians, adherents of various alternative religions or secular persuasions, non-human animals, etc. In my judgment, the list of explanations of non-fits that may render them explicable in a way that reduces the damage they do to a given candidate's candidacy includes mistaken views about the capacities of various subsets of human animals or of non-human animals, the fact that the subscribers to particular conclusions believe that the fact that the conclusion is religiously "warranted" exempts it from moral scrutiny, the possibility that observers may conflate the

fact that the friends and family of a creature that used to have but no longer has the neurological capacity to take his or her life morally seriously have a moral-rights-related interest in how this "creature" is treated with the creature's being a moral-rights bearer. In my view, a sound conceptual analysis of liberalism and empirical analysis of the prescriptive-moral practices of societies that consider themselves to be liberal-moral-rights-based will reveal that liberalism (1) places a lexically-highest value on those creatures' who have the neurological prerequisites for taking their lives morally seriously having a meaningful opportunity to do so and seizing that opportunity, (2) places its governments under a moral obligation to insure both that all creatures who possess the neurological prerequisites for taking their lives morally seriously receive the resources, emotional support, formal education, experience-opportunities, etc. that will contribute significantly to their having a meaningful opportunity to do so and that such creatures are treated by other moral-rights bearers with appropriate, equal respect and appropriate concern, and (3) places all morally-responsible creatures under a moral obligation to treat each other with appropriate, equal respect and appropriate concern. In my judgment, the protocol/facts I have just elucidated support the conclusion that in liberal-moral-rights-based societies the defining attribute of moral-rights-bearers is the possession of the neurological prerequisites for taking one's life morally seriously. I should note that economists have never addressed the issue "what attributes must a creature possess for its equivalent-dollar gains and losses to count in any economic-efficiency calculation." See Markovits, R. (2020), pp. 153–184, 228–248, and 302–303.

17. I should note that, although it is morally impermissible for the government of a liberal-moral-rights-based society to adopt an official conception of the moral good, the fact that liberalism implies that all members of any liberal-moral-rights-based society have a moral right that their moral-good positions have an influence on government decisions that is proportionate to the percentage of the society's members who share their positions (I recognize that more specification is required) implies that the governments of a liberal-moral-rights-based society do have moral-good-related duties.
18. I am ignoring the fact that many self-styled libertarians also believe that it is morally good or just for individuals to be allowed to keep desiderata they obtained through luck (say, by finding them luckily), gift, or bequest. The claim that it is morally good or just for individuals to be allowed to keep what they obtained through gift or bequest assumes that it was morally good or just for the donor or testator to own the desiderata he or she gave or bequeathed to another and claims that it is morally good or just for individuals whose ownership of a desideratum was morally good or just to be able to dispose of the desideratum any way he or she wants. If the above assumptions were true, I would find the claim in question persuasive, but, as I will argue below, there is little reason to believe that the assumptions are true. The claim that it is morally good or just for individuals to be allowed to keep what they obtained through luck is doubtful. The fact that a person who, through luck, found something that was not

previously owned by anyone else establishes that the finder's keeping what he found did not violate anyone else's property right, but it does not provide a positive moral justification for the finder's keeping what he found through luck. Thus, a finder's keeping what he found through luck cannot be justified or established to be morally good by arguing that an individual has a moral right to keep or that it would be morally good to allow individuals to keep desiderata they obtained without reducing others' opportunities to secure desiderata because the lucky finder's conduct did reduce the relevant opportunities of others by precluding them from finding and keeping the desiderata the lucky finder found and kept.

19. I acknowledge that this usage is non-standard: economists use the expressions "marginal product"—more accurately, "marginal revenue product" and "marginal allocative product" (see below)—to refer to the referenced dollar value of the last unit of labor in a specified category that was performed, not to the dollar value of all units of labor performed by the last worker in a specified category to be hired. I hope that this footnote prevents my non-standard usage from being misleading.
20. I am simplifying and will continue to simplify by assuming either (1) that relevant individuals do not differ in their capacities to obtain utility from resources or in those attributes other than the material resources at their disposal that could affect their respective relevant opportunities or (2) that subscribers to these non-utilitarian-egalitarian conceptions of the more good are not concerned with inequalities that are attributable to such interpersonal differences. The only possible (non-expositional) justifications for these simplifications are the difficulty or impossibility of ascertaining the facts they ignore.
21. It might be of some interest to provide a few crude generalizations about the relationship between the impact of particular categories of antitrust-policy-coverable business conduct, respectively, on economic efficiency and total utility. Firm decisions to use complicated pricing-techniques (such as perfect price discrimination in any of its forms, the combination of lump-sum fees and supra-marginal-cost per-unit prices, or inter-buyer price discrimination) rather than charge a single per-unit price to all prospective customers reduce both economic efficiency and total utility (because they reduce economic efficiency by increasing allocative transaction costs, creating incentives to engage in arbitrage, [in the case of conventional price discrimination] by generating conventional consumption-optimum misallocation, and by increasing economic-inefficiency-generating poverty and material inequality by redistributing income from buyers [who are poorer] to shareholders [who are richer]). Horizontal price fixing (what I call "contrived-oligopolistic pricing") reduces economic efficiency and utility in virtually all cases (once again because the practice almost always reduces economic efficiency and almost always has a distributive impact that is undesirable from a utilitarian perspective—increases material inequality by distributing income from buyers, who are poorer, to shareholders, who are better off). Predatory conduct reduces economic efficiency and decreases total utility in virtually all cases (for the same

general reasons that the use of fancy pricing-techniques and horizontal price fixing do so). Horizontal mergers and acquisitions may either increase or decrease economic efficiency (depending on whether [1] the economic-efficiency gains they yield by substituting a resulting firm that is more-organizationally allocatively efficient for participants that would have been less-organizationally allocatively efficient as separate entities after the date on which the merger or acquisition was/would be consummated *exceed* [2] the economic-efficiency losses they generate [A] by freeing the participants from each other's price-competition (and thereby increasing not only prices but derivatively equilibrium QV investment in the ARDEPPS of consummation and poverty and hence poverty-related misallocation) and [B] by concentrating the seller side of the ARDEPPS of consummation and hence the expenditures its sellers make to influence government decisions and the influence its sellers have on government decisions) and may either increase or decrease total utility will increase total utility if they increase economic efficiency sufficiently to overcome the fact that their winners will tend to be better-off than their losers and will decrease total utility if they increase economic efficiency by too small an amount to overcome the fact that their distributive impact would be undesirable from a utilitarian perspective if they would have no impact on economic efficiency or would decrease economic efficiency. Part II will provide more-detailed analyses of the determinants of the economic efficiency and distributive impact both of the practices whose effects this footnote addresses and of the other categories of antitrust-policy-coverable conduct on which this footnote has not commented.

22. I am simplifying not only by ignoring the considerations footnote 20 referenced but also by ignoring or deeming irrelevant to the notion of "opportunity" interpersonal-capacity differences that may affect the "opportunities" that different individuals have.
23. I ignore my view that this libertarian position is morally indefensible.

References

Kaplow, B., & Shavell, S. (2001). Fairness versus welfare. *Harvard Law Review, 114*, 961–1388.

Markovits, R. (1998). *Matters of principle: Legitimate legal argument and constitutional interpretation*. New York University Press.

Markovits, D. (2004). Contract and collaboration. *Yale Law Journal, 113*, 1417–1518.

Markovits, R. (2006a). Liberalism and tort law: On the content of the corrective-justice-securing tort law of a liberal, rights-based society. *University of Illinois Law Review, 2006*, 243–300.

Markovits, R. (2006b). On the economic inefficiency of a liberal-corrective-justice securing law of torts. *Illinois Law Review, 2006*, 525–569.

Markovits, R. (2020). *Welfare economics and second-best theory: A distortion-analysis protocol for economic-efficiency analysis*. Springer.

Rawls, J. (1971). *A theory of justice*. Harvard University Press.

Extant and Possible Tests of Antitrust Illegality

3

This study will often make reference to the various tests of illegality promulgated by U.S. antitrust law, the various test of illegality promulgated by E.U. competition law, and other tests of antitrust legality that could be promulgated and that might be morally desirable. Thus, the various chapters of Part II frequently reference the U.S./E.U. tests of antitrust-law/competition-law illegality to characterize particular exemplars or all exemplars of the type of conduct on which they respectively focus; the various chapters of Part II and Chap. 18 (the second chapter of Part III) refer to tests of antitrust illegality that neither U.S. antitrust law nor E.U. competition law promulgate when analyzing respectively the moral desirability of various possible responses governments could make to the type of conduct on which each focuses and the relative moral desirability of U.S. antitrust law and E.U. competition law as correctly interpreted and applied as matters of law. Unfortunately, none of these extant or possible tests of antitrust illegality has self-declaring meaning. Chapter 3 provides clear operational definitions of the tests of illegality that are promulgated by U.S. antitrust law and/or E.U. competition law and of various other tests of antitrust illegality that could be promulgated.

3.1 The Tests of Illegality Promulgated by U.S. Antitrust Legislation,[1] the Competition-Law Provisions of the E.U. Treaty,[2] and the European Merger Control Regulation[3]

3.1.1 The Specific-Anticompetitive-Intent Test of Illegality

This test of illegality prohibits covered conduct by one or more covered actors if and only if its perpetrator's or perpetrators' ex ante perception that the conduct would be at least normally profitable was critically affected by its or their belief that it would or might reduce the absolute attractiveness of the most attractive offers

R. S. Markovits, *Welfare Economics and Antitrust Policy - Vol. I*,
https://doi.org/10.1007/978-3-030-79812-3_3

against which it or they would have to compete in one or more ways that would render at least normally profitable conduct that would be economically inefficient in an otherwise-Pareto-perfect world (or, more generally, "that would be economically inefficient if its profitability would not otherwise be distorted").[4] This test of illegality is promulgated by the U.S. Sherman Act (by its Section 1 prohibition of "[e]very contract, combination…or conspiracy in restraint of trade" and by its Section 2's declaration that "[e]very person who shall monopolize, or attempt to monopolize, or combine or conspire with any other person or person, to monopolize…should be deemed guilty of a felony").[5] This test of illegality is also promulgated (in addition to other tests of illegality) by two Articles of the 2009 Treaty of Lisbon—by Article 101(1)'s prohibition of "agreements between undertakings, decisions by association of undertakings or concerted practices" that "have as their object…the prevention…[or] restriction…of competition within the common market"[6] and by Article 102's prohibition of "[a]ny abuse by one or more undertakings of a dominant position within the internal market or a substantial part of it" (or at least by this provision's prohibition of "exclusionary abuses").[7]

Before proceeding, I should point out that neither the Sherman Act nor Articles 101(1) and 102 make this test applicable to all categories of business conduct or all categories of business actors. At least 3 points or sets of related points of this sort should be made. First, Article 101(1) does not cover single-firm conduct, and Article 102 does not cover the conduct of any firm that does not occupy "a dominant position within the internal market" (though a dubious interpretation of Article 102 asserts that it does cover individual firms that do not individually occupy such a dominant position if they belong to a set of "collectively-dominant" firms [whatever "collectively dominant" means]). Second, there is good reason to believe that, correctly interpreted as a matter of U.S. law, the Sherman Act does not cover unsuccessful specific-anticompetitive-intent-motivated attempts to enter into contracts. Specifically, this conclusion is favored by the facts that (1) Section 1 does not refer to *attempts to enter into* "contracts, combinations or conspiracies in restraint of trade" and (2) U.S. courts generally refuse to correct even obvious legislative-drafting errors when interpreting statutes that define criminal offenses—facts that persuade most of the U.S. criminal-law and constitutional-law scholars with whom I have discussed this issue that it would be incorrect as a matter of U.S. law to conclude that Section 2's "attempt to monopolize" language covers unsuccessful attempts to enter into a contract, combination or conspiracy in restraint of trade even when the unsuccessful attempt had real-world effects (as would an attempt to secure a contrived-oligopolistic margin by making an offer to enter into a unilateral contrived-oligopolistic-pricing contract that the prospective contract-partner rejects by beating the initiator's contrived-oligopolistic-price-containing offer with an offer that was less attractive to the relevant buyer than the highest-non-oligopolistic-price-containing offer the contriver [the buyer's privately-best-placed supplier] could have made would have been). Third, given the liberal-moral-rights-related interest that members of a liberal-moral-rights-based society have in participating in their government's elections and legislative, administrative, and adjudicative processes, it may be correct as a matter of law to give the Sherman Act and Articles

101 and 102 constitutionality-saving constructions that allow firms to participate in its society's elections and government-decisionmaking processes even by committing acts motivated by their specific anticompetitive intent so long as they "play fair" when doing so[8]—for example, do not tell lies, pay supposedly-neutral experts or non-experts to participate in a relevant process without revealing that they are on the relevant party's payroll, raise objections in administrative processes or make claims in adjudicative settings that they know are without merit.[9]

3.1.2 The Lessening-Competition Test of Illegality

This test of illegality prohibits covered conduct by one or more covered actors if the conduct inflicts a net equivalent-monetary loss on the customers of its perpetrator(s) and the customers of its (their) product-rivals by reducing the absolute attractiveness of the most-attractive offers they respectively receive from any potential supplier that is privately-worse-than-best-placed to supply them where the baseline for measuring the competitive impact of any conduct whose legality is at issue is the situation that would prevail if the defendant(s) took no relevant action at all (not the situation that would prevail if the defendant[s] made the most-pro-competitive choice it [they] could make or some other specific choice that would increase competition relative to the status quo ante). This test of illegality is the test promulgated by all but one of the operative clauses of the U.S. Clayton Act, which prohibit the conduct they cover if its "effect...may be substantially to lessen competition or tend to create a monopoly," by the part of Article 101(1) of the 2009 Treaty of Lisbon that prohibits covered conduct by a covered actor if the covered conduct has as its "effect the prevention...[or] restriction of competition within the common market," and by the EMCR, which prohibits any "concentration" that "would significantly impede effective competition in the common market or a substantial part of it" (at least if I omit the following language that appears after the enquoted material: "in particular as a result of the creation or strengthening of a dominant position"). Five explanatory or supplementary comments or related sets of comments need to be made.

I start with the "explanation." The test specifies that the conduct must impose a net equivalent-monetary loss on relevant buyers *by reducing the absolute attractiveness of the best offers they respectively receive from any worse-than-privately-best-placed supplier* because it does not deem illegal conduct that would not have imposed an equivalent-monetary loss on the relevant buyers had it not enabled its perpetrator(s) to reduce the amount by which it or they charged its or their customers lower prices than they could obtain, given the attractiveness of the best offers these buyers respectively received from any worse-than-privately-best-placed suppliers (say, by enabling the actors in question to do a better job of estimating the highest prices they can secure).

I turn next to two fairly-straightforward supplementary points. Variants of the lessening-competition test of illegality can be distinguished by (1) differences in the probability they require to be established that the conduct will lessen competition for the conduct to be illegal and (2) differences in the amount by which the conduct must be predicted to lessen competition or shown to have lessened competition for the conduct to be illegal. Some lessening-competition tests that have been promulgated or proposed would require no more than that the effect of the covered conduct "may be" to lessen competition; some declare the conduct illegal only if there is a "reasonable possibility" that it will lessen competition (whatever that means); some declare the covered conduct illegal only if "a dangerous probability" (whatever that is) of its lessening competition is established; and some declare covered conduct illegal only if it is shown that the conduct will lessen competition beyond a reasonable doubt where the phrase "reasonable doubt" is ambiguous—is sometimes understood to refer to the minimum number that the trier-of-fact must assign to the probability of guilt for a decision of guilt to be warranted is is sometimes understood to indicate that doubts of guilt can justify a vote for innocence only if a reason can be given for them, and is sometimes understood to refer to some poorly-specified combination of the preceding two considerations. I will assume that in a civil case covered conduct is supposed to be found to have violated the lessening-competition test only if the trier-of-fact concludes that "more probably than not" it lessened competition and that in a criminal case covered conduct is supposed to be found to have lessened competition only if the trier-of-fact concludes that the conduct lessened competition beyond a reasonable doubt. Actual "lessening competition" tests of illegality also differ in the magnitude of the lessening of competition that is required for illegality. The Clayton Act refers to a "substantial" lessening of competition, and the EMCR condemns concentrations that would "significantly impede" "effective competition": I am even less able to operationalize "effective competition" than to operationalize "effectively impede." I assume the objective of the supporters of the "lessening-competition" test of illegality who support the addition of these requirements is to induce the antitrust-policy-enforcement authorities to prohibit conduct that they think may lessen competition if but only if they think that something like the weighted-average-expected reduction in competition is sufficiently large to make the enforcement-effort worthwhile (a calculation that, regrettably, one cannot make without understanding the moral-rights-related and moral-good-related objectives of policies that are designed to deter conduct that may lessen competition). This study will assume (arbitrarily) that the lessening-competition test declares illegal all conduct that is expected on the weighted average to lessen competition (unless, as I will argue next, that conclusion is critically affected by the conduct's increasing the organizational allocative efficiency of its perpetrator[s]).

I turn now to the organizational-allocative-efficiency defense that I will assume qualifies the lessening-competition test of illegality (in U.S. but not in E.U. law). Under this defense, a covered defendant whose covered conduct has been shown to lessen competition will be able to exonerate itself by establishing that its conduct would not have imposed a net equivalent-monetary loss on relevant buyers had it not (1) increased the defendant's or defendants' organizational economic efficiency (e.g., by lowering its or their marginal private and allocative costs), (2) on that account improved the defendant's array or defendants' arrays of competitive positions, (3) on that account and concomitantly worsened one or more of the defendant's rival's or defendants' mutual rivals arrays of competitive positions, (4) on that account and concomitantly reduced the profits that one or more of its or their rivals can earn from a normal or supernormal quantity to a subnormal quantity, (5) on that account caused one or more of its (their) rivals to exit, and (6) on that account inflicted an equivalent-monetary loss on the customers of the defendant(s) and the customers of its (their) rivals "combined."

I address finally an attribute of the Clayton Act's lessening-competition test of illegality that I will ignore. The Clayton Act's various provisions (each of which focuses on a different subset of business conduct) speak of lessening competition or tending to create a monopoly "in any line of commerce" or "in any line of commerce in any section of the country." This language is often interpreted to require private plaintiffs or the State to define relevant product and/or geographic markets and establish that the conduct under scrutiny has lessened or will lessen competition in a defined market. Although I understand the textual argument for this conclusion, the fact that—as Chap. 6 demonstrates—market definitions are inherently arbitrary not just at their peripheries but comprehensively provides a sound basis for a constitutionality-saving construction of the Clayton Act under which that statute would not require any market to be defined: Note that my operationalization of the lessening-competition test of illegality does not require its applier to define any market. Although Article 101(1) focuses on effects that take place "within the common market" or motives that relate to acts that occur within "the common market" and the EMCR refers to "effective competition in the common market or a substantial part of it," this language cannot ground a textual argument for the conclusion that the predicted or post-dicted lessening of competition must be shown to occur in a defined economic or antitrust market[10] because the common market is not an economic or antitrust market.

3.1.3 The Distorting-Competition Test of Illegality

This test of illegality prohibits covered conduct by covered actors that benefits its perpetrator(s) by improving their (private) competitive positions without making them as-better-placed allocatively. Among the categories of conduct that distort competition are (1) a firm's exaggerating the quality of its product, (2) a firm's claiming that its product is the product of someone else whose products have a higher reputation ("passing off" one's product as someone else's), (3) a firm's making false negative statements about the quality of a rival product, (4) a trade association's giving a product an undeservedly-low quality-rating or safety-rating or withholding a seal of approval from a product by adopting inappropriate rating-criteria that unjustifiably disadvantage the product in question or by misapplying its appropriate quality standards or safety standards, (5) a firm's making it undeservedly difficult for a rival to obtain credit or to enter into long-term contractual relationships by falsely claiming that the target was a poor credit-risk or more likely than it is to be caught up in costly contract or IP litigation, (6) a firm's bribing a rival's supplier or employee to perform less well for the rival, and (7) a firm's illegitimately obstructing access to a rival's business. Even if such conduct is not predatory (is not directed at driving the rival out), it will distort competition. Trade-association conduct that distorts competition, agreements between undertakings to engage in conduct that will distort competition, and concerted practices that "distort competition" violate Article 101(1), which prohibits such conduct by such actors if its object or effect is "the distortion of competition"; conduct that distorts competition also violates Section 5 of the U.S. Federal Trade Commission Act, which prohibits "unfair methods of competition"; and conduct by covered actors that not only distorts competition but is critically motivated by the benefits of driving its target out of business by so doing violates the Sherman Act, the object branch of Article 101(1)'s test of illegality in that it manifests specific anticompetitive intent (though the Article 101(1) conclusion will be legally relevant only if [1] the perpetrator is an undertaking and the relevant act is an agreement between undertakings or concerted practice or [2] the perpetrator is a trade association), and the exclusionary-abuse branch of Article 102 if the perpetrator(s) is (are) dominant firms or (by dubious interpretation) members of a collectively-dominant set of rivals. (I do not know whether the exclusionary-abuse branch of Article 102 prohibits conduct that distorts competition without driving its rival out, though conduct in this category might result in its perpetrator's or perpetrators' violating the exploitative-abuse branch of Article 102's test of illegality if it results in the perpetrator's or perpetrators' realizing too high a percentage of the transaction surplus generated by some relevant set of sales it makes or they make.[11])

3.1.4 The Exploitative-Abuse (of a Dominant Position?) Test of Illegality

This test of illegality renders the pricing conduct of any seller (or of any dominant seller) illegal if it causes the seller to realize an "exploitatively-high" percentage of the transaction surplus its sales of a relevant set of products to a relevant set of buyers yield. I should state at the outset that this test of illegality would seem to many not to be a test of *antitrust* illegality—would seem to focus on a reality that should lead to the seller in question (or the set of rivals to which it belongs) being subjected to public-utility regulation or being nationalized. Perhaps that is why no U.S. statute prohibits exploitative abuses. Still, E.U. authorities seem to think that—if the concept of an exploitative abuse were justiciable (were definable in some way that would enable courts to make defensible assessments of exploitativeness)—it would be correct as a matter of law to conclude that Article 102's prohibition of dominant firms' abusing their position to have an exploitative-abuse branch. It seems to me that—as I have defined it above—the concept of an exploitative abuse is justiciable—indeed, is not more difficult to apply than the concepts of specific anticompetitive intent, lessening competition, or distorting competition. However, I see no reason why any prohibition of exploitative abuses should be limited to firms that occupy a dominant position. Indeed, since as Chap. 7 will explain there is no non-arbitrary way to define the concept of "firm dominance," any argument for forbidding dominant firms from exploitatively abusing their positions would be more persuasive if it applied to all firms. I will therefore assume that any exploitative-abuse test of antitrust illegality would apply to all sellers.[12]

3.2 Some Defensible Tests of Antitrust Illegality That Have Not Been Promulgated by U.S. Antitrust Law or E.U. Competition Law

3.2.1 Economic-Efficiency-Oriented Tests of Antitrust Illegality

Many American Industrial Organization economists who focus on antitrust law and many American academic lawyers who know some economics and specialize in antitrust law claim either (1) that the U.S. antitrust laws promulgate an economic-efficiency-oriented test of illegality or (2) that (A) the U.S. antitrust laws should be read to authorize the antitrust-enforcement authorities and courts to find antitrust-law-covered conduct illegal if and only if it would be in the public interest to do so and (B) the best way to promote the public interest in the antitrust context is to apply the extant antitrust laws in the way that is most economically efficient. (Some of the U.S. academic lawyers reject the claim that the U.S. antitrust laws promulgate any specific test of antitrust illegality because they believe that the language of the U.S. antitrust statutes is particularly "non-instructive," and some take this position because they believe that language in general or statutory language in general is incapable of conveying substantive meaning.) Obviously, I disagree with these scholars' understanding of the public interest, with some members of this group's belief that the meaning of any test or utterance is supplied by the reader or listener not by the writer or speaker,[13] and with the narrower belief of some members of this group that the texts of the extant U.S. antitrust laws have no denotation. But for current purposes, the important point is that one could promulgate two economic-efficiency-oriented tests of antitrust illegality—one that prohibits law-covered acts by one or more law-covered actors if and only if the conduct in question is economically inefficient and one that prohibits such acts by such actors if and only if the conduct's prohibition would be economically efficient (given inter alia the allocative cost of enforcing the prohibition, the allocative inefficiency that would be generated by the public financing of the drafting, passing, and implementation of the prohibition, and the allocative-efficiency gains that the prohibition would generate by securing specific and general deterrence both by penalizing offenders and by "educating" and "threatening" to penalize potential offenders).

3.2.2 "Defendant-Economic-Power-Oriented" Tests of Antitrust Illegality

At least 5 variants of this test can be distinguished. The first declares illegal the possession of more than a specific "quantity of economic power," regardless of how that power was obtained. The second declares illegal the possession of more than a specified "quantity of economic power" that was not obtained (exclusively?) through "skill, foresight, and industry," that was not "thrust upon" the power-holder, that was "not inevitable," or that was obtained in a way that was not "honestly industrial."[14] The third declares illegal failures of firms that have more than a specified quantity of economic power to help their rivals prosper.[15] The fourth prohibits conduct that increases the organizational allocative efficiency of firms with more than a specified quantity of economic power if the conduct (1) improves their array of competitive positions, (2) concomitantly worsens the array of competitive positions of "marginal established firms" and/or raises the barriers to entry/investment-expansion faced by one or more otherwise-effective (potential competitors)/(established-firm potential expanders), and (3) relatedly creates a "sufficient" (unspecified) risk that the marginal established competitors in question will exit or that the relevant potential investors will no longer be effective while declaring lawful the relevant marginal competitors' and potential investors' engaging in the organizational-allocative-efficiency-enhancing conduct in question.[16] The fifth "variant of this test of illegality" is admittedly not a test of illegality but two presumptions (sometimes irrebuttable presumptions respectively of antitrust illegality and antitrust legality): (1) that various categories of conduct will violate the specific-anticompetitive-intent test of illegality and/or the lessening-competition test of illegality if the perpetrator has more than some quantity of economic power and (2) that various categories of conduct will not violate the specific-anticompetitive-interest test of illegality or the lessening-competition test of illegality if the perpetrator(s) did not possess some quantity of economic power (often equated with "some market share") before (or after?) engaging in the allegedly-illegal conduct.[17]

I want to make 5 points about these firm-economic-power-oriented tests of illegality (or presumptions of illegality or legality). First, the practicability of defendant-economic-power-oriented tests of antitrust-legality or antitrust-illegality presumptions is severely undercut by the complexity of the concept of a firm's economic power and the impossibility of operationalizing this concept non-arbitrarily. Chapter 7 addresses these two issues. Second, the practicability of these tests of antitrust illegality and these antitrust-illegality presumptions is severely undercut by the fact that—regardless of how one defines a firm's economic power—that power will not be inferrable from the firm's share of a non-arbitrarily-defined market. Chapter 6 explains why market definitions are inherently arbitrary not just at their peripheries but comprehensively, and Chap. 7 explains why even if contrary to fact markets could be defined non-arbitrarily a firm's market share would not be an acceptably-accurate predictor of its economic power (no matter how defined). Third, in my judgment, the imposition of legal duties on firms that have some specified quantity of economic power to help their rivals will tend to decrease economic efficiency (1) by deterring firms from engaging in (on-balance-economically-efficient) conduct that will give them more than the relevant quantity of economic power, (2) by inducing firms that would otherwise be deemed to have a legal-duty-imposing quantity of economic power to make (on-balance-economically-inefficient) choices that will reduce their economic power, and (3) by inducing firms to make legally-required rival-assisting choices that will be economically inefficient—for example, to abstain from engaging in systems rivalry, which is on-balance economically efficient. Fourth, parimutuel handicapping in which well-established firms are prohibited from engaging in conduct that is not only privately profitable but economically efficient while marginal established firms and new entrants are permitted to engage in such conduct will tend to decrease economic efficiency by causing additional allocatively-inefficient QV investments to be made, by causing allocatively-inefficient QV investments to survive when they would not be replaced if they were withdrawn, and by substituting less-allocatively-efficient QV investments by marginal established firms and new entrants to be substituted for more-allocatively-efficient QV investments by well-established firms. Fifth, the presumptions that various categories of conduct are substantially and legally-critically more likely to be motivated by specific anticompetitive intent or to lessen competition when the perpetrator(s) has (have) a great deal of economic power than when it (they) have little economic power is fallacious, regardless of how "firm economic power" is defined or whether that power as defined is assumed to be inferrable from a firm's market share.

3.2.3 Utilitarian Tests of Antitrust Illegality

At least 4 such tests can be distinguished (even if one ignores the variability associated with differences in the attributes a creature must possess for its utility to count). Utilitarian tests of antitrust illegality can differ by whether they focus on impacts on the total utility of all creatures whose utility counts or impacts on the average utility of all creatures whose utility counts (a difference that may be critical when the choice to be assessed will affect the number of creatures in the set of creatures whose utility counts). Utilitarian tests of antitrust illegality can also differ according to whether they focus on the relevant impact of the business conduct whose legality is at issue or the relevant impact of prohibiting that conduct.

I want to make two points about any of these 4 utilitarian tests of antitrust illegality. First, for any of these tests to be operational, one will have to deal acceptably with the problem of mapping all affective states into units of utility and disutility. Second, I suspect that, for any of the tests to be practicable, they will have to be applied somewhat circuitously through a protocol that (1) predicts or post-dicts the equivalent-monetary gains and losses the choice to be assessed generated/would generate, (2) identifies an operationally-large random sample of the winners and losers and the distribution among each of these groups of the attributes that affect the average marginal utility of money to them over the relevant ranges, (3) calculates the average marginal utility of the equivalent-monetary units won and the average marginal utility of the equivalent-monetary units lost, (4) multiplies those average figures respectively by the associated equivalent-monetary gain and loss figures, and (5) compares the two multiplicands.

3.2.4 Equality-of-the-Distribution-of-Utility-Focused Tests of Antitrust Illegality

Various equality-of-utility-focused tests of antitrust illegality can be distinguished (1) by the attributes creatures must have for their utility to be of concern, (2) by whether the tests focus on the impact of the business conduct whose legality is at issue or the impact of efforts to prevent the business conduct in question, and (3) by the inequality-metric they incorporate (e.g., by whether they measure utility-inequality by the mean deviation of the distribution of utility or the variance of that distribution or by some other measure of inequality). The same two final points I made about the utilitarian test of illegality apply mutatis mutandis to equality-of-utility tests: (1) to render any of these tests operational, one will have to figure out how to map all affective experiences into units of utility and disutility, and (2) it will probably prove most desirable from an equality-of-utility-egalitarian perspective to use a protocol that resembles the protocol I assumed would best be used to implement any utilitarian test of illegality to implement this equality-of-utility-focused test of illegality. Of course, the analogous protocol for implementing the equality-of-utility test of illegality will have to investigate the pre-choice distributions of utility of the relevant conduct's/legal policy's winners and losers and will focus on how the relevant conduct/policy will alter the utility of an appropriately-large random sample of the winners and losers. I should acknowledge as well that, if some metrics of inequality are operative, the relevant analysis will also have to take account of the distribution of utility among relevant creatures whose utility will not be affected by the choice being evaluated.

3.2.5 Equality-of-the-Distribution-of-Resources-Focused Tests of Antitrust Illegality

These tests of illegality focus on the impact of the choice to be assessed on the equality of the distribution of relevant creatures' "buying power," measured by the allocative cost of the goods and services they are able to purchase where (I suppose) the buying power of a relevant creature depends not only on its wealth and income but also on the relationship between the prices and allocative costs of the goods and services the creature will purchase and the allocative cost of any goods or services it receives free-of-charge from the government. (I am assuming for simplicity and probably indefensibly that this egalitarian concept of the moral good does not take into account the pleasantness or intrinsic- "rewardingness" of relevant individuals' labor [though I assume it does deem relevant the amount of leisure that relevant creatures consume]. This parenthetical lies behind my enquoting "buying power" in the sentence that precedes it.)

Variants of this test of antitrust illegality will differ according to (1) whether they focus on the impact of a particular exemplar (or general category) of business conduct or on the impact of government efforts to deter a particular exemplar (or general category) of business conduct and (2) the metric for inequality they respectively adopt.

To apply this test of antitrust illegality, one will have to focus on an appropriately-large random sample of relevant creatures and (1) generate estimates for each of them of their respective pre-choice "buying power" measured by the sum of the allocative cost of what they could buy, the intrinsic private value to them of their work-experiences, and the private value to them of the leisure they consumed, (2) generate estimates of the impact of the choice in question on the "buying power" of each of these creatures, (3) estimate the post-choice "buying power" of each of the members of the sample of creatures being studied, (4) calculate the inequality of the pre-choice distribution of "buying power," (5) calculate the inequality of the post-choice distribution of "buying power," and (6) compare the estimates of the pre-choice and post-choice inequality estimates. Once more, depending on the metric for inequality that is deemed morally warranted, the calculations in Steps (3), (4), and (5) of this protocol may have to take account of the buying power of creatures in the relevant sample whose "buying power" has not been or would not be affected by the business conduct or antitrust-policy choice to be evaluated.

3.2.6 Various Other Equality-of-Opportunity-Focused Tests of Antitrust Illegality

Section 2.4.4 identified and discussed a variety of equality-of-more-specific-opportunity-focused conceptions of egalitarianism on which tests of antitrust illegality could be grounded—opportunity-focused conceptions of egalitarianism that are concerned (for example) with creatures' opportunities (1) to lead lives of moral integrity, (2) to develop and employ specified intellectual, physical, or artistic skills, (3) to perform competently important governmental functions, and (4) to perform competently important non-governmental functions. Analyses that seek to implement such tests of antitrust illegality will have to focus on (1) the pre-conduct/policy distribution of "buying power" where special emphasis is placed on the private cost of purchasing training services and material goods access to which contributes to an individual's opportunity to develop a particular skill or to perform particular performer-desired governmental and non-governmental functions, (2) the pre-choice distribution of relevant disabilities and abilities, (3) the way in which these factors interact to generate or not to generate inequalities in the relevant opportunities, and (4) the impact of the business choice or antitrust policy under review on relevant creatures' general buying power and the prices of valued-opportunity-relevant goods and services. Such analyses will also have to specify the relevant inequality-of-opportunity metric and calculate the pre-choice and post-choice inequality-of-relevant-opportunity figures. Considerations of space and reader patience have persuaded me to provide no more detail. Once more, of course, the equality-of-opportunity-focused tests on which this subsection focuses could be applied to either business conduct or antitrust policies that would prevent such conduct.

3.2.7 Tests of Antitrust Illegality That Mix in Some Way Two or More of the Tests Already Considered

I will limit myself here to indicating that mixed tests that incorporate two or more of the tests articulated in Sects. 3.1 and 3.2 are perfectly coherent. Indeed, I believe that the government of a liberal-moral-rights-based society will often be morally obligated to promulgate and implement a mixed test of antitrust illegality when different citizens (and possibly participants) hold different moral-good positions because its citizens (and perhaps its participants) have a liberal moral right to have an equal opportunity influence on governmental outcomes.

Notes

1. The relevant U.S. statutes are Sherman Act, 26 Stat. 209 (1890) (codified as amended at 15 U.S.C. Sections 1–11) (hereinafter Sherman Act), Clayton Act, 38 Stat. 730 (1914) (codified as amended at 15 U.S.C. Sections 12–27) (hereinafter Clayton Act), and Federal Trade Commission Act, 38 Stat. 717 (1914) (codified as amended at 15 U.S.C. Sections 41–45) (hereinafter FTC Act).
2. The initial version of the relevant European treaty is Treaty Establishing the European Economic Community (hereinafter Treaty of Rome), 298 U.N.T.S. 11 (March 25, 1957). The current version of this treaty is Treaty of Lisbon Amending the Treaty on European Community (hereinafter 2009 Treaty of Lisbon), 2007 OJ C306, p. 1 (December 13, 2007). The relevant provisions of the 2009 Treaty of Lisbon are Article 101(1), Article 101(3), and Article 102.
3. The citation for the E.C./E.U. Merger Control Regulation is Council Regulation 139/2004 on the Control of Concentrations Between Undertakings (May 1, 2004) (hereinafter the EMCR). Throughout this book, "E.C." stands for "European Community" and is to be distinguished from "EC" (which stands for "European Commission"), and "E.U." stands for "European Union." In British parlance, the word "concentration" stands for what Americans call "merger or acquisition" and the word "undertaking" stands for what Americans call "firm."
4. I need to explain the portion of this test that follows the words "in one or more ways." This clause is included to prevent this test from deeming illegal QV investments or PPR projects that should not be illegal because their creation/execution was not critically illicitly motivated. To simplify, I will focus on QV investments. The QV investments that the clause in question

prevents from being condemned by the specific-anticompetitive-intent test of illegality satisfy the following four conditions: (1) the sum of (A) the conventional operating profits the QV investor believed ex ante that the QV investments in question would yield because the revenues the sale of the products they respectively create would generate exceed the variable cost of producing the sold units, (B) the operating profits the QV investor believed ex ante the QV investment would yield the investor by enabling it to make profitable sales of complements to the products it would create or of other members of the product-line to which the created product belongs, and (C) the operating profits the QV investor believed ex ante that the QV investment would yield the investor by enabling it to make profitable sales of one or more unrelated products by enhancing its reputation for producing high-quality, reliable goods constitute at least a normal rate-of-return on the investment in question; (2) ex ante, the investor believed that, if the investment in question would not deter a rival QV investment, the amount by which the QV investment would reduce the profit-yields of the investor's other QV investments in the relevant area of product-space by creating a product that would take sales away from them directly and by inducing the investor's rivals to respond to the investment by making non-retaliatory price-cuts or other non-retaliatory competitive moves that reduce the profit-yields of the investor's other projects would exceed the difference between the profits the investment would yield the investor in the ways listed after "(1)" in this sentence and the amount of profits that would constitute a normal rate-of-return on the investment in question (in my terminology: if the investment would not deter a rival QV investment, the investor would face a critical "monopolistic QV-investment disincentive" to make it); (3) ex ante, the investor believed that the QV investment in question would deter a rival QV investment that would in any case have lowered the profit-yields of the investor's other QV investments in the relevant ARDEPPS by competing with those investments directly and inducing other rivals to respond in non-retaliatory ways that reduce the first investor's other project's profit-yields—i.e., would in one sense increase the profits the investor whose investment's illegality is at issue would make by reducing the absolute attractiveness of the offers against which it would have to compete by deterring a rival QV investment; and (4) ex ante, the investor believed that the fact that the QV investment whose legality is at issue would deter a rival QV investment would render at least normally profitable a QV investment that would otherwise have yielded subnormal profits (would critically reduce or eliminate the monopolistic QV-investment disincentives the relevant investor faced and might even give it a monopolistic QV-investment incentive to make the investment if the investment would lower the profits of the investor's other projects by competing against them and inducing rival responses by a smaller amount than those other projects' profit-yields would otherwise have been reduced in analogous ways by the QV investment the investment under scrutiny would deter). The final clause of the definition of the specific-anticompetitive-intent test of illegality renders lawful under this test QV investments that satisfy these conditions because, if the relevant investor was making no relevant mistake, the fact that the QV investment that satisfied these conditions would be at least normally profitable if the only effects that were considered were those listed after "(1)" in the preceding sentence implies that the QV investments in question would be economically efficient in an otherwise-Pareto-perfect economy. In the other direction, QV investments made by investors that would have perceived them to be subnormally profitable ex ante but for the investor's belief that it had a monopolistic QV-investment incentive to make them are deemed illegal by the specific-anticompetitive-intent test of illegality because the fact that the profits they would yield in the 3 allocatively valuable ways listed in "(1)" above are subnormal implies that the investments would be economically inefficient in an otherwise-Pareto-perfect world and the investor's ex ante perception that the investment would be at least normally profitable was critically affected by its belief that the investment would or might reduce the absolute attractiveness of the best offers against which it would have to compete (by deterring a rival QV investment). The justification for the clause on which this footnote focuses when the investment in question is a PPR investment is the same. The only difference in the relevant analysis relates to the conventional operating profits a production-process researcher obtains by taking advantage of its discovery: in the PPR case, those profits consist of the cost-savings the researcher secures by using the discovered process (if it produces the good to whose production process the discovery relates) *plus* any profits the researcher obtains by licensing others to use the discovered process (or by selling the patent to the process).

5. For my explanation of why it is correct as a matter of U.S. law to interpret the enquoted language to promulgate a specific-anticompetitive-intent test of illegality, see Markovits (2014a), pp. 69–71 and 602.
6. For my explanation of why it is correct as a matter of E.U. law to interpret the enquoted language to promulgate a specific-anticompetitive-intent test of illegality, see id. at 117–120.
7. For my explanation of why it is correct as a matter of E.U. law to interpret the enquoted language to prohibit what U.S. courts denominate "exclusionary conduct"—i.e., conduct that manifests specific anticompetitive intent, see id. at 131–139.
8. For discussions of this issue and the (unsatisfactory) responses that U.S. courts, the European Commission (EC), and E.C./E.U. Courts of First Instance (CFIs) have made to it, see Markovits (2014a) at pp. 621–633.
9. The preceding textual discussion has ignored clauses (a)–(e) in Article 101(1), Article 101(3), and clauses (a)–(d) in Article 102. For discussions of these "provisions," see id. respectively at 102–112, 123–127, and 129–130.
10. For the definition of the concepts of "a classical or ideal economic market" and "an antitrust market," see Markovits (2014a) respectively at pp. 167–168 and 171 and respectively at Sects. 6.1 and 6.2 infra.
11. See Sect. 3.1.4 infra.

12. I am ignoring the possibility of applying an exploitative-abuse test of antitrust illegality to buyers because I think that (1) the exercise of buying power by firms lowers their marginal costs and hence the prices they charge their customers and (2) one of the goals of antitrust or competition laws is to benefit final consumers. For discussions of these two claims, see Markovits (2014a) at pp. 490–494.
13. See, e.g., the positions taken by some members of the Critical Legal Studies group on the meaningless of legal texts. See Dalton (1985), Tushnet (1983), Kennedy (1976), and Unger (1975, 1976).
14. The enquoted phrases come from Judge Learned Hand's opinion in United States v. Aluminum Co. of America (Alcoa), 148 F. 2d 416 (2d Cir. 1945). See also Judge Wyzanski's opinion in United States v. United Shoe Machinery, 110 F. Supp, 295 (Mass. 1952).
15. Although the opinion that might have used this test is far from clear on this issue, the Supreme Court at least flirted with the idea that U.S. antitrust law imposes such a duty on firms with substantial economic power in its opinion in Eastman Kodak Co. v. Image Technical Services, 504 U.S. 451 (1992)—a systems-rivalry case focusing on a decision by Eastman Kodak to create and introduce a new camera without disclosing those of its attributes independent potential suppliers of complements would need to know to develop compatible photo-finishing equipment, to supply compatible photo-finishing services, or to create compatible film. For a discussion of this opinion, see Markovits (2014a) at pp. 711–713. In a series of reports and cases, the EC has concluded that Article 102 of the 2009 Treaty of Lisbon imposes such a duty on "dominant firms" at least in the systems-rivalry context. See, e.g., Undertakings Offered by IBM, 14th Report on Competition Policy, pp. 94–95 (1984); Decca Navigator System, OJ L43/27, pp. 108–110 (1998); Microsoft, Commission Decision COMP/37.792 (2006); Campagnie Maritime Belge, C-395/96P, ECR I-1365, pp. 132 and 137 (2000); and Microsoft v. Commission, Case T-201/04 (2007). Were it not for the possibility that the drafters and ratifiers of the Treaty of Rome may have intended what is now Article 102 of the 2009 Treaty of Lisbon to impose such a legal duty on dominant firms, I would consider these decisions incorrect as a matter of law as well as a matter of policy. On the historical possibility, see DG Competition Discussion Paper on the Application of Article 82 of the Treaty to Exclusionary Abuses, Sect. 9.1 at p. 207 (2005). On the functions and desirability of systems rivalry, see Markovits (2014a) at 695–705 and Sect. 10.1.5 infra.
16. The best U.S. example of such a parimutuel-handicapping opinion is White Motor v. United States, 372 U.S. 253 (1963)—an opinion that the U.S. Supreme Court has still not disavowed. E.U. authorities engage in similar parimutuel handicapping. Although the Block Exemption Regulations that the European Commission has promulgated under authority provided by the Council of Ministers have improved over time, they still allow firms with low

market shares (assumed to be a surrogate for economic power) to control their independent distributors through contractual clauses and sales policies that firms with high market shares are not permitted (by the BERs) to employ. For a detailed discussion of the history of the relevant BERs, see Markovits (2014b) at 436–476.

17. The U.S. courts' leverage theory of tie-ins adopts an irrebuttable presumption that tie-ins used by sellers that have "market power" in the tying-product market are illegal. In the other direction, the Supreme Court's position that—to avoid summary judgment in a variety of Sherman Act Section 2 cases—the private plaintiff or the State must establish that the defendant had market power prior to engaging in the allegedly-illegal conduct in the market in which that conduct took place or perhaps has market power in that market after engaging in the allegedly-illegal conduct (the holdings are not clear on this point) adopts the second, defendant-favoring legal presumption delineated in the text. The E.U. Block Exemption Regulations discussed previously in the immediately-preceding footnote may be better described as adopting the two legal presumptions articulated in the textual sentence to which this footnote is attached.

References

Campagnie Maritime Belge, C-395/96P, ECR I-1365.

Clayton Act, 38 Stat. 730 (1914) (codified as amended at 15 U.S.C. Sections 12–27).

Council Regulation 139/2004 on the Control of Concentrations Between Undertakings (May 1, 2004).

Dalton, C. (1985). An essay in the deconstruction of contract doctrine. *Yale Law Journal, 94*, 997–1114.

Decca Navigator System, OJ L43/27 (1998).

DG Competition Discussion Paper on the Application of Article 82 of the Treaty to Exclusionary Abuses, Section 9.1 (December 2005).

Eastman Kodak Co. v. Image Technical Services, 504 U.S. 451 (1992).

Federal Trade Commission Act, 38 Stat. 717 (1914) (codified as amended at 15 U.S.C. Sections 41–45).

Kennedy, D. (1976). Form and substance in private law adjudication. *Harvard Law Review, 89*, 1685–1778.

Markovits, R. (2014a). *Economics and the interpretation and application of U.S. and E.U. antitrust law* Vol. I *Basic concepts and economics-based legal analyses of oligopolistic and predatory conduct*. Springer.

Markovits, R. (2014b). *Economics and the interpretation and application of U.S. and E.U. antitrust law* Vol. II *Economics-based legal analyses of mergers, vertical practices, and joint ventures*. Springer.

Microsoft, Commission Decision COMP/37.792 (2006).

Microsoft v. Commission, Case T-201/04 (2007).

Sherman Act, 26 Stat. 209. (1890). (codified as amended at 15 U.S.C. Sections 1–11).

Treaty Establishing the European Economic Community, 298 U.N.T.S. 11 (1957, March 25).

Treaty of Lisbon Amending the Treaty on European Union and the Treaty Establishing the European Community, 2007 OJ C306 (p. 1) (December 13, 2007).

Tushnet, M. (1987). Does constitutional theory matter? A comment. *Texas Law Review, 65*, 777–787.

Undertakings Offered by IBM, 14th Report on Competition Policy (1984).
Unger, R. (1975). *Knowledge and politics*. Free Press.
Unger, R. (1976). *Law in modern society*. Free Press.
United States v. Aluminum Co. of America (Alcoa), 148 F. 2nd 416 (2d Cir. 1945).
United States v. United Show Machinery, 110 F. Supp. 295 (Mass, D. 1952).
White Motor v. United States, 372 U.S. 253 (1963).

Price-Competition

4

Antitrust-law scholarship and antitrust-policy scholarship often refer to the intensity of the price-competition that a seller faces on a particular product and on the impact that particular conduct will have on the intensity of such price-competition. Unfortunately, in many instances, the relevant authors either never specify the metric they think should be used to measure the intensity of such price-competition or shift among alternative metrics they appear to believe (incorrectly) are coincident. This chapter explores the complexity of the concept of the intensity of price-competition that a given buyer faces on a given product, explains why no one such metric will be optimal in all contexts, and indicates the metric for such price-competition this study uses. As this chapter reveals, the concept is complicated by the fact that the metric for the intensity of price-competition could focus on (P−MC), P/MC, ([P−MC]/P), or ([P−MC]/MC) figures, the fact that a seller may charge some buyers lump-sum fees as well as per-unit prices or use tie-ins or reciprocity agreements, and the fact that a seller may charge different buyers different prices or have to incur different marginal costs to supply different buyers. In some contexts, the operationalization of the concept is also complicated by the fact that its users may not be equally interested in (P−MC) gaps that are attributable to the seller's monopoly power over price, to the seller's contrived or natural oligopoly power over price, to the seller's rivals' monopoly power over price, or to the seller's rivals' oligopoly power over price.

4.1 "Seller Price-Competition" and "the Intensity of Seller Price-Competition"

The expression "seller price-competition" refers to the process in which product-rivals compete away their prospective profits by reducing their prices toward, to, or below their marginal costs. Not surprisingly but in some ways unfortunately, the intensity of seller price-competition has been measured in a large

R. S. Markovits, *Welfare Economics and Antitrust Policy - Vol. I*,
https://doi.org/10.1007/978-3-030-79812-3_4

number of ways. Even if, to simplify, I ignore the facts that a seller may sell multiple units of its product to a given buyer for a lump-sum fee, may charge a given buyer different per-unit prices for different units of a given product, may charge a given buyer a lump-sum fee for the right to purchase units of a particular product for a constant per-unit price or for unit-to-unit-varying per-unit prices, may engage in conventional inter-buyer price discrimination, may condition its sale of one or more units of one product on stated terms to a given buyer on the buyer's agreeing to buy a specified number of units or its full requirements of a second product on specified terms, may condition its sale of one or more units of one product on specified terms to a given "buyer" on the "buyer's" agreeing to supply "the seller" in question with one, a specified quantity, the "seller's full requirements, or the "buyer's" total output of a second product on specified terms (where "buyer" and "seller" are enquoted in the last bit because the relevant actors are acting as sellers of one product and buyers of another product), the intensity of price-competition could be and has been measured by (P−MC), P/MC, (P−MC)/P, (P−MC)/MC, the ratio of the relevant product's actual unit sales to the sales that would be made if its price were set at its marginal cost at its actual output or its transaction-surplus-maximizing output, and so on and so forth. Unfortunately but not surprisingly, there is no universally-correct way to measure the intensity of price-competition. In this study, I will say that business conduct or an antitrust policy has lessened seller price-competition if it has generated an increase in (P−MC) by reducing the absolute attractiveness of the best offer the relevant buyer has obtained from any worse-than-privately-best-placed supplier (as opposed to by reducing the extent to which the relevant seller has mistakenly charged the buyer a lower price than the buyer would have been willing to pay). This study adopts this usage of "a decrease in price-competition" because this book is about antitrust law and policy and I think that this operational definition captures the way in which it is correct as a matter of U.S. law to interpret the expression "lessen competition" as it is used in U.S. antitrust law[1] and the way in which it is correct as a matter of E.U. law to interpret the expressions conduct whose "effect" is to "prevent" or "restrict competition"[2] or to "impede effective competition"[3] when that language is used in the competition-law provisions of the operative E.U. treaty.

4.2 The Components of the Gap Between the Price a Seller Charges and Its Conventional Marginal Costs

4.2.1 The Components of the Gap Between the Price an Individualized Pricer Charges a Buyer It Is Privately-Best-Placed to Supply and the Seller's Conventional Marginal Costs

The following account assumes that the relevant seller is charging the buyer in question only a per-unit price for a unit of the product being sold—inter alia, is not charging a lump-sum fee or entering into a tie-in or reciprocity agreement with the buyer in question. I subdivide the gap between the price that the seller is charging a buyer it is privately-best-placed to supply and the conventional marginal costs the seller must incur to supply the buyer in question with the relevant unit—the (P − MC) gap in question—into three major and a larger number of smaller components. The three major components are formed by inserting a seller's "highest non-oligopolistic price" (HNOP) and "no-error highest non-oligopolistic price" (NEHNOP) between its actual price and its conventional marginal costs. In the individualized-pricing context on which this subsection is focusing, the HNOP is defined to be the highest price that would be profitable for a seller that was privately-best-placed to supply a particular buyer to charge that buyer if its rivals would always respond to its moves on the assumption that it could not react to their responses. The NEHNOP is defined to be the highest price that would be profitable for a seller that was privately-best-placed to supply a particular buyer if neither the seller, nor any of its rivals, nor any relevant buyer made any ex ante error and the seller's rivals would always respond to its moves on the assumption that it could not react to their responses.

I will now delineate the various subcomponents respectively of NEHNOP–MC, HNOP–NEHNOP, and P–HNOP in individualized-pricing situations. In such situations, the NEHNOP–MC gap is first subdivided into (1) the privately-best-placed seller's basic competitive advantage (BCA) when dealing for the patronage of the relevant buyer (say, Y) and (2) the contextual marginal costs that the privately-second-placed seller would have to incur to match (or infinitesimally beat) the privately-best-placed seller's NEHNOP-containing offer ($CMC_{\#2}$). Obviously, several terms in the preceding sentence require elucidation. I will analyze the concept "basic competitive advantage" on the assumption that neither the privately-best-placed supplier of a given buyer nor its closest rival for that buyer's patronage (the privately-second-placed supplier of that buyer) will have to incur any contextual marginal costs (see below) to supply the buyer in question on relevant terms. In this case, the privately-best-placed supplier's BCA would equal the amount by which it was (privately) better-placed than anyone else to supply the buyer in question—the amount by which it could raise its price above its conventional marginal costs of production and distribution without making it inherently profitable for any rival to "steal" the customer in question by beating its offer. This amount is equal to the sum of the buyer preference advantage (disadvantage) the privately-best-placed supplier has over its closest rival for the relevant buyer's patronage at the relevant set of prices (the $BPA_{\#1}$—the additional amount of money that it would be inherently profitable for the buyer to pay to obtain its privately-best-placed supplier's product variant or service variant rather than its privately-second-placed supplier's product variant or service variant if the buyer's preference-perception were accurate) and the privately-best-placed supplier's (conventional) marginal cost advantage (disadvantage) over its closest rival for the relevant buyer's patronage ($MCA_{\#1}$—the amount by which the marginal or incremental costs the privately-best-placed supplier of the buyer in question would have to incur to supply the buyer in question were lower than the marginal or incremental costs its closest rival for that buyer's patronage would have to incur to supply the buyer). As the preceding statement implies, a seller may enjoy a BCA in its relations with a particular buyer because it has both a BPA and an MCA, because its buyer preference disadvantage (BPD) is smaller than its MCA, or because its BPA exceeds its marginal cost disadvantage (MCD).

The second component of the NEHNOP–MC gap I find worth distinguishing in individualized-pricing contexts is the contextual marginal costs of the privately-second-placed supplier of the buyer in question ($CMC_{\#2}$). Contextual marginal costs are the extra costs a seller has to bear because the price it is charging the buyer in question might expose the seller to some risk of cross-selling (i.e., arbitrage) (to the extent that the price it is charging is discriminatory or multi-part [contains a lump-sum fee as well as a per-unit price]), might induce its other customers to intensify their bargaining (by putting the lie to its statements about its costs, by leading them to conclude that it has been treating them unfairly, or by suggesting that it can in fact be bargained down), might expose it to ex ante legal-liability costs (to the extent that the price may appear to some to involve illegal price discrimination or some other price-regulation violation), and/or might induce its rivals to retaliate. Such costs are said to be "contextual" because they depend on various features of the context in which they are charged—inter alia, on the prices the relevant seller is charging other buyers, on various features of the legal milieu (e.g., on the existence of price-discrimination prohibitions or maximum or minimum price-regulations), on what the seller has told its other customers about its own costs, etc. In individualized-pricing situations, a #2 seller (a seller that is privately-second-placed to obtain the relevant buyer Y's patronage) is likely to have to incur CMC to quote Y a price that makes #2's offer as attractive to Y overall as the NEHNOP-containing offer Y received from its privately-best-placed supplier (#1) because the price-component of #2's "matching" offer to Y is likely to be discriminatory—more specifically, is likely to be lower than the price #2 charges those buyers it is privately-best-placed to supply.

Unfortunately, once one recognizes the existence of contextual marginal costs, a series of additional, related terms have to be introduced: (1) the contextual-marginal-cost advantage or disadvantage (CCA or CCD) of a privately-best-placed-supplier in an individualized-pricing context ($CCA_{\#1} = CMC_{\#2} – CMC_{\#1}$), (2) the overall marginal cost a firm would have to incur to supply a particular buyer on specified terms (OMC = MC + CMC), and (3) the overall competitive advantage a privately-best-placed seller enjoys in its relations with a particular buyer ($OCA_{\#1} = BCA_{\#1} + CCA_{\#1}$). This study will sometimes make reference to relationships that involve these concepts—in particular, will sometimes make use of the facts that (1) $CMC_{\#2} = CMC_{\#1} + CCA_{\#1}$, (2) $OCA_{\#1} = BCA_{\#1} + CCA_{\#1}$, and (3) $(NEHNOP–MC)_{\#1} = OCA_{\#1} + CMC_{\#1}$. In the end, then, my conceptual system subdivides each of the two subcomponents of the NEHNOP–MC gap ($BCA_{\#1}$ and $CMC_{\#2}$) into two parts: $BCA_{\#1} = BPA_{\#1} + MCA_{\#1}$, and $CMC_{\#2} = CMC_{\#1} + CCA_{\#1}$.

In my scheme, the second major component of the P–MC gap for an individualized pricer that is setting a price to a buyer it is privately-best-placed to supply is the HNOP–NEHNOP gap. This gap reflects various errors that can cause a privately-best-placed seller's actual price to exceed or differ from its NEHNOP for non-oligopolistic reasons. My conceptual system distinguishes three subcomponents of the HNOP–NEHNOP gap—i.e., three categories of errors that can cause an individualized pricer's HNOP to exceed its NEHNOP: (1) buyer-error-generated HNOP–NEHNOP gaps or margins ($BEM_{\#1}$), (2) rival-error-related HNOP–NEHNOP gaps or margins ($REM_{\#1}$), and (3) privately-best-placed-supplier-error-related HNOP–NEHNOP gaps or margins (#1EM). In my system, the total extra margin a privately-best-placed seller obtains because of all relevant actors' errors is symbolized at $\Sigma EM_{\#1}$. I will now comment on each of the three subcomponents of $\Sigma EM_{\#1}$ in turn.

I will restrict my comments about the relevant buyer-error margin to a few remarks about the contestability of the usefulness of the concept. Admittedly, if the buyer preferences that played a role in the analysis of the determinants of a privately-best-placed individualized pricer's NEHNOP–MC gap are defined to refer to the buyer's perceived preferences as opposed to the preferences it would have if it were a sovereign maximizer, then the NEHNOP would already reflect any buyer errors that affected the price that a privately-best-placed individualized pricer charged the buyer in question. However, for linguistic reasons and because the reality of buyer errors is sometimes relevant to both policy analyses and the determination of existing legal rights, it is useful to assume that the buyer preferences that lie behind the BPAs that are a component of a privately-best-placed individualized pricer's NEHNOP are the monetized preferences of a sovereign maximizer and to handle separately the buyer errors that may enable such a privately-best-placed seller to obtain higher prices from the erring customer than it otherwise could (or, for that matter, that may preclude it from obtaining as high a price from a buyer it was "objectively" privately-best-placed to supply as it otherwise could).

I will confine my comments about the relevant rival-error margin to a brief account of the various types of rival errors that can cause a privately-best-placed seller's HNOP to exceed its NEHNOP. In an individualized-pricing context, a privately-best-placed seller's closest competitor for a particular buyer's patronage (#2) may make at least four different types of errors that will enable the privately-best-placed seller to obtain a price above its NEHNOP. First, #2—the rival that is privately-second-placed to obtain the relevant buyer's patronage—may overestimate the overall marginal costs #2 would have to incur to supply the buyer in question at the price it would have to charge to beat the relevant privately-best-placed-supplier's (#1's) HNOP-containing offer (in which case #2 would fail to beat #1's offer despite the fact that it would beat it if it realized the inherent profitability of doing so); second, #2 may underestimate the relevant buyer's preference for #1's product or service in circumstances in which #2 will not have the opportunity to make a second bid for the relevant buyer's patronage (in which case #2 will make an offer to the buyer in question that will fail to obtain its patronage despite the fact that #2 believed that its offer would be successful and could in fact have profited by making a more attractive offer that would have been successful); third, #2 may critically overestimate the probability that #1 will beat any undercutting offer whose acceptance #2 would find profitable because #2 overestimates the probability that #1 will have the opportunity to change its initial offer to that buyer and/or the probability that #1 will find it inherently profitable to beat any relevant underbid #2 would otherwise find profitable to make (in which case #2 will be deterred from making what would have been a successful, profitable underbid by the fact that the pricing and bidding costs it would have to incur to do so exceed its estimate of the weighted-average profits such a bid would yield it if pricing and bidding costs were zero [given its estimate of the probability that its undercutting offer will be accepted], though such bidding costs are in fact less than the weighted-average profits it should expect to make by undercutting #1's initial offer [bidding costs aside], given the actual [higher] probability that its undercutting offer will be accepted); and fourth, #2 may critically overestimate the sum of (1) the benefits #1 will allow it to obtain by engaging in reciprocal collaboration if #2 does not undercut #1's bid and (2) the costs #1 will impose on it by retaliating if #2 does undercut #1's bid (in which case #2 will be deterred from making a successful underbid that would have been profitable [strategic costs considered] by its misperception of the likelihood and/or likely extent of #1's relevant contrived oligopolistic reactions [see below] to #2's various possible responses to #1's initial price).

The third type of error that can cause a privately-best-placed individualized pricer's HNOP to exceed its NEHNOP are errors that #1 makes itself. Thus, #1 may charge an individualized supra-NEHNOP price because it has overestimated its NEHNOP (its closest rival's MC, CMC, or BPD) and/or has incorrectly concluded that its closest rival will make errors that will enable it to get away with a price contained in an offer that that rival could have profited ex ante by beating (on the current assumption that the #1 seller did not intend to engage in oligopolistic conduct).

Before proceeding to the P–HNOP component of a privately-best-placed individualized pricer's P–MC gap, two additional points should be made about the HNOP–NEHNOP gap. First, although most of the preceding discussion presupposed that any errors that the privately-best-placed individualized pricer and its rivals might make would always cause it to charge prices above the NEHNOP, that supposition is unjustified. Thus, if the privately-best-placed supplier realized that its closest rival for the relevant buyer's patronage underestimated the marginal cost that that rival would have to incur to supply the buyer in question or if the privately-best-placed supplier itself underestimated its closest rival's relevant marginal cost or its own BPA over that rival in relation to the relevant buyer, the privately-best-placed supplier would tend on those accounts to charge the buyer a price below its NEHNOP.

Second, it is important to note that although the set of errors that affect a privately-best-placed individualized pricer's HNOP–NEHNOP gap includes errors its rivals make about its oligopolistic intentions, it does not include the errors it may make that affect whether it seeks to obtain an oligopolistic margin (OM) or the size of the OM it seeks to obtain.

In my scheme, the third major component of the gap between the price an individualized pricer actually charges a buyer it is privately-best-placed to supply and the conventional marginal costs it would have to incur to supply that buyer are the oligopolistic margins it seeks to obtain from the buyer in question—i.e., the extra sum it tries to obtain from this buyer because it believes that its closest rival or rivals for the relevant buyer's patronage will be deterred from making what would otherwise be a profitable undercutting response to any price it charges above its HNOP by a correct belief that it will (or may) react to such a response in a way that makes undercutting unprofitable for them. When the privately-best-placed seller believes that its rivals will be deterred from undercutting it by their correct perception that it will have an opportunity to react to such undercutting by making a move that is inherently profitable for it and will take advantage of that opportunity, the margin that it believes its ability to react will enable it to obtain is called a natural oligopolistic margin (NOM) and the privately-best-placed seller's act of setting a price that relies on its rivals' being deterred from undercutting by their realization that it would react to their undercutting by making an inherently-profitable move that would make their undercutting unprofitable for them is called natural oligopolistic pricing (NOP). When the privately-best-placed seller believes that its rivals will be deterred from undercutting it because it induced them to perceive that it would react to their responses in one or more otherwise-unprofitable ways to render otherwise-profitable undercutting responses unprofitable—namely, by leading them to believe that it would reciprocate to their cooperation and/or retaliate against their non-cooperation, the margin the privately-best-placed seller obtained by promising to reciprocate to cooperation and/or retaliate against non-cooperation is called a contrived oligopolistic margin (COM), and the privately-best-placed conduct (its setting the contrived-oligopolistic price, its communicating promises of reciprocation and threats of retaliation, its making good on those promises and threats) and any collaborative response its rivals make) are called contrived oligopolistic pricing (COP). In my system, the total oligopolistic margin a privately-best-placed seller obtains from a buyer it is privately-best-placed to supply is symbolized as $\Sigma OM_{\#1} = NOM_{\#1} + COM_{\#1}$.

One additional point needs to be made about the situation that will prevail when $P_{\#1}$ exceeds $HNOP_{\#1}$. As you will recall, my original discussion of $CMC_{\#1}$ assumed that the privately-best-placed seller was charging its HNOP, and my discussion of $CMC_{\#2}$ assumed that the privately-second-placed seller was matching or infinitesimally beating an offer by #1 to supply the relevant buyer at #1's HNOP. If $P_{\#1}$ exceeds $HNOP_{\#1}$, that fact will affect both its CMC and the CMC its closest rival for the relevant buyer's patronage will have to incur to match #1's offer. In particular, #1's higher (supra-HNOP) price will reduce $CMC_{\#1}$ if it is less discriminatory than its HNOP or is less far below, equal to, or above a legally-required minimum price, while a $P_{\#1}$ that exceeds $HNOP_{\#1}$ will increase $CMC_{\#1}$ if it is more discriminatory or exceeds a maximum-price regulation. In general, #1's supra-HNOP price will tend to reduce $CMC_{\#2}$ by reducing the extent to which #2's matching-offer price discriminates in the relevant buyer's favor and may tend to reduce $CMC_{\#2}$ as well by reducing or eliminating any positive difference between

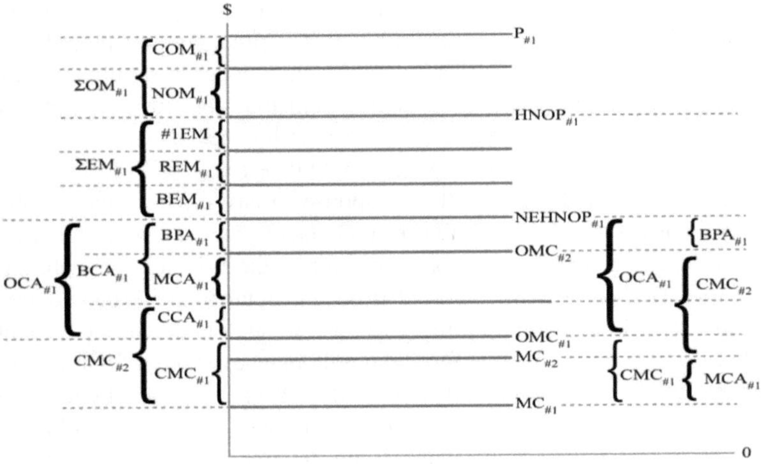

CHART 4.1

GLOSSARY OF SYMBOLS

(1) $P_{\#1}$—the privately-best-placed seller's actual price

(2) $COM_{\#1}$—the privately-best-placed seller's attempted contrived oligopolistic margin

(3) $NOM_{\#1}$—the privately-best-placed seller's attempted natural oligopolistic margin

(4) $\Sigma OM_{\#1}$—the privately-best-placed seller's attempted total oligopolistic margin=$NOM_{\#1}$+$COM_{\#1}$

(5) $HNOP_{\#1}$—the privately-best-placed seller's highest non-oligopolistic price=($P_{\#1}$–$\Sigma OM_{\#1}$)

(6) #1EM—the additional margin the privately-best-placed seller's errors about its NEHNOP, BEM, or $REM_{\#1}$ (see (7) below)—lead it to believe it can obtain non-oligopolistically

(7) $REM_{\#1}$—the additional margin the privately-best-placed seller can obtain because of errors its rivals make

(8) $BEM_{\#1}$—the additional margin the privately-best-placed seller can obtain because of errors the relevant buyer makes

(9) $\Sigma EM_{\#1}$—the total additional margin the privately-best-placed seller's actual price contains because of errors its customers make, its rivals make, or it makes on issues that do not cause it to try for additional or higher OMs=HNOP–NEHNOP (see [10] below)

(10) $NEHNOP_{\#1}$—the price that would be the privately-best-placed seller's HNOP if no-one made any relevant errors=($HNOP_{\#1}$–$\Sigma EM_{\#1}$)

(11) $BPA_{\#1}$—the privately-best-placed seller's buyer preference advantage over its closest rival for the relevant buyer's patronage

(12) $MCA_{\#1}$—the privately-best-placed seller's (conventional) marginal cost advantage over its closest rival for the relevant buyer's patronage

(13) $BCA_{\#1}$=$BPA_{\#1}$+$MCA_{\#1}$—the privately-best-placed seller's basic competitive advantage over its closest rival for the relevant buyer's patronage

Chart 4.1 The components of the gap between a privately-best-placed seller's actual individualized price and (conventional) marginal cost

(14) $CCA_{\#1}$—the privately-best-placed seller's contextual cost advantage over its closest rival for the relevant buyer's patronage when the privately-best-placed seller is charging its NEHNOP and this closest rival is matching that offer

(15) $OCA_{\#1}=BCA_{\#1}+CCA_{\#1}$—the privately-best-placed seller's overall competitive advantage over its closest rival for the relevant buyer's patronage when the privately-best-placed seller is charging its NEHNOP

(16) $CMC_{\#1}$—the contextual marginal costs the privately-best-placed seller would have to incur to supply the relevant buyer at its NEHNOP

(17) $MC_{\#1}$—the conventional marginal cost the privately-best-placed seller (#1) would have to incur to supply the buyer in question

(18) $OMC_{\#1}=MC_{\#1}+CMC_{\#1}$—the privately-best-placed seller's overall marginal cost if it charges the relevant buyer its NEHNOP

(19) $MC_{\#2}=MC_{\#1}+MCA_{\#1}$—the conventional marginal cost the privately-second-placed seller (#2) would have to incur to supply the relevant buyer

(20) $CMC_{\#2}$—the contextual marginal costs the privately-second-placed seller would have to incur to match or infinitesimally beat the privately-best-placed seller's NEHNOP-offer to the relevant buyer

(21) $OMC_{\#2}=MC_{\#2}+CMC_{\#2}=MC_{\#1}+MCA_{\#1}+CMC_{\#2}$—the overall marginal costs the privately-second-placed seller would have to incur to match or infinitesimally beat the privately-best-placed seller's NEHNOP-offer to the relevant buyer

Not Represented: the contextual marginal costs and hence overall marginal cost that the privately-best-placed seller would have to incur to make a sale or even an offer to the relevant buyer at a price that exceeded its NEHNOP or the contextual marginal and hence overall marginal cost that a privately-second-placed seller would have to incur to match or infinitesimally beat any offer by a privately-best-placed seller to the relevant buyer that contained a price that exceeded the latter's NEHNOP

N.B. $P_{\#1}-MC_{\#1}=CMC_{\#2}+BCA_{\#1}+\#1EM+REM_{\#1}+BEM_{\#1}+NOM_{\#1}+COM_{\#1}= CMC_{\#1}+OCA_{\#1}+\Sigma EM_{\#1}+\Sigma OM_{\#1}$

Chart 4.1 (continued)

the price #2 will have to charge to match #1's offer and some required minimum price though it may increase $CMC_{\#2}$ by increasing the positive difference between #2's matching-offer price and a maximum allowed price.

Chart 4.1 on page 74 presents the conceptual scheme just delineated. It is accompanied by a glossary of all the symbols my price-competition conceptual scheme involves. Before proceeding, I should point out that the preceding account of the determinants of a privately-best-placed individualized pricer's P–MC gap has ignored the reality that such a pricer's actual price may also be influenced by conventional individual-product "promotional," product-line promotional, institutional promotional, network-building, "learning-by-doing," and "keeping-in-touch" considerations.[4]

4.2.2 The Components of the Gap Between the Across-the-Board Price That an Across-the-Board-Pricing Seller Charges and Its Conventional Marginal Costs

My breakdown of the gap between an across-the-board pricer's P–MC gap is very similar to its individualized-pricing counterpart. Once more, the P–MC gap is subdivided into P–HNOP, HNOP–NEHNOP, and NEHNOP–MC components. Once more, P–HNOP = NOM + COM, and HNOP–NEHNOP = ΣEM. However, at least five differences between the across-the-board-pricing and individualized-pricing (P–MC)-gap breakdown are worth pointing out. First, because any across-the-board price that a seller charges will apply to some buyers that it is not "privately-best-placed to supply" in any sense in which that expression might be usefully defined, I use the symbol S (for seller) rather than the symbol #1 to refer to any across-the-board pricer whose HNOP or NEHNOP I am considering. Second, and relatedly, the #1EM subcomponent of the individualized HNOP–NEHNOP gap is replaced by a seller-error-margin (SEM) subcomponent in the across-the-board pricing conceptual scheme. Third, and also relatedly, although I recognize that the following usage may be confusing and therefore not advisable, in across-the-board-pricing contexts, the analysis of the breakdown of an across-the-board-pricing seller's NEHNOP–MC gap will refer to its and its rivals' across-the-board-pricing BCA/BCD distributions where each across-the-board-pricing BCA or BCD that any S has in its relations with any particular buyer is equated with the sum of its BPA or BPD in relation to that buyer and the MCA or MCD it would have in relation to that buyer *if the marginal cost that the seller in question and each of its rivals would have to incur to supply a unit of their respective products to that buyer (assuming the buyer paid the delivery costs) were equated with the marginal costs each such S would have to incur to supply the last unit of its product it would supply if all of them charged the prices that would equal their NEHNOPs if they announced their prices in the order in which they actually announced their prices*. This definition would not be problematic if, as there is some reason to believe is often the case, the MC curves of all the relevant Ses were horizontal over the relevant ranges of output. However, when the relevant MC curves are not horizontal over the relevant ranges of output, this component (though still useful as a descriptive concept) cannot be used in any protocol for identifying a particular across-the-board pricer's HNOP: if the goal is to calculate an S' HNOP, one cannot do so through a protocol of measuring the components of its HNOP–MC gap if the definition of one of these components assumes that one already knows the HNOP not only of the S in question but also of each of its rivals. Fourth and again relatedly, the across-the-board-pricing counterpart to the BCA component of the gap between a privately-best-placed seller's NEHNOP and MC in an individualized-pricing situation is the difference between the across-the-board price each across-the-board-pricing S would charge if it and its rivals knew that it could not react to its rivals' responses and they charged its customers' prices equal to their conventional marginal costs. This component will depend not just on the relevant S' across-the-board-pricing BCA/BCD distribution as defined above but also on the way in which that S' and its rivals' marginal costs vary above and below the unit outputs they would respectively produce if none behaved oligopolistically and they announced their prices in the order in which they actually did announce them. And fifth, the across-the-board-pricing counterpart to the $CMC_{\#2}$ subcomponent of the individualized-pricing NEHNOP–MC gap is replaced by an analogous subcomponent that also equals the extra margin that the seller in question finds it profitable to charge because its rivals are charging its customers prices that exceed their respective conventional marginal costs. However, whereas (1) in the normal individualized-pricing situation, a privately-best-placed supplier's closest rival will usually charge the #1's customers prices above the #2's conventional marginal costs if the #1 charges its NEHNOP to the relevant buyer because (A) the individualized price the #2 will have to charge the relevant buyer to match the #1's NEHNOP offer to that buyer will discriminate in the relevant buyer's favor and (B) sellers (including #2) will normally have to incur arbitrage-related, goodwill-related, bargaining-related, and/or law-related CMC to discriminate in favor of a buyer (to charge that buyer a lower price than the seller is charging other buyers—in particular, is charging other buyers that the seller is privately-best-placed to supply), (2) in across-the-board-pricing situations, each seller S' rivals will be charging that seller's potential customers prices above their respective conventional marginal costs because (A) by definition, in such situations these rivals will be charging their own customers the same price they are charging the relevant S' customers and (B) charging buyers that would be willing to pay them prices in excess of their respective conventional marginal costs prices equal to their respective marginal costs will be "costly" to them—i.e., because (1) each rival of each S would on this account charge supra-marginal-cost prices to that S' potential customers even if each such rival believed that the other rivals of the S in question would equate their prices with their respective marginal costs and (2) each rival of the S in question would also be charging prices that exceed the rival's marginal costs because each of them would realize that in reality its rivals (often the S' other rivals) would also be charging the relevant rival's customers (across-the-board) prices that exceed their respective marginal costs.

I will now proceed to describe the protocol for determining the NEHNOP array for a relevant set of across-the-board-pricing sellers. (For simplicity, I will henceforth assume that no relevant errors are being made and therefore focus on the NEHNOP array for such sellers.) I will then delineate and explore two simple examples that illustrate the protocol, reveal the relevance of various determinants of the gap between the prices in an across-the-board-pricing NEHNOP array and the respective seller's marginal costs, and reveal as well the fact that the NEHNOP–MC gap for across-the-board pricers will almost always substantially exceed their average and even their highest across-the-board-pricing BCA in their relations with those buyers in relation to which (on my admittedly-awkward definition) they have a (positive) across-the-board-pricing BCA.

I will start by providing an account of how one would calculate the array of across-the-board-pricing NEHNOPs for a set of across-the-board pricers.

To generate conclusions about such an NEHNOP array, one would have to know (1) the order in which the relevant sellers announced their prices, (2) each relevant seller's across-the-board BPA/BPD array, and (3) each relevant seller's MC curves over the relevant range of unit outputs.

I will start by describing the protocol for calculating the across-the-board-pricing NEHNOP array for duopolists—X1, which produces product A1, and X2, which produces product A2. I will assume that (1) X1 announces its price for A1 before X2 announces its price for A2, (2) X1 knows that X2 realizes that X1 will not react to X2's response to X1's price, and (3) X1 and X2 have perfect information about their respective BPA/BPD arrays and the shapes of their respective MC curves over the relevant range of outputs. On these assumptions, X1 will identify its profit-maximizing (HNOP) price $P1^*$ by (1) determining for each price P1 it could charge the price P2 that X2 would find most profitable to charge in response, (2) calculating the unit sales it would make if it charged the P1 in question and X2 made its profit-maximizing price-response, (3) calculating the profits that it would make by charging the particular price P1 in question, given the unit sales X1 would make at that price and its marginal costs over the relevant output-range, and (4) identifying the price $P1^*$ that would yield it the highest profits in the circumstances in question. X2 would, of course, determine the price P2 that would be most profitable for it to charge in response to any price X1 charged if X1 would not react to X2's price-response by (1) determining for each such price P2 that it could charge in response to the particular price P1 that X1 set for A1 the unit sales that it would make if it charged that P2, (2) calculating the profits it would make if it charged that price P2 in response to X1's price P1, given the marginal costs it would have to incur to supply the units it would sell if X1 charged that P1 and it responded with that P2, and (3) identifying the price that would yield it the highest profits if X1 charged the P1 in question. The relevant NEHNOP array would then consist of the price $P1^*$ that X1 would find most profitable if it could not engage in oligopolistic pricing and the price $P2^*$ that X2 would find most profitable to charge in response to X1's price $P1^*$.

The relevant protocol is more complicated but essentially no different in across-the-board-pricing situations in which three or more relevant sellers are operating. The complication is that, in the three-seller case in which X1, X2, and X3 announce their binding prices in that order, X2's calculation of the price P2 that would constitute its profit-maximizing price-response to any price P1 that X1 might charge would take into account the response that X3 would find most profitable to make if X1 charged the P1 in question and X2 responded to X1's price P1 with a particular price P2 to which X1 would not respond and neither X1 nor X2 would react to X3's response to their prices. Concomitantly, X1's calculation of its NEHNOP would have to take account of X2's prospective analysis of X3's profit-maximizing response to any price P2 that X2 could charge in response to any price P1 X1 charged on the assumption that X1 would not react to X2's and X3's responses to its price P1 and that X2 would not react to X3's response to X2's price (itself made in response to X1's price).

Although the relevant calculations will become highly complex as the number of rival sellers increases, if one had the relevant data, computer programs could be designed to generate NEHNOP-array conclusions quickly and without much expense. I should point out that there is little reason to believe that HNOP calculations will be less practicable in across-the-board-pricing contexts than in individualized-pricing contexts: the protocol I delineated for calculating individualized NEHNOPs was a protocol for calculating the NEHNOP for a privately-best-placed single individualized-pricing seller to charge an individual buyer it was privately-best-placed to supply whereas the protocol just delineated for calculating the NEHNOP array in an area of product-space in which across-the-board prices are being charged is a protocol for determining the prices that all relevant sellers in that area of product-space would be charging all relevant buyers. I do not want the wrong conclusion to be inferred from the preceding point. The fact that I do not think that it would be less practicable to determine the NEHNOPs of all the sellers that operate in a given area of product-space if they are setting across-the-board prices than if they are setting individualized prices has no bearing on whether I think it practicable to calculate such NEHNOP arrays in either type of pricing context. In fact, I do not think it practicable to calculate NEHNOPs in either pricing context—i.e., I do not think that in either individualized-pricing or across-the-board-pricing contexts, it will be cost-effective to determine whether a seller is charging an oligopolistic price by comparing its actual price with an estimate of its NEHNOP.

In another study,[5] I developed and explored two highly-simplified examples (1) to illustrate the NEHNOP-calculation protocol respectively in duopoly and three-seller cases, (2) to reveal that, as the preceding discussion of the across-the-board-pricing counterpart to the $CMC_{\#2}$ component of a privately-best-placed individualized pricer's HNOP–MC gap implied, the across-the-board-pricing NEHNOP–MC gaps for across-the-board pricers will almost always be higher not only than the average across-the-board-pricing BCA any such pricer enjoys in its relations with those buyers for which it has such a BCA but also than the highest such BCA an across-the-board pricer enjoys, and (3) to demonstrate that the (NEHNOP − MC) gaps of the members of a set of across-the-board-pricing rivals depends inter alia on the order in which they announce their prices—in particular, that such a set of rivals' NEHNOP–MC gaps will tend to be higher the greater the extent to which the firms for which the following ratio is low announce early in the relevant sequence: the ratio of (the frequency with which the relevant firm has an across-the-board-pricing BCA) to (the frequency with which it has the lowest or close-to-lowest across-the-board-pricing BCD). This conclusion reflects the fact that any seller for which this ratio is lower has more of an incentive than its rivals to undermine their prices since the amount of potential profits it will lose by charging a lower across-the-board price to buyers that would have been willing to pay it a higher price will be small relative to the amount of additional sales and related profits it will be able to make by charging (roughly speaking) a lower price than its earlier-announcing rivals charged. (Space-constraints preclude one from including these examples in this chapter.)

Notes

1. This expression is used in the U.S. Clayton Act, 38 Stat. 730 (1914) (codified as amended 15 U.S.C. Sections 12–27).
2. This language appears in what is now Article 101(1) of the Treaty of Lisbon Amending the Treaty on European Union and the Treaty Establishing the European Community (hereinafter 2009 Treaty of Lisbon), 2007 OJ C306 p.1 (December 13, 2007).
3. This language appears in the European Community's Merger Control Regulation, Council Regulation 139/2004 on the Control of Concentrations Between Undertakings, OJ L24/1 (May 1, 2004) (hereinafter EMCR).
4. A seller is properly said to be engaging in (conventional single-product) "promotional pricing" at time t(0) when it lowers the price of its product A at t(0) to a level that would not otherwise be profitable because it expects the additional sales of product A that the price-reduction enables it to make at t(0) to increase the profits it makes at t(1…n) by increasing the demand it will face in relation to product A at t(1…n) for any or all of the following three reasons: (1) because it increases the demand that the additional buyer(s) to which the price-reduction enables it to make sales at t(0) will have for product A at t(1…n)—"try it, you'll like it," (2) because it increases the demand that other buyers will have for product A at t(1…n) by increasing the positive information they receive about A from the additional buyer(s) to which its price-reduction enabled it to sell (A) at t(0) or from someone with whom these buyers talked or who observed these buyers' using A or by observing themselves the way in which A performed for these additional buyers, and/or (3) because it increases the demand that other buyers will have for A at t(1…n) because they want to be identified with the additional buyers to which its price-reduction enable it to sell A at t(0) or with particular attributes of these buyers. A seller is properly said to be engaging in product-line promotional pricing of product A1 at time t(0) when it charges a lower price for A1 because it expects that the additional sales of A1 that the reduction in A1's price will enable it to make of A1 at time t(0) will increase the demand curve it faces for products A2…n that are product A1's product-line at time t(0) and subsequently because buyers have a preference for multiple members of the same product-line in that (1) they find a matching set more aesthetically attractive than an unmatched collection, (2) the proper way to use each member of a given product-line is the same while the proper method of using different product-lines varies from product-line to product-line and it is costly to learn how to use the products in a product-line whose products one has not yet used, and/or (3) the members of any given product-line have the same strengths and weaknesses and such strengths and weaknesses differ among rival product-lines and it is costly to learn the strengths and weaknesses of a product-line whose products one has not yet used. I should add that the benefits of product-line promotional pricing will tend to be higher to the extent that the additional purchases of A2…n made by a buyer of A1 that has been induced to purchase A1 by a reduction in its price induces other buyers to purchase a member of the product-line A1…n. A seller is properly said to be engaging in

institutional promotional pricing if it charges a lower price for product A at time t(0) than it otherwise would have found profitable because it expects that the extra sales the price-reduction will enable it to make of A will increase the demand it faces for all its products (regardless of whether they are in the same product-line as A) in that product A is a good product and any buyer that consumes it will revise upward its estimate of the quality of all of the seller's products as will anyone that is told of its performance by its actual consumer or that observes its performance by its actual consumer in circumstances that enable the observer to evaluate its performance. A seller is properly said to be engaging in network-building pricing of product A when it charges a lower price for product A than it would otherwise find profitable because the objective value of product A to an individual buyer increases with the number of other buyers (i.e., users) of the product. A seller is properly said to be engaging in "learning-by-doing" pricing when it lowers its price at t(0) because it expects the additional sales that the price-reduction enables it to make at t(0) will increase the profits it makes at t(1…n) because the production of the additional units of A at t(0) will reduce the costs it will have to incur to produce various relevant outputs of its product at t(1...n) or by enabling it to discover a somewhat-different product variant that it could produce at t(1…n) on which it would face a more attractive DD/MC combination. A competitive inferior is properly said to be engaging in "keeping-in-touch" pricing if it incurs the cost of making a bid that it knows will not be accepted to secure the advertizing-like benefits such a bid will generate by making it more likely that the buyer will solicit bids from it in the future and/or to pay more attention to its bids in the future by inducing the buyer to have a better opinion of it than the buyers otherwise would have.

5. See Markovits 2014 at pp. 29–39.

References

Clayton Act, 38 Sat. 730 (914) (codified as amended 15 U.S.C. Sections 12–27).

Council Regulation 139/2004 on the Control of Concentrations Between Undertakings, OJ L24/1 (May 1, 2004).

Markovits, R. (2014). *Economics and the interpretation and application of U.S. and E.U. antitrust law* Vol. I. *Basic concepts and economics-based legal analyses of oligopolistic and predatory conduct*. Springer.

Treaty of Lisbon Amending the Treaty on European Union and the Treaty Establishing the European Community, 2007 OJ C306. (13 Dec 2007).

QV-Investment Competition (and PPR Competition)

5

Antitrust-law scholarship and antitrust-policy scholarship have rarely paid attention to the concept of the intensity of investment-competition in any relevant area of product-space. This study reveals that this omission is unfortunate—that some conduct may be rendered illegal or lawful, economically inefficient or efficient, liberal-moral-rights-violative, or undesirable or desirable from the perspective of one or more conceptions of the moral good by its impact on the intensity of investment-competition. This chapter explores the complexity of the concept of the intensity of investment-competition, explains why no one metric for the intensity of such competition will always be optimal, specifies the metric for the intensity of such competition this study uses, analyzes the determinants of the intensity of such competition, and demonstrates that the subsets of those determinants that are operative in any situation will depend on whether the relevant ARDEPPS' entry-barred expansion-preventing investment-quantity exceeds, equals, or is lower than its entry-preventing investment-quantity.

5.1 "Seller QV-Investment Competition" and "the Intensity of QV-Investment Competition"

In my usage, the expression "quality-or-variety-increasing-investment (QV-investment) competition" refers to the process by which the firms in an arbitrarily-defined portion of product-space (hereinafter "ARDEPPS") compete away their potential supernormal profits by making additional QV investments in that area of product-space—more specifically, by creating additional product variants, additional distributive outlets, and/or additional capacity or inventory (that enables its owner to provide buyers with faster average speed-of-supply throughout a fluctuating-demand cycle) in an ARDEPPS. Production-process-research (PPR) competition refers to the process by which production-process researchers (firms whose products are production-process discoveries) compete away their

R. S. Markovits, *Welfare Economics and Antitrust Policy - Vol. I*,
https://doi.org/10.1007/978-3-030-79812-3_5

potential profits by executing additional PPR projects that relate to production processes that could be used to produce one or more products produced in a given ARDEPPS. This chapter focuses on QV-investment competition, but everything it says about QV-investment competition applies mutatis mutandis to PPR competition.

The intensity of QV-investment competition in any ARDEEPPS could be measured in a variety of different ways, including (1) the highest supernormal profit-rate generated over its lifetime by any QV investment in the relevant ARDEPPS, (2) the weighted-average (weighted by the monetary-unit size of the QV investments in question) lifetime supernormal profit-rate generated by all QV investments in the relevant ARDEPPS, (3) the ratio (average ratio through time) of the equilibrium QV-investment quantity in the ARDEPPS in question at each point in time to the quantity of QV investment that at the relevant point in time would result in the ARDEPPS' most-supernormally-profitable QV investments generating just a normal rate-of-return (what I sometimes refer to as the "actual, competitive QV-investment quantity in the ARDEPPS" where the word that precedes the comma indicates the assumption that is being made about the prevailing intensity of price-competition and the word that succeeds the comma indicates the assumption that is being made about the prevailing intensity of QV-investment competition), (4) the ratio of the difference between the (weighted-average) actual, competitive QV-investment quantity and the (weighted-average) equilibrium QV-investment quantity to the actual, competitive QV-investment quantity, (5) the weighted-average ratio of the difference articulated after "(4)" above to the equilibrium QV-investment quantity, or (6) the absolute difference specified after "(4)" above. None of these metrics for "the intensity of QV-investment competition" is best in all contexts. This study uses the last (the sixth) of these metrics because the associated conception of "the intensity of QV-investment competition" is the conception that is most useful both for analyzing the legality of business conduct under a lessening-competition test of illegality and for executing analyses of the economic efficiency of any antitrust-policy-coverable business conduct and of any antitrust policy.

5.2 The (Possible) Intermediate Determinants of the Intensity of QV-Investment Competition in an ARDEPPS and the Subset or Subsets of Those Factors That Determine the Intensity of QV-Investment Competition in an ARDEPPS in Different Types of Situations

This definitional and analytic work is long overdue. Although economists do sometimes refer to one set of the relevant determinants—"barriers to entry," different economists define "the barriers to entry" to which they refer differently, and all economists that use this concept do so to analyze the supposed effect of such barriers on the competitiveness of prices (usually, on whether so-called "limit pricing" is practiced) rather than on the competitiveness of QV investment. Moreover, to my knowledge, no economist has ever focused on the other two major categories of intermediate determinants of the intensity of QV-investment competition—viz.—(1) barriers to established-firm QV investment expansion and (2) monopolistic or natural oligopolistic QV-investment disincentives and monopolistic QV-investment incentives. Indeed, to my knowledge, no economist has ever attempted to execute an analysis of competition that focuses separately on QV-investment competition. These omissions are important not just because QV-investment competition is a significant social phenomenon but also because (1) the determinants of the intensity of QV-investment competition are different from the determinants of the intensity of price competition and given practices or transactions can increase price-competition while decreasing QV-investment competition or vice versa, (2) increases in QV-investment competition will often reduce economic inefficiency in our Pareto-imperfect economy while increases in price-competition will always or virtually always increase economic efficiency in our Pareto-imperfect economy, and (3) increases in QV-investment competition have a different distributive impact from that of increases in price-competition and, from various value-perspectives, this difference will sometimes critically affect the desirability of increasing one or the other of these types of competition.

5.2.1 The Intermediate Determinants of the Intensity of QV-Investment Competition

I have found it useful to distinguish eleven intermediate determinants of the intensity of QV-investment competition—four barriers to entry, four counterpart barriers to established-firm QV-investment expansion, the monopolistic QV-investment incentives or disincentives that a potential QV-investment expander may face, and the natural oligopolistic QV-investment disincentives that two or more potential QV-investment expanders may face. All barriers to entry and expansion cause the "nominal" or "conventional book" supernormal profit-rate a potential entrant or expander would expect to realize on its new QV investment to be lower than the lifetime supernormal rate-of-return that would be generated by the most-supernormally-profitable QV investments in the relevant area of product-space at the original (pre-new-investment) QV-investment quantity. In this last sentence, the word "nominal" and the expression "conventional book" indicate the fact that the relevant calculations ignore any monopolistic QV-investment incentives or disincentives and any natural-oligopolistic QV-investment disincentives a potential expander may have to make a particular QV investment (see below). Somewhat optimistically, I am assuming that "conventional book" supernormal-profit calculations will take into account any positive contribution a relevant QV investment makes to the profit-yields of one or more of the investor's other QV investments by generating traditional joint cost-reduction economies, increasing the demand for its other products by filling out its product-line or increasing its reputation for quality, and/or enabling it to make profitable sales of complements to the product created. The monopolistic QV-investment incentives, monopolistic QV-investment disincentives, and (natural) oligopolistic QV-investment disincentives a QV investor faces on a particular QV investment all reflect the fact that, for reasons that will be delineated below (reasons that are unrelated to its generating traditional joint-cost economies or increasing the demand for the investor's other products), the QV investment in question will affect the profit-yields of the investor's other projects and, in the case of natural-oligopolistic QV-investment disincentives, will yield lower nominal profits itself because it will induce the execution of a rival QV investment that would not otherwise have been made. After defining the four different types of barriers to entry or expansion that a QV investor may face, this subsection defines the monopolistic QV-investment incentives and disincentives and the natural-oligopolistic QV-investment disincentives a QV-investment expander may face.

The profit-rate-differential (Π_D) barrier faced by a particular potential entrant or expander on the most-privately-attractive QV-investment project available to it at the relevant point in time indicates the amount by which the weighted-average lifetime rate-of-return[1] gross of capital costs that that project would be expected to generate in the absence of retaliation at any relevant ARDEPPS QV-investment quantity would be lower than its counterpart at that ARDEPPS QV-investment quantity for the most-supernormally-profitable QV-investment project or projects already in the relevant area of product-space.[2] I will first discuss Π_D barriers to entry and then discuss Π_D barriers to expansion.

Π_D barriers may confront potential entrants—even-best-placed potential entrants—for a wide variety of reasons: (1) because the established firms were able to occupy some locations in product-space including geographic-space that were inherently more profitable than any the privately-best-placed (hereinafter: best-placed) potential entrant could occupy (without paying additional costs for the locations in question that totally offset their greater appeal), (2) because the established firms were able to obtain patents at a lower cost than the cost the best-placed potential entrant would have to incur to invent around them, buy them, or buy the right to use them, (3) because the established firms were able to obtain natural resources more profitably than the best-placed potential entrant can now obtain them, (4) because the established firms had more profitable reputation-building options available to them than are available to the potential entrant that is best-placed to enter the ARDEPPS in question at a particular point in time (because, e.g., it was cheaper and more feasible for a pioneer to establish a reputation for quality and reliability than for the potential competitor that is best-placed to enter at some point in time to match it—that the advantages of being an old reliable are greater than the disadvantages of being lumbered with a reputation for low or inconsistent quality long after the pioneer's product-quality and quality-control improved), and/or (5) because the managers of the ARDEPPS' pioneers have managed and will manage its most-supernormally-profitable projects better over their lifetimes than their managerial counterparts for the ARDEPPS' best-placed potential competitor will manage its most-privately-attractive project and only part of the managerial-productivity difference in question is offset by compensation-differences (a possibility that reflects two facts: the fact that the pioneers' managers learned the business in competition with other neophytes [a factor that is admittedly offset by the copy-cat's ability to learn from the pioneers' early experience] as well as the fact that, since part of any company's managers' knowledge is company-specific, managers cannot obtain compensation equal to their contribution to their company's profits [their compensation aside]). In practice, the size of the Π_D barrier facing an ARDEPPS' best-placed potential entrant will tend to be lower when that firm is not an entirely-new business but a well-established firm operating in a related field or geographic area that is considering product or geographic diversification.

Π_D barriers may also confront firms established in the relevant ARDEPPS that are considering QV-investment expansions. The Π_D barrier to expansion facing a firm that is established in the relevant ARDEPPS on the privately-most-attractive QV-investment project it could introduce into that ARDEPPS is defined precisely the same way as the Π_D barrier to entry facing a potential competitor.

The Π_D barrier facing an ARDEPPS' best-placed potential expander at any point in time will tend to be smaller than the Π_D barrier facing its best-placed potential entrant at that time because the experience of operating in an ARDEPPS contributes to the insider's ability to conceive and execute new projects in it. However, this difference will tend to be smaller when the best-placed potential entrant is an established firm operating in a related area. It will also tend to be smaller when the QV investment in question would not be the first that the best-placed potential expander would be making in a relatively short time-period. A firm that is expanding rapidly will face a higher Π_D barrier on an additional expansion both because the nth-best project a management devises will usually be worse than its (n-1)th-best project and because firms execute projects less efficiently when they are expanding rapidly.

Although the Π_D barrier facing an ARDEPPS' best-placed potential expander at any point in time—$(\Pi_D)_E$ where the subscript E stands for "established firm"—will *tend to be* lower than the Π_D barrier facing its best-placed potential entrant at that point in time—$(\Pi_D)_N$ where the subscript N stands for "new entrant," there clearly will be situations in which $(\Pi_D)_N$ is lower than $(\Pi_D)_E$. In particular, this relationship may prevail in two types of situations: (1) when a potential competitor has made a technological, promotional, or distributive breakthrough and (2) when equilibrium QV investment is rising rapidly in the ARDEPPS in question (because "ARDEPPS demand" is rising rapidly and/or costs are falling rapidly). In this latter case, the Π_D barriers facing the established firm that is best-placed at the relevant point in time to execute an expansion that would deter an entry may be high because all the established firms may have had to expand quite rapidly to raise QV investment in the ARDEPPS to the prevailing non-equilibrium quantity.

In my usage, the risk barrier to entry or expansion (R) indicates the amount by which in the absence of retaliation the normal rate-of-return for the project in question would be higher than its counterpart for the relevant most-supernormally-profitable projects. A best-placed potential competitor will confront a risk barrier to entry to the extent that the profitability of its project is more uncertain than was the lifetime profitability of the most-supernormally-profitable projects in the ARDEPPS in question, to the extent that the best-placed potential competitor is more risk-averse than the established owners of an ARDEPPS' most-supernormally-profitable projects, and to the extent that the best-placed potential entrant is less able than the owners of the ARDEPPS' most-supernormally-profitable projects to make investment-portfolio moves that reduce the contribution of the project in question to their respective overall risk. In practice, once more, the size of the relevant R is likely to be lower when the best-placed potential entrant into the ARDEPPS in question is a large established firm that sells similar goods or services in the same territory or the same goods or services in other territories: such potential entrants will tend to be less uncertain about the outcomes of their contemplated entry, less risk-averse, and more able to reduce risk by compiling appropriate investment-portfolios than are entirely-new potential entrants.

Not only potential entrants but also potential QV-investment expanders can face R barriers. For the same reason that the Π_D faced by a potential expander will tend to be lower than the Π_D barrier faced by an already-established firm that is not operating in the ARDEPPS in question and for the same reason that these latter barriers in turn tend to be lower than the Π_D barrier faced by an entirely-new company, the R barrier faced by established firms will tend to be lower than those facing potential entrants that are established elsewhere and a fortiori than those facing entirely-new-firm potential entrants. Once again as well, the R barrier that an established firm will face on an nth expansion in any time-period will tend to increase with n both because the nth expansion will tend to be inherently more risky than the (n-1)th new project and because the nth new project will tend to be executed with less experienced personnel whose performance is riskier than the performance of the personnel that would execute the (n-1)th new project.

The scale barrier to entry or expansion (S) indicates the amount by which the relevant new entry or expansion would reduce the supernormal profit-rate generated by all projects in the relevant area of product-space (assuming, for simplicity, that the new project has an equal effect on all such projects)[3] by increasing the amount of QV investment and (in the case of new entry) the number of independent sellers that the ARDEPPS contains. Any QV investments that are added to an ARDEPPS will decrease their predecessors' rates-of-return by reducing the average BPA of best-placed products in the ARDEPPS in question, relatedly by reducing the frequency with which its firms can obtain NOMs, by lowering the average contrived oligopolistic margin in the ARDEPPS, and (usually) by increasing the average total cost of each product in the ARDEPPS by reducing the quantity of each that is sold. Although a potential competitor or expander could reduce S by reducing the scale of its entry or expansion below the minimum scale that would minimize the (Π_D + R) barriers it faced, I will assume that no entrant or expander will do so—that each entry and expansion takes place at or above the scale that minimizes the sum of the investor's Π_D and R barriers. Admittedly, this assumption is not consistent with my current static assumptions. However, it is quite realistic in the normal "dynamic" case in which "demand" for each relevant set of products increases through time since the prospect of such increases and the concomitant tendency of equilibrium QV investment to rise through time in the relevant area of product-space reduces the benefits of investing at less than minimum efficient scale by implying that in the medium or long run the larger magnitude of a QV investment of minimum efficient scale will not reduce the supernormal rate-of-return it generates by increasing total QV investment in the ARDEPPS in which it is located. The S barrier faced by potential entrants that are well-established in related fields and a fortiori the S barrier faced by potential established expanders will tend to be lower than those facing entirely new companies because the Π_D-cost to the former two types of firms of investing at lower scales will tend to be lower than those facing entirely new companies—i.e., because such established firms may be able to take advantage of joint economies in production, promotion, and distribution.

The retaliation or L barrier facing a potential entrant or potential expander indicates the amount by which the expected supernormal rate-of-return for the new QV investment in question is reduced by the possibility of retaliation. I will assume for simplicity that the supernormal rate-of-return that will be generated by the set of most-supernormally-profitable projects in the ARDEPPS will not be reduced by retaliation. On this assumption, L_N and L_E at any ARDEPPS QV-investment quantity will respectively equal the amount by which the prospect of retaliation will reduce the supernormal rate-of-return the best-placed potential competitor or the best-placed potential expander at that QV-investment quantity should expect to realize on the most-privately-attractive QV investment it can make in the ARDEPPS in question. For simplicity, I will also assume that the prospect of retaliation will affect the attractiveness of making a QV investment exclusively by reducing the potential competitor's or expander's gross-of-capital-cost expected rate-of-return on that investment—i.e., I will ignore the fact that the prospect of retaliation will increase the risk costs of making the QV investment in question. It is difficult to tell whether the retaliation barriers facing a potential entrant that is well-established in other areas or by a potential expander will be lower than those facing an entirely-new potential entrant. On the one hand, already-established firms may have "Don't Tread on Me or Don't Try to Deter Me" reputations, the ability to survive retaliation, or the ability to retaliate against retaliators that deter retaliation. On the other hand, well-established potential entrants and a fortiori potential expanders provide retaliators with more targets.

The monopolistic QV-investment incentives and disincentives ($M > 0$ and $M < 0$) a potential expander may face reflect the effect the relevant QV investment has on the profit-yields of the expander's pre-existing (or, more generally, pre-existing and other future) projects in the relevant ARDEPPS not by generating joint-cost economies or increasing the demand for the investor's other products by filling out its product-line or enhancing its reputation for quality but (1) by taking sales away from those projects directly, (2) by inducing established rivals to make non-retaliatory responses that do not involve their increasing their QV investments in the relevant area of product-space but that do reduce the expander's pre-existing projects' profit-yields, and (3) by deterring established or potential competitors from making additional QV investments in the relevant area of product-space.

When a potential expander's QV investment would do more damage to its pre-existing projects' profit-yields in the above ways (in comparison with the status quo ante) than would have been done by any monopolistic QV investments it deters others from making, the potential expander will face a QV-investment disincentive equal to the amount by which these effects reduce the actual supernormal rate-of-return its project should be expected to generate ex ante below the supernormal rate-of-return it should have been expected to generate absent these effects. When the project in question will do less damage in the above ways to the profit-yields of the relevant expander's pre-existing projects than would otherwise have been done by the QV investments of others that its expansion would deter, the potential expander will have a monopolistic QV-investment incentive.

A potential expander will be said to face natural-oligopolistic QV-investment disincentives ($O < 0$) when, rather than deterring others from making QV investments, its expansion will induce an established rival to make a QV investment that that firm would otherwise not have made. I need to delineate the conditions under which two or more firms will confront each other with natural-oligopolistic investment-disincentives that deter each of them from making an investment it would otherwise have made. For simplicity, I will focus on situations in which *two* firms cause each other to face critical natural-oligopolistic investment-disincentives. Two firms will deter each other from making an investment each would otherwise have made by confronting each other with natural-oligopolistic investment-disincentives when 3 conditions are fulfilled: (1) each firm would have found that an investment in a particular area of product-space would have yielded it at least a normal rate-of-return if the investment would not induce anyone else to invest in the area of product-space in question, (2) each firm would not find it profitable to make a first additional investment in that area of product-space if its investment would induce a rival to make a second investment in that area of product-space because that second investment in that area of product-space would reduce the profits yielded by all the investments the first investor owned in the relevant area of product-space by more than the amount by which the first investment would have increased the supernormal profits yielded by all the investor's projects in the relevant area of product-space if it would not induce anyone else to invest in that area of product-space, and (3) each of the two prospective investors would find it profitable to add a second investment to the relevant area of product-space if the other had already added a first investment to that area of product-space inter alia because in that situation the potential maker of the second additional investment in the relevant area of product-space could not deter its rival from making the first investment in that area of product-space by not making an investment in that area of product-space (because, given that fact, the second firm would find that adding the second investment to the relevant area of product-space would increase the supernormal profits it earned in that area of product-space, regardless of whether it owned other investments in that area of product-space). On my definition, the *O*s a potential expander faces on a particular investment equals the amount by which the investment's anticipated super-normal profit-rate is reduced by the facts that it (1) will reduce the investor's pre-existing projects' profit-yields (A) by taking sales away from those projects directly and inducing others to make QV investments that take sales away from those projects directly and (B) by inducing established rivals to make non-retaliatory, non-QV-investment responses to the investment-expansion in question and the expansions it induces others to make and (2) the QV investment the relevant QV investment induces others to make will reduce the "nominal profits" the relevant QV investment generates both directly and by inducing still others to react to the induced QV investment by making non-retaliatory changes in their prices and other non-QV-investment choices. This definition implies that the "nominal profits" yielded by an expansion that will induce someone else to make a QV investment that actor would not otherwise have made are defined to equal the profits the expansion in question would yield if, counterfactually, it would not cause any additional QV investments to be made in the relevant area of product-space and the *O*s that will be said to face a potential expander in this position will be defined to equal the amount by which the supernormal rate-of-return the expansion in question should be expected to generate ex ante will be reduced by the four effects just listed.

5.2.2 The Three Different Types of QV-Investment Equilibria and the Ways in Which Different Subsets of the Intermediate Determinants of the Intensity of QV-Investment Competition Interact (or Do Not Interact) to Determine the Intensity of QV-Investment Competition in Each of Them

I will now use the preceding concepts to analyze three different types of QV-investment equilibria it is useful to distinguish. I begin by defining four different QV-investment-quantity concepts and explaining two diagrams that play important roles in the analyses that follow. The first relevant QV-investment quantity is the lowest equilibrium QV-investment quantity in a given ARDEPPS. The adjective "lowest" is included because, given the presence of economies of scale in making a QV investment, there will often be a range of ARDEPPS QV-investment quantities at which all QV investments that have been made are profitable and no QV investment that has not been made would be profitable. In the text that follows, the expression "equilibrium QV-investment quantity" will always refer to the lowest equilibrium QV-investment quantity in the ARDEPPS in question.

Second, some of the analyses that follow will make reference to the (lowest) entry-preventing QV-investment quantity. This is the lowest quantity of QV investment that will render unprofitable the most-supernormally-profitable QV investment any potential competitor could introduce into the ARDEPPS at the time of analysis.

Third, some of the analyses that follow will make reference to the relevant ARDEPPS' (lowest) entry-barred expansion-preventing QV-investment quantity. This quantity is calculated on the normally-counterfactual assumption that something (usually a legal prohibition or bar) prevents any new entry from being executed at or after the time of analysis even if one or more potential competitors would otherwise have found entry profitable. In many situations, the relevant ARDEPPS' entry-barred expansion-preventing QV-investment quantity is higher than the quantity of QV investment in the ARDEPPS at the time of analysis—i.e., some expansions will have to be executed after the time of analysis to raise total QV investment in the ARDEPPS to the entry-barred expansion-preventing QV-investment quantity.

The fourth and final QV-investment quantity to which some of the analyses that follow will refer is the "actual, competitive" QV-investment quantity. As I indicated previously, this is the quantity of ARDEPPS QV investment at which the ARDEPPS' most-supernormally-profitable projects will generate a normal rate-of-return over their lifetimes, given the relationship that will prevail between price and marginal cost at different QV-investment quantities in the ARDEPPS in question. As I also indicated previously, the first adjective in the expression "actual, competitive QV-investment quantity" refers to the assumptions that are being made about the competitiveness of pricing at different ARDEPPS-QV-investment quantities, and the second refers to the assumption that is being made about the competitiveness of QV investment.

I now turn to the two figures I will use to illustrate the analysis of the three types of QV-investment equilibria it is useful to distinguish. Figures 5.1 and 5.2 illustrate the individual determinants of the intensity of QV-investment competition in any ARDEPPS, the different types of QV-investment equilibria that can be established in any ARDEPPS, and the complex relationship between the various individual determinants or sets of determinants in question on the one hand and the three types of equilibria I will distinguish on the other.

Figure 5.1 contains two highest-profit-rate (HΠ) curves and two normal-profit-rate (NΠ) curves. I will begin by analyzing the HΠ curves and then proceed to the NΠ curves.

$H\Pi_E$ (recall: the subscript "E" stands for "established firms") indicates the relationship between the equilibrium QV-investment quantity in the ARDEPPS and the "gross" weighted-average-expected lifetime rate-of-return (gross of capital costs) the established owner(s) of the most-supernormally-profitable QV-investment project(s) in the ARDEPPS would expect to realize on these project(s) if they faced no retaliation barriers and faced neither monopolistic nor natural oligopolistic QV-investment disincentives nor monopolistic QV-investment incentives on the investments in question.[4] It should be emphasized at the outset that the height of the $H\Pi_E$ curve at any given QV-investment quantity does not in general indicate the gross lifetime rate-of-return expected to be yielded by the QV investment that would bring ARDEPPS QV investment to that quantity. Indeed, the gross rate-of-return that its owner should expect this last QV investment to generate over its lifetime at the relevant ARDEPPS QV-investment quantity will equal the height

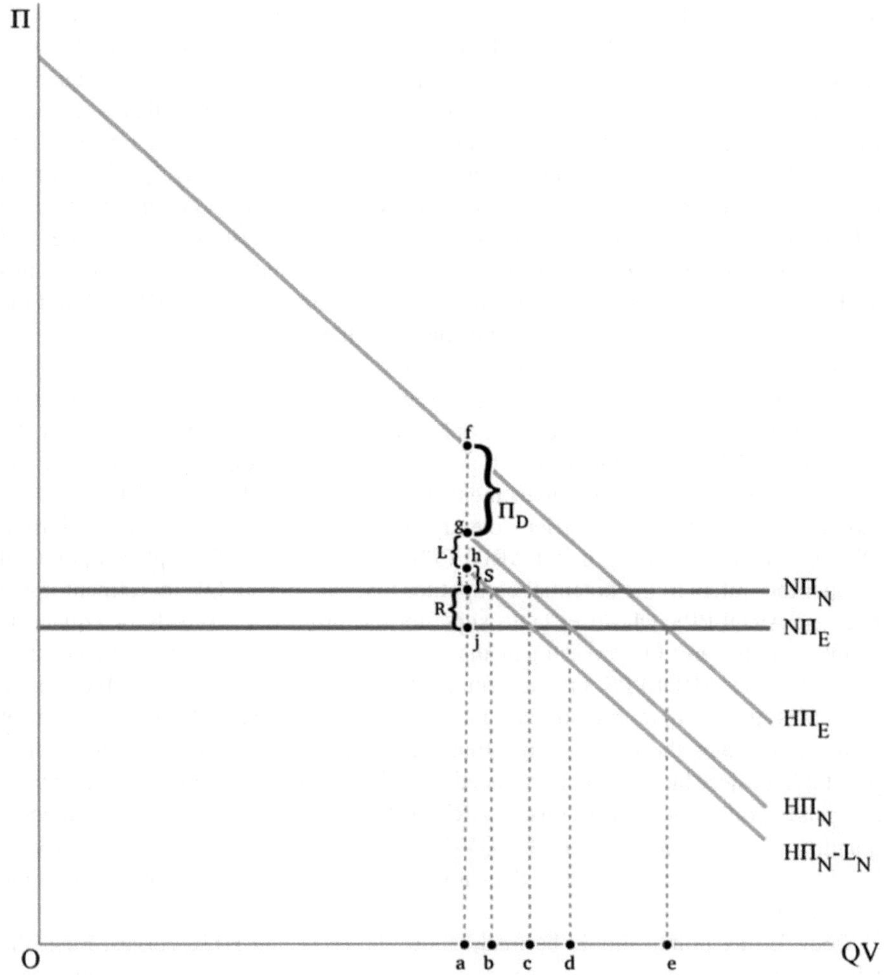

Fig. 5.1 Figure that illustrates the analysis of the entry-preventing QV-investment quantity

of the $H\Pi_E$ curve at that QV-investment quantity only if the investment in question belongs to the set of most-supernormally-profitable QV-investment projects in that ARDEPPS. In most situations, the analysis of the relationship between the equilibrium-QV-investment quantity and the actual, competitive QV-investment quantity (the QV-investment quantity at which the ARDEPPS' most-supernormally-profitable QV investments yield just a normal rate-of-return—Oe in Fig. 5.1, the QV-investment quantity at which the $H\Pi_E$ curve cuts the $N\Pi_E$ curve [see below] from above) will focus on the height of the $H\Pi_E$ curve at QV-investment quantities that exceed the sum of the QV investments in the ARDEPPS that are most profitable. I have stressed this point because this feature of the $H\Pi_E$ curve distinguishes it from the demand curves with which economists are accustomed to dealing. The height of the demand curve at any quantity indicates the price for which the unit that raises the relevant output to that quantity can be sold. By way of contrast, the height of the $H\Pi_E$ curve at any QV-investment quantity does not in general tell you the gross (of capital costs) rate-of-return that is expected to be generated by the QV investment that raises total QV investment in the ARDEPPS to that quantity: the height of the $H\Pi_E$ curve at any QV-investment quantity will equal the gross rate-of-return yielded by the QV that brings the ARDEPPS' total QV investment to the quantity in question only if the QV investment that brings the ARDEPPS' QV-investment total to that quantity belongs to the set of most-supernormally-profitable investments in that ARDEPPS and the normal rate-of-return on all these investments is the same.

$H\Pi_N$ (recall: the subscript "N" stands for "new entrant") indicates the relationship between (1) the "gross" weighted-average-expected lifetime rate-of-return (gross of capital costs) that the potential entrant that was best-placed to enter the relevant ARDEPPS at the time of analysis should anticipate realizing on the most-privately-attractive QV investment it could make within the ARDEPPS if it did not face any retaliation barriers to entry and (2) various hypothetical equilibrium QV-investment quantities in that ARDEPPS. The expression "best-placed potential competitor" refers to the potential competitor that can make a QV investment in the relevant ARDEPPS whose ex ante supernormal profit-rate exceeds or equals its counterpart for any QV investment that any other potential competitor can introduce into the ARDEPPS in question at the time of analysis. The $H\Pi_N$ curve resembles the $H\Pi_E$ curve in that its height at any ARDEPPS-QV-investment quantity indicates the rate-of-return that a given project (the most-supernormally-profitable project that can be introduced by any potential competitor at the time of analysis) would yield if it raised ARDEPPS QV investment to the indicated quantity—i.e., the identity of the QV-investment project to which the varying height of the $H\Pi_N$ curve applies does not vary as one moves to the right along the $H\Pi_N$ curve.[5]

Four further points should be made about the $H\Pi_E$ and $H\Pi_N$ curves. First, the height of the $H\Pi_E$ and $H\Pi_N$ curves at any given QV-investment quantity increases as the prices of the products in the ARDEPPS rise from the competitive price to the monopolistic price (from the products' respective marginal costs to the prices that maximize the total supernormal profits that the ARDEPPS' QV investors realize, given the quantity of QV investment in the ARDEPPS). The $H\Pi_E$ and $H\Pi_N$ curves in Fig. 5.1 (and the $H\Pi_E$ curve in Fig. 5.2) are constructed on realistic assumptions about the prices that will be charged at different QV-investment quantities in the relevant ARDEPPS—i.e., are in this sense actual $H\Pi_E$ and $H\Pi_N$ curves.[6] Second, relatedly, and somewhat inconsistently, my construction of the $H\Pi_E$ and $H\Pi_N$ curves in Fig. 5.1 assumes that their heights at any given QV-investment quantity will not depend on the percentage of ARDEPPS QV investment that has been made by new entrants as opposed to by expanding established firms. This clearly unrealistic assumption is made for expositional reasons and is relaxed when appropriate —for example, when analyzing QV-investment incentives and disincentives.[7]

Third, the downward slope of both the $H\Pi_E$ and $H\Pi_N$ curves reflects the fact that the introduction of additional product variants, outlets, inventory, or capacity will lower the rates-of-return generated by the ARDEPPS' pre-existing QV investments (including those that are "most-supernormally-profitable") both (1) by reducing the prevailing array of prices in the ARDEPPS (by reducing BCAs and perhaps NOMs and/or COMs as well) and (2) by increasing the "per-unit" average total cost of using the pre-existing QV investments because the unit-sales the new QV investment takes from its predecessors exceed the additional units the new QV investment's introduction causes its predecessors to sell both by inducing the owners to lower their prices and by increasing variety and/or quality. I should note that the expression "per-unit" is enquoted in the preceding sentence to reflect the fact that when demand fluctuates through time the relevant "product" will change when the average rate of capacity-utilization drops since this drop will be associated with an increase in the average speed of supply through a fluctuating-demand cycle and the "average speed with which a seller supplies its customers" is an attribute of the product the seller is supplying.[8]

Fourth, Fig. 5.1's assumption that the $H\Pi_E$ and $H\Pi_N$ curves are linear and parallel is not intended to be realistic. This assumption has been adopted solely to ease construction and facilitate textual exposition. It does not critically affect any significant conclusion. The distance between $H\Pi_E$ and $H\Pi_N$ at any given QV-investment quantity equals the profit-rate-differential (Π_D) barrier to entry faced by the relevant ARDEPPS' best-placed potential competitor at the time of analysis. Figure 5.1's construction of $H\Pi_N$ parallel to $H\Pi_E$ assumes that this Π_D barrier to entry will not vary with the ARDEPPS' QV-investment quantity, assuming (as I will) that variations in the pre-existing relevant QV-investment quantity will not change the identity of the ARDEPPS' most-supernormally-profitable projects or the most-privately-attractive project that could be introduced by any potential competitor. In Fig. 5.1, $\Pi_D = fg$.

As I have already indicated, Fig. 5.1 also contains two $N\Pi$ curves. $N\Pi$ indicates the normal rate-of-return (the minimum weighted-average-expected rate-of-return needed to induce investment, which varies inter alia with the riskiness of the QV-investment project in question). $N\Pi_E$ indicates the rate-of-return that owners of the ARDEPPS' most-supernormally-profitable projects will consider normal on these investments. $N\Pi_N$ indicates the rate-of-return that the ARDEPPS' best-placed potential entrant would find normal for the most-privately-attractive project it could execute to enter the ARDEPPS in question if that entry would generate no retaliation. Figure 5.1's construction of the two $N\Pi$ curves as horizontal implies that the riskiness of the relevant QV investments will not vary with the QV-investment quantity of the ARDEPPS. This assumption will not always be realistic—e.g., would be unrealistic if an ARDEPPS' constituent firms would clearly be able to contrive OMs when QV investment is low (because only a few firms are in the relevant ARDEPPS at such times), would clearly be unable to contrive OMs when QV investment is high (because the additional QV investments are made by new entrants and most or all products in the ARDEPPS other than the product that is privately-best-placed in relation to each relevant buyer are privately-second-placed or close-to-privately-second-placed to obtain the patronage of the buyer in question), and may or may not be able to contrive OMs when QV investment is middling (to the extent that in such situations the number of firms that are privately-second-placed or privately-close-to-second placed is middling). In such situations, the relevant NΠ curves would be horizontal at low and high QV-investment quantities but have a bubble in the middle. The assumption that the NΠ curves are horizontal is adopted primarily for expositional reasons but also because, as we shall see, the three generalizations in the preceding sentence are extremely crude. In any event, Fig. 5.1's assumption that the NΠ curves are horizontal does not critically affect any significant conclusion. The vertical distance between $N\Pi_N$ and $N\Pi_E$ in Fig. 5.1 indicates the risk barrier to entry (R). The assumption that $N\Pi_N$ and $N\Pi_E$ are horizontal implies that this risk barrier will not vary with the ARDEPPS' QV-investment quantity. In Fig. 5.1, R = ij. Figure 5.1 is also based on the simplifying assumption that, at any ARDEPPS-QV-investment quantity, each member of the set of most-supernormally-profitable QV investments in the ARDEPPS will generate the same gross rate-of-return and will be associated with the same normal rate-of-return.

Figure 5.1 also illustrates the remaining two barriers to entry I find useful to distinguish—the retaliation barrier to entry (L or L_N where the subscript "N" indicates that the relevant barrier relates to the position of a new entrant) and the scale barrier to entry (S or S_N). I will assume that the owners of the ARDEPPS' most-supernormally-profitable projects face no retaliation barriers on those QV investments. On that assumption, L_N indicates the amount by which the best-placed potential entrant's ex ante supernormal rate-of-return is reduced by the possibility that the established firms may retaliate against its entry. Although in reality the prospect of retaliation will reduce the best-placed potential competitor's ex ante supernormal rate-of-return both by reducing its weighted-average-expected gross rate-of-return and by increasing its risk costs, for simplicity Fig. 5.1 assumes that the L_N barrier will affect only the weighted-average-expected gross rate-of-return of the best-placed potential competitor—that the possibility of retaliation will not raise the best-placed potential entrant's R barrier. For this reason, the L_N barrier in Fig. 5.1 is represented as a vertical distance (hi) between the $H\Pi_N$ and $(H\Pi_N{-}L_N)$ curves. Also for simplicity, Fig. 5.1 assumes in addition that the L_N barrier does not vary with the ARDEPPS' QV-investment quantity. In Fig. 5.1, L = gh. (To increase readability, Fig. 5.1 omits the subscript N not only to L but also to Π_D, R, and S.)

The final barrier to entry is the scale barrier (S_N). It reflects the fact that, since entry is lumpy (since there are economies of scale in entry), any QV investment a potential competitor finds profitable to introduce will reduce not only the supernormal rate-of-return it realizes on its new entry (below the rate it would have realized post-entry on its entry if its entry would not raise total QV investment in the ARDEPPS) but the supernormal rate-of-return generated by all pre-existing QV investments in the ARDEPPS by raising the ARDEPPS' QV-investment quantity. In a static world, a potential competitor might well find it profitable to reduce the S_N barrier it faced by entering with a smaller QV investment whose size causes it to face higher (Π_D + R) or (Π_D + R + L) barriers than it would face if it entered with a larger QV investment. However, since in our actual, dynamic world ARDEPPS $H\Pi_E$ and $H\Pi_N$ curves tend to rise through time because "ARDEPPS demand curves"[9] tend to rise through time and ARDEPPS cost curves tend to decrease through time, the S-barrier advantage such a choice would yield is unlikely to survive long enough to make such a trade-off worthwhile (since the extra QV the larger entry would introduce will reduce the amount of additional investment by others the relevant increase in demand will stimulate). I will therefore assume that potential competitors will always choose to enter on a scale that is at least large enough to minimize the sum of the (Π_D + R) barriers they face (hereinafter the "minimum efficient scale"). In Fig. 5.1, the minimum efficient scale is assumed to be ab and the associated scale barrier—S—equals (ab *times* the slope of the $H\Pi_N$ curve [which Fig. 5.1 assumes does not vary with the ARDEPPS' QV-investment quantity]) = hi.

It should now be possible to use Fig. 5.1 to illustrate some of the QV-investment quantities that play a significant role in the analysis that follows. First, in Fig. 5.1, Oe—the quantity of QV investment at which $H\Pi_E$ and $N\Pi_E$ intersect—is the actual, competitive quantity of QV investment (where the first adjective refers to the competitiveness of pricing at the relevant QV-investment quantity and the second, to the competitiveness of QV investment at that QV-investment quantity). QV investment is said to be "competitive" when it is at the quantity at which any firm that owned a most-supernormally-profitable project would realize a normal rate-of-return on that project. Second, in Fig. 5.1, Oa (actually, a QV-investment-quantity infinitesimally above Oa)—the quantity of QV investment that equals the difference between the quantity at which ($H\Pi_N$-L_N) falls just below $N\Pi_N$ (Ob) and the minimum efficient scale of entry (ab)—is the "entry-preventing QV-investment quantity, the lowest quantity of QV investment whose attainment would result in the best-placed potential competitor's confronting an ex ante sub-normal rate-of-return on its most-privately-attractive project.

Thus, Fig. 5.1 indicates that in the circumstances it portrays the relevant barriers to entry permit the established firms to restrict their QV investment (infinitesimally less than) ea below the actual, competitive quantity Oe without making it profitable for any potential competitor to enter. Of this amount ea, de reflects the profit-rate-differential barrier Π_D (the difference between the intersection of $H\Pi_E$ and $N\Pi_E$ on the one hand and $H\Pi_N$ and $N\Pi_E$ on the other); cd reflects the risk barrier R (the difference between the intersection of $H\Pi_N$ and $N\Pi_E$ on the one hand and $H\Pi_N$ and $N\Pi_N$ on the other); bc reflects the retaliation barrier L (the difference between the intersection of $H\Pi_N$ and $N\Pi_N$ on the one hand and [$H\Pi_N - L_N$] and $N\Pi_N$ on the other); and ab reflects the scale barrier S (assuming that ab is the minimum efficient scale of entry in QV-investment terms and that entry will always take place at at least minimum efficient scale).

Figure 5.1 also indicates that in the circumstances it portrays the established firms can realize a supernormal rate-of-return infinitesimally below (fj = $[\Pi_D + R + S + L]_N$) on their most-supernormally-profitable projects without making it profitable for a potential competitor to enter their ARDEPPS. In brief, this conclusion reflects the fact that $(\Pi_D + R + L + S)_N$ equals the difference between the established firms' pre-entry lifetime supernormal profit-rate on their most-supernormally-profitable projects and the best-placed potential competitor's expected post-entry lifetime supernormal profit-rate—the lifetime supernormal profit-rate the best-placed entry would generate if its execution would bring the ARDEPPS into equilibrium. A numerical example might make this point more comprehensible. Assume that the lifetime supernormal profit-rate that the established firms that owned most-supernormally-profitable QV investments would realize on these projects if the pre-entry QV-investment quantity in the ARDEPPS were the ARDEPPS' equilibrium QV-investment quantity was 8.25% and that $(\Pi_D + R + S + L)_N = (5\% + 2\% + 1\% + 0.26\%) = 8.26\%$. In such a case, the fact that the established firms would realize a lifetime supernormal profit-rate of 8.25% on any most-supernormally-profitable projects they owned if the pre-entry QV-investment quantity were the equilibrium QV-investment quantity would not imply that new entry would be normally profitable: in fact, the best-placed potential competitor would anticipate realizing a lifetime profit-rate that was 0.01% subnormal if it entered. Thus, if $N\Pi_E = 10\%$ and the established firms' lifetime gross rate-of-return would therefore be 18.25% on any most-supernormally-profitable projects they owned if QV investment were in equilibrium at the pre-entry quantity, entry would not be at least normally profitable because the best-placed potential competitor's weighted-average-expected gross rate-of-return $(18.25\%–[\Pi_D]_N–S_N–L_N = 18.25\%–5\%–1\%–0.26\% = 11.99\%)$ would be lower than the normal rate-of-return for the privately-best project it could introduce into the ARDEPPS in question $(N\Pi_E + R_N = 10\% + 2\% = 12\%)$.

Figure 5.2 illustrates the various barriers to expansion, monopolistic QV-investment incentives, and monopolistic and natural-oligopolistic QV-investment disincentives that may confront the established firms that are successively-best-placed to add QV investments to their ARDEPPS after the time of analysis. In fact, Fig. 5.2 illustrates the *M*s and *O*s that the relevant successive, best-placed potential expanders will face both given the actual entry-situation and on an artificial (usually counterfactual) assumption that entry is barred (e.g., because some law effectively prohibits entry, regardless of whether entry would be profitable absent the law in question). Figure 5.2 also illustrates the determinants of the entry-barred expansion-preventing QV-investment quantity (the quantity of QV investment at which expansion would cease if entry were barred at the time of analysis), given the $H\Pi_E$ and $N\Pi_E$ curves in question. In combination, Figs. 5.1 and 5.2 will also be used to illustrate the analysis of (1) the conditions under which potential competition is "effective" (i.e., the conditions under which the entry-preventing QV-investment quantity is higher than the entry-barred expansion-preventing QV-investment quantity), (2) whether and the extent to which an ARDEPPS' established firms will find it profitable to respond to potential competition by making QV investments whose profitability is critically affected by the fact that they would deter new entry, and relatedly (3) the relationship between (A) the entry-preventing QV-investment quantity and the entry-barred expansion-

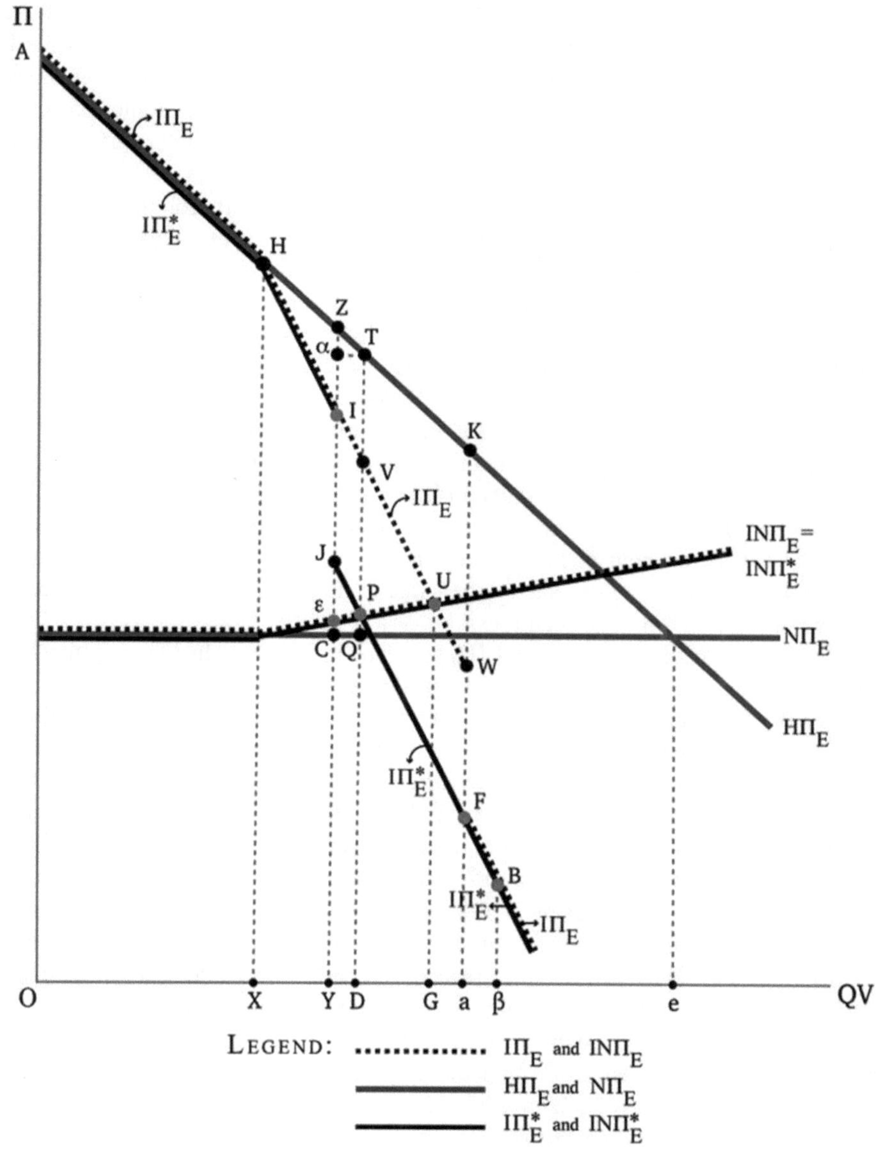

Fig. 5.2 Figure that illustrates the analysis of the entry-barred expansion-preventing QV-investment quantity

preventing QV-investment quantity on the one hand and (B) the equilibrium QV-investment quantity in the ARDEPPS in question on the other hand.

Figure 5.2 incorporates the $H\Pi_E$ and $N\Pi_E$ curves that Fig. 5.1 contains. In addition, Fig. 5.2 contains three "incremental" curves—the $I\Pi_E$* curve, the $I\Pi_E$ curve, and the $IN\Pi_E = IN\Pi_E$* curve. The $I\Pi_E$* curve indicates the actual incremental (hence "I") lifetime rate-of-return (gross of capital costs) that the established firm that would be best-placed to expand the ARDEPPS' QV investment to various quantities if no entry could take place after the beginning of the analysis-period—i.e., if entry were barred (hence the asterisk)—should expect to realize on the successive expansions in question. The $I\Pi_E$ curve indicates the same information, given the actual position of potential competitors. The $IN\Pi_E$ and $IN\Pi_E$* curves respectively indicate the normal rate-of-return for the successive best-placed QV-investment expansions that could be executed by the relevant ARDEPPS' established firms, respectively on actual-condition-of-entry and entry-barred assumptions. For simplicity, I have assumed that these two normal rates-of-return are equal—that the $IN\Pi_E$ = $IN\Pi_E$* curves coincide. It is critical to emphasize that the different points on the $I\Pi_E$, $I\Pi_E$*, and $IN\Pi_E$ = $IN\Pi_E$* curves provide information about the different, successive, most-privately-attractive expansions the ARDEPPS' established firms would or could undertake. In this respect, the incremental curves resemble demand curves rather than $H\Pi_E$, $N\Pi_N$, $N\Pi_E$, and $N\Pi_N$ curves, whose points indicate the gross rate-of-return that *a given, unchanging* QV investment or group of investments—the most-supernormally-profitable QV investment or investments in the relevant ARDEPPS—would generate or would have to be expected to generate to be privately attractive at different equilibrium QV-investment quantities.

I will now consider the $I\Pi_E$ and $I\Pi_E$* curves in Fig. 5.2. In Fig. 5.2, the $I\Pi_E$ curve is the disjointed line AHIVUWFB, while the $I\Pi_E$* curve is the disjointed line AHIJPFB. As I have already indicated, by definition, the $I\Pi_E$* curve differs from the $I\Pi_E$ curve in that the $I\Pi_E$* curve is the incremental profit-rate curve that would be applicable if (usually counterfactually) entry were barred while the $I\Pi_E$ curve is the incremental profit-rate curve that actually is applicable—i.e., that is constructed on realistic assumptions about the entry-preventing QV-investment quantity (in Fig. 5.2, Oa). This difference causes the two curves to diverge whenever the monopolistic QV-investment incentives, monopolistic QV-investment disincentives, or natural-oligopolistic QV-investment disincentives confronting the ARDEPPS' best-placed potential expander at a relevant QV-investment quantity are affected by the possibility of entry—viz., in virtually all situations in which the established firm that would be best-placed to expand ARDEPPS QV investment from some quantity below the entry-preventing quantity would face *M* disincentives, *M* incentives, or *O* disincentives if entry were barred. This conclusion reflects the fact that in the vast majority of such cases the possibility of entry will affect the existence or magnitude of the incentives and disincentives in question. I will return to this issue when explaining the divergence between the $I\Pi_E$ and $I\Pi_E$* curves between QV-investment quantities OY and Oa.

I will discuss separately three pairs of segments of the $I\Pi_E$ and $I\Pi_E$* curves that Fig. 5.2 contains. The first pair of segments contains the portions of the curves between ARDEPPS QV-investment quantities zero and OY. Between these two quantities, the $I\Pi_E$ and $I\Pi_E$* curves coincide. Their coincidence reflects an assumption that the established firms that would be successively best-placed to raise ARDEPPS QV investment from zero to OY would not have an *M* incentive,

M disincentive, or *O* disincentive to make the investments in question, regardless of whether the entry-preventing QV-investment quantity was Oa or entry was assumed to be barred. Figure 5.2 constructs the $I\Pi_E$ and $I\Pi_E$* curves to coincide with the $H\Pi_E$ curve between QV-investment quantities zero and OX. This construction assumes not only that (*M* or *O*) and (M^* or O^*) are zero between those QV-investment quantities but that Π_D and L are also zero over this QV-investment range—that the projects that create the first OX in QV investment in the ARDEPPS in question are all most-supernormally-profitable projects (given the diagram's assumption [see below] that R is also assumed to be zero for the QV investments in question) and that the relevant established firms face no retaliation barriers on the QV investments in question. However, although Fig. 5.2 also constructs the $I\Pi_E$ and $I\Pi_E$* curves to coincide with each other between QV-investment quantities OX and OY, it constructs both to be progressively lower than the $H\Pi_E$ curve as one moves from QV-investment quantity OX to QV-investment quantity OY. This divergence could reflect the fact that Π_D becomes increasingly positive for the ARDEPPS' successive best-placed potential expanders as one moves progressively above OX, the fact that L becomes increasingly positive for the ARDEPPS' successive best-placed potential expanders as one moves progressively above OX, or the fact that (Π_D + L) becomes increasingly positive for the ARDEPPS' successive best-placed potential expanders as one moves progressively above OX. However, for simplicity, I will assume that L_E is zero throughout and that all the divergences between the $H\Pi_E$ curve and the $I\Pi_E$ or $I\Pi_E$* curves at all QV-investment quantities above OX that cannot be attributed to *M* disincentives (see below) reflect Π_D barriers.

The second segments of the $I\Pi_E$ and $I\Pi_E$* curves in Fig. 5.2 contain the portions of the curves between QV-investment quantities OY and Oa. In Fig. 5.2, the $I\Pi_E$* curve diverges from the $I\Pi_E$ curve at QV-investment quantity OY. In particular, although the $I\Pi_E$ curve drops continuously progressively below the $H\Pi_E$ curve to the right of QV-investment quantity OY, the $I\Pi_E$* curve first jumps discontinuously from point I to point J at QV-investment quantity OY before declining continuously to the right of point J in precisely the same way that the $I\Pi_E$ curve does. (The $I\Pi_E$* curve is parallel to the $I\Pi_E$ curve between QV-investment quantities OY and Oa.) This construction reflects three assumptions.

First, it assumes that although the established firms that would be best-placed to add the successive QV investments to the ARDEPPS in question that would raise its QV-investment quantity to OY would not face *M* incentives, *M* disincentives, or *O* disincentives on those investments even if entry were barred (because, I am assuming, their failure to make an additional QV investment would induce an established rival to make an equally-large QV investment that would be equally damaging to the actual investor's other QV investments' profit-yields as its own expansion would be [relative to the status quo ante]), at QV-investment quantity OY, each successive best-placed potential expander would face *M* disincentives if entry were barred because each would know that it was the only established firm that could earn nominally normal returns on any additional project it introduced into the relevant area of product-space—i.e., that its decision not to expand would not induce any established rival to expand instead. I hasten to point out that, given that the entry-preventing QV-investment quantity in Fig. 5.2—Oa—is higher than OY, no similar *M* disincentives will cause the $I\Pi_E$ curve to drop continuously at point I: at least if one assumes that the new entry that would actually take place because the established firm that was best-placed to raise ARDEPPS QV investment above OY failed to do so would be equally damaging to the profit-yields of this potential expander's other projects, the relevant potential expander would face no *M* disincentives (and no *M* incentives) at QV-investment quantity OY on the realistic entry assumptions on which the $I\Pi_E$ curve's construction is based, though it would face them on the counterfactual entry-barred assumption on which the $I\Pi_E$* curve's construction is based.

Second, the $I\Pi_E$* curve's construction between QV-investment quantities OY and Oa is based on the assumption that the successive best-placed expanders in question would face the same *M* disincentives on their QV-investment projects. This assumption is unrealistic (since on our assumptions the successive expansions in question will be made by the same firm, the *M* disincentives that firm faces will tend to increase as one moves to the right because the number of pre-existing projects it owns [whose profit-yields an expansion will reduce] will increase as one moves to the right), but the assumption's lack of realism does not affect any significant conclusion I generate.

Third, the construction of the $I\Pi_E$ and $I\Pi_E$* curves between OY and Oa also reflects the continuance of our assumptions that Π_D increases progressively as one moves to the right of OX and that L equals zero.

The third segments of the $I\Pi_E$ and $I\Pi_E$* curves in Fig. 5.2 contain the portions of the curves that lie between QV-investment quantities Oa and Oβ. The critical point is that between QV-investment quantities Oa and Oβ, the $I\Pi_E$ curve coincides with the $I\Pi_E$* curve once more—i.e., that at QV-investment quantity Oa, the $I\Pi_E$ curve drops discontinuously from point W above the $I\Pi_E$* curve to point F on the $I\Pi_E$* curve. This drop reflects the fact that, once the entry-preventing QV-investment quantity Oa is reached, the entry-barred assumption becomes irrelevant since the established firm's failure to expand the ARDEPPS' QV investment beyond Oa will not induce entry. The fact that the coincident segments of the $I\Pi_E$ and $I\Pi_E$* curves to the right of QV-investment quantity Oa continue to drop further below $H\Pi_E$ between points F and B (between QV-investment quantities Oa and Oβ) reflects my continuing assumptions that Π_D rises progressively as one moves to the right beyond QV-investment quantity OX and that L is zero throughout.

Finally, since as already stated the $IN\Pi_E$ and $IN\Pi_E$* curves indicate the normal rates-of-return for the expansions that would successively be the most-privately-attractive expansions any established firm could execute if entry respectively were not and were barred, R_E and R_E* at any QV-investment quantity will respectively equal the difference between the heights of $IN\Pi_E$–and $N\Pi_E$ and the $IN\Pi_E$*–$N\Pi_E$ curves at that QV-investment quantity. In what follows, I will assume that the height of the $IN\Pi_E$ curve equals the height of the $IN\Pi_E$* curve and that R_E therefore equals R_E*. For simplicity, Fig. 5.2 is also constructed on the assumption that the risk barrier to expansion appears at precisely the same QV-investment quantity as the quantity at which the Π_D barrier to expansion appears—that the first QV-investment expansion for which the height of $I\Pi_E$ curve is lower than the height of the $H\Pi_E$ curve (because $\Pi_D > 0$) is the first QV-investment expansion for which the height of $IN\Pi_E$ curve is lower than the height of the $N\Pi_E$ curve (because $R_E > 0$). In particular, in Fig. 5.2, the QV-investment expansion for which these two barriers appear is the expansion that would raise the total amount of QV investment in the ARDEPPS to a quantity above OX.

In order to use Fig. 5.2 to illustrate the determinants of the lowest entry-barred expansion-preventing QV-investment quantity, one additional piece of information must be supplied—information on the scale of the expansion that would be best-placed to raise total QV investment in the ARDEPPS above the entry-barred expansion-preventing QV-investment quantity. Figure 5.2 assumes that this scale will be YD, the minimum efficient scale of expansion. YD is constructed to be slightly lower than ab in Fig. 5.1 because the minimum efficient scale of expansion will tend to be lower than the minimum efficient scale of entry (ab) since established firms will be more able than potential competitors to take advantage of economies of scale in production, promotion, and distribution by producing, promoting, and distributing their new products together with their old. In any event, if the expansion that would be best-placed to raise QV investment in the ARDEPPS in question above the entry-barred expansion-preventing QV-investment quantity would take place at a scale of YD, the (lowest) entry-barred expansion-preventing QV-investment quantity would be infinitesimally above OY = OD–YD where OD is the QV-investment quantity at which the $I\Pi_E$* curve cuts the $IN\Pi_E$* curve from above (at point P) and YD is the minimum scale at which any expansion of ARDEPPS QV above OD would take place if entry were barred. In what follows, I will assume that the entry-barred expansion-preventing QV-investment quantity in the ARDEPPS in question is (infinitesimally above) OY—i.e., that the lumpiness of QV investments will not cause this quantity to diverge from OY. At a QV-investment quantity (infinitesimally above) OY, the established firms that owned most-supernormally-profitable projects would be realizing a supernormal profit-rate infinitesimally below ZC on these QV investments. Despite this fact, no established firm would find it profitable to expand because the sum of the barriers to expansion and monopolistic QV-investment disincentives that the best-placed potential expander at OY would face would equal ZC. Thus, in Fig. 5.2, the value of the barriers and disincentives that would affect this next expansion are as follows: S_E for an expansion of scale YD equals Zα (the difference between the vertical coordinates of points Z and T on the $H\Pi_E$) curve,[10] $(\Pi_D + L^*)_E$ = TV (the vertical distance between the $H\Pi_E$ and $I\Pi_E$ curves at QV-investment quantity OD), M^* = VP (the vertical distance between curves $I\Pi_E$ and $I\Pi_E$* at QV-investment quantity OD), and R = PQ = εC + (PQ–εC) (the vertical distance between curves $IN\Pi_E$* and $N\Pi_E$ at QV-investment quantity OD). An inspection of Fig. 5.2 reveals that ZC = Zα + TV + VP + PQ.

Now that Figs. 5.1 and 5.2 and the various barriers, (dis)incentives, and QV-investment quantities they illustrate have been explained, it should be possible to analyze the determinants of the equilibrium QV-investment quantity in an

ARDEPPS with a given actual, competitive QV-investment quantity and correlatively the determinants of the lifetime supernormal profit-rate that will be generated in equilibrium by the most-supernormally-profitable QV investments in the ARDEPPS in question. In addition to the assumptions on which (as I have explained) the construction of Figs. 5.1 and 5.2 are based, the analysis that follows is based on four further assumptions.

The first is that at the time of the analysis QV investment in the ARDEPPS in question has not yet attained its static equilibrium quantity. New QV investments that are introduced into this ARDEPPS may be introduced either by already-established firms (in which case they will be described as QV-investment expansions) or by potential entrants (in which case they will be described as new entries). QV-investment expansions that would not have been executed but for their tendency to deter someone else (either an established firm or a potential competitor) from making a QV investment will sometimes be described as "limit investments."

The second is that, although I will continue to assume generally that QV investments are introduced into any ARDEPPS in the order of their profitability, I will also assume (somewhat inconsistently) that whenever an established firm finds an expansion profitable and a potential competitor finds an entry profitable, any relevant QV investment that is executed will be made by the established firm (regardless of whether it is more profitable than the deterred QV investment of the potential competitor). This expositionally-useful assumption has some basis in reality. Although the following justification is somewhat undercut by the fact that an ARDEPPS' best-placed potential competitors are normally existing companies operating in nearby geographic "markets" or related product "markets," I suspect that established firms usually learn of QV-investment opportunities (i.e., that a QV investment that would create a particular type of product or distributive outlet would be profitable) sooner than do potential competitors and can commit themselves to making or completing the relevant type of QV investment before outsiders can do so.

The third additional assumption is that QV investments are sufficiently immobile that it will never be inherently profitable for someone to make a QV investment on the assumption that its execution will induce an established QV investment to be withdrawn. This third assumption will be more realistic the more use-specific the established QV investments. Thus, QV investments in product or outlet design are least likely to be withdrawn because they cannot be converted into alternative uses. QV investments in physical distributive outlets will be more likely to be withdrawn to the extent that they can be (profitably) used to distribute either products that would be rivalrous with the product their creator built them to distribute or completely-different, non-rivalrous products. QV investments in capacity-increasing machinery will be more likely to be withdrawn to the extent that the machinery can be used equally well to produce other products, to the extent that their alternative users are geographically proximate to the actor that invested in them, and to the extent that the cost of transporting them any distance is low. QV investments in capacity-increasing plants will be more likely to be withdrawn to the extent that the plants are physically and geographically equally-suitable for producing other products.

The fourth and final additional assumption is that all the expansions that could be made in or entries that could be made into the ARDEPPS in question after the time of analysis will have the same QV-investment magnitude. This assumption is made purely for expositional reasons: it enables me to refer to the number of entries that could be made absent established-firm expansions and the number of expansions that would deter a given number of entries rather than the total monetary magnitudes of the investments in question.

On the above assumptions, I will analyze first the determinants of the lifetime supernormal rate-of-return that will be generated by an ARDEPPS' most-supernormally-profitable projects in equilibrium and second (derivatively and more relevantly in the current context) the determinants of the difference between the actual, competitive QV-investment quantity in a relevant ARDEPPS (Oe in Fig. 5.2) and the equilibrium quantity of QV investment in that ARDEPPS (both when the conduct under review changes the ARDEPPS' actual, competitive QV-investment quantity and when it does not change that quantity). This difference (which is the metric this study uses to measure "the intensity of QV-investment competition" in any ARDEPPS) is salient in the context of this study not only (1) because it is the parameter that is relevant to assessing whether conduct that changes it tends on that account to violate a lessening-competition test of illegality (in that increases in this difference will be associated with equivalent-monetary losses sustained by the customers of the perpetrator(s) and its (their) product-rivals in part because increases in this difference will be associated with a lowering of the absolute attractiveness of the best offer these buyers respectively receive from any inferior supplier but primarily (2) because it is the intensity-of-QV-investment-competition-related parameter that is most relevant to the economic efficiency of any antitrust-policy-coverable conduct or antitrust policy that affects QV-investment competition (in that, for reasons that Sect. 8.4 will explain, reductions in an ARDEPPS' equilibrium QV investment will tend to increase economic efficiency by reducing the amount of misallocation generated by economically-inefficient resource allocations from UO production and PPR execution to QV-investment creation in the ARDEPPS in question). I should add that, in my judgment, for reasons that Sect. 8.4 will also explain, the fact that antitrust-policy-covered conduct would reduce the intensity of PPR competition in the sense of increasing the difference between the quantity of PPR devoted to discovering a cheaper way to produce relevant quantities of one or more products at which the most-supernormally-profitable projects in this set would yield just a normal rate-of-return and the equilibrium quantity of the relevant PPR executed will be relevant to the economic efficiency of that conduct (and of antitrust policies that would prevent that conduct) because any increase in that difference would disfavor the economic efficiency of that conduct and favor the economic efficiency of antitrust policies that would prevent the conduct because, from the perspective of economic efficiency, resource allocations from PPR execution to UO production and QV creation are economically inefficient.

As we shall see, the determinants of both the supernormal profit-rate just referenced and the QV-investment difference just referenced—i.e., the subset or subsets of the previously-discussed possible determinants of these figures—will vary according to whether the entry-barred expansion-preventing QV-investment quantity exceeds, equals, or is lower than the entry-preventing QV-investment quantity. If (as it does not in Fig. 5.2) the ARDEPPS' entry-barred expansion-preventing QV-investment quantity exceeds the entry-preventing QV-investment quantity (inter alia because, at the entry-preventing QV-investment quantity, the sum of the Π_D, R, L, and S barriers facing the best-placed potential entrant would have critically exceeded [1] the sum of the Π_D, R, L, and S barriers that would have faced the established firm that would have been best-placed to add a QV investment to its ARDEPPS when that ARDEPPS-QV-investment quantity equaled the ARDEPPS entry-preventing QV-investment quantity *plus* [2] any *M* disincentives the established firm in question would have faced on the most-supernormally-profitable QV-investment expansion it could have executed had entry been barred), the supernormal profit-rate that would be yielded by the ARDEPPS' most-supernormally-profitable QV investments in equilibrium will equal the sum of (1) Π_D, R, S, and L barriers that would have just deterred the firm that was best-placed to execute a QV-investment expansion at the entry-barred expansion-preventing QV-investment quantity *plus* (2) the monopolistic QV-investment disincentive it would have had to make that investment (or *minus* the monopolistic investment-incentive it would have faced to make that investment). Perhaps more relevantly, in this category of situations, the post-conduct difference between the actual, competitive QV-investment quantity in the ARDEPPS (given the different sets of prices that would be charged at different QV-investment quantities post-conduct) and the post-conduct equilibrium-QV-investment quantity will depend on the magnitudes of the parameters listed after "(1)" and "(2)" above and the average slope of the post-conduct $H\Pi_E$ curve between the ARDEPPS' post-conduct actual, competitive QV-investment quantity and its entry-barred expansion-preventing QV-investment quantity.

If (as it also does not in Fig. 5.2) the ARDEPPS' entry-barred expansion-preventing QV-investment quantity equals the ARDEPPS' entry-preventing QV-investment quantity, the supernormal profit-rate that will be generated by the ARDEPPS' most-supernormally-profitable QV investments will equal either (1) the sum of the Π_D, R, L, and S barriers facing the firm that was the ARDEPPS' best-placed potential entrant at the ARDEPPS' entry-preventing QV-investment quantity or (2) the sum of the Π_D, R, L, and S barriers facing the established firm that was the ARDEPPS' best-placed potential expander at the entry-preventing QV-investment quantity *plus* the monopolistic [or natural-oligopolistic] QV-investment disincentives it faced on the relevant expansion (*minus* the monopolistic QV-investment incentives it had to execute the relevant expansion) where the totals referenced after "(1)" and "(2)" above equal each other and the calculations are made on the assumption that both the best-placed potential entrant and the best-placed potential expander found the QV investment they considered but decided not to make infinitesimally subnormally-profitable. In this situation, the determinants of the difference between the relevant ARDEPPS' post-conduct actual, competitive QV-investment quantity and its equilibrium QV-investment quantity would be the parameters that are referenced after either "(1)" or "(2)" above and the average slope of the post-conduct $\text{H}\Pi_{\text{E}}$ curve between its post-conduct actual, competitive QV-investment quantity and its equilibrium QV-investment quantity (which in this situation equals both its entry-preventing QV-investment quantity and its entry-barred expansion-preventing QV-investment quantity).

If (as it does in Fig. 5.2) the ARDEPPS' entry-preventing QV-investment quantity (stipulated to be Oa in Fig. 5.2 because its construction assumes that the barriers to entry portrayed in Fig. 5.1 are operative in the situation Fig. 5.2 portrays) exceeds the ARDEPPS' entry-barred expansion-preventing QV-investment quantity (OY in Fig. 5.2), the list of possible determinants of the supernormal profit-rates generated by the relevant ARDEPPS' most-supernormally-profitable QV investments in equilibrium I provided will not contain all the determinants of that figure because it does not contain all the determinants of the ARDEPPS' equilibrium QV-investment quantity (inter alia, does not contain all the determinants of the difference between that ARDEPPS' actual, competitive QV-investment quantity and its equilibrium QV-investment quantity). To see why, note that, when an ARDEPPS' entry-barred expansion-preventing QV-investment quantity is lower than its entry-preventing QV-investment quantity, in equilibrium (1) the ARDEPPS will contain more QV investment than the entry-barred expansion-preventing quantity (since if the established firms stop investing at the entry-barred expansion-preventing QV-investment quantity, the best-placed potential entrant will add a QV investment to the ARDEPPS) and (2) the ARDEPPS will not contain more QV investment than the entry-preventing QV-investment quantity (since at the entry-preventing QV-investment quantity no [further] entries will take place and, given that fact, the conclusion that the entry-barred expansion-preventing QV-investment quantity is lower than the entry-preventing QV-investment quantity guarantees that if ARDEPPS QV investment had reached the entry-preventing QV-investment quantity no established firm will introduce an additional QV investment but (3) the information Fig. 5.2 provides does not suffice to reveal where between the QV investment quantities referenced after "(1)" and "(2)" in this sentence ARDEPPS equilibrium QV investment will be. Admittedly, the information that (1) the $\text{I}\Pi_{\text{E}}$ curve in Fig. 5.2 between points I and U provides about the Π_{D} barriers to expansion, monopolistic QV-investment (dis)incentives, and natural-oligopolistic QV-investment disincentives that the relevant successive best-placed potential expanders would face and (2) the $\text{IN}\Pi_{\text{E}}$ curve in Fig. 5.2 between points E and U provides about the R barriers to expansion that the relevant successive best-placed potential expanders would face reveals that the equilibrium QV-investment quantity in the ARDEPPS in question will be above OG (since OG is below the entry-preventing QV-investment quantity Oa), but, even though that information (more specifically, the part of that information that relates to the monopolistic QV-investment [dis]incentives the relevant successive best-placed potential expanders would face) reflects assumptions I have not acknowledged about the extent to which the barriers to entry facing the second-placed, third-placed, fourth-placed, etc. potential-entrant exceed their counterparts for the best-placed potential entrant (about how much QV investment potential entrants would introduce if established-firm QV investment fell different amounts below the entry-preventing QV-investment quantity), the information on which Fig. 5.2 is based does not justify any conclusion about where equilibrium QV investment in this situation will fall between OG and Oa. In short, the determinants of the difference between the actual, competitive QV-investment quantity in any ARDEPPS and its equilibrium QV-investment quantity and hence of the supernormal profit-rate its most-supernormally-profitable projects yield in equilibrium in situations in which the ARDEPPS' entry-barred expansion-preventing QV-investment quantity is lower than its entry-preventing QV-investment quantity depend not only on (1) the barriers to expansion/monopolistic QV-investment (dis)incentives/ natural-oligopolistic QV-investment disincentives faced by its best-placed potential expander at the entry-barred expansion-preventing QV-investment quantity and (2) the barriers to entry facing the ARDEPPS' best-placed potential entrant at its entry-preventing QV-investment quantity (assuming no entry has taken place after the time at which the entry-barred expansion-preventing QV-investment quantity has been calculated) but also on (3) the amount by which the sum of the barriers to expansion and monopolistic QV-investment (dis)incentives or natural-oligopolistic QV-investment disincentives increases as one moves from successively-less-supernormally profitable expansions above the entry-barred expansion-preventing QV-investment quantity and (4) somewhat relatedly, the amount by which the barriers to entry facing the successively worse-than-best-placed potential entrants rise. If the least-supernormally-profitable QV investment made in the ARDEPPS in this category of situation is made by an established firm and yielded just a normal rate-of-return, the supernormal profit-rate generated by the ARDEPPS' most-supernormally-profitable QV investments in equilibrium will equal the sum of the barriers that expander faced on this last investment *plus* any monopolistic or natural-oligopolistic QV-investment disincentives it had to make it or *minus* any monopolistic QV-investment incentive it had to make it. If the least-supernormally-profitable QV investment made in the ARDEPPS is made by a new entrant and yielded it just a normal rate-of-return, the supernormal profit-rate generated by the relevant ARDEPPS' most-supernormally-profitable QV investments will equal the sum of the barriers to entry facing the potential competitor that made it. In either event, the difference between the relevant ARDEPPS' actual, competitive QV-investment quantity and its equilibrium QV-investment quantity will depend not only on the supernormal profit-rate generated by its most-supernormally-profitable QV investments in equilibrium (and on that profit-rate's determinants) but also on the average slope of the ARDEPPS' $H\Pi_E$ curve between its actual, competitive QV-investment quantity and its equilibrium QV-investment quantity (assuming as I am that the $N\Pi_E$ curve is horizontal over the relevant QV-investment-quantity range).

Notes

1. Throughout this text, the expressions "rate-of-return" or "profit-rate" are being defined in the way that lawyers use them—viz., to refer to rates that are gross of capital costs. The expressions "supernormal" rate-of-return or "supernormal"

profit-rate refer to rates whose calculation takes capital costs into consideration (to rates that economists would use the expression "rate-of-return" or "profit-rate" to signify).

2. In my terminology, the most-supernormally-profitable QV-investment projects in any area of product-space are those with the highest, identical supernormal rate-of-return. For expositional reasons, I will assume (often counterfactually) that all these projects have the same weighted-average-expected rate-of-return (gross of capital costs) and the same normal rate-of-return.
3. This assumption is admittedly unrealistic. Indeed, the fact that projects in a given area of product-space will have different effects on the rates-of-return generated by the various other projects in that area of product-space plays a significant role in my argument for the inevitable arbitrariness of market definitions and underlies my claim that, in some circumstances, potential expanders have monopolistic QV-investment incentives to make a particular QV investment.
4. Although the identity of the projects that are most-supernormally-profitable may vary either with the equilibrium quantity of QV investment in the ARDEPPS or with changes in the ARDEPPS' structure that do not alter its equilibrium QV-investment quantity, I will ignore this possibility in the text that follows.
5. Unless otherwise indicated, the analyses that follow assume (admittedly sometimes counterfactually) that QV investments will be introduced into an ARDEPPS in the order of their profitability.
6. Thus, one might also construct a "monopolistic" and a "competitive" $H\Pi_E$ curve for a particular ARDEPPS. The former would indicate the rate-of-return the ARDEPPS' most-supernormally-profitable projects would yield as its QV-investment quantity varied if prices in the ARDEPPS were always perfectly monopolistic (maximized the profits that the ARDEPPS' constituent firms realized, given the ARDEPPS' QV-investment quantity). The latter would indicate the rate-of-return the ARDEPPS' most-supernormally-profitable projects would yield as its QV-investment quantity varied if prices in the ARDEPPS were always perfectly competitive (equaled the respective products' marginal costs). The monopolistic $H\Pi_E$ curve will tend to be higher to the extent that the monopolist is able to increase its returns on a given amount of QV investment (1) by charging supra-marginal-cost prices for its products and services and/or (2) by making a less-overlapping set of QV investments (by offering a set of products and services whose members' respective appeals overlap to a lesser extent than the appeals of its competitive counterparts). Obviously, all actual $H\Pi_E$ curves will start at the height of the monopolistic $H\Pi_E$ curve (since prices will be monopolistic when the ARDEPPS contains one QV investment) and progressively converge on the competitive $H\Pi_E$ curve as one moves to the right.
7. In practice, the rate at which any given actual $H\Pi_E$ curve converges on the lower, competitive $H\Pi_E$ curve will increase inter alia with the percentage of any additional QV investments made by new entrants.

8. Admittedly, since the presence of additional product variants or distributive outlets in the early stages of an ARDEPPS' formation may increase the sales of their predecessors by making more consumers aware of the ARDEPPS' product or by increasing consumer-confidence in the quality and reliability of all products produced by the ARDEPPS, the HΠ curves may slope upward over a low range of ARDEPPS QV investment. Figure 5.1 ignores this possibility. The text that follows also ignores the fact that new product variants may have different effects on the rates-of-return generated by what originally were the most-supernormally-profitable QV investments in the ARDEPPS.
9. A "demand curve" is a diagrammatic representation of a schedule indicating the quantity of an indicated product that will be sold at different prices. Demand curves are usually constructed in diagrams whose vertical axis measures some monetary unit (say dollars—$) and whose horizontal axis measures the quantity of the good in question (Q). Economists distinguish between the demand curve a given seller of a particular product faces when selling that product—the "firm" demand curve—and the demand curve faced by an industry whose members produce identical physical products with identical images that they distribute from an identical location—so-called industry demand curves. The text enquotes the expression "ARDEPPS demand curve" because in all or virtually all cases the sellers in a given ARDEPPS will be producing physically-different products with different "images" and be distributing them from different locations among which relevant buyers will not be indifferent. Since the "products" in the ARDEPPS are different, there will usually be no straightforward ARDEPPS counterpart for the traditional notion of an industry demand curve. My use of the concept of an "ARDEPPS demand curve" should therefore be regarded as purely heuristic.
10. I should note that one should not count as part of the scale barrier that would confront the established firm that was contemplating making a QV investment that would raise the total QV investment of the ARDEPPS in question from OY to OD the amount by which the R barrier to expansion at QV-investment quantity OD exceeds the R barrier to expansion at QV-investment quantity OY —PQ–εC—because on the assumptions of Fig. 5.2 the expansion in question will not raise the risk costs of any pre-existing QV investment. However PQ–ε C is a component of the risk barrier R faced by the established firm that is privately-best-placed to increase the ARDEPPS' QV-investment quantity from OY to OD: the other component of that risk barrier is εC (the risk barrier to the execution of the expansion that would be privately-best-placed to raise the ARDEPPS' QV-investment quantity to OY). For convenience, however, I am classifying this component of the scale barrier to the relevant expansion to be a component of the risk barrier to that expansion.

The Inevitable Arbitrariness of Market Definitions

6

Conventional analyses of the illegality and economic efficiency of many types and subtypes of antitrust-law/policy-coverable conduct focus on the magnitudes of one or more parameters whose definition presupposes the non-arbitrary definability of relevant markets—for example, of perpetrator market shares, of the sum of the market shares of the relevant market's or markets' leading 4 or 8 firms, or of the post-merger HHI of the relevant market and the merger-generated increase in that HHI figure (where HHI stands for the sum of the squares of the market shares of all firms placed in a relevant defined market). This chapter exposes the cost-ineffectiveness (indeed, the incoherence) of all such analytic protocols by demonstrating that definitions both of classical (ideal-type) economic markets and of so-called antitrust markets are arbitrary not just at their peripheries but comprehensively.

6.1 The Inevitable Arbitrariness of Definitions of Classical Economic Markets

Before the 1950s, economists implicitly used the term "market" or the expression "economic market" to refer to a set of sellers and buyers that were selling and buying products that ideally satisfied the following 3 conditions: (1) all pairs of products placed inside any such market are highly competitive with each other in the sense that each is "well-placed" (privately-second-placed or perhaps privately-close-to-second-placed) to obtain a substantial percentage of the customers that every other product in that market is best-placed to obtain, (2) each product in any such market is approximately equally competitive in the above sense with all other products in that market—that in a market containing products A1…9 products A1 and A2 are privately-well-placed to obtain the same percentage of each other's customers as are products A1 and A3, products A1 and A4, products A8 and A9, etc., and (3) each product in any such market is more competitive with any other

R. S. Markovits, *Welfare Economics and Antitrust Policy - Vol. I*,
https://doi.org/10.1007/978-3-030-79812-3_6

product placed inside the market than with any product placed outside the market. For 6 reasons, I reject the claim that one can define such "classical economic markets" non-arbitrarily.

First, one cannot generate such a non-arbitrary definition of a classical economic market because one cannot establish non-arbitrarily the minimum amount of sales that must be made of any set of rival products to a specified group of customers for the relevant products and buyers to constitute a "market."

Second, one cannot define any such classical economic market non-arbitrarily because there is no non-arbitrary way to specify whether the competitiveness of two products depends on the frequency with which each reduces the other's OCAs, (OCA + NOM)s, (OCA + NOM + COM)s and/or the amount by which each reduces the other's OCAs, (OCA + NOM)s, or (OCA + NOM + COMs)—i.e., to specify how (highly) competitive is any pair of products be they members of a set of products whose producers might be deemed to constitute the sellers in a defined market (any pair of [market] insider-insider products) or any pair of [market] insider-outsider products.

Third, one cannot define any such classical economic market non-arbitrarily because, even if one could define the competitiveness of any product-pair non-arbitrarily, one could not define non-arbitrarily "the equality of the competitiveness of all product-pairs in any given set of products" whose members might be deemed to compose the seller-side of a classical economic market. Thus, even if one could generate a non-arbitrary competitiveness-score for each product-pair in any given set of products and therefore a non-arbitrary distribution of competitiveness-scores for the product-pairs in any given set of products whose sellers might be deemed to constitute the seller-side of a classical economic market, one could not decide non-arbitrarily whether the metric for the equality of the competitiveness of all product-pairs in any given set of products is the mean deviation of the distribution of relevant-product-pair competitiveness scores, the variance of that distribution, or some other measure of the dispersion of that distribution.

Fourth, for at least 3 sets of reasons, one cannot determine non-arbitrarily the extent to which any given set of products violates the ideal requirement that each product in a given classical economic market must be more competitive with each other product in that market than with any product not in that market: (1) if one cannot define the competitiveness of two products non-arbitrarily, one will not be able to determine the identity of the product-set-insider rival with which each product is least competitive much less its competitiveness with that rival; (2) if one cannot define the competitiveness of two products non-arbitrarily, one cannot identify the product-set-outsider rival with which each product-set-insider is most competitive, how competitive each product-set-insider is with the product-set-outsider with which it is most competitive, or the amount by which each product-set insider is more competitive with the product-set-outsider rival(s) with which it is most competitive than it is with the product-set-insider rival(s) with which it is least competitive; and (3) even if the preceding difficulties can be surmounted (say, because there is a non-arbitrary way to measure the competitiveness of a pair of products), there would be no non-arbitrary way to decide which of two or more product-market definitions each of which contained at least one product that was more competitive with one or more product-set-outsiders than with one or more product-set-insiders failed to satisfy the insider-outsider competitiveness criterion to the greatest extent: whether the failures of each should be measured by the total difference between the higher insider-outsider-competitiveness scores and the lower insider-insider-competitiveness scores, the number of cases in which the insider-outsider-competitiveness scores exceed an insider-insider-competitiveness score, or some metric in which both of the above two considerations play some role.

Fifth, one cannot define classical economic markets non-arbitrarily in all those situations in which no set of product variants whose sellers might be deemed to constitute the seller-side of a classical economic market satisfies best each of the three conditions that are satisfied in classical economic markets—in situations in which no market definition dominates all of its alternatives.

The sixth and empirically-least-important reason for concluding that classical economic markets cannot be defined non-arbitrarily is that it will not be possible to define markets non-arbitrarily if more than one market definition that satisfies the minimum-volume-of-sales-necessary-to-constitute-a-market criterion satisfies equally well the three conditions that classical-economic-market definitions are ideally supposed to satisfy.

6.2 The Inevitable Arbitrariness of Definitions of "Antitrust Markets"

Starting in the 1950s, Industrial Organization economists stopped referring to what I am calling "classical economic markets" and focused on markets that were supposed to be defined in the way that would be associated with market-aggregated parameters and market-aggregated-parameter-oriented decision-rules that would play useful roles in "the best" protocols that could be devised for analyzing the illegality of antitrust-law-covered conduct or the desirability of prohibiting exemplars of such conduct. In other words, for these IO economists, the question was: "What definition of an antitrust market would be functionally best?" (It is worth pointing out that the advocates of focusing on antitrust markets as opposed to classical economic markets did not distinguish between the goal of generating antitrust-law conclusions that are correct as a matter of law and antitrust-policy conclusions that are most-morally-desirable and did not have much to say about the operative tests of antitrust illegality or the criterion or criteria for evaluating an antitrust policy).

The economists who urged scholars and antitrust officials to focus on antitrust markets rarely if ever asked whether antitrust markets could be defined non-arbitrarily. In fact, for at least 5 reasons, antitrust markets cannot be defined non-arbitrarily.

First, it may not be possible to define antitrust markets non-arbitrarily because no antitrust-market-oriented approach to any antitrust-law or antitrust-policy issue can be functionally desirable from any defensible normative perspective because the non-market-aggregated data one uses to define an antitrust market have more relevant predictive power both for the legality of any antitrust-law-covered business conduct and for that conduct's or its deterrence's moral desirability than any estimates of the market-aggregate parameters one can use antitrust-market definitions to define could have: antitrust-market-oriented approaches achieve what the British call "the remarkable double" of increasing cost (because it is extremely expensive to define markets) while decreasing accuracy. I admit that this objection can be countered by arguing that it may be possible to demonstrate that a particular antitrust-market definition is functionally the least bad such definition that could be used.

The second reason why antitrust markets cannot be defined non-arbitrarily assumes that the metric for assessing any concrete or abstract antitrust-market definition is the seriousness as a matter of law of the errors its use causes to be made. Even if as I believe it is possible to determine the categories of business actors and conduct that (say) U.S. antitrust law and E.U. competition law cover and the test(s) of illegality they apply to such actors/conduct, it will not be possible to define antitrust markets non-arbitrarily on this assumption because it will not be possible to determine non-arbitrarily the relative extents to which the legal wrongfulness of the incorrect legal decisions to which that market definition's use leads depends on (1) the number of legal decisions that are incorrect as a matter of law to which it leads, (2) some function that gives different weights to the number of incorrect exonerations and incorrect convictions to which it leads, (3) the number of lawful business-choices deterred by the legally-erroneous decisions of illegality to which it leads, (4) the number of illegal business-choices elicited by the legally-erroneous decisions of lawfulness to which it leads, (5) some parameter that takes account of the "legal-rightfulness" of the business choices condemned as unlawful or deterred by the legally-erroneous decisions to which the use of the relevant antitrust-market definition leads (the amount by which those choices did or would have benefited relevant consumers or did or would have yielded supernormal profits for their perpetrator[s] even if they would not have illicitly reduced the absolute attractiveness of the most attractive offers against which they would have to compete), (6) some parameter that takes account of the "legal wrongfulness" of the business choices found lawful and elicited by the legally-incorrect conclusions of lawfulness to which the use of the relevant antitrust-market definition leads, the extent to which the incorrect legal decisions that resulted from the use of the antitrust-market definition in question disserved the effectuation of the more-ultimate "goals" the relevant antirust law's promulgators were seeking to achieve by passing the law in question (if those goals could be ascertained), etc.

The third reason why antitrust markets cannot be defined non-arbitrarily assumes that the metric for assessing any concrete or abstract antitrust-market definition is the extent to which its use results in legally-incorrect decisions being made that disserve the ultimate goals the relevant law's promulgators passed the law to achieve. This reason is that in many situations it is not possible to identify those goals or a fortiori the trade-offs between them the relevant legislators would have deemed appropriate when relevant applications of the law disserve some of the goals and serve some other of the goals.

The fourth reason why antitrust markets cannot be defined non-arbitrarily assumes that the metric for assessing an antirust-market definition is the impact that its use to resolve antitrust cases will have on the instantiation of the moral values to which the relevant society is committed to instantiating (as opposed to the impact it will have on the securing of the goals that led the relevant source of law's promulgators to [pass the law]/[adopt the treaty-provision]). Even if one can determine whether the society whose antitrust policy is at issue is a moral-rights-based society of moral integrity and (if it is) the conception of justice it is committed to instantiating and derivatively the set of moral rights that constrain its pursuit of the operative conception of the moral good, it may not be possible to define antitrust markets non-arbitrarily because it is not possible to determine the conception of the moral good or the mixed conception of the moral good that should in the relevant society control the assessment of those choices that are neither required by nor prohibited by their (its) moral-rights commitments.

Fifth, and least important empirically, even if one has determined the operative conceptions of justice and the moral good, there may be no non-arbitrary way to define antitrust markets because two or more antitrust-market definitions may lead to decisions that secure moral-rights-related interests and the moral good as the society in question identifies them to the same extent.

7 The Concepts of a Firm's Economic Power or Dominant Position

As applied, U.S. antitrust law makes the illegality of tie-ins depend on whether the State or a private plaintiff has proved that the tying seller has market or economic power in the so-called tying-product market and makes the disposition of monopolization and attempt-to-monopolize cases depend on whether the State or a private plaintiff has proven that the defendant had market power before (or after—the doctrine is unclear) engaging in the conduct alleged to constitute monopolization or an attempt to monopolize. Article 102 of the 2009 Treaty of Lisbon imposes special competition-law obligations on firms that occupy a dominant position in a relevant market. This chapter demonstrates the "cost"-ineffectiveness (indeed, the incoherence) of these legal positions by demonstrating that the concepts of market power or market dominance cannot be defined non-arbitrarily.

This chapter has two sections. Section 7.1 analyzes the complexity of the notion of the economic power that a firm possesses when selling a single product or a set of more-or-less-rivalrous products and the inevitable arbitrariness of the choice of metrics for measuring such power. Section 7.2 analyzes the complexity of the notion of a firm's dominance in an arbitrarily-defined portion of product-space and the inevitable arbitrariness of the choice of a metric for determining whether a firm occupies a dominant position or for measuring a firm's dominance in an ARDEPPS.

7.1 The Concept of a Firm's Economic Power When Selling a Particular Product or a Set of More-or-Less-Rivalrous Products

Why is the concept of a firm's economic power in a particular ARDEPPS complex? Let me count the ways. First, one must decide whether a firm's economic power depends solely on its ability to secure prices above marginal cost, its ability to earn supernormal profits, or on some combination of these two abilities. Second, one must decide whether the appropriate metric for a firm's economic power over price

R. S. Markovits, *Welfare Economics and Antitrust Policy - Vol. I*,
https://doi.org/10.1007/978-3-030-79812-3_7

is (P − MC), ([P − MC]/P), or ([P − MC]/MC) and whether the appropriate metric for a firm's ability to earn supernormal profits is the supernormal profit-rate it realizes on any of the QV or PPR investments it owns in the relevant ARDEPPS, on the weighted-average supernormal profit-rate it realizes on all its QV or PPR investments in the ARDEPPS, or (least attractive) on the total amount of supernormal profits it earns in that relevant ARDEPPS. Third, one must determine whether the economic power that is of interest is economic power as defined regardless of its source or economic power that derives from one or more particular sources: (1) when the relevant power-dimension is power over price, (A) from the relevant firm's own BCAs (power that derives from its monopoly power), (B) from is NOMs and COMs (power that derives from its oligopoly power), (C) from errors that relevant actors make, and/or (D) from its rivals' BCAs, NOMs, COMs, and error-related ability to secure supra-competitive prices (which determine $CMC_{\#2}$ in individualized-pricing contexts and the extent to which the seller can take a piggyback-ride on its rivals' supra-marginal-cost prices in across-the-board pricing contexts), and (2) when the relevant power-dimension is supernormal-profit-related, (A) from the difference between the weighted-average (Π_D + R) barriers the seller faces on its QV or PPR investments in the relevant area of product-space and the (Π_D + R) barriers confronting the established rival or potential competitor that is just deterred from adding a QV investment to the relevant ARDEPPS' QV-investment or PPR total, and from the monopolistic QV-investment (PPR-investment) disincentives it faced that deterred it from adding to the relevant ARDEPPS' total QV investment or PPR (power that relates to its monopoly power over QV investment or PPR), (3) from the L barriers it erected that deterred any established or potential competitor from increasing the relevant ARDEPPS' QV-investment or PPR total and from the natural-oligopolistic QV-investment disincentives or PPR disincentives it and a rival faced that deterred them from adding to the relevant ARDEPPS' QV-investment or PPR total (from its oligopoly power over investment), (C) from the monopolistic QV-investment or PPR disincentives that deterred one or more of its established rivals from increasing the relevant ARDEPPS' QV-investment or PPR total (from its rivals' QV-investment-related or PPR-related monopolistic power), and/or (D) from the retaliation barriers to QV investment or PPR one or more of its rivals erected and the natural-oligopolistic QV-investment or PPR disincentives that deterred one or more of its rivals from increasing the relevant ARDEPPS' QV-investment or PPR total (from its rivals' QV-investment-related or PPR-related oligopoly power).

Unfortunately, for two reasons, I do not know how best to define the economic power of a firm for the purpose of developing decision-rules under which a conclusion about a firm's economic power will play a constructive role in (1) the determination of whether it will be found to have violated an extant antitrust law or whether that determination should be based on other evidence and (2) the determination of whether it would be economically efficient to prevent the firm from engaging in particular conduct. The first reason is that, no matter how defined, a firm's economic power has no bearing on whether any kind of conduct had been motivated by specific anticompetitive intent, will lessen competition, or will distort competition. The second is that, no matter how defined, a firm's economic power is a very weak determinant of the economic efficiency of any antitrust-policy-coverable conduct in which it might engage and should certainly not play a critical role in determining whether it would be economically efficient to permit different firms to engage in any kind of antitrust-policy-coverable conduct. I suppose that the preceding claims that, no matter how defined, a firm's economic power cannot play a desirable role in the determination of the illegality or economic efficiency of any antitrust-law/policy-covered conduct in which it may engage implies that the best way to define a firm's economic power is to adopt a metric that minimizes the frequency with which firms are deemed to have an amount of economic power that results in its economic power's playing a role in any antitrust-law-related legal analysis or antitrust-policy-related economic-efficiency analysis. Clearly, the preceding analyses cannot contribute to the development of a metric for a firm's economic power that can play a constructive role in antitrust-law or antitrust-policy-related-economic-efficiency analysis.

7.2 The Concept of a Firm's (Undertaking's) Occupying a Dominant Position

The concept of "the dominant position that a firm can occupy in an area of product-space in which it is operating" is as problematic as the concept of a firm's economic power in such an area of product-space. I can think of two kinds of metrics that one might use to measure the dominance of a firm in an ARDEPPS.

The first would equate a firm's dominance with its economic power in that area of product-space. Section 7.1 revealed the complexity of this notion of economic power and explained why I do not think that one can resolve the associated uncertainties constructively when the concept is to be used in an antitrust-law analysis or antitrust-policy-related economic-efficiency analysis.

The second would measure the dominance of a firm's position in a given ARDEPPS by its share of all sales made in the ARDEPPS (or, perhaps, by its share of the QV investment or PPR located in that ARDEPPS).[1] This chapter's proofs that neither classical economic markets nor antitrust markets can be defined non-arbitrarily (and the related fact that the acronym "ARDEPPS" stands for "*arbitrarily-defined* portion of product-space") establishes that the choice of any market-share-oriented metric for a firm's dominance of the seller-side of an area of product-space must be arbitrary.

Volume I of my 2014 study *Economics and the Interpretation of U.S. and E.U. Antitrust Law* explains in detail why—even if markets could be defined non-arbitrarily—one could not infer any of the components of a firm's ability to charge supra-competitive prices or realize supernormal profits or a supernormal rate-of-return in a defined market from its share of that market's sales.[2] I do not have space to repeat that analysis here. However, I will point out one salient fact: a firm that makes 100% of the sales of a particular product in a particular geographic area may be charging prices that are only slightly above its marginal costs because firms that (1) are located elsewhere, (2) for transportation-cost reasons, are always slightly-worse-than-privately-best-placed to supply buyers in the geographic area in question, and (3) for that reason, make no sales in the area in question cause the local firm's OCAs and hence its NOMs to be tiny.[3]

Notes

1. The European Commission (EC) has indicated that it believes that a firm's dominance can be inferred both from its achieving supra-competitive results and from its market share, Thus, in its 2005 Discussion Paper—Director General (DG) Competition Discussion Paper on the Application of Article 82 [now Article 102 of the 2009 Treaty of Lisbon] of the Treaty to Exclusionary Abuses (December 2005)—the EC declares: "An undertaking that is capable of substantially increasing price above the competitive level for a significant period of time holds substantial market power…". Id. at Sect. 4.1. In the same Discussion Paper, the EC states: "It is very likely that very high market shares which have been held for some time indicate a dominant position. This would be the case when an undertaking holds 50% or more of the market provided that rivals hold a much smaller share of the market. In the case of lower market shares, dominance is more likely to be found in the market share range of 40–50% than below 40% although also undertakings with market shares below 40% could be considered to be in a dominant position. However, undertakings with market shares of no more than 25% are not likely to enjoy a (single) dominant position in the market concerned." Id. at Sect. 4.2.1, I should acknowledge that the Discussion Paper does indicate that conclusions of dominance will also be influenced by other factors (whose relevance [in my judgment] it either fails to explain or misapprehends): (1) market-share fluctuations, (2) product differentiation, (3) low barriers to expansion and entry (which barriers the EC does not define and whose relevance it seems to attribute to the effective potential investors' inducing established firms to limit price [an effect I doubt will result—see Markovits (2014b) at 221–234 and Sect. 12.1.2 infra]), and (4) buyer power. See id. For more detailed discussions of these EC positions, see Markovits (2014a, 267–273). The E.C./E.U. courts' position on "dominance" is the same as the EC's. See id. at 273–274.
2. See id. at 275–279.
3. I do not think one can "solve this problem" by placing the non-local firms in the relevant local market and attributing to them market shares that will result in the local firm's market share's "indicating" its OCAs. That response (which the U.S. DOJ and FTC has made in their 2010 Horizontal Merger Guidelines) deserves to be said to involve "cooking the books." For a discussion of the referenced conduct of the U.S. DOJ and FTC, see Markovits (2014b) at p. 150 note 1050, citing United States Department of Justice and Federal Trade Commission Horizontal Merger Guidelines (August 19, 2010) at Sects. 5.1 ¶1, 5.2 ¶2, 5.2 ¶5, 5.2 ¶6.

References

Director General (DG) Competition Discussion Paper on the Application of Article 82 of the Treaty to Exclusionary Abuses (December 2005).

Markovits, R. (2014a). *Economics and the interpretation and application of U.S. and E.U. antitrust law,* Vol I *Basic concepts and economics-based legal analyses of oligopolistic and predatory conduct*. Springer.

Markovits, R. (2014b). *Economics and the interpretation and application of U.S. and E.U. antitrust law,* Vol II *Economics-based legal analyses of mergers, vertical practices, and joint ventures*. Springer.

United States Department of Justice and Federal Trade Commission Horizontal Merger Guidelines (August 19, 2010).

The Study's TBLE Distortion-Analysis Protocol for Economic-Efficiency Analysis

8

This chapter delineates and argues for the ex ante economic efficiency of the "distortion-analysis" protocol this study uses to assess the economic efficiency of choices. This protocol has three distinctive features. First, it instructs the analyst to consider the impact of the choice whose economic efficiency is at issue on the magnitudes of many categories of economic inefficiency that conventional economic-efficiency analyses ignore (including the economic inefficiency generated by resource allocations between alternative QV-investment-creating uses, between alternative PPR-executing uses, among alternative unit-output-producing, QV-investment-creating, and PPR-executing uses, and among alternative final consumers). Second, it instructs the analyst to respond ex ante economic efficiently to The General Theory of Second Best's[1] demonstration that since the individual Pareto imperfections that would cause economic inefficiency in an otherwise-Pareto-perfect economy will in general be as likely to counteract each other's tendencies to cause economic inefficiency to any given extent as to compound each other's tendencies to cause economic inefficiency to that extent it is not economically efficient to infer the economic efficiency of a choice from its impact on the Pareto-imperfectness of the relevant economy. More positively, the protocol instructs the analyst to predict the impact of the choice under review on many individual categories of economic inefficiency (resource misallocation) by estimating the choice's impact on the amount of resources devoted to the associated category of resource allocations, by estimating the profits/losses that would be generated by the choice-elicited/deterred resource allocations, by developing formulas for the difference between the profits yielded by and the economic efficiency of (the "distortion" in the profits yielded by) the individual exemplars of a relevant category of resource allocations, by estimating the post-choice magnitudes of the parameters in those formulas (primarily Pareto imperfections), by calculating the distortions in the profits/losses that would be yielded by the choice-elicited/deterred resource allocations, and by combining the conclusions of the preceding analyses. Third, the protocol contains a subprotocol for determining the ex ante economic efficiency of doing any economic-efficiency-analysis-relevant work (which takes

R. S. Markovits, *Welfare Economics and Antitrust Policy - Vol. I*,
https://doi.org/10.1007/978-3-030-79812-3_8

account not only of the direct allocative cost of such efforts but also of the allocative cost of the government's financing such efforts) and instructs the analyst to do all that work but only that work whose performance is ex ante economically efficient.

It is useful to distinguish three categories of protocols for economic-efficiency/allocative-efficiency analysis and correlatively three categories of economic-efficiency/allocative-efficiency analyses. Most economic-efficiency analyses that are actually executed are "first-best-allocative-efficiency" analyses. The defining characteristic of such analyses is that they focus on the economic efficiency of changing the magnitude of one exemplar of one type of Pareto imperfection (the "target" Pareto imperfection) and assume that the target imperfection is the only Pareto imperfection in the relevant economy (both before and after the target imperfection's magnitude has been altered). In this study, I use the acronym "FBLE" to stand both for the compound-adjective "first-best-allocative-efficiency" when used to describe a category of economic-efficiency analysis or a particular economic-efficiency analysis and for "first-best allocatively-efficient" when used to describe an economic-efficiency conclusion (e.g., to describe the conclusion that it is "economically efficient" for the price of a good to equal its marginal cost at its transaction-surplus-maximizing unit output). I find this acronym apposite because "FBLE" resembles the word "fable," and such analyses and conclusions are based on the "fable" that, but for the target imperfection, the relevant economy is Pareto-perfect (or, alternatively, the fable that it is ex ante economically efficient or accuracy-costless to ignore the other Pareto imperfections the relevant economy contains). My daughter Stefanie also finds "FBLE" an appropriate acronym because it resembles the work "feeble" and FBLE economic-efficiency analyses and conclusions are feeble.

The second category of economic-efficiency or allocative-efficiency analyses and conclusions worth distinguishing are second-best-allocative-efficiency analyses and second-best-allocatively-efficient economic-efficiency conclusions. The defining characteristic of such economic-efficiency analyses and economic-efficiency conclusions is that they are perfectly-accurate—that they, respectively, incorporate and are generated by perfectly-accurate exemplars of all relevant theoretical research, all empirical research, and all efforts to determine the implications of what is known for the economic efficiency of the choice(s) under review. I use the acronym "SBLE" to reference both "second-best-allocatively-efficient" and "second-best-allocative-efficiency" because "SBLE" resembles the word "sable" and "sable" is beautiful but prohibitively expensive and SBLE analyses would be ex ante economically inefficient to execute even if they could be executed in that they would be ex ante unduly expensive from the perspective of economic efficiency.

The third category of economic-efficiency or allocative-efficiency analyses and conclusions I find useful to distinguish are economic-efficiency analyses and conclusions that are ex ante economically efficient—respectively, analyses that execute theoretical research, execute empirical research, and consider the implications of what is known or suspected if and only if such work is ex ante allocatively efficient and economic-efficiency conclusions that would be generated by ex ante economically-efficient economic-efficiency analyses. I use the acronym "TBLE" to refer to such analyses and conclusions because "TBLE" resembles the word "table" and, in my judgment, at least if one is concerned exclusively with economic efficiency, TBLE economic-efficiency analyses are the category of such analyses that one should bring to the academic or policy-evaluation "table" and TBLE economic-efficiency conclusions are the category of economic-efficiency conclusions on which policy decisions should be based.

This chapter outlines and argues for the TBLE (ex ante economic efficiency)—of the protocol for economic-efficiency analysis that this study uses. More specifically, this chapter explains that the protocol this study uses to analyze the economic efficiency of business conduct and antitrust policies corrects the three major deficiencies of the conventional economic-efficiency-analysis protocol.

First, rather than focusing solely on the impact of choices on the amount of economic inefficiency the economy in question generated (1) by producing the goods it produces in economically-inefficient proportions, (2) by using known, less-economically-efficient production-processes rather than known, more-economically-efficient production-processes, and (3) by effectuating allocations of final goods among their possible consumers that are economically inefficient for reasons unrelated to the poverty and material inequality with which the allocations are associated, the protocol this study uses focuses as well on the impacts that any choice whose economic efficiency is at issue has on the amounts of economic inefficiency the relevant economy generates inter alia in the following additional ways: (4) by allocating resources in economically-inefficient proportions among uses in which they would produce additional units of extant products, create QV investments, and execute PPR projects, (5) by misallocating resources among alternative QV-investment-creating uses, (6) by misallocating resources among alternative PPR-executing uses, (7) by allocating final goods among possible final consumers in a pattern that is associated with economic-inefficiency-generating poverty and material inequality, and (8) by generating allocative transaction costs allocative-inefficiently.

Second, rather than assuming the ex ante economic efficiency of basing economic-efficiency predictions on the assumption that any choice that decreases (increases) the Pareto-imperfectness of an economy will on that account increase (decrease) economic efficiency, the economic-efficiency-analysis protocol this study uses responds ex ante economic efficiently to the reality that in general individual Pareto imperfections are as likely to counteract as to compound their respective tendencies to cause economic inefficiency in an otherwise-Pareto-perfect economy by focusing on the ways in which an economy's various possible Pareto imperfections (and some other parameters) interact to generate or not generate each category of economic inefficiency it is ex ante economically efficient to distinguish and consider separately by causing economically-inefficient resource allocations to be profitable and/or economically-efficient resource allocations to be unprofitable (in my terminology, by "critically distorting" the profitability of one or more resource allocations). (The word "ways" with an "s" appears in the preceding sentence because, unfortunately, the relevant interactions vary from category of resource allocations to category of resource allocations.) Third, rather than ignoring the fact that economic-efficiency analysis is allocatively costly, the protocol this study uses (1) instructs economic-efficiency analysts to execute those and only those economic-efficiency-relevant theoretical and empirical research-projects whose execution is ex ante economically efficient, (2) instructs economic-efficiency analysts to devote resources to considering the economic-efficiency implications of what is known (or guesstimated) if but only if it is ex ante economically efficient to do so, and (3) delineates an ex ante economically-efficient protocol for assessing the ex ante economic efficiency of a work-project (which focuses inter alia on the differences between the private and allocative cost of the resources that would be directly "consumed" by any relevant work-project, the allocative transaction costs and economic inefficiency the government would generate when financing the execution of any work-project, and the allocative benefits that any relevant work-project would generate by increasing the economic efficiency not only of the government choice under consideration but also of other choices).

This chapter has six sections. Section 8.1 discusses The General Theory of Second Best and its implications for the ex ante economically-efficient protocol for predicting or post-dicting (hereinafter "predicting") the economic efficiency of a choice. Section 8.2 defines the various categories of uses to which resources can be devoted and the various categories of resource allocations that can be executed (and, relatedly, of resource misallocation that can be generated). Section 8.3 defines the concept of "the aggregate distortion in the profits yielded by any resource allocation," distinguishes two categories of formulas for any such aggregate-profit-distortion, and explains the role that aggregate-profit-distortion figures play in the protocol for economic-efficiency prediction I believe is most ex ante economically efficient. Section 8.4 explains why I believe that, from the perspective of economic efficiency, economies currently devote too many resources to QV-investment creation relative to the amounts they devote, respectively, to (1) the production and distribution of units of a less-diverse, possibly-lower-quality, and less-conveniently-and-quickly-distributed/delivered set of products and (2) the execution of PPR projects (a belief that plays a role in many of the economic-efficiency analyses Parts II and III execute). Section 8.5 delineates the TBLE distortion-analysis protocol for economic-efficiency prediction that I think is most ex ante economically efficient: Part II uses a crude version of this protocol to generate more-or-less-tentative conclusions about the economic efficiency of various categories and subcategories of antitrust-policy-coverable business conduct and of various antitrust policies, and Part III uses a crude version of this protocol to compare the economic efficiency of U.S. antitrust law and E.U. competition law as written and correctly interpreted and applied as a matter of law.

Section 8.6 illustrates the difference between the protocol for economic-efficiency prediction I claim is TBLE and the protocol that most applied welfare economists use to analyze the economic efficiency of choices by delineating and criticizing a canonical FBLE economic-efficiency analysis.

8.1 The General Theory of Second Best and Its Implications for the Economic-Efficiency-Prediction Protocol That is TBLE

According to The General Theory of Second Best, in a situation in which one or more members of a set of sufficient conditions for the achievement of an optimum cannot be or will not be fulfilled (henceforth "in a situation in which the relevant system will always contain one or more 'imperfections'—i.e., departures from the relevant set of sufficient conditions for the achievement of the specified optimum"), the elimination or reduction of any individual imperfection or set of imperfections will be as likely to worsen the relevant outcome by any given amount as it will be to improve the outcome by that amount if it leaves one or more imperfections in place. The basic rationale for this conclusion is that, in the absence of a correct general argument to the contrary (which has never been made for the case in which the relevant optimum is "maximum economic efficiency" and whose existence for that case I doubt), one must assume that, in general, the imperfection(s) that would be removed or reduced by an imperfection-reducing choice that would not eliminate all relevant imperfections would be as likely to have counteracted the relevant net-optimum-disserving effects of the remaining imperfections in the system to any given extent as they would be to have compounded the net-optimum-disserving effects of the remaining imperfections in the system to the same extent.[2] The General Theory of Second Best applies both when the relevant maximand (objective function) is economic efficiency and when it is a maximand in which economic efficiency (1) is not valued at all or is not the only desideratum and (2) is not monotonically related to the relevant maximand (objective function).

Admittedly, The General Theory of Second Best would not have much bearing on the protocol for economic-efficiency analysis that is ex ante economically efficient if the ex ante most-economically-efficient way to predict the impact of a choice on economic efficiency was either (1) to identify all of the choice's winners and losers and estimate and sum these parties' respective equivalent-monetary (henceforth equivalent-dollar) gains and losses or, less ambitiously, (2) to identify a TBLE-large, random sample of the choice's winner and losers, estimate their respective equivalent-dollar gains and losses, and derive a final estimate of the choice's economic efficiency by multiplying the difference between the sums of the studied parties' equivalent-dollar gains and losses by the ratio of (the total number of winners and losers in the relevant society) to (the total number of winners and losers identified and studied). In fact, however, for three reasons or sets of reasons, the approaches just described would not be ex ante economically efficient: (1) the incentives that the beneficiaries/victims of any choice have, respectively, to exaggerate the magnitude of the equivalent-dollar gains/losses it would confer/impose on them (to the extent that their doing so increases the probability that any government choice in question will be made/rejected or any non-government choice in question will be allowed/prohibited) would make it impracticable to estimate relevant winners'/losers' equivalent-dollar gains/losses by asking them to testify to the equivalent-dollar impact the choice at issue would have on them even if they could estimate that impact accurately, (2) the winners and losers of many choices will often not be well-placed to predict or even post-dict their equivalent-dollar effect on them, and (3) at least in my judgment, no method of estimating a choice's winners'/losers' equivalent-dollar gains/losses that does not rely on their "testimony" would be acceptably accurate or ex ante economically efficient. I am therefore not surprised that, to my knowledge, no concrete analysis of the economic efficiency of any choice (no "applied Welfare Economics" analysis) has ever proceeded by identifying all or a random sample of its winners and losers and estimating their equivalent-dollar gains and losses.

However, The General Theory of Second Best does have important implications for (indeed, invalidates) the protocol that the overwhelming majority of applied welfare economists use to analyze the economic efficiency of choices—a protocol that focuses exclusively on the impact of the choice on the Pareto-imperfectness of the relevant economy (more particularly that assumes that any choice that decreases/increases the Pareto-imperfectness of an economy [say, by reducing/increasing a given target Pareto imperfection] will increase/decrease economic efficiency on that account). Although this assumption (1) would almost always be true[3] if the choice in question reduced the magnitude of the only Pareto imperfection in an otherwise-Pareto-perfect economy and (2) would be ex ante economically efficient to make if it was ex ante economically efficient to assume either that the economy in question was otherwise-Pareto-perfect or that, acting together, the other Pareto imperfections the relevant economy contained would not critically affect the economic efficiency of reducing the target Pareto imperfection, economies in which one or more particular Pareto imperfections can be reduced or eliminated are never otherwise-Pareto-perfect, and no-one has ever justified the conclusion that it will be ex ante economically efficient to ignore the non-target Pareto imperfections all actual economies always contain when predicting/post-dicting the economic efficiency of increasing or decreasing a particular target Pareto imperfection (to ignore The General Theory of Second Best's demonstration that the fact that Pareto imperfections are in general as likely to counteract as to compound each other's tendencies to generate economic inefficiency in an otherwise-Pareto-perfect economy invalidates the claim that one can predict the economic efficiency of a choice from its impact on the Pareto-imperfectness of the economy in which it is made).

To be somewhat more concrete, The General Theory of Second Best invalidates the protocol for economic-efficiency analysis that most economists use[4] because it implies that, unless one can develop an argument to the contrary (which has not yet been made) it is correct to conclude that the fact that the seven Pareto-optimal conditions belong to a set of sufficient conditions for the maximization of economic efficiency does not imply that a choice that did or would reduce (1) the incidence and/or magnitudes of the imperfections in seller competition the relevant economy contains, (2) the incidence and/or magnitudes of the imperfections in buyer competition the relevant economy contains, (3) the incidence and/or magnitudes of the real externalities generated in the economy in question, (4) the incidence and/or magnitudes of the taxes on the margin of income (effectively) levied in the economy in question, (5) the incidence and/or magnitudes of any imperfections in the relevant information available to the economy's resource allocators, (6) the incidence and/or magnitudes of resource-allocator non-maximization in the economy in question, (7) the amount of buyer surplus generated in the economy in question, and (8) most comprehensively, the Pareto-imperfectness of an economy *will in general even tend to favor the conclusion that the choice did or would increase economic efficiency if the relevant economy did/would remain Pareto-imperfect post-choice.*

8.2 Categories of Resource-Uses and Categories of Resource Allocations

8.2.1 11 Categories of Resource-Uses

This study and the protocol for economic-efficiency analysis I believe is ex ante economically efficient distinguishes 11 categories of resource-uses:

(1) unit-output-producing (UO-producing) resource-uses in which resources are devoted to producing units of a given, extant product or service (defined expansively to include as part of a given product or service such desiderata as warranties of the product's proper performance),
(2) quality-or-variety-investment-creating (QV-investment-creating) resource-uses in which resources are devoted to executing an investment that (A) creates a new product or product variant or a new distributive outlet (either of which may or may not replace a pre-existing alternative) or (B) creates additional capacity or inventory (which enables its owner to supply the relevant good or distributive or non-distributive service at a higher average speed throughout a fluctuating-demand cycle),
(3) production-process-research-executing (PPR-executing) resource-uses in which resources are devoted to discovering privately and/or allocatively cheaper ways of producing relevant quantities of an existing product (research that seeks to discover a new product that is cheaper to produce than its extant alternatives is both QV-investment-creating and PPR-executing),
(4) known-production-process-effectuating resource-uses (choice-among-known-production-process-effectuating resource-uses where the expression "production process" is defined to include [A] the process of producing goods and the process of supplying non-distributive services, [B] acts of communicating to potential buyers information about a product's or service's attributes, uses, usefulness, methods of use, and/or durability, [C] the choices that producers and distributors make between having production-process functions performed by employees or by independent contractors, [D] the choices that firms that hire employees to perform various production-process functions make among the various sorts of hierarchical controls that can be used to induce their employees to make those production-process choices that maximize the firm's

profits, and [E] the choices that firms that use independent contractors to perform various production-process functions make among the contractual clauses and hiring and renewal-of-contract criteria they could employ to increase the extent to which the independent contractors with whom they contract make production-process choices that maximize the firm's profits),

(5) the resource-uses that are associated with (A) individual firms' employing particular pricing-techniques to convert what might be buyer surplus into seller surplus (non-discriminatory "single pricing," in which the firm charges the same per-unit price and no lump-sum fee to all its potential customers for each unit of its product they purchase, perfect price discrimination in one or the other of its possible forms, pricing in which the buyer is charged a combination of a lump-sum fee for the right to purchase up to a certain quantity or an unlimited quantity of the seller's product for a specified per-unit price that exceeds the marginal cost the seller would have to incur to produce the unit of its output at which the demand curve it believes it faces for that product cuts its marginal-cost curve from above, conventional price discrimination, tie-in pricing (in which a seller that may or may not also be charging a lump-sum fee conditions its agreeing to supply the relevant buyer with a stated quantity of one [so-called tying] product at a specified per-unit price or with as many units of the tying product as the buyer wishes to purchase at the specified per-unit price on the buyer's agreeing to purchase a specified quantity or its full requirements of a second [so-called tied] product at a specified per-unit price), reciprocal-trade-agreement pricing (in which one firm that may or may not also be charging another firm a lump-sum fee conditions its agreeing to supply that second firm with a stated quantity of its product or with as many units of its product as the second firm wants to purchase at the specified per-unit price on the second firm's agreeing to supply the first firm with a specified quantity, as many units as the first firm wants to purchase, the first firm's full requirements, or the second firm's total output of a second good [or an analogous reciprocity arrangement in which the relevant initiative is taken by a firm that is acting initially in its capacity as a buyer]), (B) individual firms' trying to prevent their independent distributors from making sales of rival products whose consummation is against the joint interest of the producer and the distributor in question, (C) individual firms' trying to induce their independent distributors to place mutually-profitable advertizements, to set up mutually-profitable in-store promotional-displays, to make mutually-profitable shelf-space decisions, to make mutually-profitable salesmanship efforts, to communicate to the producers mutually-profitable sales-techniques, to provide mutually-profitable post-sale repair and maintenance services perhaps to fulfill warranty obligations (by subsidizing distributor advertizing; by contractually obligating distributors to provide specified advertizements, in-store promotional-displays, and/or shelf-space allocations; or by communicating to distributors its intention not to renew their distributorships if they do not make advertizing/promotional-display/shelf-space/sales-effort/post-sales-service decisions that are in the distributor's and the producer's joint interest), and (D) individual

firms' trying to deter their distributors from charging lower prices (or higher prices) for the producer's product than is in the interest of the producer and all its distributors taken all together (e.g., by including vertical-territorial-restraint clauses, other sorts of vertical-customer-allocation clauses, and resale-price-maintenance clauses in their distributorship contracts),

(6) the resource-uses that are associated with potential buyers' considering the purchases they will choose to make, with government entities' supplying final consumers with product-information (or banning certain products altogether), with private entities' supplying final consumers with product-information and product-recommendations, and with individual producers' trying to prevent their customers from combining the producer's products with inferior complements when the buyers' doing so would reduce the basic-product-producer's profits by leading its customers to be dissatisfied and/or by tarnishing the reputation of the basic-product-producers' products because the customers and third-party observers attribute the resulting poor performance of the producer's product to the producer's product rather than to the complement with which it was combined (by contractually obligating their distributors/their products' final consumers to sell exclusively/purchase their full requirements of complements produced by the firm itself or by other suppliers the producer names or by contractually obligating [their distributors to sell]/[their customers to use] complements that have specified attributes [and monitoring their distributors'/customers' complement-choices and legally enforcing the complement-obligations in question]),

(7) the use of resources to commit (liberal) moral-rights-violating acts or illegal acts of other sorts—for example, to commit (A) acts that are motivated by specific anticompetitive intent (acts whose perpetrator[s] would not have found ex ante profitable but for its/their belief that the conduct would or might increase its/their profits by reducing the absolute attractiveness of the best offers against which it/they would have to compete in one or more ways that would render the conduct profitable though it would be economically inefficient in an otherwise-Pareto-perfect economy—price-fixing, predatory conduct of all kinds, some mergers and acquisitions, some joint ventures or functionally-analogous collaborative arrangements of other kinds, etc.), (B) deceptive or fraudulent (sometimes competition-distorting) acts, (C) libel and slander, (D) assault or battery, (E) murder, (F) kidnapping, (G) theft or conversion, (H) regulatory violations, and (I) illegal tax-evasion or lawful tax-avoidance,

(8) the use of resources by non-government and government actors (A) to prosecute, defend, participate in plea negotiations, and decide criminal cases and (B) to initiate, settle, mediate, arbitrate, litigate, and officially resolve private disputes or disputes about alleged administrative-regulation violations,

(9) the use of resources by private actors to participate in electoral politics and legislative or administrative-regulation-promulgative processes,

(10) the use of resources by governments to devise and pass legislative/administrative regulations, and
(11) the use of resources by governments to detect violations of the law, identify law-breakers, penalize offenders, collect taxes, and execute government transfers.

8.2.2 16 Categories of Resource Allocations (and Related Categories of Economic Inefficiency)

This study and the protocol for economic-efficiency analysis I believe is ex ante economically efficient distinguishes the following 16 categories of resource allocations:

(1) allocations of resources from specified UO-producing-and-using, QV-investment-creating-and-using, and PPR-executing-and-using pairs of related resource-uses in one or almost always more-than-one specified ARDEPPS to a UO-producing-and-using (consuming) use in a specified ARDEPPS or vice versa,
(2) allocations of resources from specified UO-producing-and-using, QV-investment-creating-and-using, and PPR-executing-and-using pairs of related resource-uses in one or almost always more-than-one specified ARDEPPS to a QV-investment-creating-and-using related pair of uses in a specified ARDEPPS,
(3) allocations of resources from specified UO-producing-and-using, QV-investment-creating-and-using, and PPR-executing-and-using related pairs of uses in one or almost always more-than-one specified ARDEPPS to a PPR-executing-and-using related pair of uses in a specified ARDEPPS,
(4) intra-ARDEPPS UO-to-UO resource allocations,
(5) intra-ARDEPPS QV-to-QV resource allocations,
(6) intra-ARDEPPS PPR-to-PPR resource allocations,
(7) resource allocations from the use of one known production process to another (where goods/services and hence "production processes" are defined in the expansive way in which I previously defined them)—resource allocations that may yield misallocations that entail departures from the production optimum in that they create a situation in which more of one good could have been produced without reducing the output of any other good,
(8) resource allocations from various specified uses in one or usually more-than-one specified ARDEPPS to uses in which specified producers use them to (A) implement pricing-techniques designed to convert into seller surplus what would otherwise be buyer surplus, (B) try to prevent their independent distributors from selling rival products, (C) try to induce their independent distributors to place mutually-profitable advertizements, set up mutually-profitable in-store promotional-displays, make mutually-profitable

shelf-space decisions, make mutually-profitable sales-efforts, communicate to the relevant producer mutually-profitable sales-techniques, and provide mutually-profitable post-sale (repair and maintenance)/warranty services, and (D) try to deter its distributors from driving down the price charged for the producer's product to an "organizationally"-unprofitable level by competing against each other;

(9) resource allocations from various alternative uses in one or usually more-than-one specified ARDEPPS to uses in which (A) final consumers try to identify the consumption choice that is privately-best for them, (B) governmental or non-governmental entities supply consumers with relevant product-information or recommendations, (C) the government bans certain products altogether, and (D) producers try to prevent their customers from combining their respective products with inferior complements whose use by the buyers in question disserves the joint interest of the respective buyers and basic-product producers,

(10) resource allocations in which final goods that have been produced are allocated to one final consumer rather than to another (when the allocation that is made does not affect the extent of poverty or resource-ownership inequality the relevant economy generates)—i.e., that can cause conventional consumption-optimum-related misallocation, and

(11) resource allocations from various specified uses in one or usually more-than-one ARDEPPS to uses in which they execute the following categories of conduct: (A) conduct by private entities that is motivated by specific anticompetitive intent (conduct that would not have been perceived to be ex ante profitable by its perpetrator[s] had the perpetrator[s] not believed that it would or might increase its [their] profits by reducing the absolute attractiveness of the best offers against which it [they] would have to compete in one or more ways that would render the conduct ex ante economically inefficient in an otherwise-Pareto-perfect economy—most often, contrived-oligopolistic and predatory conduct and mergers, acquisitions, joint ventures, and other types of collaborative conduct when it is motivated by specific anticompetitive intent), (B) conduct by private entities that violate the law because it is prohibited by statutes that deem such conduct illegal if it "lessens competition" in the sense of imposing a net equivalent-dollar loss on the combination of its perpetrator's or perpetrators' customers and the customers of the (their) product-rivals by reducing the absolute attractiveness of the best offer they, respectively, receive from any worse-than-privately-best-placed supplier (at least if this outcome was not critically affected by the conduct's driving a perpetrator-rival out or deterring a perpetrator-rival from making a QV or PPR investment by increasing the organizational allocative efficiency of the perpetrator[s]), and (C) conduct by private entities that distort competition (give its perpetrator[s] a private advantage that does not reflect its [their] allocative superiority by persuading buyers that the perpetrator's product [perpetrators' products] has [have] good qualities that they do not possess or that their rivals' products have bad qualities that they do not possess or by misleading buyers into

underestimating the lifetime costs of their products or overestimating the lifetime cost of their rivals' products),

(12) resource allocations from various specified uses in one or usually more-than-one ARDEPPS to uses in which they execute various types of liberal-moral-rights-violating conduct not delineated in Item (11) of this list or to tax or regulation avoidance or evasion,

(13) resource allocations from various specified uses in one or usually more-than-one ARDEPPS to uses by government to devise and promulgate legislation/administrative regulations/Presidential or Prime Ministerial decrees that have the force of law and to detect violations of these "laws,"

(14) resource allocations from various specified uses in one or usually more-than-one ARDEPPS to prosecuting alleged criminal offenses, defending those accused of criminal wrongdoing, negotiating plea-deals, adjudicating criminal cases, penalizing those found guilty of criminal behavior, making civil-law claims, defending those accused of civil-law violations, negotiating civil-law settlements, using mediation or arbitration to resolve or help the parties to settle civil-law disputes, adjudicating civil-law cases, executing settlements, and enforcing civil-law judgments,

(15) resource allocations from various specified uses in one or usually more-than-one specified ARDEPPS to uses in which the government transfers money to claimants eligible for the transfer, and

(16) resource allocations from various specified uses in one or usually more-than-one ARDEPPS to uses by the government to devise and implement the various revenue-raising measures it adopts to finance its operations.

8.3 The Concept of the Aggregate Distortion in the Profits Yielded by a Resource Allocation, Two Types of Formulas for an Aggregate Profit-Distortion, and the Role That Aggregate-Profit-Distortion Figures Play in the Economic-Efficiency-Analysis Protocol I Claim Is Ex Ante Economically Efficient

8.3.1 The Definition of the Aggregate Distortion in the Profits Yielded by a Resource Allocation

In my terminology, a profit figure, private-benefit figure, or private-cost figure is said to be "distorted" if and by the number of dollars by which it diverges from its allocative counterpart. Thus, the profits yielded by a resource allocation are said to be "distorted" if and by the number of dollars by which they differ from the economic efficiency of the resource allocation; similarly, the private benefits that a resource-use confers on the resource-user are said to be "distorted" if and by the number of dollars by which they differ from the (net) allocative benefits yielded by the resource-use[5]; and the private cost of a resource-use to a resource-user is said to be distorted if and by the number of dollars by which it differs from the allocative benefits that those resources would have generated in their sacrificed uses. More specifically, in my terminology, a private figure is said to be "inflated" if it exceeds its allocative counterpart and to be "deflated" is it is lower than its allocative counterpart.[6] In my usage, the *aggregate* distortion in any private figure is the distortion in that figure that is generated by the interaction of all extant exemplars of all types of Pareto imperfections and of any of the other factors that affect its magnitude.

8.3.2 Two Types of Formulas for the Aggregate Distortion in the Profits Yielded by any Resource Allocation (or for the Aggregate Distortion in any Private-Benefit or Private-Cost Figure)

Two types of equivalent formulas can be used to calculate the aggregate distortion in the profits yielded by any resource allocation—"onesy" (1E) formulas and "step-wise-distortion"—(SW)D—formulas. The defining characteristic of any "onesy" formula for the aggregate distortion in any private figure is that such formulas take account "all at once" or in "one go"—hence "onesy"—of the way in which the various determinants of the relevant aggregate distortion interact to determine the magnitude of that distortion.[7] For example, the onesy formula for the aggregate distortion in the profits yielded by an allocation of resources from the production of less-than-one, one, or more-than-one just-extra-marginal units of product B to the production of a marginal unit of product A is $MC^*_A([P^*_B/MC^*_A] - [P^*_A/MC^*_A])$. In this formula, MC^*_A and MC^*_B are adjusted-marginal-cost figures created by adjusting, respectively, MC_A and MC_B to take account of the way in which the relevant economy's various Pareto imperfections interact to cause or not cause (MC_A/MC_B) to diverge from the marginal rate of transformation of B into A—i.e., to generate a (MC^*_A/MC^*_B) ratio that equals the marginal rate of transformation of B into A . Similarly, in this formula, P^*_A and P^*_B are adjusted-price figures created by adjusting, respectively, P_A and P_B to take account of the way in which the relevant economy's various Pareto imperfections interact to cause or not cause (P_A/P_B) to diverge from the marginal rate of substitution of B for A—i.e., to generate a (P^*_A/P^*_B) ratio that equals the marginal rate of substitution of B for A. By way of contract, the step-wise-distortion—(SW)D—formula for the aggregate distortion in any private figure does not present the interactions of the various sources of the possible distortion in the private figure in question all in "one go." To the contrary, the step-wise-distortion formula for the aggregate distortion in any private figure presents this distortion as the sum of seven single-type-of-Pareto-imperfection-oriented step-wise distortions, each of which is calculated on two assumptions: (1) the (almost-always-unrealistic) assumption that the extant exemplars of the other six types of Pareto imperfections the relevant economy contains do not affect the contribution that the extant exemplars of the type of Pareto imperfection on which the aggregate-profit-distortion-formula formula-component of interest makes to the aggregate profit-distortion and (2) the almost-always-unrealistic assumption that the extant exemplars of the type of Pareto imperfection on which the aggregate-profit-distortion-formula formula-component of interest focuses do not affect the aggregate profit-distortion by affecting the incidences and magnitudes of any of the six other types of Pareto imperfections. To illustrate the second of these two unrealistic assumptions, let me point out that the calculation of the step-wise-monopoly-distortion component of the formula for the aggregate distortion in the profits yielded by an allocation of resources from the production of one, less-than-one, or more-than-one just-extra-marginal unit(s) of B to the production of one (marginal) unit of A ignores the possibility that the relevant economy's imperfections in seller price-competition may alter the aggregate profit-distortion in question by altering the external costs that would have been generated by the production of the sacrificed unit(s) of B and/or the external costs that were generated by the production of the marginal unit of A by altering, respectively, the output of B and the output of A. I hasten to add that this feature of each of the seven components of the step-wise-distortion formula does not undermine the formula's accuracy because the effects that each component ignores are picked up in the calculation of the other components of the overall formula. Thus, in the preceding example, the failure of the step-wise-monopoly-distortion component of the step-wise-distortion formula for the relevant aggregate profit-distortion to reflect the impact that imperfections in seller price-competition have on that aggregate distortion by altering the amounts of distortion-relevant externalities that would have been generated by the production of the sacrificed unit(s) of B and that were generated by the production of the marginal unit of A is rendered inconsequential by the fact that the calculation of the step-wise-externality-distortion component of the relevant step-wise aggregate-profit-distortion formula takes full account of the impact that the extant imperfections in seller price-competition have on the externalities that would have been generated by the production of the sacrificed B and were generated by the production of the marginal unit of A.

I have analyzed elsewhere both the onesy and the step-wise-distortion formula for the aggregate distortion in the profits yielded by an allocation of resources from the production of one, less-than-one, or more-than-one just-extra-marginal unit(s) of one product B to the production of a marginal unit of product A.[8] Space-constraints deter me from repeating this analysis here.

I think it will be both convenient and informative to delineate the symbols I use to stand for the 1E and (SW)D formulas for the aggregate distortion (ΣD) in the (private) profits (Pπ) yielded by an allocation of resources from the production and use (consumption) ("C" for creation and "U" for use) of just-extra-marginal units of B to the production and consumption of a marginal unit of A. The (unfortunately-complicated) symbol I use to refer to the relevant onesy formula is $1E(\Sigma D)(P\pi_{(C+U)\Delta UOA/(C+U)\Delta UOB})$ where the two components of the subscript indicate respectively and sequentially the uses to which the relevant resource allocation devotes resources and the uses from which the relevant resource allocation withdraws resources. The equally-complicated symbol I use for the step-wise-distortion formula for the same aggregate profit-distortion is $(SW)\Sigma D(P\pi_{(C+U)\Delta UOA/(C+U)\Delta UOB})$. The possibly-instructive point is that this step-wise-distortion symbol can be replaced by a lengthier symbol that references the seven step-wise-single-type-of-Pareto-imperfection-oriented figures whose sum equals the relevant aggregate profit-distortion: $(SW[M])D(P\pi_{(C+U)\Delta UOA/(C+U)\Delta UOB})$ + $(SW[MS])D(P\pi_{(C+U)\Delta UOA/(C+U)\Delta UOB})$ + $(SW[X])D(P\pi_{(C+U)\Delta UOA/(C+U)\Delta UOB})$ + $(SW[T])D(P\pi_{(C+U)\Delta UOA/(C+U)\Delta UOB})$ + $(SW[NS])D(P\pi_{(C+U)\Delta UOA/(C+U)\Delta UOB})$ + $(SW[NM])(P\pi_{(C+U)\Delta UOA/(C+U)\Delta UOB})$ + $(SW[BS])D(P\pi_{(C+U)\Delta UOA/(C+U)\Delta UOB})$ where "M" stands for "monopoly" (actually, imperfections in seller competition), "MS" stands for "monopsony," "X" stands for "(real) externalities," "T" stands for "taxes on the margin of income," "NS" stands for "resource-allocator non-sovereignty," "NM" stands for resource-allocator "non-maximization," and "BS" stands for "buyer surplus" (thank you very much).

8.3.3 The Role That Aggregate-Profit-Distortion Figures Play in the Distortion-Analysis Protocol for Economic-Efficiency Prediction I Claim is TBLE

Estimates of the aggregate distortions in the profits yielded by various resource allocations play an important rule in the economic-efficiency-prediction protocol I claim is ex ante economically efficient because that protocol proceeds in part by predicting or post-dicting the economic-efficiency gains or losses the choice whose economic efficiency is at issue would generate by inducing or deterring resource allocations by predicting or post-dicting (1) the resource allocations that the choice whose economic efficiency is at issue would or did induce and deter, (2) the profits that the resource allocations the choice would or did induce would or did yield and the losses the resource allocation the choice did or would deter would have generated, and (3) the post-choice aggregate distortions in those profits and losses. Of course, since the protocol for economic-efficiency analysis I am recommending is TBLE, it will instruct analysts to do work related to these three tasks if and only if that work is ex ante allocatively efficient.

8.4 The Reasons Why I Believe That, From the Perspective of Economic Efficiency, Contemporary Economies Devote Too Many Resources to QV-Investment Creation and Not Enough to UO Production and PPR Execution

Part II's analyses of the economic efficiency of many antitrust-policy-coverable business-choices and of many antitrust policies will be significantly influenced by my belief that not only the marginal but many intra-marginal resource allocations to QV-investment creation and use from UO production and use (consumption) and

PPR execution and use are economically inefficient primarily because their profitability is "critically inflated"—i.e., primarily because the economy's relevant Pareto imperfections cause the resource allocations to be profitable despite their economic inefficiency. Section 8.4 explains why I subscribe to this position—in particular, why I believe that (1) the step-wise-imperfections-in-seller-price-competition (hereinafter "step-wise-monopoly") distortion in the private benefits that the production of a unit of output confers on its producer—(SW[M])D($PB_{(U)UO}$) where the subscript "(U)" refers to "use"—is negative, (2) the step-wise-monopoly distortion in the private benefits that a QV-investment creator obtains by using its QV investment—(SW[M])D($PB_{(U)QV}$)—is positive, (3) the step-wise-monopoly distortion in the private benefits that a production-process researcher obtains by using its research—(SW[M])D($PB_{(U)PPR}$)—is negative, (4) the step-wise-monopoly distortion in the private cost of creating a QV investment with resources withdrawn from UO-producing and PPR-executing uses—(SW[M])D($PC_{(C)QV/(C+U)UO \text{ and } (C+U)PPR}$)—is negative, (5) the step-wise-monopoly distortion in the profits yielded by a resource allocation that withdraws resources from UO-producing (and consuming) uses and PPR-executing-and-using uses and devotes them to creating and using an additional QV investment is positive, and (6) the components of the step-wise-distortion formula for the aggregate distortion in the profits yielded by such resource allocations that refer to the step-wise distortions in those profits that are yielded by the other six types of Pareto imperfections will almost certainly not fully counteract the inflating effect of imperfections in seller price-competition and imperfections in QV-investment competition—indeed, seem unlikely in general to reduce the positive aggregate profit-distortion in question.

I address first the step-wise imperfections-in-seller-price-competition-generated (SW[M]) distortion in $PB_{(U)UO}$. The text focuses on the simplest and (probably) the most common case—viz., the case that assumes that the production and sale of the relevant unit of output does not increase the producer's profits by increasing the future demand for the good in question, by increasing the demand for one or more of the producer's other products (be they complements of the good in question or unrelated goods whose consumer-perceived quality is enhanced by the contribution that the good in question's quality makes to the producer-company's general reputation for producing high-quality goods), by lowering its costs (learning-by-doing [if you believe in it]), or by yielding it any kind of advantage that could be generated by a retaliatory or predatory price.

In this simple case, (SW[M]D)$PB_{(U)UO}$ equals the difference between the pre-tax-price the seller did/would obtain for the unit in question and the conventional marginal revenue the seller did/would obtain by selling that unit at that price. I hasten to add that this (P − MR) difference depends not just on the demand and marginal-cost curves the seller faces but also on the pricing-technique the seller did/would use when pricing the relevant good and, derivatively, on all the determinants of the profitability of using different pricing-techniques and on the private cost to the seller of using each such pricing-technique. Thus, P = MR for each unit of output sold by a seller that faces a downward-sloping demand curve if that seller

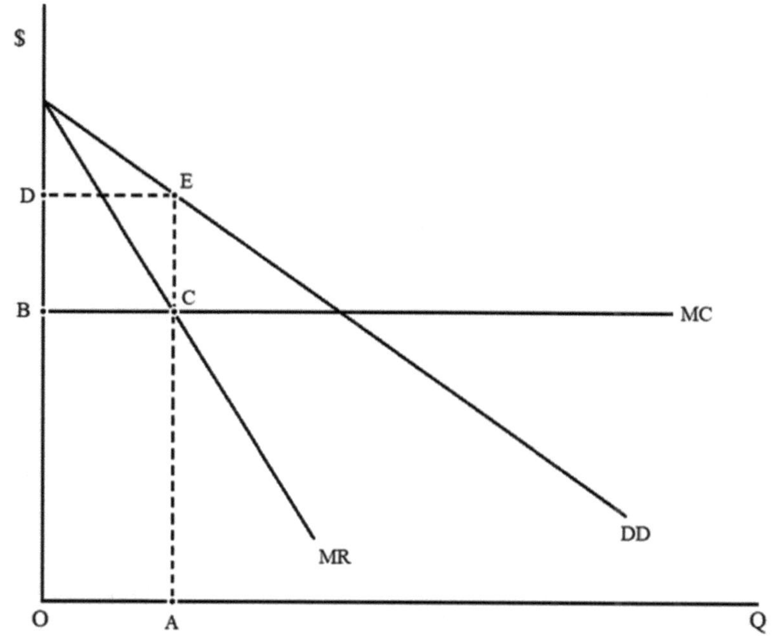

Fig. 8.1 Figure that illustrates the analysis of the imperfections-in-seller-price-competition-generated (SW[M]) distortion in PB_{UO} or $PB_{(U)UO}$

can and does practice perfect price discrimination perfectly accurately when selling the relevant product to each of its customers without incurring any pricing-costs.

Figure 8.1 illustrates the analysis of the imperfections-in-seller-price-competition (monopoly) distortion in the private benefits that a decision to produce a unit of output confers on the producer on the assumptions that those benefits equal conventional marginal revenue and that the relevant producer sells its product by setting a single per-unit price for it and allowing potential buyers to purchase as many units as they wish at that price (engages in what I call "single pricing"). This second assumption is manifest in the construction of the MR curve (in the fact that, given the linearity of the DD curve, MR is constructed to be halfway between the vertical axis and the DD curve). Figure 8.1 reveals that, on the assumptions on which it is based, (SW[M])D($PB_{\Delta UO}$) for the marginal unit of the product in question equals (−EC) since on the assumptions on which step-wise distortions are calculated the DD curve for the relevant product coincides with the marginal allocative value curve [MLV] for that product)[9]—i.e., since on those assumptions the allocative benefits generated by the production (and consumption) of the marginal unit of the product in question equals its price (EA), which exceeds the marginal revenue the sale of that unit generated because, in order to sell that last unit at the price EA, the relevant single-pricing producer reduced the price it charged and hence obtained for all its intra-marginal units of the good in question.

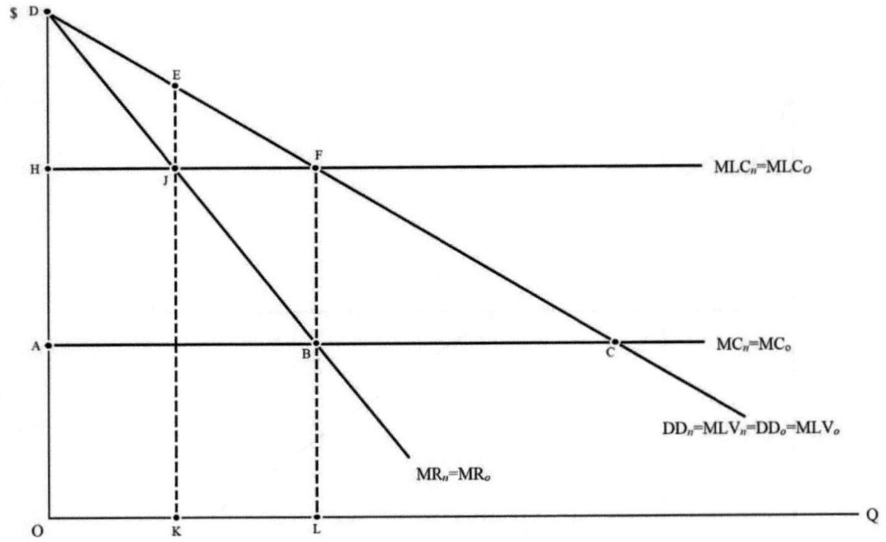

Fig. 8.2 Figure that illustrates the analysis of the imperfections-in-seller-price-competition-generated (SW[M]) distortion in $PB_{(U)QV}$

I turn now to the step-wise-monopoly distortion in the private benefits that the use of a QV investment confers on a QV investor (that uses the QV investment in question itself). To simplify the relevant analysis, I will assume (1) that the profits generated by the use of the QV investment equal the difference between the conventional variable costs of using the QV investment and the conventional revenue yielded by the use of the QV investment (that the sale of the newly-created product generates no repeat-purchase-related, no complement-sales-related, no general-promotional-benefit-related, no-learning-by-doing-related [cost-related], and no reputation-for-engaging-in-strategic-conduct-related benefits) and that the relevant QV investor had neither a monopolistic QV-investment incentive nor a monopolistic or natural-oligopolistic QV-investment disincentive to make the investment in question)—i.e., $PB_{(U)QV}$ equals the conventional operating profits generated by the use of the QV investment in question—and (2) that the QV investor engages in single pricing.

Figure 8.2 illustrates the relevant analysis, though its construction reflects some additional assumptions that are unrealistic and whose significance will be subsequently discussed. To start, in Fig. 8.2, the subscript "*n*" indicates that the curve to whose symbolic representation it is attached provides information that relates to the new product, distributive outlet, capacity, or inventory ("*n*" for "new") created by a relevant QV investment, and the subscript "*o*" indicates that the curve to whose symbolic representation it is attached provides information that relates to each and all of the old "products" ("*o*" for "old") whose output is reduced when a unit of the new product is produced. Figure 8.2 assumes that $DD_n = DD_o$ for each old product, relatedly that $MR_n = MR_o$ for each old product, that $MC_n = MC_o$ for each old product, and that $MLC_n = MLC_o$ for each old product (where the MLC curve indicates the marginal allocative cost that would be generated by the production of successive units of *n* and each old product *o* whose output is reduced by the production of *n* if the assumptions of step-wise-monopoly-distortion analysis were accurate). Figure 8.2's assumptions that $DD_n > MLV_n$ and that $DD_o > MLV_o$ also reflect the fact that the diagram is being used to illustrate a step-wise-monopoly-distortion analysis, which makes assumptions that imply that the respective DD and MLV curves will coincide. Figure 8.2 does not distinguish the various old products whose unit output is reduced when the created QV investment is used—i.e., Figure 8.2 assumes that each of the DD, MR, MC, and MLC curves for each of these old products is the same. Figure 8.2 also assumes that the DD, MR, MC, and MLC curve for each old product is the same as its counterpart for the new product. Figure 8.2 assumes as well that the relevant DD = MLV curves are linear and, less consequentially, that the MC and MLC curves are horizontal. In addition, Figure 8.2 (more specifically, Fig. 8.2's assumption that the output [OL] at which $MR_n = MR_o$ cuts $MC_n = MC_o$ from above [at point B] equals the output at which $MLC_n = MLC_o$ cuts $DD_n = MLV_n = DD_o = MLV_o$ from above [at point F] —i.e., that the post-QV-investment outputs of *n* and each *o* are economically efficient). Figure 8.2 also assumes that (1) all the resources that are combined with the QV investment in question to make use of it (that are expended as variable costs) are withdrawn from the production of one unit of each of the other old products in the new QV investment's ARDEPPS and (2) the post-QV-investment P/MC ratios of each of the other products in the new QV investment's ARDEPPS equal both each other and the P/MC ratio of the product created by the QV investment in question[10]—i.e., Figure 8.2's construction ignores the possibilities (1) that some of the resources "consumed" as variable costs when the QV investment in question is used may be withdrawn from QV-investment-creating and/or PPR-executing uses, (2) that some of the resources that are withdrawn from UO-producing uses when the created QV investment is used may be withdrawn from the production of extant products that are not located in the newly-created product's ARDEPPS, (3) that the use of the created QV investment may reduce the output of some products in the ARDEPPS by more than one unit and of other products in the ARDEPPS not at all, and (4) that the post-QV-investment P/MC ratios of the in-ARDEPPS products whose outputs are reduced when the created QV investment is used may differ both from each other and from the P/MC ratio of the product created by the QV investment in question.

On the assumptions of Fig. 8.2, (1) $(SW[M])D(PB_{(U)QV})$ = area HFBA − area DFH where area HFBA equals the deflation that imperfections in seller-price-competition generate in the variable cost of producing the OL = AB units of the product created by the QV investment (the positive difference between the total variable allocative costs of producing those units—area HFLO—and the total [private] variable cost of producing those units—area ABLO), and area DFH equals the imperfections-in-seller-price-competition-generated buyer-surplus deflation in the revenue generated by the sale of the new product (the positive difference between the allocative value of those units—are DFLO—and the revenue the QV investor obtained by selling those units at price FL per unit—area HFLO) and (2) the absolute value of the former amount—i.e., the (SW[M]) deflation in variable (operating) costs and related equal inflation in $PB_{(U)QV}$ is twice the absolute value of the latter amount—i.e., the buyer-surplus deflation in the revenue the QV investor obtained by selling *n* and the related equal deflation in $PB_{(U)QV}$.[11]

Of course, if the assumptions on which the construction of Fig. 8.2 is based are relaxed, the preceding conclusions will obtain only fortuitously. Thus, if each of the products whose outputs are reduced by the use of the QV investment have their outputs reduced by more than one unit, the absolute value of the negative imperfections-in-seller-price-competition-generated (SW[M]) distortion in the private cost of using the QV investment will be less than twice the absolute value of the negative imperfections-in-seller-price-competition (SW[M]) distortion in the revenues generated by the use of the QV investment (though the absolute value of the former distortion will still be higher than the absolute value of the latter). If the demand curves for the new and old products in question are identical but convex or concave to the origin, the ratios of the two negative (SW[M]) distortions in question will, respectively, be smaller or greater than 2 if all the other assumptions continue to obtain. If the resources that are combined with the QV investment to produce units of the new product are withdrawn exclusively from the production of *o*s in the new product's ARDEPPS but the demand curves and marginal-cost curves for the new product and the products whose outputs are reduced by the new product's sales are different, the relevant differences could either increase or decrease the distortion ratio just referenced by causing the weighted-average P/MC ratio for the relevant *o*s to be higher or lower than P_n/MC_n. If some of the resources that are combined with the QV investment to produce units of the new product are withdrawn from the production of units of extant products that are not in the new product's ARDEPPS, that reality will increase/decrease the distortion ratio in question if the weighted-average P/MC ratio for the out-of-*n*'s-ARDEPPS products whose sales are reduced when *n* is produced is higher than/lower than P/MC for the new product: If one can assume that the weighted-average P/MC ratio for the "out-of-ARDEPPS" products in question equals the weighted-average P/MC ratio for all products in the economy, the fact that some of the resources that are combined with the QV investment to produce units of the new product are withdrawn from the production of products in a random sample of other ARDEPPSes will increase the relevant distortion ratio if P_n/MC_n exceeds its weighted-average economy-wide counterpart and will decrease the relevant distortion ratio if P_n/MC_n is lower than its weighted-average economy-wide counterpart. If some of the resources used to produce units of the new product once the QV investment that created it is completed are withdrawn from QV-investment-creating uses whose $(SW[M])D(PB_{(U)QV})$ is positive, the distortion ratio previously referenced will be lower (since MLC_n/MC_n will be lower). And if some of the resources employed to use the QV investment are withdrawn from PPR-executing uses, I am not sure how that reality will affect the (SW[M])D ratio in question because, although for reasons that will be discussed next, $(SW[M])D(PB_{(U)PPR})$ is negative, it is not clear whether, across all relevant cases, the percentage (negative) (SW[M])D($PB_{(U)PPR}$) is higher or lower than the percentage negative (SW[M])D($PB_{(U)UO}$). Nevertheless, although I acknowledge that the following conclusion depends on a number of empirical assumptions that will certainly be contested and may even be contestable, I am confident that the step-wise-imperfections-in-seller-price-competition-generated distortion in $PB_{(U)QV}$ will always or virtually always be positive. For reasons that will be articulated below, I am even more confident that the step-wise (imperfections-in-seller-price-competition *plus* imperfections-in-investment-competition) distortion in $PB_{(U)QV}$ is positive. Those reasons are as follows:

(1) in my judgment, QV investors have monopolistic QV-investment-incentives to make the QV investments they make far more often than they have monopolistic or natural-oligopolistic QV-investment disincentives to make them;
(2) monopolistic QV-investment-incentives inflate the private benefits of the QV investments with which they are associated (the fact that an investor's QV investment is less competitive with its other projects than the rival investments it deters would have been increases the investment's profit-yield without changing its ex ante economic inefficiency [because the investor's investment will be more competitive with its rivals' projects than the investment it deters would have been] and the fact that an investor's QV investment will induce its established rivals to make non-retaliatory responses that reduce the investor's other projects' profits less than the non-retaliatory responses the rivals would have made to the deterred investment would have reduced those profits increases the profits the investment yields the investor while reducing the investment's economic efficiency in that the deterred additional competitive responses would probably have increased economic efficiency by lowering prices and hence both poverty and the relevant ARDEPPS' and [more relevantly] the economy in question's equilibrium-QV-investment quantities); and
(3) although the imperfections in PPR competition that production-process researchers face will tend to inflate $PB_{(U)PPR}$ because production-process researchers will tend to have monopolistic PPR incentives to execute PPR projects more often than they have monopolistic or natural-oligopolistic PPR disincentives to execute them and those monopolistic investment-incentives are private-benefit-inflating, the associated reduction in the deflation in the variable cost of using QV investments is almost certainly smaller than the inflation in the benefits of (creating and) using QV investments associated with the QV investor's having a monopolistic QV-investment-incentive to make it.

I turn now to the just-mentioned step-wise imperfections-in-seller-price-competition-generated (SW[M]) distortion in the net private benefits yielded by the use of investments in PPR—in particular, to my reasons for believing that this distortion is negative. Figure 8.3 illustrates the argument for this conclusion that would apply when the use of the relevant discovery would reduce the marginal-cost curve for producing the good to whose production process the discovery relates even if the production-process researcher that executed the PPR project in question used the resulting discovery exclusively itself[12]—more specifically, my reasons for believing that, all tolled, the relevant imperfections in seller price-competition generate a negative (SW[M]) distortion (1) in the private-cost savings that a cost-reducing production-process discovery will enable its user to secure when producing the output of the good *G* to whose production process the relevant discovery relates that would have been produced had the discovered production process not been used, (2) in the profits that a marginal-cost-reducing production-process discovery would enable its user to realize by expanding its unit output of *G*, and hence (3) in $PB_{(U)PPR}$.

Figure 8.3 contains six curves. The first is a $DD_G = MLV_G$ curve for the good *G* to whose production process the relevant PPR project relates. For reasons I indicated previously when discussing Fig. 8.2's assumption that its DD curves coincide with its MLV curves, the labeling of the MLV_G curve is actually misleading: The MLV_G curve that Figure 8.3 contains is actually the MLV_G curve that would be operative if the unrealistic step-wise-monopoly-analysis practice of

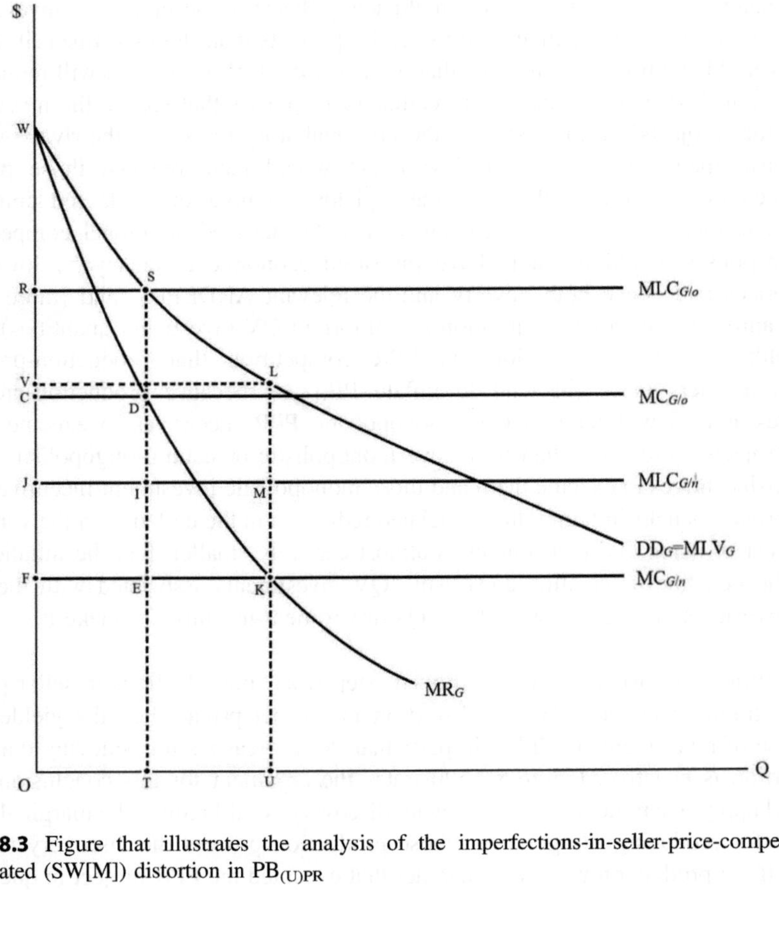

Fig. 8.3 Figure that illustrates the analysis of the imperfections-in-seller-price-competition-generated (SW[M]) distortion in $PB_{(U)PR}$

ignoring the distorting effects of all exemplars of all types of Pareto imperfections other than imperfections in seller price-competition made no difference. The fact that $DD_G = MLV_G$ is constructed to be convex to the origin plays no critical role in the analysis that follows.

The second curve in Fig. 8.3 is MR_G. Like its counterparts in Figs. 8.1 and 8.2, MR_G in Fig. 8.3 is a conventional MR curve that is constructed on the assumption that G is sold at a single per-unit price that applies to all units of the product and all potential buyers of the product and that the sale of units of G does not increase the seller's profits in any way other than by yielding it revenue on the sale of G. The single-pricing assumption does affect the quantitative conclusion the following analysis reaches because it guarantees that the use of any marginal-cost-reducing production process a relevant PPR project discovers will tend to yield a negative (SW[M]) distortion in $PB_{(U)PPR}$ by increasing the amount of buyer surplus generated by the sale of G.

The third and fourth curves in Fig. 8.3 are the $MC_{G/o}$ and $MC_{G/n}$ curves. These curves indicate the marginal cost of producing successive units of G using, respectively, (1) the new (hence subscript "*n*") production process the PPR project in question (did discover)/(would have discovered) and (2) the old (hence subscript "*o*") production process that (presumably) was/(would be) replaced by the new production process that the PPR project in question (did discover)/(would have discovered). $MC_{G/n}$ is lower than $MC_{G/o}$ in Fig. 8.3 (FO < CO) because the analysis that Fig. 8.3 illustrates assumes (as I believe is typically the case) that the use of the new production process will reduce the marginal cost of producing G.[13]

The fifth and sixth curves in Fig. 8.3—$MLC_{G/n}$ and $MLC_{G/o}$—indicate the marginal allocative cost of producing successive units of G using, respectively, the new production process that the PPR project in question (did discover)/(would have discovered) and the old production process that the new production process (did replace)/(would have replaced)—more precisely, the $MLC_{G/n}$ and $MLC_{G/u}$ curves that would be operative if the step-wise imperfections-in-seller-price-competition distortion-analysis protocol of ignoring the distorting effects of all exemplars of all types of Pareto imperfections other than imperfections in seller price-competition would not affect the relationship between $MLC_{G/n}$ and $MLC_{G/o}$. Figure 8.3 constructs its $MLC_{G/n}$ curve below its $MLC_{G/u}$ curve on the assumption that the relevant imperfections in seller price-competition would generate negative (SW[M]) distortions in both the private marginal cost of producing each unit of the output of G that would be produced if the old production process was used (output OT—the output at which $MR_{G/o}$ cuts $MC_{G/o}$ from above at point D) and the extra units of G that the use of the new production process would make it profitable for the producer of G to produce (TU where OU is the output at which MR_G cuts $MC_{G/n}$ from above at point K). In Fig. 8.3, the height of the $MLC_{G/o}$ curve (RO) exceeds the height of the $MC_{G/o}$ curve (CO) by the same percentage as the percentage by which the height of the $MLC_{G/n}$ (JO) curve exceeds the height of the $MC_{G/n}$ curve (FO). This construction manifests an assumption that the relevant imperfections in seller price-competition will yield the same negative (SW[M]) percentage-distortion in MC both when the old production process is used and when the new production process is used—i.e., that $(MLC_{G/o}/MC_{G/o}) = (MLC_{G/n}/MC_{G/n}) > 1$.

Figure 8.3 illustrates the fact that on the assumptions on which it is constructed and on the further assumption that the researcher that executed the relevant PPR project will/would use any discovery it will/would yield exclusively itself, the use of the discovered process will (1) increase the profits the production-process researcher would realize if it produced the output of *G* it would produce if it used the old production process (output OT) by area CDEF, (2) increase allocative efficiency by reducing the allocative cost of producing output OT by area RSIJ where area RSIJ *exceeds* area CDEF, (3) increase the profits that the production-process researcher can earn by expanding its unit output from OT to OU by area DKE (the area between MR_G and $MC_{G/n}$ between outputs OT and OU), and (4) increase allocative efficiency by inducing the production-process researcher to increase its output of *G* from OT to OU by area SLUT (the allocative value of the extra units of output) *minus* area IMUT (the allocative cost of producing the extra TU units of *G* with the new production process), which equals area SLMI and is larger than area DKE (the area that equals the profits that the discovery will enable the production-process researcher to realize by expanding its unit output of *G* from OT to OU).

I will now explain why I have constructed Fig. 8.3 to assume (1) that $MLC_{G/n}$ exceeds $MC_{G/n}$ and that $MLC_{G/o}$ exceeds $MC_{G/o}$, (2) that $(MLC_{G/n}/MC_{G/n}) = (MLC_{G/o}/MC_{G/o})$, (3) that therefore the allocative-cost savings that the use of the discovered process would generate when employed to produce the output of *G* that the producer of *G* would have produced if required to use the old production process (area RSIJ in Fig. 8.3) *exceeds* the private-cost savings that the use of the discovered process would have enabled the producer of *G* to obtain had it produced the output of *G* it would have produced if required to use the old production process (area CDEF in Fig. 8.3) equals (area CDEF) *times* the ratio of $(MLC_n/MC_n) = (MLC_o/MC_o) > 1$, and (4) that the profits that a marginal-cost-reducing discovery will enable its user to realize by expanding from OT to OU its output of *G* (area DKE in Fig. 8.3) will be lower than the allocative-efficiency gains that output-expansion will be deemed to generate if one assumes $MLV_G = DD_G$ (area SLMI in Fig. 8.3) if one makes the neutral assumption that the producer of *G* produced the quantity of *G* that would be economically efficient for it to produce on the (SW[M])-distortion-analysis assumptions when using the old production process (the output OT = RS at which MLV_G cut $MLC_{G/o}$ from above).

To start, I believe that $MLC_{G/n}$ exceeds $MC_{G/n}$ and that $MC_{G/o}$ because (1) the vast majority of the resources used to produce *G* both with the new production process and with the old production process is withdrawn from alternative UO-producing uses, a far smaller percentage of the resources used to produce *G* both with either the new or the old production process is withdrawn from QV-investment-creating uses, and an even smaller (indeed, a significantly-smaller) percentage of the resources used to produce *G* with either the new or the old production process is withdrawn from PPR execution, (2) the (SW[M]) distortion in the private benefits that the sacrificed UO production would have conferred on the sacrificing UO producers and hence in the PC of the withdrawn resources in question to the producer of *G* is negative, the (SW[M]) distortion in the private benefits that the sacrificed QV-investment creation(s) would have conferred on the sacrificing QV investor(s) and hence in the PC of the withdrawn measurers in question to the producer of *G* is positive, and the (SW[M]) distortion in the private benefits that the sacrificed PPR would have conferred on the sacrificing production-process researcher(s) and hence in the PC of the withdrawn resources in question to the producer of *G* is negative, and (3) although I am confident that the percentage-(SW[M]) inflation of the cost to the producer of *G* of the resources that the production of *G* withdraws from PPR execution is far higher than the absolute values of the percentage-(SW[M]) deflations in the cost to the producers of *G* of the resources it withdraws, respectively, from UO production and QV-investment creation to produce *G*, I am reasonably sure that the sum of the percentages of the resources used to produce *G* that are withdrawn from UO production and PPR execution is sufficiently higher than the percentage of these resources withdrawn form QV-investment creation to more than offset the fact that the percentage-inflation in $PB_{(U)QV}$ is several times the absolute value of the weighted-average percentage-deflation in $PB_{(U)UO}$ and $PB_{(U)PPR}$. (This last belief reflects [1] my guesstimates of the percentages of the economy's resources that are devoted, respectively, to UO-producing, QV-investment-creating, and PPR-executing uses and [2] my belief that the percentage of the resources used to produce *G* that is withdrawn from QV-investment creation is likely to be lower than the percentage of the economy's resources devoted to QV-investment creation, though I admit that this difference is reduced by the fact that a small percentage of QV investments are knowledge-creating [that only a small percentage of the resources devoted to creating QV investments of all kinds are specialized, scientifically-and-technologically knowledgeable/skilled resources that are unlikely to be devoted to UO production (though they might be devoted to PPR execution)].)

Second, my belief that $(MLC_{G/n}/MC_{G/n}) = (MLC_{G/o}/MC_{G/o})$ reflects the absence of any reason to believe that the shift to the new production process will tend to change either the percentages of the resources used to produce *G* that are withdrawn, respectively, from UO-producing, QV-creating, and PPR-executing resource-uses or the sign or percentage-distortions in the private benefits that the sacrificed resource-uses would have conferred on the three categories of sacrificing resource-users.

Third, the fact that the amount by which the switch to the new production process would reduce the allocative cost of producing the output of *G* its producer would have produced if required to use the old production process exceeds the amount by which the switch would reduce the private cost to *G*'s producer of producing that output follows from the points made in the preceding two paragraphs: If (1) the producer of *G* can produce the output in question with 30 units of input using the new production process when it would have had to use 40 units of input to produce that output with the old production process and (2) the private cost of each input was $1 when its allocative cost was $1.50, the private-cost saving would be $10, but the allocative-cost saving would be $15.

Fourth and finally, to see why the (SW[M]) distortion in the private benefits a marginal-cost-reducing production-process discovery will confer on the discoverer that uses it by making it profitable for that resource allocator to increase its unit output of the product *G* to whose production process the discovery relates (from OT to OU in Fig. 8.3) is negative, one will have to explain either (1) why the positive (SW[M])-distortion in those profits that relevant imperfections in seller price-competition generate by causing $MC_{G/n}$ to be lower than $MLC_{G/n}$ over the relevant output-range (area IMKE) is lower than the negative (SW[M])-distortion in those profits that the imperfection in price-competition faced by the seller of *G* when selling that product yields by increasing the buyer surplus that seller's sales of *G* generates (area RSLV in Fig. 8.3) or (2) (more promisingly) why area DKE (the profits yielded by the relevant increase in output—the area between MR_G and $MC_{G/n}$ between outputs OT and OU) is lower than area SLMI (the increase in economic efficiency generated by the production and consumption of the extra TU units of *G*—the area between $DD_G = MLV_G$ and $MLC_{G/n}$ between outputs OT and OU). In brief, to see why area DKE is lower than area SLMI, note that (1) DE (the shift-to-the-new-production-process-generated reduction in the height of the MC_G curve) is lower than SI (the associated reduction in the height of the MLC_G curve) (inter alia because marginal cost is lower than marginal allocative cost) and (2) the absolute average slope of the MR_G curve between outputs OT and OU is higher than the absolute average slope of the $DD_G = MLV_G$ curve between outputs OT and OU. I have now explained why on what I take to be the plausible or neutral assumptions of Fig. 8.3 imperfections in seller price-competition will generate negative (SW[M]) distortions in both components of $PB_{(U)PPR}$ and hence in $PB_{(U)PPR}$.

The next issue I need to address is the step-wise-monopoly distortion in the private cost of creating a QV investment with resources withdrawn from UO production and PPR execution. I have already explained why the (SW[M]) distortions in $PB_{(U)UO}$ and $PB_{(U)PPR}$ are negative. Since the private cost to any resource-user of the resources it withdraws from a UO-producing use or a PPR-executing use equals (infinitesimally exceeds) the private benefits the resources in question would have conferred on their alternative users while the allocative cost of any resource-user's withdrawing resources from any UO-producing or PPR-executing resource-use equals the allocative benefits they would have generated in those sacrificed uses, the conclusion that the relevant imperfections in seller price-competition would deflate $PB_{(U)UO}$ and $PB_{(U)PPR}$ implies that these imperfections will deflate the private cost of creating a QV investment with resources withdrawn from UO-producing and PPR-executing uses.

I have now explained why I believe that the step-wise-imperfections-in-seller-price-competition distortion in the private benefits that the use of a QV investment confers on the QV investor is positive and that the step-wise-imperfections-in-seller-price-competition distortion in the private cost of creating a QV investment with resources withdrawn from UO production and PPR execution is negative. Obviously, if these two conclusions are correct, the step-wise-imperfections-in-seller-price-competition distortion in the profits yielded by resource allocations that

(1) withdraw resources from UO-producing and PPR-executing uses and devote them to QV-investment-creating uses and (2) withdraw resources primarily from UO-producing uses and to far-lesser extents from QV-investment-creating and PPR-executing uses and devote them to using the created QV investments will be positive. Obviously, ceteris paribus, this conclusion provides support for my belief that, from the perspective of allocative efficiency, economies devote too many resources to QV-investment creation relative to the amounts they devote to UO production and PPR execution.

Admittedly, however, Second-Best Theory reveals the problematic character of assuming that all relevant ceteris are paribus. My argument for the conclusion that too many resources are devoted to QV-investment creation from the perspective of economic efficiency would be undermined if, for example, resource-users tended to underestimate the profitability of QV investments, tended to overestimate the profitability of UO production or PPR execution, and/or tended to make mathematical errors that led them to reject QV-investment projects whose profitability was established by the information they possessed and/or that led them to make decisions to produce units of extant products or execute PPR projects whose unprofitability was established by the information they possessed. My argument for the conclusion that economies devote an economically-inefficiently-large amount of resources to QV-investment creation relative to the amounts of resources they devote to UO production and PPR execution would also be undermined by evidence that suggests that the other-Pareto-imperfection-oriented components of the (SW) distortion formula for the aggregate distortion in the profits yielded by resource allocations from UO production and PPR execution to QV-investment creation are negative.

I have already (partially) addressed and dismissed one such possibility—viz., that imperfections in QV-investment competition and PPR competition might generate negative step-wise distortions in the profits yielded by the relevant category of resource allocations.[14] I will now discuss briefly (to a less-than-third-best-allocatively-efficient extent if one could focus on long-run consequences) other possibilities.

The first additional (SW[…])D I will discuss is connected to the reality that some QV investors do not use their QV investments (i.e., the scientifically-innovative product their respective QV investments discovered or the branded non-scientifically-innovative product or distributive service their respective QV investments created) exclusively themselves and that some production-process researchers do not use the production process their respective PPR projects discovered exclusively themselves. Thus, some QV investors license others to produce and sell the product they discovered (say, in certain geographic areas or to certain classes of customers defined non-geographically), sell the patents their QV investments yielded, or franchise others to operate distributive outlets in the branded chain their QV investment created, and some production-process researchers license others to use their discovered production process or sell their related IP rights to others. To the extent that the purchasers of any

QV-investment-related license, patents, or franchises secure buyer surplus on their purchases (either because they have buyer [monopsony] power in the relevant context or because the cost to the investor of identifying the highest price that individual buyers would be willing to pay for a relevant license, patent, or franchise makes it profitable for the investor to make choices that allow such customers to obtain buyer surplus on their purchases), the resulting negative step-wise (buyer-surplus/monopsony) distortion in the private benefits of using the created QV investment will counteract the step-wise-monopoly component of the aggregate distortion in the profits yielded by resource allocations from UO-producing and PPR-executing resource-uses to QV-investment creating-and-using resource-uses. And to the extent that the prospective purchasers of any license and patents that would have been generated by any PPR project that would be sacrificed to the creation and use of a QV investment would have obtained buyer surplus on such purchases, such prospective buyer surplus would further deflate the private benefits of using the sacrificed PPR, would on that account further deflate the private cost to the QV investor of the resources it withdrew from PPR to create and use its QV investment, and would therefore compound the positive (SW[M]) distortion in the profits yielded by the resource allocations in question.

The next effect of these possibilities will clearly vary from resource allocation to resource allocation within this category of (UO-producing and PPR-executing) to QV-creating resource allocations. I have four observations or guesses that bear on this matter. First, in my judgment, the vast majority of QV investments do not create either patentable knowledge or a valuable, distinctive product or distributive brand—i.e., do not create anything that can be licensed, sold, or franchised. Second, I suspect that most if not the vast majority of product-discoveries are made by firms that produce the discovered product exclusively themselves. Third, I suspect that the vast majority of the franchisees of the branded distributive chains that some QV investments create do not obtain significant amounts of buyer surplus on their franchise-purchases (because there typically are a large number of equally-well-placed prospective purchasers of the relevant individual franchises). Fourth, I suspect that (1) a quite high percentage of production-process discoverers do not use the discovered process exclusively themselves either because the discovery is made by an independent research-firm that does not produce the product to whose production process the discovery relates and does not find it profitable to integrate forward into product-production or because the discoverer is a producer of the product to whose production process the discovery relates but produces far from all of the output of that product and (2) many of the potential buyers of the right to use a discovered production process have buyer power in the relevant negotiations (have no equally-well-placed established or potential purchasing-rivals in the subarea of product-space in which they are operating). If these admittedly-highly-contestable guesses are correct, this additional buyer-surplus possibility will not significantly undermine my conclusion that, from the perspective of economic efficiency, too many resources are devoted to QV-investment creation relative to the amounts allocated to UO production and PPR execution.

The next three additional (SW[…])Ds I will consider are all subcategories of step-wise externality-distortions—(SW[X])Ds. I should indicate at the outset that the tax-law and public-subsidy-law assumptions that the following treatment of externalities implicitly adopts might be deemed inconsistent with the claim that these analyses are step-wise-externality-distortion analyses. However, in my defense, I will assert that my assessments of the incidences and magnitudes of the relevant "non-internalized externalities" (admittedly an expression that contains a redundancy) reflect what I take to be realistic assumptions about the extent to which the relevant societies' "potential externalities" are internalized or prevented by its tort law, environmental law, zoning law, tax law, and public-subsidy laws.

The second additional (SW[…])D that needs to be discussed is the step-wise externality-distortion that is generated by the conventional external costs that are generated, respectively, by UO production, QV-investment creation, and PPR execution—i.e., is the (SW[PX])D where "PX" stands for "production externalities." To start: in my judgment, there is no reason to believe that, across all relevant resource-uses, the following four ratios are equal: (1) the ratio of (the external variable allocative cost of just-extra-marginal UO production) to (the [internal] variable cost of such UO production), (2) the ratio of (the total external allocative cost of QV-investment creation) to (the total private cost of QV-investment creation), and (3) the ratio of (the total external allocative cost of just-extra-marginal PPR projects) to (the total private cost of such PPR projects) where the external allocative costs of QV-investment creation primarily consist of the non-internalized air-pollution, water-pollution, noise-pollution, and road-congestion costs generated when pilot plants, final production-plants, distributive outlets, capacity, inventory, and research facilities are constructed/produced, and the external allocative costs of PPR execution primarily consist of the uninternalized air-pollution, water-pollution, noise-pollution, and road-congestion costs generated when research facilities, pilot plants to try out the discovered process, and final production facilities that use the discovered production process are constructed. Over the long run, it would almost certainly be TBLE to devote a substantial amount of resources to estimating the three ratios just referenced. My current guess would be that the relevant ratio is (1) highest for UO production and QV investments that create inventory, (2) second-highest for QV investments that create non-artistic products, distributive outlets, and capacity, (3) considerably lower for PPR projects (because most do not require pilot plants to be constructed or existing production-plants to be replaced), and (4) lowest for artistic QV investments. The combination of these guesses and my additional belief that resource allocations from UO production and PPR execution to QV-investment creation withdraw far more resources from UO production than from PPR execution (because the percentage of the economy's resources that are devoted to UO production is far higher than the percentage devoted to PPR execution and because most QV investments do not make use of the significantly-technologically-knowledgeable human resources that would be more likely to be withdrawn from PPR) imply that the production-externality step-wise distortion in the profits yielded by the allocations of resources on which I am now focusing is negative (that the number of dollars by which the non-internalization of the external costs that would have been generated by the UO-producing uses and PPR-executing uses sacrificed to the creation and use of QV investments would have inflated the benefits that these sacrificed resource-uses would have conferred on the sacrificing resource-users and concomitantly inflates the private cost of these resources to the relevant QV investors and hence deflates by the same amount the profits the QV investors realize by creating and using the relevant QV investments *exceeds* the number of dollars by which the non-internalization of the external costs that were generated by the creation and use of the relevant created QV investments inflates the profits yielded by the creation and use of those QV investments [by deflating the private cost of both creating and using those QV investments])—that the "production"-externality step-wise-distortion component of the step-wise-distortion formula for the aggregate distortion in the profits yielded by exemplars of the categories of resource allocations on which the current analysis is focusing counteracts the (SW[M])-distortion component of that formula.[15]

The third additional (SW[…])D that merits consideration is the step-wise externality-distortion that is generated by what might broadly be classified as consumption externalities—(SW[CX])D where "CX" stands for "consumption externality." I will focus here on (1) the external costs that the consumption of a QV-investment-created new product imposes on buyers who place a positive value on owning and/or being seen to own "the latest thing," (2) the external costs that the use of a literary, visual, or musical "product" to produce a derivative work generates by rendering the original work trite or altering its meaning in a way that reduces its dollar value to its potential and actual consumers, and (3) the external costs and benefits that are generated by the use of a QV-investment-created distributive outlet. Obviously, the non-internalization of any external costs that the consumption (perhaps even the creation—i.e., the existence) of a new product imposes on owners of old products that value owning "the latest thing" and on owners of unsold old products whose potential buyers value owning "the latest thing" creates a positive step-wise externality-distortion in the profits yielded by the creation and use of a QV investment created with resources withdrawn from UO-producing and PPR-executing uses. Equally obviously, any non-internalized external costs that any (QV-investment-created) derivative literary, visual, or musical work of art generates by reducing the allocative value of the original work from which it derives is also associated with a positive step-wise distortion in the private benefits and profits yielded by the QV investment in question and the resource allocations that its creation entailed.

The analysis of the step-wise externality-distortion that is associated with the use of a QV-investment-created distributive outlet is more complicated because the use of such distributive outlets can generate both external benefits and external costs and it is not clear whether all things considered the use of the additional distributive outlet created by a QV investment generates net external costs or net external benefits. Thus, the use of an additional distributive outlet will

(1) generate external benefits by eliminating the external costs its customers would have generated when making shopping-visits to other stores that their visit to the new outlet cause them to abandon or shorten,
(2) will generate non-internalized external benefits to the extent that (in crude terms) it reduces the miles its customers travel to do their shopping and hence the non-internalized air-pollution, noise-pollution, accident, and road-congestion external costs they generate when traveling to shop (because the new outlet is closer to them than are the outlets they would otherwise have patronized and the greater convenience of driving to the more-proximate outlet does not lead them to increase the number of shopping trips they make sufficiently to increase the total number of miles they drive to shop), and
(3) will generate non-internalized external costs if, by decreasing the distance its customers must drive to do a single shop, it increases the number of shopping trips they choose to make sufficiently to increase the miles they drive to shop.

I should admit that the preceding "analysis" ignores the possibilities that the creation of an additional distributive outlet may also affect the amount of shopping-trip-travel externalities that are generated by changing the residential-location decisions of relevant shoppers and the business-location decisions of these shoppers' potential employers and so on and so forth. My own clearly-contestable conclusion is that, all tolled, the use of QV-investment-created distributive outlets generates net external benefits—that this step-wise externality-distortion reduces the positive magnitude of the aggregate distortion in the profits yielded by resource allocations to relevant QV-investment-creating uses from UO-producing and PPR-executing uses (even if one takes account of the possibility that some of the resources employed to use a created distributive outlet might be withdrawn from the creation of another distributive outlet).

The fourth and last additional (SW[…])D that I will address is the step-wise knowledge-creation-related (KCR) externality-distortion, which can be a subcomponent of the step-wise aggregate-profit-distortion formula for the small minority of QV investments that yield allocatively-valuable knowledge (usually scientific or technological knowledge but occasionally commercial knowledge [say, of the kind generated by the first person to recognize the complementarity of laundromat-services and bar-services—of establishing suds and suds "stores"]) and by all PPR (since all successful PPR generates scientific or technological knowledge). If (1) such discoverers cannot keep their discoveries secret (by contractually obligating their employees not to reveal any discovered information to anyone who has not paid the discoverer for it and enforcing those contractual obligations, by preventing potentially-revealing communications from being discovered by outsiders and (perhaps) by constructing production facilities with attributes that cause outsiders to misapprehend attributes of a discovered production process [strategies that are more likely to preserve the secrecy of production-process discoveries than of product-discoveries]), (2) the government does not prevent non-discoverers from using discoveries (for the appropriate period of time after the discovery was made—see below) without paying the discoverer for the right to do so by giving discoverers an effective IP right and/or prosecuting IP-right violators, and (3) the State does not pay actual discoverers monetary awards equal to the allocative value of their discoveries or prospective researchers monetary awards equal to the expected allocative value of their proposed research while permitting non-discoverers to use the discoveries, the non-internalized KCR external benefits that are generated by knowledge-creating QV investments will yield a negative (SW[(KCR)X])D in the profits yielded by any resource allocation to the creation of such QV investments, and the non-internalized KCR external benefits that would have been generated by the unpaid-for use of the production-process discoveries that were sacrificed to the creation (and possibly the use) of any QV investment (be it knowledge-creating or not) will, by deflating the prospective private benefits of using the sacrificed production-process decisions, inflate the private profits of the resource allocations on which I am now focusing by deflating the private cost both of creating them and of using them. These results imply that, if the three conditions previously specified are fulfilled, (writing broadly) the step-wise KCR-externality-distortion component of the step-wise formula for the aggregate distortion in the profits yielded by allocations of resources from UO-producing and PPR-executing uses to QV-investment-creating uses will tend to be positive for QV investments that do not create knowledge and negative for QV investments that do create knowledge.

Unfortunately, the "appropriate period of time" parenthetical in my statement of the second relevant condition points to an issue that is difficult to resolve. The easiest-to-comprehend way to do so is to assume that (1) there are no relevant risks and no relevant risk costs, (2) more than one researcher may be attempting to make the discovery in question, (3) each researcher's efforts advance the date on which the relevant discovery will be made,[16] and (4) the number of research-projects that will be economically efficient to have executed is the number associated with a last research-project whose allocative cost is lower than the allocative benefits it should be expected to yield ex ante by advancing the date of the discovery in question. Even on the assumption that no exemplar of any other type of Pareto imperfection is present, the calculation of the length (and breadth) of the IP protection that would be ex ante economically efficient is quite complicated.[17] For current purposes, the relevant points are that (1) all relevant societies' IP laws as applied could either "over-internalize" or "under-internalize" what would be the external benefits of R&D in their absence and (2) it is difficult to determine the length and breadth of such protection that would be just right from the perspective of internalization (even if one ignores the tendency of IP protection to generate economic inefficiency by deterring economically-efficient uses of discoveries). For what it is worth, although I fully acknowledge that I lack both the scientific knowledge and the legal-practice knowledge (about the conditions under which IP protection is granted and the breadth of the IP protection that is granted) that one should possess to even guess about these matters, I am inclined to think that, from the perspective of economic efficiency, if the distorting influence of all other types of Pareto imperfections was ignored, (1) from the perspective of economic efficiency, in an otherwise-Pareto-perfect world, current IP law as applied would provide too much protection to both product-discoveries and production-process discoveries, (2) the positive (SW[KCR(X)])D component of the step-wise-distortion formula for the aggregate distortion in the profits yielded by resource allocations from UO-producing and PPR-executing resource-uses to knowledge-creating QV-investment-creating resource-uses compounds the positive (SW[M])D component of that formula, and (3) the positive (SW[KCR(X)])D component of the step-wise-distortion for the aggregate distortion in the profits yielded by resource allocations from UO-producing and QV-investment-creating resource-uses to PPR-executing resource-uses offsets but does not fully offset the negative (SW[M])D component of that formula.

Section 8.4 executes a large number of theoretical analyses[18] but also contains a large number of empirical conjectures. My conclusions that (1) the profits yielded by resource allocations from UO-producing and PPR-executing uses to QV-investment-creating uses tend to be significantly inflated and (2) from the perspective of economic efficiency economies currently devote too many resources to QV-investment creation and not enough to UO production and PPR execution are derived from the combination of these theoretical analyses and empirical guesses. Although some of the conclusions Part II reaches about the economic efficiency of categories or subcategories of antitrust-policy-coverable business conduct and the economic efficiency of various possible antitrust policies and some of the conclusions that Part III reaches about the relative economic efficiency of U. S. antitrust law and E.U. competition law correctly interpreted and applied as matters of law depend on the above resource-allocation-economic-efficiency conclusions, the third-best allocative efficiency and moral desirability of my approach to antitrust-policy analysis does not do so.

8.5 The Distortion-Analysis Protocol for Economic-Efficiency Prediction That I Believe Is TBLE

This subsection explains in very broad terms the protocol that would be TBLE for an economic-efficiency analyst to use to determine the ex ante economic efficiency of doing any work that would bear on the economic efficiency of the choice under review. The protocol for economic-efficiency analysis that I am recommending (that I claim is TBLE) instructs the analyst (1) to estimate and sum the estimates of all the allocative costs of any work he or she could do—the allocative benefits that the resources that any such work would use up would have generated in their alternative uses *plus* the allocative transaction costs the government would generate to finance the work *plus* any economic inefficiency that the public financing of the work would generate (related allocative transaction costs aside) *plus* any economic inefficiency the work would generate by delaying the government decision on the choice under review, (2) to estimate and sum the allocative benefits any such work would generate—any increase in economic efficiency the work would generate by altering the government's decision on the choice under review *plus* any increase in economic efficiency the work would generate by yielding information and/or information-relevance insights that increase the economic efficiency of other government and non-government decisions, and (3) to compare the two sums just referenced and do work if and only if the sum of the predicted allocative benefits exceeds the sum of the predicted allocative costs. Before proceeding, an admission that relates to this pervasive feature of the protocol for economic-efficiency analysis that I claim is TBLE. As decision-theorists have long recognized, the instruction I have just delineated creates an infinite-regress problem that cannot really be overcome: An analyst who has been instructed to do that work and only that work he or she concludes is ex ante economically efficient must ask not only whether it would be ex ante economically efficient to do some specified work but also whether it would be ex ante economically efficient to think about whether it would be ex ante economically efficient to do that work and whether it would be ex ante economically efficient to think about whether it would be ex ante economically efficient to think about whether it would be ex ante economically efficient to do that work and so on and so forth. My somewhat-lame response is an *assertion* that at some point the analyst will intuit that it is not ex ante economically efficient to dive deeper into this rabbit-hole and that differences in the relevant intuitions of different analysts are unlikely to make a significant difference in their research-choice/information-consideration decisions or a fortiori in their economic-efficiency conclusions.

The approach to economic-efficiency analysis I claim is TBLE instructs economic-efficiency analysts to predict/post-dict the impact of any choice on the amounts of economic inefficiency generated in the whole economy by following a protocol that has six major components in addition to the general instruction to do that work but only that work whose performance is ex ante economically efficient.

The first major component of the protocol for economic-efficiency analysis I claim is TBLE focuses on the impact of the choice under review on 7 of the 16 categories of economic inefficiency an economy can generate—in particular, on those categories of economic efficiency that are associated with categories (1)-(6) and (10) in Subsection 8.2.2's list of categories of resource allocations and economic inefficiency. This major component of the protocol instructs the economic-efficiency analyst to analyze the impact of the choice under review on any of the seven categories of economic inefficiency in question by taking the following seven steps:

(1) define a random subset of the economy's ARDEPPSes that is third-best-allocatively-efficient large—i.e., whose definition and use in this protocol would be TBLE;
(2) identify the private cost and more specific characteristics of each of the exemplars of the resource allocations in the functional categories on which this component of the protocol is focusing to or in each of the ARDEPPSes defined in Step (1) that the choice under review would/did deter/induce;
(3) estimate the profits that were/would be generated by each of the resource allocations in the fully-specified categories on which this component of the

protocol is focusing that Step (2) concludes the choice did/would induce and the losses that would have been/would be generated by each of the fully-specified resource allocations on which this component of the protocol is focusing that Step (2) concludes the choice did/would deter;

(4) estimate the aggregate distortion in the profits/losses that the analyst estimated was/would be yielded by each resource allocation in the category on which this component is focusing to each ARDEPPS being studied that the analyst predicted the choice under review did/would induce/deter by combining the different correct formulas for the aggregate distortion in the profits yielded by any exemplar of each of the relevant functional categories of resource allocations with estimates of the post-choice magnitudes of the parameters in the formulas in question (estimates that are themselves generated from information that the analyst possesses ab initio and information that the analyst obtains by doing TBLE research into the post-choice magnitudes of the parameters in question [when the choice under review has already been made, the relevant research will be empirical research on the post-choice magnitudes of the parameters; when the choice under review has not yet been made, the relevant research may include additional empirical research on the pre-choice magnitudes of the parameters in question, theoretical research to identify the determinants of the impact of the choice on the relevant parameters and the way in which those factors interact to change the parameters in question, and empirical research on the magnitudes of those factors]);

(5) for each functional category of resource allocation to or in each ARDEPPS that is being studied, combine the conclusions generated in Steps (2)-(4) to yield estimates of the impacts that the choice under review would have on the quantity of the associated functional category of economic inefficiency each studied ARDEPPS contains (note that the definition that equates "the aggregate distortion in the profits yielded by a specified resource allocation" with the difference between the profits yielded by and the economic efficiency of that resource allocation implies that the allocative efficiency of any resource allocation equals the profits it yielded *minus* the aggregate distortion in those profits);

(6) sum the conclusions reached in Step (5) for each studied ARDEPPS to yield an estimate of the impact that the choice under review did/would have on the total amount of each of the categories of economy inefficiency on which this portion of the protocol is focusing that was/would be generated *in all the studied ARDEPPSes combined* by decisions to execute economically-inefficient resource allocations in the relevant functional category to or in them and decisions not to execute economically-efficient resource allocations in the relevant functional category to or in them; and

(7) estimate the impact of the choice under consideration on the amounts of economic inefficiency generated in the whole economy by decisions to execute economically-inefficient resource allocations and decisions not to execute economically-efficient resource allocations in each referenced category of resource allocations by multiplying (the Stage (6) estimates of the impacts of

the choice under review on the total amount of resource misallocation in each such functional category in all studied ARDEPPSes) by (the respective ratios of [the private cost of the resource allocations in that category the choice did/would induce/deter in the economy as a whole] to [the private cost of the resource allocations in that category the choice did/would induce/deter in the studied ARDEPPSes]).

Before commenting on this component of the protocol for economic-efficiency prediction that I believe is TBLE, I want to illustrate it diagrammatically. Figure 8.4 serves this purpose.

The vertical axis of Fig. 8.4 measures dollars, and the horizontal axis measures in dollars the total allocative cost (TLC) of the resources devoted to the specified resource allocation (RA). The relevant "resource allocation" is specified in the subscript of the $RATLC_{.../...}$ symbol that appears just below the end of the horizontal axis. The entry that replaces the ellipsis that appears before the forward-slash in the subscript specifies the related pair of resource-uses (producing and consuming a unit of output, creating and using a QV investment, executing a PPR project and using the discovery it yields) and the ARDEPPS to which the indicated resource allocation devotes resources. The "entry" (actually series of entries) that replaces the ellipsis that appears after the forward-slash in the subscript specifies the various uses and ARDEPPSes from which the relevant resource allocation withdraws resources. In virtually all exemplars, the sacrificed uses in question will vary

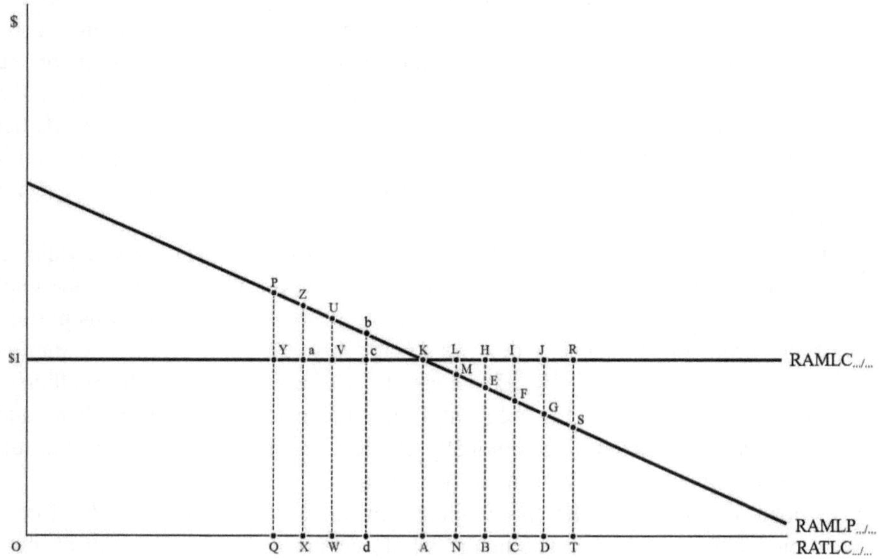

Fig. 8.4 Figure that reveals the basis of an important component of the protocol for economic-efficiency analysis the author believes is TBLE

as successive allocations to a specified pair of uses in a specified ARDEPPS are executed.

Figure 8.4 contains two curves. The first is the "resource allocation marginal allocative product" (RAMLP) curve. Unlike standard "marginal allocative product" curves, which indicate the allocative value generated by the devotion of successive units of a given input to a particular purpose, the RAMLP$_{\ldots/\ldots}$ curve indicates the marginal allocative value generated by the devotion to a specified related pair of uses in a specified ARDEPPS of the successive batches of inputs (resources) that would be devoted to the specified related pair of resource-uses in the specified ARDEPPS. (Like their counterparts in the RATLC$_{\ldots/\ldots}$ symbol, the entries that will replace the first and second ellipses in the subscript to the RAMLP$_{\ldots/\ldots}$ symbol specify, respectively, the uses and ARDEPPSes to which the relevant resource allocation devotes resources and the uses and ARDEPPSes from which the relevant resource allocation withdraws resources.) In Fig. 8.4, the RAMLP$_{\ldots/\ldots}$ curve is constructed to be downward-sloping. That assumption is realistic both (1) because successive exemplars of any related pair of resource-uses (the consumption of the successive units of a given product, the use of successive QV investments in a given ARDEPPS, and the use of successive production-process discoveries in a given ARDEPPS) will generate progressively-lower allocative value and (2) because the allocative product in their sacrificed uses of the successive batches of resources whose allocative cost is (say) \$1 that the relevant resource allocation withdraws from sacrificed uses rises (both because resources are specialized and because the goods or services that are sacrificed by successive allocations have progressively-higher allocative values). In Fig. 8.4, the RAMLP$_{\ldots/\ldots}$ curve is also constructed to be linear. There is no reason why this should be the case. Unfortunately, this linearity assumption is consequential. If accurate, it would enable an analyst to determine whether a given choice would increase or decrease the amount of economic inefficiency generated by all economically-inefficient choices to execute or not execute resource allocations in a particular category to a particular ARDEPPPS from (accurate) estimates of the choice's impact on the absolute value of the aggregate distortion in the profits yielded by the economics-marginal resource allocation in the relevant category to the ARDEPPS in question even when the choice changes the sign of the operative aggregate profit-distortion.[19]

The second curve that Fig. 8.4 contains is the "resource allocation marginal allocative cost" curve—RAMLC$_{\ldots/\ldots}$. The entries that replace the two ellipses in its subscript are the same as their counterparts for the RATLC$_{\ldots/\ldots}$ and RAMLP$_{\ldots/\ldots}$ symbols. Figure 8.4 is constructed on the arbitrary assumption that RAMLC$_{\ldots/\ldots}$ = \$1.

In Fig. 8.4, the economic efficiency of allocating successive batches of resources whose allocative cost is \$1 to the to-be-specified functional use-category to the to-be-specified ARDEPPS equals the distance between the heights of the RAMLP$_{\ldots/\ldots}$ and RAMLC$_{\ldots/\ldots}$ curves at the RATLC$_{\ldots/\ldots}$ quantity that would be generated by the allocation in question. In Fig. 8.4, successive allocations in the to-be-specified category up to a RATLC$_{\ldots/\ldots}$ quantity of OA would be economically efficient, and further allocations would be economically inefficient.

Thus, a choice that would increase the equilibrium $RATLC_{.../...}$ quantity for the to-be-specified functional category of resource allocation to the to-be-specified ARDEPPS from OX to Od would increase economic efficiency by area Zbca by reducing by area Zbca the amount of economic inefficiency generated by economically-inefficient decisions not to execute the resource allocations that would raise the $RATLC_{.../...}$ figure for the to-be-specified category of resource allocation from OX to Od without causing any relevant economically-inefficient resource allocation to be executed. Similarly, a choice that would increase the equilibrium $RATLC_{.../...}$ quantity for the to-be-specified category of resource allocation from ON to OC would increase the amount of economic inefficiency generated by economically-inefficient exemplars of choices to execute or not to execute resource allocations in the to-be-specified category by area LIFM by raising from AN to AC the allocative cost of the economically-inefficient resource allocations in the to-be-specified category that were executed without affecting the amount of economically-efficient resource allocations in that category that are executed (if, as I am assuming [contestably—see below] the economic efficiency of the resource allocations in that category that were unaffected is not affected by the choice in question).[20] Or a choice that would increase the equilibrium $RATLC_{.../...}$ quantity from OW to ON would increase economic efficiency by area UKV *minus* area KLM by causing WA in economically-efficient resource allocations in the to-be-specified category to be executed and AN in economically-inefficient resource allocations in the to-be-specified category to be executed (where the magnitude of the relevant resource allocations is measured by their allocative cost) on the same assumption articulated in the parenthetical that appears at the end of the preceding sentence.

I should also note that if the last (economics-marginal) resource allocation in the to-be-specified category yields just a normal rate-of-return[21]—if $P\pi_{.../...} = 0$ for that resource allocation, $\Sigma D(P\pi_{\Delta.../\Delta...})$ for that last (marginal) resource allocation will equal $(-LE_{\Delta.../\Delta...})$ for that resource allocation (since by definition $\Sigma D(P\pi_{.../...}) \equiv P\pi_{.../...} - LE_{.../...}$). And, if the economics-marginal resource allocation in the to-be-specified category is infinitesimally small, $\Sigma D(P\pi_{\Delta.../\Delta...})$ for that resource allocation will equal the negative difference between the heights of the $RAMLP_{.../...}$ curve and the $RAMLC_{.../...}$ curve at the $RATLC_{.../...}$ quantity to which the resource allocation in question brings the ARDEPPS' $RATLC_{.../...}$ quantity.

If it were allocative-costless to do so, one would estimate the impact of a choice on the amount of economic inefficiency generated by economically-inefficient choices to execute and/or not to execute exemplars of any to-be-specified functional category of resource allocations to a to-be-specified ARDEPPS by "estimating" perfectly accurately its $RAMLP_{.../...}$ curve, the impact of the choice whose economic efficiency is at issue on the $RATLC_{.../...}$ quantity for the to-be-specified functional category of resource allocations to the to-be-specified ARDEPPS, and any impact that the choice in question had on the relevant $RAMLP_{.../...}$ curve. Given the allocative cost of executing the associated empirical research, it would almost certainly be TBLE not to try to do a perfect job of making these estimates.

If one concludes that the choice whose economic efficiency is an issue will/did not change the sign of the relevant $\Sigma D(P\pi_{\Delta\ldots/\Delta\ldots})$ figure, it might be TBLE to make use of the fact that the choice would decrease/increase the amount of economic inefficiency economically-inefficient decisions to execute and/or not to execute exemplars of a functional category of resource allocation to the ARDEPPS in question by estimating its impacts on (1) the operative $\Sigma D(P\pi_{\Delta\ldots/\Delta\ldots})$ figure and (2) the allocative cost of the resources devoted to the resource allocation in question. If one concludes that the choice whose economic efficiency is at issue will/did change the sign of the operative $\Sigma D(P\pi_{\Delta\ldots/\Delta\ldots})$ figure, that conclusion would strengthen the economic-efficiency case for estimating the shape of the $RAMLP_{\ldots/\ldots}$ curve. I suspect that it will rarely be TBLE to consider the possibility that the choice whose economic efficiency is at issue will alter the relevant $RAMLP_{\ldots/\ldots}$ curve over the relevant $RATLC_{\ldots/\ldots}$ range, but clearly, it would be TBLE for an economic-efficiency predictor to devote a TBLE amount of resources to considering the TBLE of pursuing this issue.

It may be worthwhile to make six additional points about this first major component of the protocol for economic-efficiency analysis I claim is TBLE. First, in some situations, it may be analytically convenient (TBLE for "practical reasons") to decompose the first three categories of resource allocation in the preceding list of categories of resource allocations (and the associated categories of economic inefficiency) into their inter-ARDEPPS UO-to-UO, inter-ARDEPPS QV-to-QV, inter-ARDEPPS PPR-to-PPR, UO-to-QV or QV-to-UO, UO-to-PPR or PPR-to-UO, and QV-to-PPR or PPR-to-QV components. Second, the members of the listed set of economic-inefficiency categories whose economic efficiency will be affected by a given choice will vary from choice to choice. Third, even those choices that affect the magnitudes of the same categories of economic inefficiency may affect those magnitudes not only by different amounts and by different percentages but also in different directions. Fourth, the preceding exposition assumes (unrealistically) that economic-efficiency analysts will have allocatively-costless access to perfectly-accurate formulas for the aggregate distortion in the profits yielded by any exemplar of any category of resource allocations, to all pre-existing data on the pre-choice magnitudes of any parameter that appears in any of the aggregate-profit-distortion or choice-impact formulas in question (as well as to any known information that relates to the accuracy of that data), to any theoretical or empirical work that has been done that bears on the impact of the choices whose economic efficiency they are predicting/post-dicting will have on the parameters whose magnitudes will affect the choice's effect on any relevant aggregate-profit-distortion figure, and to any theoretical or empirical work that has been done on any parameter that affects the impact that a choice under review will have on the amount of resources devoted to the categories of resource allocations (and economic inefficiency) on which this first component of the protocol for economic-efficiency analysis I am recommending focuses—categories (1)-(6) and (10) in the preceding list of categories of resource misallocation: As I suggest at the end of the immediately-preceding paragraph, it will be TBLE for such analysts to consider the TBLE of their executing various relevant theoretical research and empirical research-projects and of their devoting additional resources to considering the implication of what they know for the economic efficiency of the choices whose economic efficiency is at issue. Fifth, the third-best allocative efficiency of the economic-efficiency analyst's collecting additional data on any relevant parameter will depend inter alia on the contribution that the additional data would make to the accuracy of the analyst's prediction/post-diction of the impact that the choice under review and all other choices that will be at issue would/did have on each of the categories of economic inefficiency to whose analysis that data is relevant: thus, even if it would not be TBLE to collect additional data on the externalities generated pre-choice by the production and consumption of two same-ARDEPPS products between whose production the choice whose economic efficiency is at issue allocates resources (say, a choice that would accurately internalize the externalities in question) if that data's only relevance were to the impact the choice would have on intra-ARDEPPS UO-to-UO misallocation in the instant "case," it might well be TBLE to collect additional data on such externalities if such data were also relevant (say) (1) to the instant choice's impact on the amounts of economic inefficiency generated by the allocation of resources between or among known production processes, (2) to the instant choice's impact on the amount of economic inefficiency generated by the allocation of resources between UO-producing-and-using uses and QV-investment-creating-and-using uses, and/or (3) to other choices' impacts on economic efficiency. Sixth and finally, a point that I hesitate to include both because it would be expositionally inadvisable to justify it at this juncture and because it is disfavored by its immediate predecessor in this list: I suspect that it will be TBLE to do more empirical research on more types of Pareto imperfections when predicting/post-dicting the impact of choices on the three categories of economic inefficiency associated, respectively, with the first three categories of resource misallocation that appear in the preceding list of categories of resource allocation and misallocation than when analyzing the impact of choices on the other 13 categories of economic inefficiency in that list—thus, although intra-ARDEPPS UO-to-UO misallocation can be caused by differences in the externalities generated by the production and consumption of units of same-ARDEPPS product variants between whose production a choice whose economic efficiency is at issue may allocate resources, by differences in the tax-rates that apply to the sale of such product variants, and by errors that buyers make when choosing between such product variants (by consumer non-sovereignty and/or non-maximization), I would not be surprised if it turned out to be TBLE for analysts of the impact of a choice on intra-ARDEPPS UO-to-UO allocation to concentrate overwhelmingly or even exclusively on whether the choice in question increases or decreases such misallocation by increasing or decreasing conduct that results in sales being made by privately-worse-than-best-placed suppliers that are also allocatively-worse-than-best-placed (specifically, on whether the choice increases or decreases (1) predatory pricing and (2) price-fixing [what I called contrived-oligopolistic pricing], which leads to sales being made by privately-worse-than-best-placed potential suppliers that are also allocatively-worse-than-best-placed when the contrived-oligopolistic offer of the privately-best-placed firm is beaten by a non-cooperating competitive inferior, when the price-fixer retaliates against the privately-worse-than-best-placed rival that has taken the price-fixer's customer, and when the rival against which the price-fixer has retaliated engages in defensive retaliation against the retaliating price-fixer).

The second major component of the protocol for economic-efficiency analysis I claim is TBLE focuses on the impact of the choice under review on the amount of economic inefficiency the relevant economy generates by using less-economically-efficient, known production processes rather than more-economically-efficient, known production processes—i.e., by generating economic inefficiency in the category that is associated with category (7) of resource allocations in the preceding list of categories of resource allocations. I should state at the outset that the 7-Step protocol for economic-efficiency prediction/post-diction that I argued is TBLE to follow when analyzing the impact of choices on categories (1)-(6) and (10) of resource misallocations in the preceding list could also be TBLE when the goal is to determine the impact of a choice on choice-among-known-production-process-generated misallocation. I distinguish the current component of the overall protocol for economic-efficiency prediction/post-diction from its predecessor because choice-among-known-production-process-generated misallocation is far more likely than the categories of economic inefficiency on which the preceding component focuses to be generated by government prohibitions and regulations, a possibility that merits separate treatment. Thus, choice-among-known-production-process-generated misallocation is often caused (1) by government prohibitions of mergers, acquisitions, joint ventures, and other types of collaborative arrangements, which prohibitions preclude firms from using production processes that would involve their combining resources owned by different firms that are complementary for scale or non-scale reasons, (2) by fair-rate-of-return public-utility-pricing regulations that equate the highest price the regulated firm may charge for any regulated product with the price that will yield it just a "fair" (in practice, somewhat supernormal) rate-of-return on its investment ("rate-base"), thereby giving regulated utilities whose conventional profit-maximizing prices are higher than their highest originally-allowed regulated price an incentive to make otherwise-unprofitable decisions to expand their rate-bases (inter alia, to make intrinsically-unprofitable decisions to use known, more-privately-and-allocatively-expensive, more-capital-intensive production processes rather than known, less-privately-and-allocativley-expensive, less-capital-intensive production processes in order to expand their rate-bases and thereby put themselves in a position to persuade the regulatory authority to grant them permission to charge the higher prices they would find more profitable [the higher prices that would enable them to realize the allowed "fair rate-of-return" on their expanded rate-base]), and (3) by government prohibitions of firms' using various types of contractual arrangements (resale-price-maintenance clauses, vertical territorial restraints or other sorts of customer-allocation clauses, single-brand exclusive-dealership arrangements, slotting/shelf-space-specifying/advertizing-specifying clauses, tie-ins, and reciprocity agreements) or related sales-policies to control their independent distributors or customers (e.g., to induce their independent distributors to supply customers with repair and maintenance services or make good on warranty clauses as allocative-efficiently as possible). I acknowledge that some of these sorts of government prohibitions and policies can also cause the categories of economic inefficiency on which the first major component of the protocol I claim is TBLE focuses: Thus, merger prohibitions can prevent economically-efficient QV-investment or PPR projects from being executed by preventing mergers that would create merged firms that could execute more-economically-efficient QV and PPR investments, and fair-rate-of-return public-utility-pricing regulation can generate QV-investment-related misallocation by making it profitable for the regulated firm to execute inherently-unprofitable QV investments that are also allocatively inefficient and can generate PPR-related misallocation by making it profitable for regulated firms to execute less-inherently-profitable/less-economically-efficient PPR projects that are designed to discover more-capital-intensive production processes rather than more-inherently-profitable/more-economically-efficient PPR projects that are designed to discover less-capital-intensive production processes. However, although I do think that it will sometimes be TBLE for analysts to consider such possibilities when analyzing the impact of choices on the categories of economic inefficiency on which the first component of my protocol focuses, my intuition is that these possibilities are sufficiently more important when choice-among-known-production-process-generated misallocation is at issue to justify my delaying my discussion of this source of misallocation until my analysis of choice-among-known-production-process misallocation.

The third major component of the distortion-analysis protocol for economic-efficiency prediction/post-diction that I think is TBLE focuses on the TBLE way for analysts to predict/post-dict the impact that a choice will have on economic efficiency by altering the extent of poverty and/or material inequality the economy in question generates. I should admit at the outset that (1) most of the categories of economic inefficiency whose magnitudes are affected by poverty and material inequality are categories on which the previous components of this account focus and (2) to avoid double-counting, I should amend my previous account of the first two major components of the protocol I am proposing and recommending by acknowledging that the approaches I argued would be TBLE to use to predict/post-dict the impact of choices on the categories of economic inefficiency on which these components of my protocol focus are deficient in that they ignore the impacts that choices have on those categories of resource misallocation by changing the amounts of poverty and material inequality the economy in question generates. This third major component of my proposed protocol is designed to remedy this omission. This component of the protocol instructs the analyst (1) to identify the various ways in which poverty and/or material inequality can increase economic inefficiency—inter alia, by increasing the amount of economic inefficiency generated (A) by failures to make economically-efficient investments in human capital (in pre-natal and postnatal nutrition and medical care, in clothing and housing, in parenting, in formal and informal education, in job-training, etc.), (B) by economically-inefficient consumption choices caused by (i) consumer non-sovereignty and/or consumer non-maximization that result in the buyers' making consumption choices against their individual interest that are also economically efficient and (ii) the fact that poor consumers find it individually advantageous to purchase or rent cheap goods (say, ugly, breakdown-prone, noise-and-air-polluting, accident-prone cars or ugly and disease-and-fire spreading housing-units) whose consumption is more prone to generate external costs than is the consumption of their more-privately-expensive alternatives when the relevant external-cost differences render the relevant consumers' privately-advantageous consumption choices economically inefficient, (C) by choices to commit economically-inefficient crimes (poverty and material inequality increase such crime by increasing poor individuals' non-sovereignty and non-maximization and social alienation [which increases the extent to which they fail to internalize the equivalent-dollar losses their possible criminal acts would impose directly on others] and by reducing the difference between the attractiveness to poor potential criminals of life inside prison and the life they could lead outside prison if they did not engage in crime), (D) by economically-inefficient decisions to perform non-criminal, dangerous labor (increases in poverty increase the number of such decisions that are made both because increases in poverty increase relevant potential-worker non-sovereignty and non-maximization and because in at least some societies the incidence and magnitude of government transfers to poor individuals who are injured or killed at work and/or to their families are higher than the incidence and magnitude of such transfers to the better-off and their families [i.e., because in some societies increases in poverty increase government subsidization of dangerous labor]), (E) by economically-inefficient government decisions (because government decisionmakers place less weight per person on the equivalent-dollar effects of their choices on the poor and relatively-less-well-off and more weight per person on the equivalent-dollar effects of their choices on the wealthy and relatively-better-off [since for a variety of reasons, the per-person political power of better-off individuals exceeds the per-person political power of worse-off individuals]), and (F) by increasing the net equivalent-dollar losses the society's distributions of income and wealth generate by dissatisfying the "external preferences" of its members and participants (their non-parochial preferences for others' having resources and opportunities)—I acknowledge that this last claim may reflect my unwarranted optimism about the extent to which the relevant society's members and participants share my distributive values, (2) to estimate/guesstimate the impact of the choice under consideration on poverty and/or material inequality, and (3) to estimate/guesstimate the effect that the choice's estimated/guesstimated impact on poverty and material inequality would have on economic efficiency in each of the ways in which it could affect economic efficiency if the government did nothing to combat the effects in question.

The fourth major component of the protocol for economic-efficiency analysis I claim is TBLE instructs the analyst (1) to estimate/guesstimate the impact of the choice on the private costs that final consumers incur to determine the purchases that best promote their respective goals, the "private" cost to the government of supplying information about products (or banning some products), the private cost to non-government actors of supplying product descriptions and evaluations, and the private cost to producers of controlling the complements their customers combine with their products and (2) to analyze and estimate/guesstimate the magnitudes of the factors that determine the ratios of the above private costs to their allocative counterparts.

The fifth major component of the protocol for economic-efficiency analysis I claim is ex ante economically efficient instructs the analyst (1) to consider the impact of the choice on allocative transaction costs—i.e., both (A) the choice's impact on the private transaction costs that non-government actors incur to implement pricing-techniques designed to convert what would otherwise be buyer surplus into seller surplus, to induce their employees and the independent contractors they use to make choices in the actor's interest, to engage in and conceal various types of illegal conduct, and to respond to civil and criminal claims made against them and that government actors incur to promulgate and implement laws and regulations, to negotiate plea-deals and try related cases, to adjudicate criminal and civil cases, to collect fines, and to implement the incarcerative sentences and non-incarcerative restrictions imposed on those found liable or guilty, and to raise the resources required to finance government operations and (B) all those factors that affect the ratio of (the impact of the choice on the *allocative* transaction costs associated with these private costs) to (its impact on the private transaction costs in question)—inter alia, the proportions of the resources used up as transaction costs that are withdrawn, respectively, from UO-producing-and-using, QV-investment-creating-and-using, and PPR-executing-and-using uses, the Pareto imperfections that distort the private benefits those resources would have generated for their alternative users in each of the pairs of functionally-related uses from which they would be withdrawn, and the different ways in which those Pareto imperfections interact to distort the private benefits that those resources would have generated, respectively, in their alternative pairs of functionally-related uses, (2) to estimate/guesstimate the choice's impact on risk-cost-related allocative costs—i.e., both on (A) the risk costs the members of and participants in the relevant society incur and the private costs such actors incur to reduce such risk costs and (B) the factors that influence the ratio of the allocative cost of any choice-induced or choice-deterred allocative risk-cost-avoidance moves to their private counterparts and the ways in which those factors interact to determine that ratio (which vary with the nature of the alternative uses from which the resources devoted to risk-cost avoidance are withdrawn), (3) to estimate/guesstimate the non-allocative-transaction-cost-related allocative costs or benefits the choice would generate by increasing/decreasing moral-rights-violating conduct (e.g., the allocative cost of the injuries/deaths the choice would cause/deter, the allocative cost that the libel/slander the choice would cause/deter would generate/would have generated [both by causing/deterring direct harm to its target and those who value the target's welfare and indirectly by deterring/causing economically-efficient transactions/relationships with the target], the non-allocative-transaction-cost allocative cost of the thefts the choice would/did cause/deter by generating/deterring transfers of goods from their higher-dollar-valuing owners to their lower-dollar-valuing "transferees" and by inducing/deterring potential victims of theft to make/from making otherwise-allocatively-inefficient choices to protect themselves against theft [to install burglar alarms, to place valuables in safe-deposit boxes, to purchase fewer durable goods (which can be stolen), to work less and consume more leisure), and (4) when the choice in question affects government expenditures, to estimate the resource misallocation the choice would generate on this account even if no allocative transaction costs had to be generated to finance relevant government expenditures—i.e., (A) analyze the ways in which the government will respond to that fiscal reality (inter alia, by raising various taxes, increasing the prices it charges for various government-supplied goods and services, increasing government debt and/or inflation, and eliminating other expenditures) and (B) analyze the economic efficiency of each of these predicted responses (by using a protocol that responds ex ante economic efficiently to The General Theory of Second Best).

The sixth and final component of the protocol for economic-efficiency prediction/post-diction that I claim is TBLE instructs the analyst to add together all of his or her estimates of the impacts of the choice on the categories of economic inefficiency and other allocative costs the preceding components of this protocol reference to generate a prediction/post-diction of the overall impact of the choice under review on economic efficiency.

I want to close this account of the protocol for economic-efficiency prediction I claim is ex ante economically efficient by reiterating the pervasive feature of the protocol that renders it ex ante economically efficient—i.e., *third-best* economically efficient. At each stage of the associated analysis, the protocol instructs the analyst to consider whether, everything considered, it would be ex ante economically efficient to execute additional empirical or theoretical research-projects or to devote additional attention to the implications of the available information and to continue to do such additional work until the analyst concludes that it is TBLE to stop.

8.6 A Critique of a Canonical, Standard FBLE Analysis of the Economic Efficiency of a Series of Horizontal Mergers That Convert a Purely-Competitive Industry Into a Pure Monopoly While Creating a Resulting Firm That Faces a Lower Marginal-Cost Curve Than the Participants Would Have Faced and the Same Fixed Costs as the Participants Would Have Faced

In 1968, Oliver Williamson (1968) published a canonical analysis of what he called the "*welfare* trade-off" and I would denominate "some of the *economic-efficiency* trade-offs" that have to be made to assess the economic efficiency of the series of horizontal mergers described in this subsection's heading.[22] I will close this chapter by summarizing and criticizing Williamson's argument, which is based on a standard, FBLE economic-efficiency analysis, and contrasting it with the analysis of the economic efficiency of such a series of mergers that I think would be TBLE.

Figure 8.5 contains seven curves: nothing significant turns on its constructing them as straight lines. Williamson's analysis references only four of these curves: (1) the industry demand curve for the product produced by all participants in the series of horizontal mergers whose economic efficiency he is analyzing—DD_{IND}, which coincides with the demand curve the purely-monopolistic firm F that will be operating after (A) the series of mergers in question is consummated $(DD_F)_A$; (2) $MR_{IND} = (MR_F)_A$, which indicates the industry marginal-revenue curve (MR_{IND}) and the post-series-of-mergers marginal-revenue curve that will face the firm F that exists after the mergers are consummated (assuming as he assumes and I will accept ad arguendo that the resulting pure-monopoly firm engages in what I call single pricing); (3) the marginal-cost curve the industry faces before the mergers are consummated—$(MC_{IND})_B$; and (4) the lower marginal-cost curve that will face the industry and the firm F that exists after the mergers are consummated —$(MC_{IND})_A = (MC_F)_A$. Because Williamson's analysis is FBLE, the diagram he uses does not include the remaining three curves Fig. 8.5 contains (1) MLV_{IND}, which indicates the marginal allocative value of the successive units that could be produced of the product the relevant industry produces, (2) the industry marginal-allocative-cost curve for that product before the series of horizontal mergers whose economic efficiency is at issue was consummated—$(MLC_{IND})_B$, and (3) the marginal-allocative-cost curve facing the industry and the resulting firm F (which constitutes the seller-side of the industry after the relevant series of mergers is consummated)—$(MLC_{IND})_A = (MLC_F)_A$. Let me be more specific: Williamson does not include these last three curves because his FBLE economic-efficiency analysis implicitly assumes that DD = MLV and that MC = MLC. Figure 8.5 includes these three additional curves because, on realistic assumptions about the Pareto imperfections that any actual economy contains for reasons I offered in Sect. 8.4 and have explained in more detail in Markovits (2020) at pp. 140–149 and 186–191, $(MLC_{IND})_B$ will exceed $(MC_{IND})_B$ and $(MLC_{IND})_A = (MLC_F)_A$ is likely to exceed $(MC_{IND})_A = (MC_F)_A$ (as Figure 8.5 assumes, probably by the same percentage as the percentage by which MLC_B exceeds MC_B), and MLV_{IND} will exceed $(DD_{IND})_B = (DD_F)_A$ (by a percentage that equals the sales tax-rate or excise tax-rate that is levied on the sales of the product the participating firms produce [if one assumes unjustifiably that, taken together, the relevant externalities of consumption, buyer errors, and buyer monopsony power do not affect the relationship between DD_{IND} and MLV_{IND} either before or after the relevant mergers are consummated]). Figure 8.5 contains $(MLC_{IND})_B$, $(MLC_{IND})_A = (MLC_F)_A$, and MLV_{IND} curves that take account of these divergencies by making the MLC curves 50% higher than the MC curves (admittedly, a percentage whose only justification is visual) and by making the MLV_{IND} curve exceed the DD_{IND} curve by about 10% (a percentage that is slightly higher than the weighted-average U.S. sales/excise tax-rate but is below the weighted-average E.U.-member-nation value-added tax-rate).

I will use Fig. 8.5 to illustrate the first of two criticisms I will make of Williamson's analysis of the economic efficiency of the series of horizontal mergers whose economic efficiency he is analyzing—the criticism that he misanalyzes both of the economic-efficiency effects on which he focuses. According to Williamson,

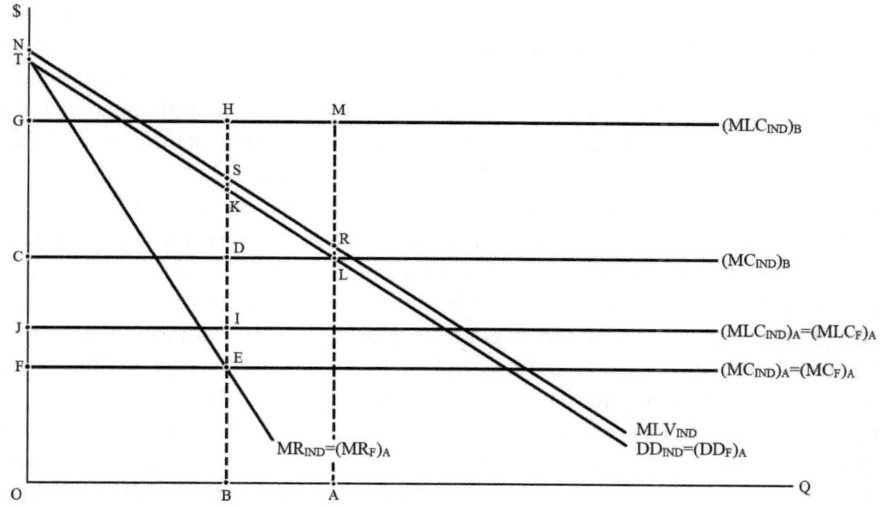

Fig. 8.5 Figure that illustrates some of the most important differences between standard, FBLE economic-efficiency analyses of antitrust-policy-coverable conduct and the protocol for such economic-efficiency analyses the author believes is TBLE

the series of mergers whose economic efficiency he is analyzing will affect economic efficiency in two ways: (1) by creating a resulting firm whose profit-maximizing output—in Figure 8.5, OB (the output at which the single-pricing resulting firm's MR curve [$(MR_{IND}) = (MR_F)_A$] cuts its after-merger-series MC curve [$(MC_{IND})_A = (MC_F)_A$] from above at point E)—is lower than the industry's before-merger-series output—in Figure 8.5, OA (the output at which the industry's MR curve [MR_{IND}] cuts its before-merger-series MC curve [$(MC_{IND})_B$] from above) and (2) by creating a resulting firm that had to incur lower variable costs—equal to area FEBO—to produce its post-merger-output OB than the industry had to incur—area CDBO—to produce that output (the first OB units of its product it produced prior to the merger-series). According to Williamson, the first, unit-output-related impact of the series of mergers in question just referenced would reduce economic efficiency by the area between DD_{IND} and $(MC_{IND})_B$ between output OB and OA—in Fig. 8.5, by area KLD—while the second, reduction-in-variable-cost-of-producing the post-merger-series output of the product in question would increase economic efficiency by the area between $(MC_{IND})_B$ and $(MC_{IND})_A$ between output zero and output OB—by area CDEF. However, even if one assumes that the merger-series in question would create a resulting firm whose unit output would be lower than the unit output the industry would have produced absent the mergers (an assumption whose accuracy depends on the size of the MC reduction, the shape of the DD_{IND} curve, and the pricing-technique the merger partners and the resulting firm would employ), the associated economic-efficiency loss will equal area KLD only if (1) $DD_{IND} = MLV_{IND}$ and $(MC_{IND})_B =$

$(MLC_{IND})_B$ or, fortuitously, (2) the departures from these two assumptions happen to cancel each other out. On the admittedly-quantitively-arbitrary assumptions of Fig. 8.5 (which do imply that the merger-series will reduce the relevant product's unit output), the reduction in unit output from OA units to OB units that the merger-series would generate would *increase* economic efficiency by area HMRS —the area between $(MLC_{IND})_B > (MC_{IND})_B$ and $MLV_{IND} > DD_{IND}$ between output OA and output OB, not *decrease* economic efficiency by area KLD.

Figure 8.5 reveals as well that on its assumptions Williamson will also have misanalyzed the impact that the relevant merger-series will have on economic efficiency by creating a merged firm that can produce the industry's product more cheaply than the merger partners could have done as separate entities—by lowering the industry's MC cost curve from CO to FO. Even if I accept Williamson's acceptable assumption that the mergers will not affect the relevant fixed costs of production, Fig. 8.5's assumptions that $(MLC_{IND})_B$ exceeds $(MC_{IND})_B$ and that $(MLC_{IND})_A$ exceeds $(MC_{IND})_A$ imply that, by reducing the operative MC curves, the merger-series will increase economic efficiency by reducing the allocative cost of producing the resulting firm's output by area GHIJ, which is greater than the associated private-cost reduction (area CDEF). Williamson assumes that the private-cost savings the merger-series he is investigating will enable the resulting firm to achieve will equal the allocative-cost savings the merger will generate because he assumes that the economy in which the merger-series whose economic efficiency he is investigating is oPp—that is, because he ignores either the reality that actual economies are Pareto-imperfect and/or the possibility that the Pareto imperfections that actual economies contain may distort the private-cost savings he is assuming the mergers he is studying will generate. Figure 8.5 takes account of the Pareto-imperfectness of actual economies—indeed, assumes for reasons I have already explained that those imperfections will deflate both MC_B and MC_A by the same percentage and concomitantly will deflate the private-cost savings Williamson's mergers will generate by that percentage. Thus, in Fig. 8.5, the economic-efficiency gain the merger-series will generate by reducing MLC_{IND} (area GHIJ) exceeds the private-cost savings the merger-series will generate by reducing MC_{IND} (area DCEF) by the same percentage that MLC_B (GO) exceeds MC_B (CO) and MLC_A (JO) exceeds MC_A (FO). Williamson's first-best assumptions have led him to overestimate the economic-efficiency loss that the merger-series he is analyzing will generate by changing the relevant industry's unit output and to underestimate the economic-efficiency gain that the merger-series he is analyzing will generate by creating a resulting firm that can produce the industry's product more cheaply (to tend to underestimate on both these accounts the economic efficiency of the merger-series whose economic efficiency he is investigating).

In essence, the preceding criticism of Williamson's analysis focuses on the fact that it ignores The General Theory of Second Best—that it is a FBLE analysis. The second criticism I have of Williamson's analysis is that it ignores many categories of economic inefficiency whose magnitudes the merger-series he is considering will affect and many categories of economic-efficiency-related effects the merger-series in question will have. I will consider here four such ignored categories of efficiency-related effects.

First, Williamson ignores the fact that, if the relevant "market's" "product" or "products" (see below) are created by QV investments, the merger-series in question will probably affect economic efficiency by altering equilibrium QV investment in the area of product-space in which the mergers in question are consummated. I suspect that Williamson ignored this possibility not just because economists in general ignore QV-investment effects but also because he was explicitly assuming that prior to the mergers the relevant industry was perfectly competitive and believed on that account that QV investment in that industry would be invariant. In fact, this last belief, though common, is incorrect. For perfect price-competition to prevail, two conditions must be fulfilled: (1) no seller must have a competitive advantage when competing for the patronage of any buyer, and (2) the number of sellers that are privately-equal-best-placed to supply any buyer must be sufficiently high to preclude any seller from obtaining a contrived-oligopolistic margin from any buyer. Both these conditions will be fulfilled if the relevant "industry" contains a large number of sellers all of which produce with identical cost-structures physically-identical products with identical images that are distributed to buyers whose quantity-demands do not vary through time from locations among which all relevant buyers are indifferent. Under such conditions, QV investment will be invariant. However, both these conditions can also be fulfilled if products are differentiated either materially or by virtue of their images, speed of delivery, and/or distributive-geographic-location so long as no seller is uniquely-privately-best-placed to supply any buyer because, for example, any buyer preference advantage any non-worse-than-privately-best-placed seller has over all its rivals in its relations with any buyer is perfectly offset by a marginal-cost disadvantage it suffers relative to a relevant rival in its relations with that buyer and the number of sellers that are privately-equal-best-placed to secure the patronage of any buyer is too high to enable any to obtain a contrived-oligopolistic margin (I know I am simplifying—see Sect. 9.1) The point is that when the conditions for perfect price-competition are satisfied for this second set of reasons, perfect price-competition is compatible with equilibrium QV investment's varying.

The series of mergers whose economic efficiency Williamson is analyzing could either increase or decrease equilibrium QV investment in the area of product-space in which they are consummated. The series will tend to increase that ARDEPPS' equilibrium-QV-investment quantity by increasing the height of its $H\Pi_E$ curve. The series will tend to decrease the relevant ARDEPPS' equilibrium-QV-investment quantity by substituting for a situation in which no established firm faced a monopolistic QV-investment disincentive at any relevant ARDEPPS QV-investment quantity a situation in which (at least if potential competition is not effective post-mergers) the pure monopolist that the relevant series of mergers creates has a monopolistic QV-investment disincentive to make or renew any but its first QV investment in that area of product-space. Even if I adopt Williamson's implicit assumption that the pure monopolist the merger-series he is analyzing will create will not face effective potential competition at any ARDEPPS

QV-investment quantity and ignore the possibility that the series of mergers in question may generate dynamic as well as static efficiencies, I would not be able to predict whether Williamson's merger-series would increase or decrease equilibrium QV investment in the ARDEPPS in which it takes place (an issue that will be more important if one substitutes for my current implicit static assumptions a more-realistic set of assumptions that takes account of the fact that the $H\Pi_E$ curves for most ARDEPPSes increase through time as the relevant society's population and per-capita wealth increase through time). The failure of Williamson to address the impact of the merger-series whose economic efficiency he is analyzing on the relevant ARDEPPS' equilibrium QV-investment quantity is rendered salient by the fact that an ARDEPPS' equilibrium-QV-investment quantity can either be too high or too low from the perspective of economic efficiency.

Second, Williamson's economic-efficiency analysis is incomplete because it ignores the fact that if the "product" or "products" produced by the industry in which his series of mergers is consummated are "production processes," the merger-series in question can affect equilibrium PPR in that industry and economic efficiency by doing so. The analysis of this possibility parallels the QV-investment-oriented analysis just executed.

Third, Williamson ignores the possibility that the merger-series whose economic efficiency he is analyzing may tend to decrease economic efficiency by concentrating the seller-side of the industry in question and thereby increasing the expenditures its sellers or seller (originally many and, post-mergers, one) make on political parties/campaigns/candidates and government-decision-making-process participation.

Fourth, Williamson ignores the possibility that his merger-series may generate economic inefficiency by increasing poverty and material inequality by raising the prices charged for the industry's "product" and perhaps reducing its equilibrium-QV-investment quantity.

I want to close this discussion of Williamson's canonical antitrust-policy-related economic-efficiency analysis by pointing out two additional features of his study that reduce its policy-relevance, though they do not render it inaccurate. Both reflect the fact that Williamson was not trying to develop a complete economically-efficient protocol for government to use to respond to the type of merger-series whose economic efficiency he was analyzing. (Yes, I know: one step at a time. One can make a valuable contribution without doing everything that needs to be done to develop an economically-efficient government-decision-making protocol.) First, Williamson does not consider the allocative cost and allocative benefits of economic-efficiency analysts' doing additional theoretical and empirical research on various issues. Second, Williamson does not consider the allocate cost of government's financing various protocols for analyzing the economic efficiency of the type of merger-series on which he focuses or the possible TBLE of different approaches to determining the economic efficiency of such merger-series.

I hope that this section has served its purpose—has provided substantial reason to believe that the protocol for economic-efficiency analysis that I am arguing would be ex ante economically efficient for government to use when analyzing the economic efficiency of antitrust (or other sorts of) policies is significantly more economically efficient than the FBLE economic-efficiency-analysis protocol that the vast majority of applied welfare economists use, even when the latter protocol is employed by an extremely intelligent, accomplished economist.

Notes

1. This is the title of a deservedly-famous article by Lipsey and Lancaster (1956).
2. A non-economic example may make the Second-Best-Theory argument more comprehensible. Assume that there is an ideal way to drive a car around a corner (I will not specify the associated maximand or objective function [whatever it is that would ideally be maximized])—viz., to drive the car 15 miles per hour and turn the steering wheel in the appropriate direction 40 degrees per second. If the car is being driven 15 miles per hour, the optimal rate at which to turn the steering wheel will be 40° per second because, if one turns the steering wheel 40 degrees per second in the appropriate direction, both (all) of the optimal conditions will be fulfilled, and the optimum will be achieved. However, what if the accelerator is jammed, the car is moving 85 miles per hour, and nothing can be done about those facts? Will it be (second-best) optimal to turn the steering wheel 40° per second in the direction that would be optimal in the absence of any imperfections? Almost certainly not. Although it might turn out that fulfilling the second optimal condition (turning the steering wheel 40° per second in the direction that a first-best analysis would recommend) is second-best optimal, any such reality will be fortuitous in the sense that it will not follow from the fact that turning the steering wheel 40° per second in the direction that a first-best analysis would recommend is an optimal condition (belongs to a set of sufficient conditions for the achievement of the relevant optimum). To determine the best way to turn the steering wheel when the car is traveling 85 miles per hour, one would have to examine how departures from the two optimal conditions interact to cause sub-optimal outcomes both in general and in the particular relevant context—for example, the presence of a steel-reinforced concrete wall 50 yards from the road may play an important role in the relevant analysis even if it would play no role in determining the optimal way to drive the car around the corner in question. The pertinent points are: (1) once one of two optimal conditions is not fulfilled, there is no general reason to believe that fulfilling or more closely approximating the second optimal condition will even tend to improve the outcome, and (2) in order to determine whether to fulfill or more closely approximate the fulfillment of the second of two optimal conditions when the first is not fulfilled (or, more generally, what to do about a second of two outcome-determinants when the magnitude of the first outcome-determinant is not first-best), one must combine an appropriate theoretical analysis with context-specific empirical findings.
3. I write "almost always" because the amount of economic inefficiency in an economy that contains only one Pareto imperfection may depend not only on the magnitude of that imperfection but also on the distributions of income and wealth in the economy in question and a choice that reduces the magnitude of the only Pareto imperfection in a given economy could increase the amount of

economic inefficiency it contains if it alters the distributions of income and/or wealth in that economy in a way that increases the amount of resource misallocation that would be generated by a Pareto imperfection of the relevant kind of different relevant magnitudes.

4. I recognize that some applied welfare economists do take some account of The General Theory of Second Best. For example, some public-finance economists examine how the impact of a particular tax on the amount of one category of economic inefficiency that is generated would be affected by the presence of an exemplar of one or two types of non-tax Pareto imperfections in the relevant economy. However, although these pieces of scholarship are useful, taken collectively, this body of useful scholarship does not respond appropriately to The General Theory of Second Best. For a more-detailed discussion, see Markovits (2020), pp 36–79.
5. For example, the private benefits yielded by a decision to produce a marginal unit of the output of some good (in the simple case, the conventional marginal revenue generated by the sale of that unit) will not be distorted (will not differ from the allocative benefits generated by the consumption of that unit) if either (1) the seller faced perfect price-competition, no sales tax, excise tax, or value-added tax were levied on the relevant sale, the buyer of the unit was a non-monopsonistic sovereign maximizer who obtained no buyer surplus on the purchase, and the buyer's consumption of the unit generated no [real] externalities or (2) two or more of the above conditions were not fulfilled but the departures from those conditions perfectly counteracted each other.
6. I recognize that some economists use the word "distortion" differently to reference any possible cause or source of what I call a profit-distortion, private-benefit distortion, or private-cost distortion—in practice, to reference any Pareto imperfection. I think my usage is more consistent with ordinary language: in ordinary language, one would say that a Pareto imperfection is (possibly) distorting, not that it is a "distortion." But for current purposes, the important point is not the relative attractiveness of my usage and its alternatives. What is important is that readers understand the way in which I define "distortion.".
7. I use the word "onesy" to refer to the indicated type of formula because in ordinary language a "onesy" is an item of clothing (usually, infant-wear) that integrates into one continuous garment clothing—"components" (such as a pair of pants and a shirt) that are usually separate.
8. See Markovits (2020), pp. 136–140 and 140–149, respectively.
9. I am ignoring the complications that might be introduced by the wealth-effects' of reductions in the price of the good in question affecting the value of intra-marginal units of the relevant product to their respective buyers.
10. This second condition would be fulfilled, for example, if the demand curve for the new product and the demand curves for each of the "old" products in the new product's ARDEPPS were identical, the marginal-cost curve for each product in that ARDEPPS was the same, and all the producers of products in the ARDEPPS engaged in single pricing.

11. To see why this is the case when the relevant DD curve is linear and the seller prices its product by setting a single per-unit price and allowing buyers to purchase as much as they want at that price, note that, under those conditions: (1) buyer surplus equals either area DFH or area DFB (the sum of the differences between the heights of the DD and MR curves between output zero and the actual output AB), (2) both these areas contain area DFJ, (3) area DFH also contains area DJH while area DFB contains area JFB, (4) both of these areas are right triangles whose angles have the same magnitudes (thus, angle BJE equals angle DJH), and (5) area DJH will equal area JFB (so that area DFH equals area DFB [in both cases, the buyer surplus generated]) if and only if HJ = JR (the bases of the two right triangles are equal).
12. If the relevant production-process researcher does not use its production-process discovery itself, any buyer surplus secured by its licensees or the actors to which it sold any related IP rights (attributable either to these buyers' monopsony power or to the fact that the cost the discoverer would have to incur to ascertain precisely the value of its discovery to its prospective individual licensees or buyers and to charge these parties different prices render it unprofitable for the discoverer to remove all these buyers' buyer surplus) would further increase the negative distortion in $PB_{(U)PPR}$.
13. For an analysis that considers the case in which the use of the discovered production process would increase MC_G, see Markovits (2008), pp. 220–222.
14. I wrote "partially" because the text that addressed this issue considered only a few of the imperfection-in investment-competition-related possibilities. For a more complete discussion, which does not yield conclusions that undermine this text's conclusion that imperfections in investment competition increase the positive value of the (SW[M])-distortion component of the step-wise-distortion formula for the relevant aggregate profit-distortion, see Markovits (2020), pp. 173–183.
15. I should note that this conclusion cuts against the economic efficiency of internalizing all external costs of production, though I have no doubt that, all things considered, policies that internalize such externalities "non-patchily" will increase economic efficiency (primarily because they will encourage producers to shift to known, less-external-cost-prone, more-economically-efficient production processes, induce the execution of economically-efficient PPR into less-external-cost-prone production processes, and [though this is more contestable] reduce poverty and material inequality, which cause economic inefficiency).
16. The alternative way of modeling the problem is to assume that each additional researcher's efforts increase the probability that the discovery will be made, (to simplify) that all relevant researchers are equally likely to make the discovery (first), and that the probability that each researcher will make the discovery is lower than the amount by which each researcher's efforts will increase the probability that the discovery will be made.
17. For an example in which such a calculation is made, see Markovits (2002).

18. I might also have analyzed the step-wise tax-distortion (SW[T])D in the profits yielded by the allocations of resources on which this section focuses–the distortion that is generated by differences in the effective tax-rates applicable to the profits yielded respectively by the production of units of existing products, the creation and use of QV investments, and the execution of PPR projects and the use of the discoveries they yield (differences that result inter alia from tax rules allowing research-expenditures to be expensed rather than depreciated at an economically-realistic rate).
19. I examine the relevance of a RAMLP$_{.../...}$ curve's being concave or convex to the origin elsewhere at Markovits (2020) at pp. 330–332.
20. I examine the possible consequences of relaxing this assumption and the possible TBLE of making it at id. at p. 344.
21. I examine the consequences of relaxing this assumption and argue for the TBLE of making this assumption at id. at 332–344.
22. Williamson (1968). In 1977, Williamson revisited this issue in a contribution to a special issue the University of Pennsylvania Law Review devoted to his original article on the occasion of its tenth anniversary. Williamson (1977).

References

Lipsey, R., & Lancaster, K. (1956). The general theory of second best. *Review of Economic Studies, 24*, 11–32.

Markovits, R. (2002). On the economic efficiency of using law to increase research and development: A critique of various tax, antitrust, intellectual property, and tort law rules and policy proposals. *Harvard Journal of Legislation, 39*, 63–120.

Markovits, R. (2008). *Truth or economics: On the definition, prediction, and relevance of economic efficiency*. Yale University Press.

Markovits, R. (2020). *Welfare economics and second-best theory: A third-best-economically-efficient distortion-analysis protocol for economic-efficiency analysis*. Springer.

Williamson, O. (1968). Economies as an antitrust defense: The welfare trade-off. *American Economic Review, 58*, 18–36.

Williamson, O. (1977). Economies as an antitrust defense revisited. *University of Pennsylvania Law Review, 125*, 699–736.

Part II
Introduction to Part II: The Morally-Relevant Effects of Specific Categories of Antitrust-Policy-Coverable Conduct and the Ability of Government to Secure Better Outcomes

Part II applies the concepts and analytic protocols that Part I defines and discusses to a succession of categories of antitrust-law-coverable conduct. Chapter 9 focuses on oligopolistic conduct; Chap. 10, on predatory conduct; Chap. 11, on horizontal mergers and acquisitions; Chap. 12, on conglomerate mergers and acquisitions; Chap. 13, on surrogates for vertical integration; Chap. 14, on vertical mergers and acquisitions; Chap. 15, on joint ventures and functionally-analogous collaborations of other sorts; and Chap. 16, on internal growth. Each of these chapters analyzes the functions that exemplars of the category of conduct on which it focuses can perform for its perpetrator(s), the impact that exemplars of such conduct will have on economic efficiency, the ability of the government of a liberal-moral-rights-based society to increase economic efficiency by responding appropriately to exemplars of the relevant category of conduct, the liberal-moral-rights-violativeness of different exemplars of such conduct, the ability of the government of such a society to secure liberal-moral-rights-related interests by responding appropriately to such conduct, the impact of various exemplars of the relevant category of conduct on the instantiation of the utilitarian, various non-utilitarian-egalitarian, and various mixed egalitarian conceptions of the moral good, and the ability of the government of a liberal-moral-rights-based society to instantiate one or more of these pure or mixed conceptions of the moral good by responding appropriately to various exemplars of the category of conduct on which the chapter in question focuses.

Part II is divided between the two volumes of this study. Volume I contains Chaps. 9–10. Volume II contains Chaps. 11–16. Part II is divided to reduce the difference between the lengths of the two volumes of this study. The particular division selected is attributable to the fact that Chaps. 12 and 14 (respectively on conglomerate and vertical mergers and acquisitions) rely heavily on analyses executed in Chap. 11 (on horizontal mergers and acquisitions).

9 Oligopolistic Conduct

This chapter focuses on "oligopolistic conduct." In my terminology, "oligopolistic conduct" always involves one or more perpetrators' making a move that it or they would not have found ex ante profitable but for its or their belief that one or more of its or their rivals' responses would or might be influenced by its/their rivals' belief that the initiator would react to its/their response in one or more ways that would render unprofitable for the rival a response that the rival would otherwise have found profitable. Thus, in the sense in which I define this concept, "oligopolistic conduct" involves more than simple recognized interdependence. In my terminology, the category "oligopolistic conduct" includes not only initiating moves of the type just defined but also any cooperative response such an initiating move elicits, any reciprocatory act the initiator makes to a cooperative move by a rival, and any retaliatory act that an initiator commits to impose a loss on a non-cooperative rival.

I distinguish two subcategories of any category of oligopolistic conduct. Oligopolistic conduct in any category is said to be "contrived" if the initiator's rivals anticipate the imitator's reacting to their cooperative and/or non-cooperative responses in one or more ways that would render unprofitable non-cooperative responses the rivals would otherwise have found profitable despite the fact that the anticipated reactions would be inherently unprofitable for the initiator because the initiator has communicated to its rivals its intention to react to their non-cooperation by engaging in (inherently-unprofitable) retaliation and/or to react to their cooperation by reciprocating (by foregoing otherwise-profitable opportunities to beat any contrived-oligopolistic-margin-containing offers they make to their own customers). Oligopolistic conduct is said to be natural if the initiator's rivals anticipate its reacting to any non-cooperative response they make to its initial offer by making any inherently-profitable move that renders their response unprofitable because they believe that the relevant buyer(s) will give the initiator an opportunity to rebid and that the initiator will find it inherently profitable to make a move that renders their response unprofitable.

R. S. Markovits, *Welfare Economics and Antitrust Policy - Vol. I*,
https://doi.org/10.1007/978-3-030-79812-3_9

This chapter has five sections, which respectively focus on (1) seller-practiced oligopolistic pricing, (2) oligopolistic interactions that result in sellers' not revealing to prospective buyers information the sellers possess about attributes of their products that lower the products' dollar value to the buyers or increase the lifetime cost to the buyers of the sellers' durable products or in sellers' not revealing to government officials information about the mistakes that their products' purchasers may make when deciding whether to buy their products or what price to pay for their products and/or about the external accident-and-pollution losses generated by the production and/or consumption of their product that would result in the officials' making regulatory decisions that were adverse to the sellers' interests, (3) oligopolistic interactions that result in their seller-perpetrators reducing equilibrium QV investment or equilibrium PPR in their ARDEPPS, (4) contrived-oligopolistic conduct in which potential investors in an area of product-space engage to induce each other to make investments that are less duplicative and on that account increase the profits the investors can make on a given total amount of investment, and (5) buyer-practiced oligopolistic pricing.

Each section of this chapter has three subsections. The first focuses on the economic efficiency of the conduct the section analyzes and the economic efficiency of the government's responding to such conduct and the prospect of its occurrence in various ways (that are not liberal-moral-rights-violative). The second subsection focuses on whether the conduct that the section analyzes is liberal-moral-rights-violative and on whether the government of a liberal-moral-rights-based society has a moral duty to allow the conduct, to prohibit and deter the conduct, to give victims of exemplars of the conduct that are liberal-moral-rights-violative an appropriate opportunity to obtain legal redress, and/or a moral duty to deter the conduct if it is not liberal-moral-rights-violative that derives from a more abstract moral duty to give appropriate, equal weight to each of its society's members' (or members' and participants') moral-good positions. The third subsection focuses on the impact of the conduct in question on the instantiation of the various morally-defensible conceptions of the moral good I distinguish and on whether it might be morally good from the perspective of one or more of these conceptions of the moral good for a government of a liberal-moral-rights-based society that has no moral duty to deter such conduct or a subset of such conduct to do so.

Before proceeding, some bad news and some good news. The bad news is that this chapter will be not only exhaustive but exhausting. The good news is that it will enable me to devote less space to analyzing the analogs to the issues that this chapter addresses that are salient in relation to the other categories of business conduct and antitrust policies with which Chaps. 10, 11, 12, 13, 14, 15, and 16 are concerned.

9.1 Seller-Practiced Natural-Oligopolistic and Seller-Practiced Contrived-Oligopolistic Pricing

I begin by delineating the acts that seller-practiced natural-oligopolistic pricing and seller-practiced contrived-oligopolistic pricing entail or involve. I focus first on the three types or sets of acts that a seller that is trying to obtain one or more NOMs will or may commit to put itself in a position to obtain NOMs or to practice natural-oligopolistic pricing. Temporally, the first such acts are otherwise-unprofitable acts the firm commits to put itself in a position to obtain NOMs naturally by increasing the profits it would have earned had it originally charged the price it would have to charge to beat any non-cooperative response of a rival to its initial NOM-containing offer and thereby to increase the probability that it would be inherently profitable for it to outbid any rival that beat its original NOM-containing offer. If I assume for simplicity that the relevant reduced price equals the natural-oligopolistic pricer's HNOP,[1] the relevant gross profits will equal the firm's OCA in individualized-pricing situations and will tend to increase with the gap between its HNOP and average MC for the sales the relevant price-reduction will enable it to obtain in across-the-board-pricing situations (though I acknowledge that the preceding claim ignores the relevance of the ratio of the unit sales the natural-oligopolistic pricer would have obtained at its initial, undermined NOM-containing price to the unit sales it will gain by lowering its initial undermined price and the magnitude of the price-reduction it would find most profitable to make if its initial NOM-containing price were undermined). In individualized-pricing situations, the extra costs the seller must incur to lower its initial price include the cost of investigating whether a buyer that has reported receiving a superior offer is telling the truth, the costs that improving its initial bid will impose on it because the relevant buyer(s) had lied to it when they claimed to have received a superior offer from one or more of its rivals and would have accepted the seller's initial offer had the natural-oligopolistic pricer stuck with it, the cost of calculating and communicating the second bid, the costs that improving its initial bid will impose on it by encouraging future buyers to demand concessions and perhaps to delay their purchases to extract concessions, and the goodwill costs that improving its initial bid to one or more buyers will impose on it by alienating buyers to whom it did not and/or will not make improved second offers. In across-the-board-pricing situations, the extra costs the natural-oligopolistic pricer must incur to lower its initial price include the cost of altering its advertizements to change the price-information they contain, the cost of changing the prices posted on store-shelves, stamped on product-packages, and entered into distributive-outlet computers, the cost of inducing future buyers to delay their purchases in future pricing-rounds in the hope of obtaining similar price-reductions, and the goodwill-loss costs of alienating buyers who paid the firm's initial price. The otherwise-unprofitable moves that a firm might make to enable itself to obtain OMs naturally by increasing its OCAs include

(1) shifting to a known production process whose use lowers the firm's MC curve while raising its average total cost,
(2) executing PPR that is designed to discover lower-MC-curve-associated production processes whose use will lower their relevant marginal costs but will raise ATC (if one counts the cost of the relevant PPR as part of the fixed cost of producing the product in question),
(3) substituting otherwise-less-profitable QV investments that are associated with higher OCAs for otherwise-more-profitable QV investments that are associated with lower OCAs to increase the NOMs it can secure,
(4) making otherwise-unprofitable QV investments or PPR investments that yield it high OCAs (that on this account put it in a position to sell non-production-process products, distributive services, or production processes on which it can obtain NOMs),
(5) engaging in predation to drive out a rival investment, prevent the creation of a rival investment, or induce a rival to change the product-space location of its extant or planned investment to one that was less competitive with the predator's project to increase the predator's OCAs and hence its NOMs,
(6) consummating otherwise-unprofitable horizontal mergers or acquisitions that eliminate as an independent entity a firm that reduced its OCAs and NOMs,
(7) consummating otherwise-unprofitable exemplars of any category of M or A to prevent a participant from making an investment that would lower its OCAs and NOMs,
(8) consummating otherwise-unprofitable vertical mergers or acquisitions or using contractual or sales-policy surrogates for vertical integration to increase its OCAs and NOMs, and
(9) participating in joint ventures that increase the firm's OCAs and NOMs because the joint-venture agreement explicitly prohibits the parents from entering the joint venture's ARDEPPSes, the joint venture from entering the parents' ARDEPPSes, and/or the parents from entering each other's ARDEPPSes and/or relies on the parent's partial ownership of the joint venture to deter them from making investments in the joint venture's ARDEPPSes.

The second set of otherwise-unprofitable acts that a firm could commit to put itself in a position to obtain OMs naturally do so by reducing the cost to the firm of changing its initial price or of determining whether it needs to change its initial price to retain the patronage of a buyer that has claimed that it has received a superior individualized offer from a worse-than-privately-best-placed potential supplier. These moves include executing

(1) otherwise-unprofitable mergers or acquisitions in individualized-pricing situations that increase the resulting firm's NOMs above those the participants could realize by creating a resulting firm that can take advantage of one participant's greater ability to determine whether a buyer in an individualized-pricing context is lying about the offers it has received,

(2) otherwise-unprofitable mergers, acquisitions, or decisions to grow internally that are participated in or made by firms that are setting across-the board-prices that create a resulting firm that will obtain higher NOMs than the participants would have obtained because the resulting firm can take better advantage of economies of scale in changing initially-announced prices in advertizements, on shelves, on packages, and in computers,
(3) otherwise-unprofitable mergers, acquisitions, or decisions to grow internally that are participated in or made by firms that are or a firm that is setting across-the-board-prices that increase the NOMs the perpetrator(s) obtain because the resulting firm is more prominent and on that account is more able than the (M or A)-participating individual firms or the smaller version of the internally-growing firm to organize its and its rivals' announcing and locking themselves into prices in a sequence that increases their HNOP array or making and implementing "premature" price-announcements that enable them to progressively lock themselves into natural-oligopolistic prices at times at which the private cost to them of reducing their initially-announced prices is lower, and
(4) various otherwise-unprofitable moves to induce rivals to make and implement "premature" price-announcements that enable the actors to obtain NOMs by reducing the private cost they must incur to change their initially-announced prices.

Temporally, the second act that a firm may commit in the course of practicing natural-oligopolistic pricing is one that it must commit to do so—charging a natural-oligopolistic price. Admittedly, it is not more private-transaction-costly or allocative-transaction-costly for a firm to set individualized natural-oligopolistic prices or an across-the-board natural-oligopolistic price than to set HNOPs.

Temporally, the third act or set of acts that a firm may commit in the course of practicing natural-oligopolistic pricing is the act or set of acts it may commit if the relevant buyer(s) reject the natural-oligopolistic pricer's initial offer—perhaps but necessarily because they have received a superior offer or claim to have a received a superior offer to the NOM-containing offer the natural-oligopolistic pricer initially made. As we shall see, one or more rivals of a natural-oligopolistic pricer may beat its initial offer(s) and try to persuade relevant buyer(s) to forego the opportunity to obtain yet-better offers from the natural-oligopolistic pricer to deter it and its future counterparts from charging the buyer(s) natural-oligopolistic prices in the future. If this happens, the natural-oligopolistic pricer will have to incur/generate private/allocative transaction costs in an individualized-pricing situation to determine whether the buyer(s) are misrepresenting the offers they received and to rebid and in across-the-board-pricing situations to calculate the price-change it wants to execute and to change the prices in its advertizing, on its store-shelves, and in its checkout-counter computers.

I focus next on the three types of acts or related sets of acts that a natural-oligopolistic pricer's (worse-than-privately-best-placed) rivals may commit in response to its charging a natural-oligopolistic price. First, any firm can choose to investigate whether a rival that has made an offer it could profitably beat if the rival would not react is in fact in a position to secure an OM naturally—whether the rival will be given a chance to rebid and will find it inherently profitable to beat any superior offer the firm makes. Second, if the firm determines that a seller has charged a natural-oligopolistic price, the firm could choose to report the natural-oligopolistic pricing to the public authorities (if such pricing is illegal or to persuade them to make it illegal) and/or to the relevant buyers (to damage the natural-oligopolistic pricer's goodwill). Third, if the rival determines that the natural-oligopolistic pricer is in a position to obtain an OM naturally, it could choose to beat the natural-oligopolistic pricer's initial offer nevertheless perhaps to build up goodwill but possibly by combining its own initially-superior offer with efforts to induce the buyer to accept that offer to deter the natural-oligopolistic pricer and its future potential counterparts from charging the buyer natural-oligopolistic prices in the future.

I focus finally on the three acts that a buyer can commit in response to its being charged a natural-oligopolistic price. First, the relevant buyer can investigate whether the price it is being charged is oligopolistic (contrived-oligopolistic or natural-oligopolistic)—conduct in which the buyer will engage only if it thinks it could respond profitably or desirably to its discovering that the price it was charged was oligopolistic. Second, the buyer could choose to respond to its discovery that it had been charged a natural-oligopolistic price by informing the public authorities of this fact, by informing the natural-oligopolistic pricer that it knew that the relevant seller's price was natural-oligopolistic and threatening the seller not to pay that price in the hope of eliciting a better offer from the natural-oligopolistic pricer, and/or by informing its worse-than-privately-best-placed suppliers that it knew it had been charged a natural-oligopolistic price and that it would accept an offer from them that was (sufficiently) superior. Third, a buyer that had been charged a natural-oligopolistic price could listen to and/or accept a superior offer it received from a worse-than-privately-best-placed supplier.

I turn now to the behaviors that may be or will be generated by seller-practiced contrived-oligopolistic pricing. I start with ten sets of behaviors in which one or more seller-initiators of contrived-oligopolistic pricing may or will engage.

The first such set of acts contains ten types of sometimes-inherently-profitable but in the relevant instances otherwise-unprofitable acts in which a firm may engage to increase the profits it can subsequently make by practicing contrived-oligopolistic pricing:

(1) shifting to a known, otherwise-less-profitable-to-use production process whose adoption lowers the firm's marginal-cost curve and thereby increases the profits it can realize by engaging in contrived-oligopolistic pricing by (A) increasing the equivalent-dollar benefits the "shifter" can confer on one or more potential cooperators by reciprocating to their cooperation by increasing the frequency and/or average amount by which the "shifter" is those potential cooperators' closest rival for the patronage of buyers the potential cooperator is best-placed to supply and (B) decreasing the dollar-losses the shifter must

suffer to inflict relevant dollar-losses on one or more non-cooperators by retaliating against their non-cooperation by increasing the frequency with which the shifter is privately-second-placed or given small amounts worse-than-privately-second-placed to supply buyers that potential non-cooperators are privately-best-placed to supply,

(2) executing otherwise-unprofitable PPR that is designed to discover a marginal-cost-curve-reducing production process whose adoption will increase the profits the shifter can realize by practicing contrived-oligopolistic pricing in the same ways that the conduct referenced in Item (1) can do so,

(3) substituting an otherwise-less-profitable QV investment for an otherwise-more-profitable QV investment when the substitution increases the profits the investor will make by practicing contrived-oligopolistic pricing by increasing the frequency with which and the average amount by which the investor is privately-second-placed to secure the patronage of one or more potential cooperator's customers and/or the frequency with which the investor is privately-second-placed or various relevant amounts worse-than-privately-second-placed to supply their customers,

(4) creating an otherwise-unprofitable QV investment that it will add to its existing stock of QV investments that is rendered profitable by its increasing the profits the investor can obtain by practicing contrived-oligopolistic pricing because the investment will increase the frequency and/or average amount by which the investor is privately-second-placed to supply buyers that one or more potential cooperators are privately-best-placed to supply or the frequency with which the investor is privately-second-placed or various relevant amounts worse-than-privately-second-placed to supply buyers that one or more potential non-cooperators are privately-best-placed to supply,

(5) engaging in otherwise-unprofitable predation that is rendered profitable by its increasing the profits the predator can obtain by practicing contrived-oligopolistic pricing because the target is an established rival or potential competitor that would not be disposed to cooperate with the predator's contrived-oligopolistic pricing or (to which)/(against which) the prospective contriver would not be well-placed to reciprocate/retaliate because the predation will reduce the number of rivals to which the prospective contriver must communicate its contrived-oligopolistic intentions and/or reduce the cost it must incur to identify its non-cooperator in individualized-pricing situations by reducing the number of potential non-cooperators, and/or because the elimination of the target will increase the frequency and average amount by which the predator is privately-second-placed to supply buyers that one or more potential cooperators are privately-best-placed to supply and the frequency with which the predator is privately-second-placed or relevant amounts worse-than-privately-second-placed to supply buyers one or more potential non-cooperators are privately-best-placed to supply,

(6) executing otherwise-unprofitable horizontal mergers and acquisitions that are rendered profitable by their increasing the resulting firm's ability to profit by practicing contrived-oligopolistic pricing (A) by eliminating a potential

non-cooperator—see Item (5) in this list, (B) creating a resulting firm that can take advantage of one of the participant's stronger reputation for engaging in strategic behavior and/or can take advantage of organizational economies of scale in building and maintaining a reputation for engaging in strategic conduct, (C) creating a resulting firm that, in an individualized-pricing situation, (i) can take advantage of economies of scale in using past and contemporary sales-information to infer that it had lost sales to a non-cooperator, (ii) has greater knowledge than one participant possesses of the facts other than non-cooperation by rivals that influence the relevant sales-percentages, (iii) is more able than at least one participant to execute relevant statistical analyses, (iv) can make use of the excess reciprocatory power one participant has in relation to particular cooperators and/or can take advantage of the fact that the participants are either respectively privately-second-placed and privately-third-placed or uniquely-privately-equal-second-placed to supply a cooperator's customers, and (v) can retaliate more-cost-effectively than the participants could taken together when acting separately by shifting the balance of its retaliation between its participants' operations, (D) creating a resulting firm that, in across-the-board-pricing situations, faces lower retaliation-public-good obstacles and is better-placed to orchestrate joint retaliation with those of its remaining rivals that would profit from joint retaliation, (E) generating static (marginal-cost-reducing) efficiencies that increase the benefits that the resulting firm can confer on cooperators by reciprocating to their cooperation by causing it to be privately-second-placed more often and by larger amounts to obtain the patronage of buyers that potential cooperators are privately-best-placed to supply and that decrease the losses the resulting firm must incur to inflict relevant amounts of losses on non-cooperators by retaliating against them by increasing the frequency with which it is privately-second-placed or relevant amounts worse-than-privately-second-placed to supply buyers that potential non-cooperators are privately-best-placed to supply, (F) generating dynamic efficiencies that cause the resulting firm to make an investment that neither participant would have made that will increase the frequency and average amount by which the resulting firm is the closest competitor of a cooperator or the frequency with which the resulting firm is privately-second-placed or relevant amounts worse-than-privately-second-placed to obtain the patronage of a non-cooperator's customers both when the resulting firm's additional investment does not deter a rival investment and a fortiori when it does,

(7) executing otherwise-unprofitable conglomerate mergers or acquisitions that are rendered profitable by their increasing the resulting firm's ability to profit by engaging in contrived-oligopolistic pricing (I will be more terse) (A) by eliminating an effective potential entrant, (B) by creating a resulting firm that has a stronger reputation for engaging in strategic behavior than does at least one of the participants and can take advantage of organizational economies of scale in building and maintain a reputation for engaging in strategic conduct, and (C) (i) when or particularly when the resulting conglomerate faces rivals that operate in both participants' ARDEPPSes can make relevant communications

more cheaply (because one communication covers the pricing of both participants), (ii) in individualized-pricing contexts, can infer non-cooperation from sales-evidence more-cost-effectively and can profit by practicing cross-ARDEPPS reciprocation and retaliation, and (iii) can take advantage of the relevant effects generated by the static or dynamic efficiencies the mergers or acquisitions yield,

(8) participating in otherwise-unprofitable vertical mergers or acquisitions that are rendered profitable by their increasing the profits their participants can realize by practicing contrived-oligopolistic pricing because the (M or A)s yield static or dynamic efficiencies that improve the ability of the resulting firm to reciprocate to cooperators and/or retaliate against non-cooperators and/or create a more prominent resulting company that has a stronger reputation for engaging in strategic behavior than does at least one participant, can take better advantage of organizational economies of scale in building and maintaining such a reputation, and is better-placed to orchestrate multifirm-initiated contrived-oligopolistic pricing,

(9) participating in otherwise-unprofitable joint ventures that are rendered profitable by their increasing the parents' ability to profit by practicing contrived-oligopolistic pricing on their own or as part-owners of the joint venture (A) by substituting one joint-venture investment for two parent-investments, (B) by increasing the extent to which the parents cooperate with each other (both when deciding to invest in each other's ARDEPPSes and when setting prices in those ARDEPPSes in which both parents are operating), and (C) by taking advantage of any relevant effects of the static and dynamic efficiencies the joint venture yields both for itself and for the parents, and

(10) making otherwise-unprofitable choices to grow internally when the investment in question would increase the firm's ability to profit by engaging in contrived-oligopolistic pricing in a host of ways previously referenced.

Second, a seller that wants to practice contrived-oligopolistic pricing must identify the rivals that would find it inherently profitable to beat its COM-containing offers and communicate to its potential undercutters or underminers its intention to retaliate against their non-cooperation and/or to reciprocate to their cooperation (typically, by allowing them to obtain prices from their customers contained in offers the initiator would find inherently profitable to beat). In most situations, the initiator will have to make these communications verbally (which will be both privately and allocatively transaction-costly and may provide evidence of legal transgressions). However, when the initiator's rivals are well-informed of its (HNOP + NOM) and the initiator has a reputation both for estimating its (HNOP + NOM) totals accurately and for engaging in contrived-oligopolistic pricing or strategic conduct more generally, the initiator may be able to make the necessary communications simply by setting a price that exceeds its (HNOP + NOM).

Third, when the contrived-oligopolistic pricer is setting individualized prices, it must calculate the sum of the dollar benefits it must confer on each individual cooperator and the dollar losses it must inflict on that rival should it not cooperate to deter that rival and other rivals from not cooperating in the future. That sum will depend on (1) the profits the relevant rival (would obtain)/obtained by not cooperating, (2) the number the rival would assign to the probability that the contriver would detect non-cooperation and would identify it as the non-cooperator, (3) the relevant rival's assumptions about the correlation between the contriver's reactions to its current cooperation/non-cooperation and the contriver's reactions to future acts of cooperation/non-cooperation, (4) the relevant rival's assumptions about the positions, dispositions, and likely assumptions of other rivals of the contriver, and (5) the relevant rival's risk-averseness. When the contrived-oligopolistic pricer is setting across-the-board prices, it must make a similar calculation, though in such pricing-contexts there will *usually* not be separate acts of reciprocation ("usually" because across-the-board contrivers could conceivably pay monetary bribes to cooperators or reward them by foregoing investment-opportunities).

Fourth, when the contrived-oligopolistic pricer is setting individualized prices, it must identify the firm(s) that forewent inherently-profitable opportunities to beat its offer(s) to customer(s) to which it made sales at contrived-oligopolistic prices, identify the buyers in relation to which it could reciprocate to the cooperating rival's cooperation (buyers that the cooperator is uniquely-privately-best-placed to supply and the contriver is uniquely-privately-second-placed to supply and buyers that the cooperator and contriver are uniquely-privately-equal-best-placed to supply), and either not bid for those buyers' patronage at all or charge them a higher price that loses their patronage when a lower price would have been inherently profitable.

Fifth, when the contrived-oligopolistic pricer and its rivals are setting individualized prices (which are usually secret), it must determine whether its rivals are not cooperating (are beating its offers from a position of competitive inferiority)—whether the fact that it has not made more sales to former customers, to established customers of rivals, or to new buyers in its ARDEPPS reflects non-cooperation as opposed to changes in the relevant buyers' (non-dollar) preferences, the exit/non-entrance of an unexpectedly-high number of established/new buyers, the creation of one or more new products in its ARDEPPS, and/or a macro-economic downturn: Occasionally, a seller will be able to make such determinations by soliciting information from its former customers, but usually it will have to do so by (A) collecting information about the percentage of its prior sales it retained historically, the percentage of sales to former customers of rivals it secured historically, the percentage of sales to new buyers in the ARDEPPS it made historically, the parameters other than rival non-cooperation that affected the above percentages historically, and the magnitudes of these percentages and parameters in the past and in the most-recent time-period and (B) by inferring that one or more rivals have been "stealing" buyers it was privately-best-placed to supply in the recent past from the fact that it made lower sales to these three sets of buyers than past-sales records and estimates of the magnitudes of the sales-determining parameters other than undercutting (undermining) pricing by competitive inferiors would imply it would make absent rival-undercutting from inferior competitive positions.

Sixth, when the contrived-oligopolistic pricer is setting individualized prices, it will have to identify its non-cooperators. Sometimes, it will be able to do so by asking relevant buyers but more often it will have to do so by identifying their suppliers by observing deliveries and inspecting the goods that the relevant buyers resold when they were retailers or the inputs they used when they were manufacturers and determining whether these buyers' preferences have changed or whether they have bought recently-introduced products that suit them better.

Seventh, particularly when the relevant contriver and its rivals are setting individualized prices, the contriver must determine the amount of benefits it can confer respectively on each of its cooperating rivals by reciprocating to their cooperation—([the number of unit sales it is uniquely-equal-best-placed as the relevant rival to make] *times* [the average amount by which in these instances those two firms are better-placed than are the relevant buyers' third-placed supplier]) *plus* ([the number of unit sales it is uniquely-second-placed to make to buyers the relevant rival is uniquely-best-placed to make] *times* [the average amount by which the prospective contriver is better-placed to make these sales than are these buyers' third-placed suppliers]). I think that contrivers will virtually always find it profitable to reciprocate to a rival's cooperation to the greatest extent possible because (1) such reciprocation is virtually costless, legal considerations aside—fool me once, shame on you, but fool me twice, shame on me, (2) such reciprocation generates lower law-related costs than retaliation generates (because reciprocation is harder to prove than retaliation), and (3) a contriver's reciprocation to a rival's cooperation will usually not suffice to render that cooperation profitable for the cooperator.

Eighth, the contriver must determine the amount of harm it must inflict on a non-cooperator by retaliating against its non-cooperator. Once more, I will assume that the contrivance is being practiced by a seller that is charging individualized prices. To determine the dollar-loss such a contriver will find most profitable to inflict on an identified non-cooperator by retaliating against it, such a contriver must calculate or estimate the profits the non-cooperator's non-cooperation would yield the non-cooperator if its non-cooperation would not induce the contriver to react, the loss the non-cooperator's conduct would cause the non-cooperator to sustain by causing the contriver not to allow the non-cooperator to obtain COMs from its own customers, the non-cooperator in question's and other prospective non-cooperators' estimates of the probability that its/their non-cooperation will be detected and that it/they will be identified as the non-cooperator, and the relevant non-cooperator's or non-cooperators' risk-averseness.

Ninth, the contriver must determine the set of retaliatory moves that will inflict the "requisite dollar-loss" on the non-cooperator most-cost-effectively. (The phrase "requisite dollar-loss" is misleading in that it ignores the facts that there are costs and benefits of overpunishing and underpunishing a non-cooperator by various amounts and that those costs and benefits are difficult to determine.) I will focus first on the protocol that on various simplifying assumptions[2] an individualized-pricing contriver that found it most profitable to retaliate exclusively by charging the non-cooperator's customers retaliatorily-low prices would have to use to determine the set of buyers to which it would offer retaliatory prices. On those simplifying assumptions, the contriver would proceed (1) by identifying the buyers the relevant non-cooperator (the target) was uniquely-best-placed to supply, (2) determining the target's OCAs in its relations with those buyers, (3) determining its (the contriver's) competitive positions in its relations with those buyers (whether it was their second-placed supplier or the amount by which it was worse-placed than their second-placed supplier when it was worse-than-second-placed to supply them), (4) determining for each buyer the non-cooperator was best-placed to supply the (dollar-loss-inflicted)-to-(dollar-loss-incurred) ratio for a retaliatory price-cut where (on the assumption that the contriver will obtain the non-cooperator's customer's patronage at the contriver's retaliatory price if the target charges that buyer a non-oligopolistic price and the contriver beats the target's offer by a penny) the dollar-loss inflicted equals the target's OCA in its relations with the buyer in question and the dollar-loss incurred equals one cent *plus* the amount by which the contriver was worse-than-second-placed to supply the buyer in question *plus* the other costs listed in footnote 2, (5) rank the non-cooperator's customers by the (dollar-loss-inflicted)-to-(dollar-loss-incurred) ratio that applies to each of them with the highest-ranked buyer being the buyer for which this ratio is highest, and (6) make retaliatory offers to the buyers in question, starting with the highest-ranked buyer until the total dollar-loss inflicted was requisitely high. Of course, even in individualized-pricing situations, the determination of the most-cost-effective retaliation strategy will be more complicated if, at some point before enough dollar-losses would be inflicted on the non-cooperator by price-retaliation, an exemplar of another form of retaliation (say, retaliatory advertizing) would be more-cost-effective. Across-the-board pricers will not find it easier to retaliate against one or more non-cooperators. If they retaliate by charging lower prices, they will have to respond cost-effectively to the reality that their price-cuts will apply not only to customers of the non-cooperators but across-the-board, to the possibility that cooperating rivals might misperceive their retaliation to be non-cooperation, and to the reality that coordinated price-retaliation will be more-cost-effective than individual, non-coordinated retaliatory price-responses by non-underminers. And, of course, in across-the-board-pricing situations, as in individualized-pricing situations, the identification of the most-cost-effective retaliatory response will be complicated by the possibility that it might include retaliatory advertizing as well as retaliatory pricing.

Tenth, both when the contrivance-initiator is setting individualized prices and when the contrivance-initiator(s) is (are) setting across-the-board prices, it or they may choose to retaliate against any defensive retaliation that a non-cooperating rival practices in response to the contriver's or contrivers' offensive retaliation against the non-cooperator's non-cooperation.

I turn next to the behavior that a firm's attempt to contrive an oligopolistic price may elicit from its rivals: (1) reporting or not reporting the contriver's contrivance-efforts to buyers (to cost the contriver goodwill) and to the authorities, (2) not beating (not undermining) the contriver's contrived-oligopolistic-price-containing individualized (across-the-board) price; (3) in individualized-pricing contexts, combining the conduct indicated after "(2)" in this list with charging higher prices to their own customers to take advantage of the contriver's offer to reciprocate to their cooperation; (4) beating the contriver's COM-containing individualized price or undermining the contriver's or contrivers' contrived across-the-board price(s), and (5) defensively retaliating against any retaliatory moves the contriver(s) made in reaction to the rival's non-cooperation (by placing retaliatory advertizements or charging the contriver's customers retaliatory [inherently-unprofitable] prices).

I address finally the behaviors in which a buyer that is being charged contrived-oligopolistic prices may engage: (1) choosing to purchase or not purchase various units of the contriver's product at the contriver's contrived-oligopolistic price and (2) if it recognizes or suspects that it is being charged a contrived-oligopolistic price, reporting this fact to public authorities and/or, if its society's legal regime gives it an opportunity to obtain legal redress, suing the contriver for the loss it sustained as a result of its having paid higher prices for the product-units of the contriver it purchased and for the buyer surplus it lost because the contriver's contrived-oligopolistic price deterred the buyer from purchasing one or more units of the contriver's product the buyer would otherwise have bought.

9.1.1 The Economic Efficiency of Seller-Practiced Natural-Oligopolistic and Contrived-Oligopolistic Pricing and the Economic Efficiency of a Government's Prohibiting Each of These Subtypes of Oligopolistic Pricing and Implementing That Prohibition in Various Ways

9.1.1.1 The Economic Efficiency of Seller-Practiced Natural-Oligopolistic and Contrived-Oligopolistic Pricing

This section's analysis will proceed on the following seven assumptions/ conclusions:

(1) relevant sellers' practice of contrived-oligopolistic pricing will not affect the extent to which they engage in any other type of contrivance or any type of individual or joint predation;
(2) the Pareto imperfections the relevant economy contains cause the allocative costs that are associated with any private transaction costs that are generated to exceed those private transaction costs;
(3) the Pareto imperfections the relevant economy contains cause it to allocate too many resources to QV-investment creation from the perspective of economic efficiency;
(4) the Pareto imperfections the relevant economy contains cause it to devote too few resources to PPR from the perspective of economic efficiency;

(5) choices that increase poverty and/or material inequality will tend to increase economic inefficiency on that account (because the incidences and magnitudes of some of the Pareto imperfections the relevant economy contains will vary with the society's income/wealth distribution);
(6) both natural-oligopolistic pricing and contrived-oligopolistic pricing virtually always increase poverty and material inequality because (A) both types of oligopolistic pricing tend to impose equivalent-dollar losses on the relevant ARDEPPS' buyers and to confer equivalent-dollar gains on the oligopolistic pricers (and in some instances on their rivals) and (B) the class of relevant buyers almost always[3] contains more poor or near-to-poor individuals/families than does the class of shareholders/creditors/managers/employees of the relevant pricers and as classes the relevant buyers will almost always be less-materially-well-off than the relevant pricers' shareholders/creditors/managers/employees, and
(7) the expenditures that firms make on political parties/campaigns/candidates and on government-decisionmaking-process participation tend to decrease economic efficiency (and increase poverty and material inequality).

The Economic Efficiency of Seller-Practiced Natural-Oligopolistic Pricing

Natural-oligopolistic pricing can affect economic efficiency in at least eight ways. First, the prospect of practicing natural-oligopolistic pricing tends to increase economic inefficiency by inducing firms that would like to obtain NOMs to make otherwise-unprofitable decisions of various types to enable themselves to obtain OMs naturally. The introduction to Sect. 9.1 listed the relevant types of decisions. Although some exemplars of most of these types of decisions could be profitable even if they did not allow their perpetrator(s) to obtain OMs naturally, the fact that the exemplars on which I am now focusing are otherwise-unprofitable favors the conclusion that they are economically inefficient. Some of the types of decisions that firms make to put themselves into a position to obtain OMs naturally are also economically inefficient because they would be economically inefficient even if they were otherwise-profitable and did not increase the incidence of natural-oligopolistic pricing. For example, as Chap. 10 will explain, decisions to practice predation fall into this category.

Second, natural-oligopolistic pricing can increase/decrease economic efficiency by lowering/raising the private transaction costs that sellers incur when making bids to potential customers and hence the (higher) allocative transaction costs they generate when doing so. Thus, in the one direction, if in individualized-pricing situations the awareness of sellers that are worse-than-privately-best-placed to supply a buyer that its privately-best-placed supplier is in a position to secure an OM naturally deters one or more worse-than-privately-best-placed suppliers from bidding, it might be appropriate to credit the practice of natural-oligopolistic pricing with the associated allocative-transaction-cost saving. But, in the other direction, if in an individualized-pricing situation a worse-than-privately-best-placed seller responds to the privately-best-placed seller's NOM-containing offer by beating that offer and trying to persuade the buyer to accept it (to forego the opportunity to secure a yet-better offer from its privately-best-placed potential supplier) and a fortiori if the relevant buyer decides to let its privately-best-placed potential supplier rebid, the natural-oligopolistic pricing will decrease economic efficiency by increasing the allocative transaction costs that relevant sellers generate when bidding for buyers' patronage and trying to persuade them to accept offers. Natural-oligopolistic pricing will also increase allocative transaction costs in across-the-board-pricing contexts if one or more non-initiators undermine an initiator's natural-oligopolistic price and the initiator reacts by rebidding (which will happen only if the rival can obtain a goodwill advantage from doing so or hopes to persuade the buyer to accept its offer to deter suppliers from charging the buyer NOPs). Natural-oligopolistic pricing will also generate extra private and allocative transaction costs if a rival of a natural-oligopolistic pricer or (more likely) a buyer that realizes it is being charged a natural-oligopolistic price complains to its natural-oligopolistic-pricing supplier or reports this fact to the authorities, perhaps in the hope of securing the practice's prohibition (I am assuming for the moment that the practice is not illegal).

Third, if natural-oligopolistic pricing leads to a rival of the natural-oligopolistic pricer's making a sale to a buyer in relation to which it is operating with an OCD because it underbids the natural-oligopolistic pricer and convinces the buyer to accept its lower offer, the natural-oligopolistic pricing will on this account tend to cause intra-ARDEPPS UO-to-UO misallocation if (as I believe) sellers that are worse-than-privately-best-placed tend to be worse-than-allocatively-best-placed as well.

Fourth, if the product for which a natural-oligopolistic price is being charged is a product created by a QV investment, natural-oligopolistic pricing will tend to decrease economic efficiency by raising the relevant ARDEPPS' $H\Pi_E$ and $H\Pi_N$ curves and hence its equilibrium QV investment.

Fifth, if the product for which the natural-oligopolistic price is being charged is a production process or the right to use a production process for which the natural-oligopolistic pricer has IP rights, natural-oligopolistic pricing will tend to increase economic efficiency by raising the relevant ARDEPPS' $H\Pi_E$ and $H\Pi_N$ curves and hence its equilibrium PPR.

Sixth, if I am correct in assuming that natural-oligopolistic pricing will increase poverty and material inequality, it will tend to increase economic inefficiency on this account.

Seventh, whether natural-oligopolistic pricing increases/decreases economic efficiency by increasing/decreasing the expenditures the sellers in the ARDEPPS of practice make on political parties/campaigns/candidates and government-decisionmaking-process participation depends on whether it increases or decreases the concentration of the seller-side of the ARDEPPS of practice (on whether the additional investment it causes to be made in the ARDEPPS of practice is made by firms with "higher-than-average" shares of the relevant ARDEPPS' sales or by new entrants or established firms with lower-than-average shares of the relevant

ARDEPPS' sales): Although I have my suspicions, they are not sufficiently-well-grounded for me to want to speculate on this issue.

Eighth, to the extent that the sloppiness with which firms operate and the overall compensation they pay their managers and employees increase with the super-normal rate-of-return they could realize on their investment if they operated as proficiently as possible and did not pay their managers and employees more than they would otherwise pay them, natural-oligopolistic pricing will—by increasing its practitioner's "potential supernormal profit-rate"—cause economic inefficiency by resulting in the practitioner's generating higher allocative costs than it would otherwise generate to perform its operations and (to the extent that the natural-oligopolistic pricer passes on some of its related potential profits to its managers and employees) by inducing its managers and employees to make additional economically-inefficient substitutions of untaxed or lower-taxed working-conditions and fringe-benefits for the goods they would have purchased with the money they could have been paid had they chosen not to obtain more attractive, untaxed working-conditions and lower-taxed fringe-benefits by increasing the marginal tax-rate levied on their taxable earnings.[4]

Before proceeding to seller-practiced contrived-oligopolistic pricing, I want to indicate my belief about the overall economic efficiency of seller-practiced natural-oligopolistic pricing. I believe that even when the good that is being priced is a production process or the right to use a production process and the practice of natural-oligopolistic pricing does not increase allocative transaction costs (because no rivals of the firm that is trying to secure an NOM beats its offer and tries to persuade the relevant buyer not to accept any underbid the natural-oligopolistic pricer makes in reaction to the rival's initially-superior offer) and the practice of natural-oligopolistic pricing does not lead to intra-ARDEPPS UO-to-UO misallocation by leading to a natural-oligopolistic-pricer rival's making a sale, natural-oligopolistic pricing will decrease economic efficiency. The remainder of Sect. 9.1 proceeds on the assumption that natural-oligopolistic pricing is economically inefficient.

The Economic Efficiency of Seller-Practiced Contrived-Oligopolistic Pricing

Seller-practiced contrived-oligopolistic pricing can affect economic efficiency in each of the eight ways in which seller-practiced natural-oligopolistic pricing can do so. However, it is important to note three economic-efficiency-related differences between seller-practiced contrived-oligopolistic and natural-oligopolistic pricing. Two of these differences favor the conclusion that seller-practiced contrived-oligopolistic pricing is more economically inefficient than is seller-practiced natural-oligopolistic pricing, and one favors the conclusion that seller-practiced contrived-oligopolistic pricing is less economically inefficient than is seller-practiced natural-oligopolistic pricing.

First, even when seller-practiced contrived-oligopolistic pricing does not involve acts of offensive and defensive retaliation, it is likely to be far more privately and allocatively transaction-costly than seller-practiced natural-oligopolistic pricing. As the introduction to Sect. 9.1 indicated, a seller that is charging individualized prices will have to execute a lot of transaction-costly tasks to do so even if it is not undercut by a privately-worse-placed rival (even if it does not have to engage in offensive retaliation against non-cooperators). Admittedly, because across-the board prices are usually public, seller-contrivance of across-the-board prices may be less transaction-costly if it does not involve retaliation (though across-the-board-price contrivance may involve allocative-transaction-costly discussions of the prices that different participants may charge).

Second, seller-practiced contrived-oligopolistic pricing is likely to be more economically inefficient than seller-practiced natural-oligopolistic pricing because it does sometimes result in offensive retaliation against non-cooperation and defensive retaliation against offensive retaliation and both offensive and defensive retaliation are allocative-transaction-costly and prone to generate intra-ARDEPPS UO-to-UO misallocation (to the extent that the retaliator ends up making the sale despite the fact that it is not only privately but also allocatively worse-placed to supply the buyer[s] in question).

Third, I suspect that the prospect of being able to profit by contriving COMs is less likely to induce sellers to make otherwise-unprofitable, economically-inefficient decisions to increase the profits they can realize by practicing contrived-oligopolistic pricing than the prospect of obtaining NOMs is to induce sellers to make otherwise-unprofitable, economically-inefficient moves to enable themselves to obtain OMs naturally. I base this conclusion on the fact that the otherwise-unprofitable decisions a seller could make to increase its ability in various ways to profit by engaging in subsequent contrived-oligopolistic pricing will simultaneously decrease the ex ante profitability of its practicing contrived-oligopolistic pricing in the future by increasing the OCAs it enjoys in its relations with and the NOMs it can obtain from buyers it is privately-best-placed to supply and hence the safe profits it must put at risk to try to secure any COM.

Everything considered, in my judgment, seller-practiced contrived-oligopolistic pricing is economically inefficient even when the good whose price is being contrived is a production process or the right to use a production process—indeed, is more economically inefficient than seller-practiced natural-oligopolistic pricing.

The preceding analyses focus on the economic efficiency of the conduct of all the parties that play a role respectively in natural-oligopolistic and contrived-oligopolistic pricing. Because any firm that initiates natural-oligopolistic or contrived-oligopolistic pricing is a cause-in-fact of the responses that its rivals and relevant buyers make to its conduct, it seems appropriate to attribute to such oligopolistic-pricing initiators the economic-efficiency effects of all such actors' associated conduct. However, it may be of interest to analyze (and speculate on the net) economic-efficiency effects of the various possible decisions that the rivals of the initiator and the buyers in the ARDEPPS of practice make in response to the initiator's conduct.

I focus first on the initiator's rivals. Although I acknowledge the contestability of this conclusion, I am inclined to conclude that it would be economically efficient for a rival of a natural-oligopolistic pricer to report the initiator's oligopolistic pricing to the authorities, to sue oligopolistic pricers if the legal system in question gives them the right to obtain legal redress, to undercut/undermine the initiator's individualized/across-the-board NOP, to try to persuade the relevant buyer(s) to accept its initially-superior offer (even though any such conduct is allocative-transaction-costly and will generate intra-ARDEPPS UO-to-UO misallocation if it is successful), to undercut/undermine the initiators' across-the-board COPs, and to retaliate defensively against a contrived-oligopolistic pricer's offensive retaliation against its non-cooperation (once more, even though such conduct is allocative-transaction-costly and will generate intra-ARDEPPS UO-to-UO misallocation if it leads to the defensive retaliator's making one or more sales). Obviously, my conclusions that several of the categories of rival-behaviors that oligopolistic pricing can elicit are economically efficient are based on my belief that such rival-responses will tend to deter natural-oligopolistic or contrived-oligopolistic pricing, which I believe are always or almost always misallocative.

The same considerations that led me to conclude that it is allocatively efficient for the *rivals* of oligopolistic pricers to report contrived and natural-oligopolistic pricing to the authorities, to sue oligopolistic pricers, to undercut/undermine COPs and NOPs, and to defensively retaliate against contrivers' offensive retaliation lead me to conclude that it would be economically efficient for the actual and potential *customers* of contrived-oligopolistic pricers to report their suppliers' natural-oligopolistic and contrived-oligopolistic pricing to the authorities (despite the allocative transaction cost of doing so), to refuse to pay natural-oligopolistic prices and contrived-oligopolistic prices (e.g., to accept an inferior supplier's undercutting/undermining response to an individualized/across-the-board natural or contrived-oligopolistic price) despite the fact that the purchase would generate intra-ARDEPPS UO-to-UO misallocation, and to sue oligopolistic pricers if the legal system entitles them to obtain legal redress.

9.1.1.2 The Economic Efficiency of a Government's Prohibiting Seller-Practiced Contrived-Oligopolistic and Natural-Oligopolistic Pricing and Implementing Such a Prohibition in Various Ways That Are Not Liberal-Moral-Rights-Violative

Section 9.1.1.1 established the economic inefficiency of both seller-practiced contrived-oligopolistic pricing and seller-practiced natural-oligopolistic pricing. If the mere prohibition of these types of pricing (unaccompanied my any effort to implement it) would deter such pricing and would not deter sellers from charging their HNOPs because doing so would create a risk that they might be mistakenly perceived to have violated the prohibition, Sect. 9.1.1.1's economic-efficiency conclusions would imply the economic efficiency of a government's promulgating such a prohibition. Obviously, the more salient and contestable issues are: What would be the most-economically-efficient way for a government that was constrained by its society's liberal-justice commitment to implement a prohibition of seller-practiced contrived and natural-oligopolistic pricing and would such a government's efforts to implement such prohibitions as economic efficiently as they could be implemented increase economic efficiency? I will analyze these issues on the assumption that the liberal conception of justice implies that (1) to win a civil suit against a seller alleged to have engaged in (prohibited) oligopolistic pricing, the government or a private plaintiff must prove that more probably than not the defendant engaged in the practice, (2) to win a criminal case against a seller accused of having engaged in (prohibited) oligopolistic pricing, the government must establish the defendant's guilt "beyond a reasonable doubt,"[5] (3) government may not secure evidence in a variety of liberal-moral-rights-violative ways (e.g., by coercing confessions), and (4) government may not impose ex post burdens or "costs" on convicted wrongdoers that exceed the wrongfulness of the wrongdoer's conduct (that in this sense "the total sanctions imposed on an individual found to have violated a prohibition of oligopolistic pricing must fit the seriousness of the [criminal offense/civil wrong])." By definition, the implementation-approach that does not violate these liberal-moral-rights-related constraints that will be most economically efficient will be the liberal-justice-permissible approach that maximizes the positive difference between the allocative benefits and allocative costs generated by the implementation of the prohibition of seller-practiced contrived-oligopolistic and natural-oligopolistic pricing.

I will begin by discussing the probativeness of the various types of evidence that academics and judges claim can be used to prove oligopolistic pricing as well as the probativeness of various other types of evidence I think can be used to establish the requisite probability that sellers accused of practicing oligopolistic pricing actually engaged in the practice. This discussion is relevant to the allocative cost of investigating and proving seller-practiced oligopolistic pricing because many of the types of evidence that academics have proposed using and judges have actually used to determine whether a seller has practiced oligopolistic pricing are less probative than those experts/officials claim and, in some instances, are far more allocative-costly to use than they claim. Although I think that some types of evidence that these scholars and officials have ignored can be used to prove seller oligopolistic pricing, I fear that in most cases it will be extremely difficult and allocative-costly to prove that a seller has engaged in oligopolistic pricing even if, as I am now assuming, the law prohibits both seller-practiced natural-oligopolistic pricing and seller-practiced contrived-oligopolistic pricing.[6]

I start by listing and explaining briefly why the various types of evidence that scholars have claimed can be used cost-effectively to prove seller-practiced oligopolistic pricing and/or that judges have claimed can establish that a defendant has engaged in oligopolistic pricing are not so probative and (in some instances) not so allocatively-inexpensive to collect and use as these experts and officials believe.[7] I begin with evidence-proposals or evidence-use practices that must be rejected because they ignore the related facts that (1) sellers that are not pure monopolists can obtain supra-competitive prices without engaging in oligopolistic pricing, (2) the (HNOP–MC) differences for an individualized-pricing seller in its relations with those buyers it is privately-best-placed to supply vary at any given time among the buyers it is privately-best-placed to supply at that time, and (3) a seller's across-the-board HNOP will vary through time. The proposals in this set include proposals to infer a seller's or a set of rival-sellers' practice of oligopolistic pricing from the fact that (1) the seller engaged in inter-buyer price discrimination (which is far more likely to manifest inter-buyer differences in the seller's BPAs and hence OCAs and HNOPs than inter-buyer differences in the seller's OMs), (2) the seller(s) raised its (their) prices by more than can be accounted for by contemporaneous increases in its (their) marginal costs (a fact that is far too likely to be attributable to the seller's or sellers' BPAs increasing through time [say, because of a rival's exit or the seller's improving its product] for such evidence to have much probative value), (3) the seller(s) failed to reduce its (their) prices in response to a decline in (A) the demand curve(s) for its (their) product(s) or its (their) rate(s) of capacity-utilization (facts whose probative value is undercut by the reality that many of the referenced decreases in demand are concentrated in the lower-price-range part of the relevant demand curves—i.e., are associated with much larger decreases in the seller's or sellers' smaller BPAs and OCAs than in its or their larger BPAs and OCAs), (4) price-changes' in the seller's ARDEPPS' (in my terminology) being smaller than the weighted-average price-changes in the economy as a whole (a proposal that is likely to be prohibitively-allocative-costly to implement and in any event ignores the fact that many of the causes of ARDEPPS price-changes [changes in marginal cost, changes in BPAs generated by exits and entries, changes in demand for the ARDEPPS' products]) vary substantially from ARDEPPS to ARDEPPS—that changes in ARDEPPSes' OMs account for a small percentage of changes in their prices), (5) prices have changed relatively infrequently in the accused seller's or sellers' ARDEPPS (a proposal that fails for the same or analogous reasons to those that undermine its immediate predecessor), (6) the shares of sales made by the ARDEPPS' individualized sellers have remained unusually constant over a substantial period of time (a fact that is more likely to be attributable to the homogeneity of the ARDEPPS' products and the constancy of its equilibrium QV-investment quantity than to its members' practicing [contrived] oligopolistic pricing), (7) the ARDEPPS' sellers' prices have moved together through time (which is more likely to reflect their experiencing similar changes in their marginal costs or similar changes in their arrays of BPAs because of rival exits and QV investments than to their having made similar or identical changes in their OMs), and (8) each member's of a set of rivals that produce homogeneous products for similar or equal marginal production costs charging a lower price to one or more buyers and higher prices to all other buyers when each relevant buyer gets the lowest price it is offered from only one seller (the claim is that this pattern manifests a horizontal customer-allocation scheme [which might be said to obviate or in fact to manifest contrived-oligopolistic pricing] is undercut by the facts that [1] delivery costs constitute a high percentage [say 30%] of the marginal costs of the delivered product [say, one-pound loaves of sliced white bread], [2] the buyers [say school districts] value [insist on] early delivery of the relevant product, [3] each seller can satisfy that buyer-preference without incurring substantial extra delivery costs when supplying the schools in the district in which its bakery is located but would have to incur twice the delivery costs to put on an extra truck to effectuate the timely delivery of the product to schools in other school districts, and [4] each bakery happens to be located in a different school-district). (In the early 1970s, I consulted in a case that involved precisely this fact-pattern.)

The second set of evidence-proposals for proving oligopolistic pricing contains two that fail because they would be prohibitively-allocative-costly to implement and because the probativeness of the evidence whose use they recommend is undercut both by the fact that increases in the OMs obtained in an ARDEPPS will increase its equilibrium investment-quantity (i.e., will lead to established-firm investment-expansions or new entries) and by the fact that the amount by which an ARDEPPS' equilibrium investment-quantity falls below its actual, competitive investment-quantity is largely attributable to factors that are different from and not positively correlated with the size of the OMs its sellers obtain (by the determinants of its [HNOP–MC] gaps at various relevant ARDEPPS-investment quantities and by the barriers to entry, barriers to expansion, and monopolistic investment-incentives or monopolistic or natural-oligopolistic investment-disincentives that relevant potential investors face). The first evidence-proposal that must be rejected for these reasons is that courts infer that sellers have engaged in oligopolistic pricing from the sellers' persistent realization of (presumably) unusually-large amounts of supernormal profits. I assume that this proposal's proponents are actually urging courts to draw the relevant inference from the sellers' in a relevant ARDEPPS (I ignore the difficulty of delineating a relevant set of sellers—the inevitable arbitrariness of market definitions) realizing unusually-high supernormal profit-rates (though even this specification is inadequate in that it does not indicate whether the relevant referent is the highest supernormal-profit-rate generated by any investment in the relevant ARDEPPS or the weighted-average supernormal-profit-rate generated by all investments in the relevant ARDEPPS). Specification-deficiencies aside, this proposal must be rejected for two reasons. To begin with, it would be extremely allocative-costly to implement: It is allocative-costly to determine the supernormal profit-rate a QV investment or an investment in PPR generates because it is allocative-costly to estimate acceptably accurately the dollar-magnitude of any such investment and this proposal requires the estimation of the supernormal profit-rates generated either by the most-supernormally profitable or all investments in the defendants' ARDEPPS. (If the proposal is that triers-of-fact infer sellers' practice of oligopolistic pricing from evidence that the supernormal profit-rate generated by the most-supernormally-profitable investments or all investments in their ARDEPPS is higher than its weighted-average economy-wide counterpart, the implementation of this proposal will be even more allocative-costly because it will require estimates to be made of the supernormal profit-rate yielded by the most-supernormally-profitable or all investments in a TBLE-large, random sample of the economy's ARDEPPSes.) In addition and more interestingly from the perspective of this study's economic analysis, the inference this proposal instructs triers-of-fact to draw would be unjustified even if accurate estimates of the relevant supernormal profit-rates could be made at low allocative cost. Admittedly, increases in the OMs secured in an ARDEPPS will tend to cause the highest supernormal-profit-rate generated by any investment located in it to rise by raising the ARDEPPS' $H\Pi_E$ and $H\Pi_N$ curves, hence its equilibrium investment-quantity, and hence the barriers to entry and expansion that are operative at that investment-quantity. However, inter-ARDEPPS variations in the OMs that sellers obtain when using their individual investments in an ARDEPPS (even relative to the dollar cost of those individual investments) account for too low a percentage of variations in the supernormal profit-rates generated by the respective ARDEPPSes' highest supernormal profit-rates for it to be justifiable to infer oligopolistic pricing from the highest-supernormal-profit-rates generated by any investment in the ARDEPPS: More specifically, the supernormal profit-rates generated by the most-supernormally-profitable investments in any ARDEPPS depend far more on (1) the ratio of (the total [HNOP–MC] gaps for all units sold of the individual products created by or of all sales of the right to use production processes discovered by the individual investments in an ARDEPPS) to (the dollar cost of those individual investments), (2) the rate at which the sum of the barriers to expansion and monopolistic investment-incentives or monopolistic or natural-oligopolistic investment-disincentives that would face the individual established firms that would be privately-best-placed to increase the ARDEPPS' investment-quantity at various pre-existing investment-quantities rises as the pre-existing ARDEPPS-investment-quantity rises, and (3) the rate at which the sum of the barriers to entry facing the (often different) potential competitors that would be privately-best-placed to enter the ARDEPPS in question at various pre-existing ARDEPPS-investment-quantities rise as the pre-existing ARDEPPS-investment-quantity rises. I should add that the variant of this proposal that instructs triers-of-fact to infer a group of sellers' practice of oligopolistic pricing from their realization of a high weighted-average supernormal-profit-rate on all their investments in an ARDEPPS would in any event be unsound because, even if the magnitude of the sellers' OMs were not only a significant but a strong predictor of the highest supernormal-profit-rates generated by any investment in an ARDEPPS, it would not be a good predictor of the average supernormal-profit-rate generated by all investments in the relevant ARDEPPS, given that increases in the OMs that would be secured (or in the HNOP–MC] gaps that would be generated) in an ARDEPPS at relevant ARDEPPS-investment quantities will, by increasing the ARDEPPS' equilibrium-investment quantity, tend to cause decreases in the percentage of the ARDEPPS' investments that are most-supernormally-profitable and may on that account tend to cause decreases in the weighted-average supernormal-profit-rate yielded by all investments in an ARDEPPS even if they raise the supernormal-profit-rate generated by the ARDEPPS' most-supernormally-profitable investments.

The second evidence-proposal that must be rejected because the argument for it ignores the facts that (1) increases in an ARDEPPS' OMs will lead to increases in its equilibrium-investment quantity and (2) many factors other than the magnitudes of the OMs an ARDEPPS' sellers secure affect the difference between its actual, competitive investment-quantity and its equilibrium investment-quantity is the proposal that sellers be found to have practiced oligopolistic pricing if they have possessed substantial "excess capacity" for a prolonged period of time. The same two types of objections can be made against this evidence-proposal as were made against its immediate predecessor. The first is that, even if the inference this proposal urges decisionmakers to draw were justified, this proposal would almost certainly be prohibitively-allocative-costly to implement (1) because it is allocative-costly to determine the capacity of an ARDEPPS whose sellers produce goods and/or services as opposed to production processes (whether and when it would be profitable or economically efficient for the owner of moth-balled capacity to bring it on line) and (2) because—when speed of supply is allocatively valuable and quantity-demand for a good or service defined independent of the speed with which it is supplied varies through time (think of personal protective equipment and ICU facilities [including ventilators] or, less dramatically, of restaurant meals)—it is difficult to determine the average rate-of-capacity-utilization through time that is economically inefficient (the capacity quantity that is "excess"). The second objection to this proposal is to the inference it urges decisionmakers to draw: Although when practiced in ARDEPPSes whose investments are QV investments seller-practiced oligopolistic pricing will tend to increase the ARDEPPS' capacity (equilibrium QV investment) and reduce the average rate of capacity-utilization in that ARDEPPS to an even greater extent (since it will also tend to reduce the ARDEPPS' unit sales), inter-ARDEPPS variations in seller-OMs would account for too low a percentage of inter-ARDEPPS variations in the extent of "excess capacity" (even if the allocative value of increasing the average speed of supply could be ignored) to make the proposed inference justified: Once more, this second conclusion reflects the fact that inter-ARDEPPS differences in (individualized-product total [HNOP–MC] gaps) to (individual-QV-investment cost) ratios and of inter-ARDEPPS differences in the magnitudes of the determinants of an ARDEPPS' "intensity of QV-investment competition" as I have defined that concept that are not attributable to inter-ARDEPPS differences in individual-product OMs and are not highly-positively-correlated with the determinants of such OMs almost certainly account for far more of inter-ARDEPPS differences in the excessiveness of capacity than do inter-ARDEPPS differences in individual-product OMs.

The third set of evidence-proposals that some believe are acceptably accurate and allocative-cost-effective are proposals that have been adopted by U.S. courts (though they consider many of these types of evidence to be "plus factors" that favor a finding that the defendants [whose prices have varied together?] have engaged in oligopolistic pricing as opposed to being decisive on their own). These proposals must be rejected for a variety of reasons. Thus, the fact that the defendant in an oligopolistic-pricing suit has been convicted for practicing oligopolistic pricing in the past is much less probative than at least some courts seem to believe: True, this history may favor a finding of guilt by implying that oligopolistic pricing was feasible and profitable for the defendant in the past but (1) many offenders do not repeat their offenses, and (2) a past conviction may reduce the profitability of oligopolistic pricing for the defendant by increasing the likelihood that enforcement-authorities and relevant buyers will scrutinize the convicted offender's subsequent conduct for illegality and by increasing the likelihood that triers-of-fact who know about the preceding conviction will be inclined on that account to find the convicted offender guilty in subsequent trials. Courts also appear to give undue weight to the evidence on market-structure factors that they think favor the feasibility and profitability of oligopolistic pricing. In part, the allocative efficiency of drawing inferences from evidence on market-structure factors is undermined by the inevitable arbitrariness of market definitions; in part, it is undermined by the fact that firms do not engage in illegal conduct in the majority or vast majority of cases in which it would be profitable for them to do so; and, in part, it is undermined by the courts' and antitrust-law-enforcement-authorities' misunderstanding of the relationship between the "structural" factors on which these judicial practices focus —product homogeneity, the number of sellers in the "market" the judges have defined, the concentration of the seller-side of the markets they have defined, the height of the barriers to entry into those markets, and the frequency of entry into those markets—and the profitability of seller-practiced oligopolistic pricing. (U.S. antitrust courts and [with one possible exception, the statement in Section 7 ¶ 2 of the 2010 U.S. DOJ/FTC Horizontal Merger Guidelines] U.S. antitrust-law-enforcement authorities do not recognize natural-oligopolistic pricing as a separate phenomenon and therefore have not addressed the relationship between the "structural" factors they deem relevant and the feasibility of natural-oligopolistic pricing.)

I will proceed one by one to consider the U.S. courts' and antitrust-law-enforcement authorities' positions on the relevance of the "structural" factors they claim it is appropriate to take into account when determining whether a defendant has engaged in oligopolistic pricing. I start with product homogeneity. The U.S. courts and antitrust-law-enforcement authorities believe that product homogeneity favors the profitability of oligopolistic pricing. Here is what I think: If product homogeneity includes locational homogeneity,

(1) product homogeneity disfavors the feasibility of natural-oligopolistic pricing by reducing the relevant sellers' OCAs,
(2) as U.S. courts and U.S. (and E.U.) antitrust-law-enforcement authorities emphasize, product homogeneity favors the profitability of contrived-oligopolistic pricing by simplifying the associated price-fix (if product heterogeneity is associated with greater inter-product differences in marginal costs and quality, the fixing of the prices of heterogeneous products will be more complicated because different cartel-members will have to be allowed to charge different prices),
(3) product homogeneity favors the profitability of contrived-oligopolistic pricing by reducing OCAs and therefore NOMs and hence the safe profits a seller must put at risk to try to obtain COMs,
(4) product homogeneity disfavors the profitability of contrived-oligopolistic pricing, given the number of independent sellers in the relevant ARDEPPS, by increasing the percentage of such sellers that are well-placed to obtain the patronage of each buyer (to which necessary communications must be made and that might be the actual non-cooperator [a consideration that is relevant in an individualized-pricing context, in which prices are typically secret]),

(5) product homogeneity disfavors the profitability of contrived-oligopolistic pricing by reducing the rewards a contriver can give a cooperator by abstaining from beating the cooperator's COM-containing price by reducing the amount by which a contriver that wants to reciprocate to cooperation is privately-better-placed than the privately-third-place supplier of buyers the reciprocation-beneficiary is privately-best-placed to supply and the reciprocator is privately-second-placed to supply and of buyers the reciprocation-beneficiary and the reciprocator are uniquely-privately-equal-best-placed to supply,
(6) product homogeneity probably disfavors the profitability of contrived-oligopolistic pricing by lowering the harm-inflicted to loss-incurred ratio for inflicting given relevant amounts of harm on a non-cooperator by engaging in price-retaliation (by lowering the non-cooperator's OCAs in its relations with buyers it is privately-best-placed to supply and the prospective retaliator is privately-second-placed or close-to-privately-second-placed to supply), though this effect will be offset by product homogeneity's tendency to lower the amount by which the undercut contriver is worse-than-privately-second-placed to supply those of its non-cooperator's customers to which the contriver wants to charge retaliatory prices, and
(7) product homogeneity makes across-the-board price-retaliation less-cost-effective by precluding across-the-board-price retaliation from imposing more costs on non-cooperators than on cooperators (given their respective sales) and by precluding a retaliator from obtaining a percentage of the benefits that its retaliation confers on the contrivers that exceeds its share of the ARDEPPS' sales.

Although I do not know whether, all tolled, product homogeneity favors or disfavors the profitability of oligopolistic pricing, I do know that the academic and antitrust-enforcement-authority view that it favors the profitability of such pricing is not well-grounded.

U.S. courts and antitrust-law-enforcement authorities believe that the profitability of seller-practiced oligopolistic pricing is inversely related to the number of sellers in the "market" they have defined. If I ignore ad arguendo the inevitable arbitrariness of any relevant-market definition, this belief could be correct for natural-oligopolistic pricing to the extent that, ceteris paribus, the magnitude of each seller's BPAs and hence OCAs in its relations with those buyers it is privately-best-placed to supply will be inversely related to the number of sellers in the ARDEPPS in question (though of course, the relevant ceteris [e.g., the degree of product homogeneity] will not always be paribus). For two reasons, the belief that the profitability of contrived-oligopolistic pricing is inversely related to the number of sellers in the defined market is also less-well-founded than its subscribers believe: (1) to the extent that privately-best-placed sellers' OCAs are inversely related to the number of sellers in their market, it is not clear that the magnitude of a seller's OCAs is directly related to the profitability of its engaging in contrived-oligopolistic pricing, and (2) the relevant belief fails to take account of the fact that the percentage of the sellers placed in given defined markets that are reasonably-well-placed to obtain the patronage of each buyer in those markets varies considerably from defined market to defined market. This last reality undercuts the relevance of the number of sellers in defined across-the-board-pricing markets to the profitability of contrived-oligopolistic pricing in those "markets" (to the severity of the public-good obstacle to the practice of contrived-oligopolistic pricing in such markets) as much as it undercuts that number's relevance to the profitability of contrived-oligopolistic pricing in individualized-pricing "markets."

The fact that the average competitiveness (however defined) of the different pairs of products placed in given defined markets varies from defined market to defined market also reduces the relevance of the "concentration" of the seller-side of a defined market (no matter how measured) to the profitability of its sellers' practicing contrived-oligopolistic pricing.

The soundness of the relevant officials' belief that the profitability of an ARDEPPS' sellers' practicing contrived-oligopolistic pricing will increase with the height of the barriers to entry facing its best-placed potential competitor is also called into question by two facts. First, there is little correlation between the height of the barriers to entry facing an ARDEPPS' privately-best-placed potential competitor and the probability that that firm is an effective potential competitor (will enter if nothing that would otherwise be unprofitable is done to prevent its doing so). Second, the presence of an effective potential competitor has less bearing on the profitability of contrived-oligopolistic pricing than one might suppose: (A) Even if contrived-oligopolistic pricing will not result in entry, it may result in established-firm investment-expansions, and (B) the fact that a particular exemplar of contrived-oligopolistic pricing will lead to an increase in the relevant ARDEPPS' equilibrium investment-quantity will often not cause it to be unprofitable when it would otherwise have been profitable, especially if the additional investments are made by contrivers.

Some scholars, judges, and antitrust-law-enforcement officials also believe that contrived-oligopolistic pricing is more likely to be profitable in ARDEPPSes into which entry has been infrequent. This belief is less justified than they suppose not only because contrived-oligopolistic pricing can be profitable even when it does lead to entry but also because infrequency of entry may be attributable not to the ineffectiveness of potential competition but to the established firms' being in position to take advantage of and taking advantage of their ability to forestall entry by making limit investments (investments they would not have found profitable to make but for the fact that the investments would deter entry)—to learn of the existence of a profitable investment-opportunity before any potential competitor does so.

Some judges and antitrust-enforcement officials also find probative of seller contrived-oligopolistic pricing evidence that the members of a set of rival retail-distributors have agreed to the inclusion of minimum-price-setting resale-price-maintenance clauses in their respective contracts with their respective suppliers. These officials appear to suspect that the retailers in question are using these clauses to effectuate their own horizontal price-fix: that the retailers are inducing their suppliers to set the fixed price(s) in what appear to be vertical minimum-resale-price clauses and to enforce the retailers' horizontal price-fix by suing or cutting off retailers that violate what appears to be the vertical minimum-resale-price clauses to which they have agreed. I would find that claim dubious even if the courts and antitrust-law-enforcement authorities did not (mistakenly) consider such vertical RPM arrangements to be of dubious legality because it is rare that retailers are better-placed than their suppliers to engage in contrived-oligopolistic pricing.

Finally, some antitrust courts and antitrust-law-enforcement authorities think that evidence that a set of rivals has tried to standardize or succeeded in standardizing their products favors the conclusion that they practiced contrived-oligopolistic pricing. I do not find such evidence probative of contrived-oligopolistic pricing primarily because, as I indicated earlier, all things considered, product homogeneity probably does not render contrived-oligopolistic pricing more profitable but also because there is sometimes a legitimate reason for rivals' wanting to standardize their products: Such standardization may be legitimately profitable when (1) buyers value not having to evaluate the differences among heterogeneous products and (2) buyers may be dissatisfied with their product-choice because they have chosen the wrong complement to combine with the differentiated product variant they purchased in a situation in which the complement that is most compatible with each member of a series of heterogeneous product variants differs from product variant to product variant.

The point of the preceding discussion is not to establish that antitrust-law judges and enforcement-authorities have totally misunderstood the factors that affect the profitability of oligopolistic pricing in general and contrived-oligopolistic pricing in particular. As I will point out when discussing the types of evidence that do favor the conclusion that defendants have engaged in oligopolistic pricing, the relevant authorities have correctly assessed the relevance of some types of such evidence. The point I am making here is that many of the types of evidence that some scholars and enforcement-officials have claimed can establish requisite probabilities that sellers have engaged in oligopolistic pricing at relatively-low allocative cost cannot do so because those types of evidence are less probative than these scholars and officials claim and/or are more-allocative-costly to collect than the proponents of their use appear to believe.

I turn now to the five types of evidence that I believe can be used to determine whether a business accused of practicing oligopolistic pricing should be found to have done so in a civil suit or a criminal prosecution. The first type of relevant evidence contains eyewitness testimony, audio or audio/visual recordings, or documentary evidence of contrived-oligopolistic communications, of statements of contrived-oligopolistic intentions, or of admissions of contrived-oligopolistic pricing. I want to make five points about such evidence. First, in some, perhaps many instances, the credibility of eyewitnesses is reduced by the fact that they are disgruntled employees or former employees who have been fired. Second, unofficial minutes of meetings in which contrived-oligopolistic-pricing plans were discussed (sometimes after the official minutes indicate that "the lawyers have left the room") are available more often than one might think: Some managers like to keep complete records. Third, even when official minutes of meetings or incriminating e-mails have been deleted, some employees keep printouts of them, and it is sometimes possible to recover these e-mails from hard-drives. Fourth, many statements that appear to be incriminating turn out to be far more ambiguous than private plaintiffs or prosecutors claim. And fifth and finally, when credible evidence of any of these types is available, the introduction of such evidence will often be the most-allocatively-efficient way to prove oligopolistic pricing.

The second type of evidence that can be used to prove oligopolistic pricing has two components: (1) evidence about the price or prices the defendant(s) charged one buyer or a set of buyers in one region at one point in time and (2) evidence that enables the trier-of-fact to determine the defendant's or defendants' HNOPs to the buyer(s) in question. Taken together, such evidence enables the trier-of-fact to determine whether the price(s) that the defendant(s) charged exceeded the relevant seller's or sellers' HNOP(s). For at least three reasons, I doubt that it will often be possible or economically efficient to use such evidence to establish the requisite probability that one or more defendants have practiced oligopolistic pricing. The most important is that, even if one could assume that no relevant mistakes were made (so that the relevant comparison was between the actual price the seller charged and its HNOP), it would be difficult and extremely allocative-costly to generate acceptably-accurate estimates of the relevant HNOPs. As we saw, to do so for sellers charging individualized prices, one would have to establish not only their customer-by-customer BPAs and MCAs but also their customer-by-customer ($CMC_{\#2}$)s, which would require the plaintiff to determine the amount by which the #2 s' prices to their own customers were supra-competitive and the magnitudes of all the other determinants of the CMC of the respective #2 s' practicing price discrimination in favor of the alleged contriver's customers to any given extent. As we saw, to do so for sellers charging across-the-board prices, one would have to establish the BCA distributions of each seller, of each such seller's product-rivals, and of each such seller's product-rivals' product rivals (and so on and so forth) as well as the order in which each seller and its product-rivals announced their prices. Although, these days, it may be possible (1) to obtain BPA-relevant information from distributor-computer records of the prices that the distributors charged for the members of the relevant set of products on various individual days and the quantities of the individual products in question that were sold on those days and (2) to obtain MCA-relevant information (A) from accounting records of what accountants call "average direct (i.e., variable) costs" if average variable costs do not deviate significantly from marginal costs or (B) from engineering studies, I am not optimistic on either account. I acknowledge the moral permissibility of (1) ignoring the possibility that a seller that underestimated its HNOP might have engaged in oligopolistic pricing (i.e., intended to charge an oligopolistic price) even though it did not charge a price that exceeded its NEHNOP and (2) dealing with the possibility that a seller that charged a price that exceeded its NEHNOP might have done so by mistake (not with the intention of securing an OM) by entitling defendants to exonerate themselves by establishing such a defense. But still, I do not think that this "straightforward" way of proving oligopolistic pricing will often be practicable or economically efficient.

The third type of evidence that might be used to prove oligopolistic pricing also has two components: (1) evidence on the prices that one or more sellers have charged for a given product or a given set of rival-products at different times in the same geographic location (region) or at the same time in different geographic locations and (2) evidence on the relationship between the magnitudes of the determinants of the HNOPs for the product(s) in question at different times in the same location or at the same time in different locations. Such evidence is probative because, if it can be shown (1) that the prices charged for a product or set of rival-products at Time 2 exceed the prices charged for it or them at Time 1 by more than the relevant product's or products' estimated HNOPs at Time 2 exceed their estimated HNOPs at Time 1, (2) that the prices charged for a product or set of rival-products in Region 2 exceed the prices charged for it or them at the same time in Region 1 by more than the estimated HNOPs in Region 2 exceed the estimated HNOPs in Region 1, or (3) that the prices charged at Time 1 or in Region 1 equal the prices charged at Time 2 or in Region 2 when the estimates of the HNOPs at the two times or in the two regions were different, it might be appropriate to conclude that the relevant sellers were obtaining OMs or higher OMs at Time 2 or in Region 2 in the first two cases or at one of the times or in one of the regions in "case (3)" (though the defendants should clearly be allowed to exonerate themselves by demonstrating that the proffered actual-price and HNOP-related evidence was critically inaccurate or that the price-differences or price-equalities in question reflected inter-temporal or inter-regional differences in relevant seller-errors or the fact that the seller or sellers had reduced their prices at Time 1 or in Region 1 but not or not to the same extent at Time 2 or in Region 2 to promote their products, to promote their respective companies, to enable themselves to make profits on complements or other members of the same product-line, and/or to obtain learning-by-doing cost-advantages).[8] I do think that an approach that focuses on evidence on (1) the relationship between prices that were charged for a set of rivalrous products at two times in one region or at one time in two regions and (2) the relationship between the magnitudes of the determinants of the relevant products' HNOPs at the two times in question or in the two regions in question is more promising than any approach that compares the actual prices and estimated HNOPs. It will often be possible to estimate actual-price differences and HNOP differences more allocative-cheaply and accurately than to estimate the actual prices and HNOPs themselves. But I do not want to be Pollyannish about the prospects for proving oligopolistic pricing through such "comparative" evidence acceptably-reliably and economic-efficiently. I will say no more than that I suspect that in some cases the use of such comparative evidence will not be liberal-moral-rights-violative and will be allocatively efficient.

The fourth type of evidence whose introduction and consideration in oligopolistic-pricing cases will sometimes be liberal-moral-rights-non-violative and ex ante economically efficient is behavioral evidence that does not focus directly on whether the price(s) charged is (are) oligopolistic. I should acknowledge at the outset that some scholars, courts, and antitrust-law-enforcement authorities have recognized the usefulness of some subtypes of this type of evidence. I include in this set of evidence-types (1) evidence that a seller has not bid for the patronage of a buyer whose patronage it could have profited from securing, given the offers made by the seller's rivals, or has offered a price to a buyer that it knew or should have known the buyer would reject when the seller knew that it could have supplied the buyer in question profitably at a lower price, (2) evidence that a buyer has made side-payments to one or more of its rivals, (3) evidence that a seller has charged one or more of its rivals' customers low prices that are inherently unprofitable, and (4) evidence that a set of rivals have made otherwise-unprofitable agreements (perhaps through a trade association) to engage or not engage in certain behaviors that facilitate their practice of contrived-oligopolistic pricing—for example, not to grant buyers secret discounts, not to advertize, to put "price-protection clauses" into their contracts of sale (which guarantee that buyers that can prove that, post-purchase, they received a superior offer from another potential supplier will receive a rebate from their actual supplier that leaves them at least as well-off as they would have been had they accepted initially the superior offer of the alterative supplier). I also include in this set of probative evidence-types (5) evidence that the members of a group of rivals have exchanged or have agreed to exchange information about their marginal costs, the offers they have made, their inventories, their planned outputs, the prices they intend to charge in the future (which information sometimes identifies the sellers and/or buyers involved) whose dissemination clearly facilitates the practice of contrived-oligopolistic pricing by helping sellers determine whether they have been undercut by inferiors, to identify their non-cooperators, to reciprocate more-private-cost-effectively to their cooperators, to identify their non-cooperators, and to retaliate more-private-cost-effectively against their non-cooperators even if the information-exchange in question does not manifest specific anticompetitive intent (because it was rendered ex ante profitable by its enabling the participants to determine that their operations have not been so proficient as they could be, to avoid underestimating their HNOPs, to make more-profitable production-plans, which may also be more-economically-efficient). (Indeed, information-exchanges that identify the sellers and buyers involved in particular transactions may be even less likely to manifest specific anticompetitive intent on that account because the inclusion of such additional information increases the legitimate profits the exchange generates for its participants [at the same time that it increases the contribution the exchange makes to the probability that the participants can profit by engaging in contrived-oligopolistic pricing]). The set of probative types of evidence also includes (6) evidence that the alleged contrivers had the opportunity to engage in face-to-face communication (say, at a trade-association meeting) (though I do not find this type of evidence highly probative and believe that antitrust scholars, enforcement-authorities, and courts overestimate its probativeness). I also include in this set of probative evidence (7) evidence that alleged oligopolistic pricers have committed other acts that (1) increased the profits they could make by practicing contrived-oligopolistic pricing and/or increased the OMs they could obtain naturally that (2) would have been ex ante unprofitable had they not increased the profits the actors should have been predicted to make by practicing contrived-oligopolistic and/or natural-oligopolistic pricing. I have already listed the various kinds of conduct some of whose exemplars might be rendered profitable by the contribution they make to the profits their perpetrator will realize by practicing contrived-oligopolistic pricing and/or natural-oligopolistic pricing.

Before proceeding, I want to make five points that relate to the behaviors in which firms may engage to increase the profits they can make by practicing contrived-oligopolistic and natural-oligopolistic pricing:

(1) as I indicated at the beginning of my discussion of these possibilities, the profitability of exemplars of all these types of behavior may or may not depend on their increasing their perpetrators' COM *plus* NOM total;
(2) because horizontal mergers and acquisitions and many joint ventures increase their participants' OCAs by freeing them from each other's competition, I suspect (A) that very few exemplars of such conduct increase the profits their participants will expect to secure by practicing contrived-oligopolistic pricing and (B) that the perpetrator-perceived ex ante profitability of even fewer exemplars of such conduct is critically affected by the perpetrators' belief that such conduct will increase the profits they will make by practicing contrived-oligopolistic pricing;
(3) I do think that the perpetrator-perceived ex ante profitability of a substantial number of the exemplars of such conduct is critically increased by the perpetrator's or perpetrators' belief that the conduct will increase its (their) NOMs;
(4) I think it will rarely be practicable or cost-effective to use this type of evidence to prove oligopolistic pricing: It will almost always be too difficult to prove that the defendants' perception that the conduct was ex ante profitable was critically affected by their belief that it would increase their COMs and/or NOMs for the use of this type of evidence to be economically efficient; and
(5) these possibilities are still relevant because they affect the ex ante economic efficiency of seller-practiced oligopolistic pricing as well as the economic efficiency of efforts to deter it.

The fifth and last type of evidence that bears on whether sellers accused of oligopolistic pricing did in fact engage in this practice is "structural" evidence where "structural" is enquoted because (1) the standard reference to "structural evidence" is to features of the relevant sellers' relevant "market" that increase the likelihood that they will find it profitable to contrive oligopolistic prices and (2) I believe that market definitions are inherently arbitrary. I have already discussed the factors that determine (1) the feasibility of natural-oligopolistic pricing for a given seller, (2) the probability that an individualized pricer will find contrived-oligopolistic pricing profitable, and (3) the probability that a set of rival across-the-board pricers will find contrived-oligopolistic pricing profitable. I have also already explained why I think that the various types of "structural" evidence that scholars, courts, and antitrust-law-enforcement officials claim are probative and allocatively-cost-effective to use are far less probative and allocatively-cost-effective to use than they believe. At this juncture, I will restrict myself to asserting that the situational (as opposed to structural) evidence that relates to the potential profitability of contrived-oligopolistic pricing is far more refined and difficult and allocative-costly to collect and use than those who advocate the use of structural evidence believe.

I will now discuss in the following order the allocative cost of the government's preventing oligopolistic pricing, the allocative benefits of its doing so, and finally the allocative efficiency of its doing so. Hopefully, the mere prohibition of oligopolistic pricing will deter many businesses from its practice even when such pricing would be profitable: At least, this conclusion will be correct if, as I would like to think, the CEOs, other high-level executives, and relevant employees of most companies are law-abiding and will not violate the law even when it would be profitable for them to do so. (I acknowledge that the government may have to make some effort to persuade some of these individuals that natural-oligopolistic pricing is morally indefensible to bolster their disposition to obey the law by not engaging in such pricing.) However, I have little doubt that a significant number of firms will practice oligopolistic pricing even if it is legally prohibited so long as its practice is ex ante profitable for the companies (and, perhaps more relevantly, for the relevant company-personnel). To deter such companies (individuals) from engaging in oligopolistic pricing, the government must not only prohibit the practice but make the ex ante law-related cost of engaging in it sufficiently high to render ex ante unprofitable oligopolistic pricing that would otherwise be ex ante profitable (taking account of the risk cost associated with violating the law). The certainty-equivalent cost (weighted-average-expected cost *plus* risk cost) of violating a law prohibiting oligopolistic pricing depends inter alia on (1) the probability that the violation will be detected, (2) the probability that the government (and/or in some legal regimes one or more private plaintiffs) will bring a civil suit or criminal prosecution against the firm whose oligopolistic pricing they believe they have detected,[9] (3)(A) the probability that any civil suit will be settled, the distribution of possible settlement-amounts, the probability that any criminal prosecution will be plea-bargained, and the distribution of possible criminal fines that would be levied in and non-custodial and/or prison sentences that would be imposed in the plea-bargain agreement and (B) the probability that the civil or criminal case will go to trial, the probability that the defendant will be found guilty, and the distributions of possible civil fines that will be levied, criminal fines that will be levied, and non-custodial or prison sentences that will be imposed if the defendant is found guilty, (4) the lawyering-costs associated with the possible civil-settlement/criminal-plea negotiations/trials in question, and (5) the non-attorney-fee private transaction costs that a defendants employees'/managers'/directors' participation in related discussions with lawyers, submissions of documents, and participation in pre-trial discovery, dispute-negotiations, and trials would impose on the company (or on relevant individual company-personnel).

The government can alter the preceding defendant-costs (1) by varying the amount of resources it devotes to uncovering oligopolistic pricing, (2) by varying the "awards" that non-government actors can obtain by providing the government with relevant evidence or suing on their own behalf (say, by allowing buyers that oligopolistic pricing has harmed to recover compensatory or treble damages and providing such buyers with relevant evidence and testimony), (3) by varying the amount of resources it devotes to negotiating civil settlements or plea-bargaining or trying individual cases, (4) by varying (A) the civil and criminal fines that the law permits courts to impose on companies convicted of oligopolistic pricing, (B) the civil and criminal fines the courts can impose on individuals convicted of participating in a company's oligopolistic pricing, (C) the damage-awards that injured victims of oligopolistic pricing are entitled to obtain from companies that and/or individuals who have imposed losses on them by engaging in oligopolistic pricing, and (D) the length of the prison sentences, unpleasantness of the prison-conditions, and duration and onerousness of the non-custodial restrictions that can be imposed on individuals convicted of oligopolistic pricing, and (5) the "hardness" of the "ball" they play when negotiating with defendants and submitting civil-fine and criminal-sentence recommendations to judges.

The allocative cost that the government must generate to deter any given amount of oligopolistic pricing depends on (1) the number of potential oligopolistic pricers that would engage in the practice if doing so would be predicted (ex ante) to yield them respectively different amounts of profits, taking law-related costs into consideration, (2) the profits these various companies or individuals would expect to realize by practicing oligopolistic pricing if there were no law-related costs of doing so, and (3) the allocative cost of the government's making the decisions that would cause the law-related costs of relevant firms' and individuals' practicing oligopolistic pricing to be sufficiently high to render the practice ex ante unprofitable for them.

Obviously, the analysis of the allocative cost of the most-economically-efficient set of decisions a liberal-justice-constrained government could make to deter oligopolistic pricing would be extremely complicated even if I ignored the complications introduced by the need to estimate the allocative benefits that would be generated by deterring various amounts of oligopolistic pricing (which will be discussed below). I will limit myself to discussing four points.

First, the allocative cost of a government's enforcing a prohibition of oligopolistic pricing in a particular way includes (1) the allocative transaction costs associated with the private transaction costs the government will incur to implement the oligopolistic-pricing prohibition in that way—the allocative transaction cost of doing the associated investigations, of negotiating relevant civil settlements and plea deals, of trying relevant cases, of requiring judges and juries to devote their time to the cases in question, and of supervising or incarcerating those individuals convicted of oligopolistic pricing on whom non-custodial or custodial sentences have been imposed, (2) the allocative "cost" that imprisoning price-fixers generates by imposing losses not only on those convicted but also on their family and friends and by sacrificing the allocative product that imprisoned oligopolistic pricers would have generated had they not been imprisoned, (3) the allocative transaction costs that oligopolistic pricers generate to defend themselves or to negotiate private-law settlements and criminal-law plea-deals, (4) any extra allocative transaction costs that the enforcement of the prohibition induces oligopolistic pricers to generate by giving them an incentive to arrange and enforce their price-fix in less-detectable/provable but more-allocative-costly ways (though this effect will be offset by any allocative-transaction-cost savings the enforcement of the prohibition generates by deterring [allocative-transaction-costly] oligopolistic pricing), (5) the allocative transaction cost the government generates to finance its enforcement-efforts (e.g., to change the tax law and to collect the extra taxes), and (6) the economic inefficiency (allocative-transaction-cost-effects aside) generated by the decisions the government makes to finance its oligopolistic-pricing-prohibition-implementation expenditures (decisions to raise taxes, to raise the prices it charges for goods and services it sells, to print money, or to cancel other expenditures).

Second, it is important to recognize that many of the allocative transaction costs just referenced will equal their private counterparts only fortuitously and rarely. The ratio of the relevant allocative-to-private transaction costs will depend primarily on (1) the percentages of the resources "consumed" as private transaction costs that will be withdrawn respectively from UO-producing-and-consuming, QV-investment-creating-and-using, and PPR-executing-and-using uses and (2) the percentage-distortions in the private benefits that the resources withdrawn from these alternative uses would have generated in each of these categories of sacrificed uses. For reasons I explained earlier, I assume that the relevant allocative transaction costs exceed their private counterparts.

Third, the amount of private/allocative transaction costs the government will have to incur/generate to create any probability that it will be able to detect and prove given firms' or individuals' practice of oligopolistic pricing depends (1) on the availability of eyewitness testimony by credible observers, pertinent audio or audio/visual recordings, pertinent documents, etc., (2) on the availability of evidence that the suspect(s) engaged in oligopolistic-pricing-practice conduct other than charging oligopolistic prices—for example, evidence that (A) the suspect(s) failed to make inherently-profitable individualized offers to buyers that apparently-cooperative rivals were privately-best-placed to supply, (B) the suspects made cross-payments to some of their rivals, (C) the suspect(s) offered inherently-unprofitably-low prices to individualized buyers that a rival that appears not to have been cooperating was privately-best-placed to supply or executed inherently-unprofitable reductions in their across-the-board prices in response to a rival's responding to its/their initial price(s) by charging an undermining price, (3) the availability of comparative evidence that would enable the government to prove oligopolistic pricing by showing that the relationship between one or more sellers' actual prices at different times in the same region or in different regions at the same time could not be attributed to the relationship between those sellers' HNOPs in the same region at different times or in different regions at the same time, (4) on the availability of evidence that the suspect(s) had made otherwise-unprofitable choices that would increase the profits they could make by practicing contrived-oligopolistic pricing and/or the OMs they could obtain naturally, and/or (5) the availability of evidence that the suspects had made "premature" price announcements (usually in trade journals) and related price-"postings" in media read by final consumers and on their products' packages and their distributive outlets' shelves that enable them to obtain OMs "naturally" by allowing each to delay locking itself into an NOM-containing price (by making it costly to change its initial price) until its rivals had locked themselves into cooperative prices.

Fourth, a point that is not really an economic-efficiency point—a point that relates to the possibility that the most-economically-efficient approach for the government to take to implementing an oligopolistic-pricing prohibition may be to allocate relatively few resources to detecting and prosecuting such offenses but to impose enormous civil and/or criminal penalties on the firms and individuals convicted of oligopolistic pricing and/or to allow victims of oligopolistic pricing to obtain (say) treble damages. The point is that, even if such an approach would maximize the positive difference between the allocative benefits that the implementation of an oligopolistic-pricing prohibition generates by deterring such behavior and other similar types of conduct and the allocative cost of implementing the probation, liberalism would deem such an implementation-approach liberal-moral-rights-violative because it treats those convicted of oligopolistic pricing as means (for reducing the allocative cost of securing relevant amounts of deterrence) rather than as ends—i.e., fails to show appropriate, equal respect for those convicted of oligopolistic pricing by subjecting them to a penalty that is more severe than is warranted by the moral-rights-wrongfulness of their crime and fails to show appropriate concern for their welfare as well. I want to make two further points about this possible conflict between economic efficiency and liberalism. First, although one might agree that any such conflict would be eliminated by the equivalent-dollar losses the Draconian enforcement-protocol under consideration would generate because, for moral reasons, the members of and participants in a liberal-moral-rights-based-society would place a high negative-dollar value on its use, I doubt (with some regret) that such an "external-preference"-based argument would be empirically successful. Second, although liberalism might not condemn the use of such an implementation-protocol if it would enable the government to secure weightier liberal-moral-rights-related interests it could not otherwise have secured by increasing economic efficiency and derivatively the resources available to the government, I also doubt that, for empirical reasons, any such argument would be persuasive.

I turn now to the allocative benefits that would be generated by an oligopolistic-pricing-prohibition-implementation policy. At least 10 categories of such allocative benefits (tendencies to increase economic efficiency) are worth distinguishing. First, because oligopolistic pricing is allocatively inefficient, suing oligopolistic pricers civilly or prosecuting oligopolistic pricers will yield allocative benefits by generating specific-deterrence-related allocative benefits—i.e., by deterring the convicted defendants from engaging in the practice in the future. Second, for the same reasons, suing or prosecuting oligopolistic pricers will yield allocative benefits by generating general-deterrence-related allocative benefits—i.e., allocative benefits by deterring others' practice of oligopolistic pricing. Third, because contrived-oligopolistic pricing is one subcategory of a broader category of conduct—conduct that manifests specific anticompetitive intent—that is economically inefficient (with one possible exception: contrived-oligopolistic QV-investment-restrictions, which may increase economic efficiency by reducing the amount of resources devoted to QV-investment creation [though the result can almost certainly be achieved more-allocative-efficiently through tax policy[10]]), suing or prosecuting sellers that engage in contrived-oligopolistic pricing will also yield allocative benefits by deterring exemplars of other categories of acts that manifest specific anticompetitive intent (predatory conduct, certain exemplars of mergers and acquisitions, certain exemplars of joint ventures and other functionally-analogous types of collaboration, certain exemplars of internal growth). Fourth, to the extent that contrived-oligopolistic pricing is a subcategory of the broader category of conduct—conduct prohibited by antitrust laws—whose exemplars tend to be economically inefficient even when they do not manifest their perpetrator's or perpetrators' specific anticompetitive intent, civilly suing or prosecuting oligopolistic pricers will also tend to yield allocative benefits by deterring antitrust-prohibited conduct that is not motivated by specific anticompetitive intent. Fifth, because firms that want to profit by engaging in contrived-oligopolistic pricing, natural-oligopolistic pricing, and predatory conduct will tend to engage in otherwise-unprofitable and presumptively-economically-inefficient conduct that increases the profits they can earn by engaging in oligopolistic and predatory conduct, civilly suing and prosecuting oligopolistic pricers will yield allocative benefits by deterring those sued and other prospective practitioners of such conduct from engaging in economically-inefficient conduct that will increase the profits they can realize by engaging in oligopolistic and predatory behavior. Sixth, because contrived-oligopolistic pricing and (I think) natural-oligopolistic pricing are liberal-moral-rights-violative and liberal-moral-rights violations are usually economically inefficient, suing and prosecuting oligopolistic pricers may yield allocative benefits by reminding the relevant society's members and participants of their liberal moral commitments and thereby disposing them to fulfill their liberal moral commitments both when making non-political decisions and when choosing which political parties and which political candidates to support. Seventh, because I think that requiring wrongdoers and law-breakers to compensate their victims generates external-preference-related equivalent-dollar gains to observers and "non-monetary" satisfaction to victims who feel entitled to redress, authorizing victims to obtain compensation from oligopolistic pricers will yield allocative benefits on those accounts. Eighth, suing/prosecuting oligopolistic pricers will tend to yield allocative benefits by decreasing poverty and material inequality (by deterring economically-inefficient conduct that increases both poverty and material inequality). Ninth, suing/prosecuting oligopolistic pricers will tend to yield allocative benefits (tend to increase economic efficiency) by reducing X-inefficiency whose generation is misallocative by reducing the profit-rate the oligopolistic pricers could realize if they did not generate X-inefficiency if firms' proclivity to generate production-optimum-misallocation-causing X-inefficiency increases with their potential profit-rate. Tenth, suing or prosecuting oligopolistic pricers will tend to increase economic efficiency by reducing the amount of misallocation that the managers and employees of the firms whose oligopolistic pricing is deterred generate by substituting untaxed or lower-taxed attractive working-conditions or fringe-benefits for the goods they would have purchased with the monetary compensation they exchanged for the working-conditions and fringe-benefits in question if the firms whose oligopolistic pricing was deterred would have shared some of the profits the deterred oligopolistic pricing would have yielded them with their managers and employees.

I turn at last to the allocative efficiency of various oligopolistic-pricing-prohibition-implementation policies. I will proceed on the assumption that it is not morally permissible in a liberal-moral-rights-based society for the government to reduce the extent to which it deters oligopolistic pricing by lowering the amount of resources it devotes to oligopolistic-pricing investigations and suits and to subject those convicted of oligopolistic pricing to civil fines and damage-awards and criminal firms and incarcerative and non-incarcerative sentences that collectively exceed the "total" that fits the moral wrongfulness of their conduct. I recognize the lack of specificity and contestability of the following conclusions, but I currently believe that it will be ex ante economically efficient for the government (1) to give the buyers and oligopolistic-pricer rivals who/that have been directly harmed by oligopolistic pricing a legal right to obtain full compensation including compensation for reasonable related legal fees from the oligopolistic pricers that have charged them OMs and to assist such victims' efforts to obtain legal redress (though treble-damage rules may be liberal-moral-rights problematic), (2) to include in its oligopolistic-pricing-prohibiting legislation civil-fine and imprisonment provisions that (taken together with the damage-awards available to victims) create total sanctions that properly reflect the wrongfulness of the conduct in question, (3) to devote a large amount of resources to detecting oligopolistic pricing in ways that do not violate the defendants' or anyone else's liberal moral rights (A) by discovering relevant witnesses, documents, and audio or audio–video evidence, (B) by executing probative comparative analyses to detect and prove oligopolistic pricing (by examining whether the relationship between the prices that are being charged for a relevant set of products at the same time in different regions or at different times in the same region matches the relationship between those products' HNOPs in the different regions at the relevant point in time or in same region at different points in time), and (C) by investigating various seller behaviors other than charging supra-HNOP prices that may favor the conclusion that the seller has engaged in contrived-oligopolistic pricing, and (4) to play hardball when negotiating civil settlements and criminal plea-deals and submitting civil-fine and non-custodial and custodial sentencing-recommendations to judges.

9.1.2 The Liberal-Moral-Rights-Violativeness of the Various Business-Choices That Seller-Practiced Contrived-Oligopolistic and Natural-Oligopolistic Pricing May Entail or Induce and the Possible Moral Duty of the Government of a Liberal-Moral-Rights-Based Society to Prevent Such Conduct and to Give the Direct Victims of any Such Conduct That Is Liberal-Moral-Rights-Violative an Appropriate Opportunity to Obtain Legal Redress

9.1.2.1 The Liberal-Moral-Rights-Violativeness of the Various Business-Choices That Seller-Practiced Contrived-Oligopolistic or Seller-Practiced Natural-Oligopolistic Pricing Always or May Entail or Induce

This section's analyses apply some of Sect. 9.2.2's conclusions about the extensions of liberalism to the choices that seller-practiced oligopolistic pricing may entail or induce. I wrote "some of Sect. 9.2.2's conclusions" for the following reasons:

(1) an oligopolistic-pricing-related choice made either by a seller-initiator of oligopolistic pricing or by a rival of such a seller in response to such an initiator-choice that would otherwise be liberal-moral-rights-violative (see below) can not be justicized in a liberal-moral-rights-based society of (perfect) moral integrity by demonstrating that the choice would confer an equivalent-dollar gain on its perpetrator that would enable it to secure its privacy rights, a meaningful opportunity to enter into and/or maintain an intimate relationship that would critically affect its opportunity to take its life morally seriously, or to purchase nutrition, clothing, housing, medical care, or anything else that would critically affect its (or its family-members') opportunity to lead a life of moral integrity (A) because the government of such a society would already have secured the relevant individuals' liberal-moral-rights-related interests (even if I ignore the likelihood that the type of choosers involved in seller-practiced oligopolistic pricing would almost always be able to secure these interests by engaging in conduct that would not contradict the prima facie liberal moral rights of others or by eliciting gifts or charitable contributions) and possibly (B) because I suspect that, in a situation of imperfect liberal justice (in which the government did not fulfill its relevant liberal moral obligations), liberalism would not approve of such an individual's securing resources to which he or she is entitled by violating the prima facie liberal moral rights of others;

(2) an oligopolistic-pricing-related choice made either by a seller-initiator of oligopolistic pricing or by a rival of such a seller in response to the initiator's choice cannot be justicized in a liberal-moral-rights-based society by demonstrating that the choice would contribute to the chooser's instantiating its

conception of the moral good because, although liberalism implies that individual liberal-moral-rights bearers have a liberal moral right to make choices that instantiate their own morally-defensible conception of the moral good (regardless of whether the choices the individual makes to do so impose equivalent-dollar losses on others that derive from others' prejudices, religious views that are not morally defensible, or contrary conceptions of the moral good), liberalism does not imply that an individual's moral-good-instantiation-related moral rights are violated by the financial constraints under which the individual is operating (or, in some cases, by the "desires" that others have not to be exposed to conduct they find disconcerting or upsetting for reasons not covered by the items in the preceding list: I realize that this parenthetical alludes to without addressing much less resolving a host of difficult issues that merit serious consideration);

(3) although I recognize that the choices that sellers make to initiate and execute contrived-oligopolistic pricing and some of the responses that the rivals of the initiator(s) may make to the initiator's/initiators' choices will impose losses on the customers of the initiator(s), the customers of one or more rivals of the initiator(s), and/or the rivals of the initiator(s) and that in some cases those losses will prevent the relevant losers from having a meaningful opportunity to take their lives morally seriously (if the government does not intervene redistributively to prevent this outcome), the relevant choices' liberal-moral-rights-violativeness will never be critically affected by their having any such effect because, for reasons that will be discussed below, the choices in question would be liberal-moral-rights-violative even if they had no such effects; and

(4) although I recognize that the choices that sellers make to initiate and execute oligopolistic pricing and some of the rival-responses that the conduct of the initiator(s) elicit will limit the contribution that affected buyers and rivals can make to the instantiation of the conception of the moral good to which they individually subscribe, the relevant choices' liberal-moral-rights-violativeness will never be critically affected by any such effect they have both because the relevant choices would be liberal-moral-rights-violative in any event and because the relevant losers' moral-good-related liberal moral rights are not violated by the existence of financial constraints that limit their ability to secure the moral good as they understand it.

The Liberal-Moral-Rights-Violativeness of the Choices Involved in Seller-Practiced Contrived-Oligopolistic Pricing

I will focus first on the choices that the initiators of a contrived-oligopolistic-pricing sequence will or may make when engaging in this practice. Before assessing the specific initiator-acts that this practice may involve, I will explain why efforts to obtain COMs from buyers would violate various buyers' liberal moral rights even if such efforts did not violate the liberal moral rights of any rival of the initiator. First, a contrived-oligopolistic-pricing initiator can offer no positive justification for any profits the practice yields it: With few if any exceptions, such conduct decreases both economic efficiency and total utility so that the contriver cannot argue that he or she deserves the profits it yields because he or she deserves moral credit for engaging in the conduct. Second, no moral justification can be made for the equivalent-dollar losses the practice imposes on the buyers on whom (successful) contrived-oligopolistic pricing imposes equivalent-dollar losses ([1] the actual and prospective customers of the initiator[s], [2] the actual and possible customers of any initiator-rival that has accepted the initiator-offer of reciprocation [in an individualized-pricing situation] or that has raised its price to take advantage of the initiator across-the-board-price increase [in across-the-board-pricing situations]), and [3] the actual and possible customers of initiator-rivals in individualized-pricing situations that have not accepted any offer of reciprocation but are taking advantage of the fact that the initiator's or initiators' obtaining COMs from its or their own customers have increased the CMCs the initiator[s] would have to incur to match various offers the relevant rivals might make) or on the perpetrator-rivals on whom some variants of the practice impose equivalent-dollar losses. Third, the successful practice of contrived-oligopolistic pricing will often leave the actual and possible customers of the contrivance-initiator(s) worse-off than they would have been had the contrivance-initiator(s) never entered the relevant business because it deters the initiator-rivals from making as attractive offers to those buyers as they would have made in the initiator's or initiators' absence, at least if the initiator(s) would have been replaced by equally-competitive alternatives that would not have engaged in such contrivance had the initiator(s) never entered the relevant business. Fourth, the successful practice of contrived-oligopolistic pricing will impose equivalent-dollar losses on the contrivers' actual and possible customers that exceed the equivalent-dollar gain it confers on the contriver(s)—given that the associated price-increase will (by reducing unit sales) destroy transaction surplus (the sum of the seller surplus and buyer surplus generated by the contriver's or contrivers' sales to their actual and possible customers). If I were to express this in terms of the Hand formula for negligence, the private cost or burden (B) to each contriver of avoiding imposing a loss on its actual and possible customers by choosing not to charge them a contrived-oligopolistic-price (COP) will be lower than the weighted-average-expected (↓PL) or (to be fancier) the certainty-equivalent (↓[PL + R] benefits the "avoidance-move" would confer on its prospective beneficiaries—the victims of loss-generating conduct where "R" stands for "risk costs," "P" for the probability of the loss, and "L" for the magnitude of the loss.

Two final introductory-observations. First, although I recognize that contrived-oligopolistic pricing does not involve the "theft" or "unlawful conversion" of property in the strictest sense of those concepts because it does not involve the removal of material objects (even currency) from its victims, the four preceding points do seem to me to warrant the conclusion that contrived-oligopolistic pricing is morally tantamount to theft. Second, the four points made in the preceding paragraph apply to all types of conduct that—like seller-practiced contrived-oligopolistic pricing—are motivated by specific anticompetitive intent.

I will now assess the more specific acts that initiators of and responders to contrived-oligopolistic-pricing efforts may commit. I will start with the five specific choices or sets of choices that the initiator(s) of contrived-oligopolistic-pricing sequence may make.

First, any choice a seller made that it would not otherwise have made because the seller believed the choice would increase the profits it would subsequently realize by practicing contrived-oligopolistic pricing would violate the liberal moral rights of its immediate victims directly even if the seller does not subsequently engage in contrived-oligopolistic pricing because any such choice manifests the chooser's specific anticompetitive intent. If any such choice did lead its perpetrator to increase the extent to which the chooser practiced contrived-oligopolistic pricing, it would be liberal-moral-rights-violative on that account as well.

Second, a contrived-oligopolistic-pricing-initiator's communicating to its rivals its intention to reciprocate to their cooperation and/or retaliate against their non-cooperation is liberal-moral-rights-violative both because it is part of a scheme to violate relevant buyers' liberal moral rights and because it violates the liberal moral rights of the communicatees to be treated with appropriate, equal respect: in the reciprocator-promise case, by attempting to induce them to commit a liberal-moral-rights violation themselves (by accepting the offer of reciprocation) and, in the retaliation case, because the threatened retaliation would violate the retaliatee's liberal moral rights. Indeed, although I recognize the contestability of this conclusion, I am disposed to think that the recipients of such communications would be morally entitled to some compensation on this account because the communication would impose a "dignity-loss" on them even if they suffered no material harm (if the threat of retaliation did not deter the communicatee from maintaining its contacts with relevant buyers by making them offers, if the threat of retaliation was never carried out, and if the public revelation of the communication of a promise of reciprocation did not [undeservedly] tarnish the communicatee's reputation for probity by raising the possibility that it had solicited or suggested its openness to such an arrangement).

Third, any act of retaliation committed by a seller in furtherance of its plan to obtain COMs would violate the liberal moral rights of its target for all the reasons that all conduct motivated by specific anticompetitive intent violates its victims' liberal moral rights. Indeed, such acts of retaliation violate the liberal moral rights not only of the target non-cooperator but also of all buyers on whom the retaliation imposes equivalent-dollar losses by deterring future non-cooperation and encouraging further contrivance by the retaliator.

Fourth, any act of reciprocation committed by a contrived-oligopolistic-pricing initiator violates the liberal moral rights not only of the buyers directly affected by their supplier's taking advantage of the contrivance-initiator's offer but also of all other buyers on whom the reciprocation imposed equivalent-dollar losses by inducing additional contrived-oligopolistic pricing or by increasing the CMCs the reciprocatee faced in relation to buyers it was or would otherwise have been privately-second-placed to supply.

Fifth, although I believe that a contrivance-initiator's choices to promise reciprocation and then renege on that promise does violate the rights of the buyers it causes to get less-attractive deals than the contrivance-initiator's relevant rivals would otherwise have offered them and that such buyers would be morally entitled to obtain redress in appropriate proportions from both the initiator and the cooperator, I do not think that rivals of any contrivance-initiator who tried unsuccessfully to take advantage of the initiator's promise of reciprocation are morally entitled to obtain compensation for the loss the relevant sequence of decisions imposed of them: Those rivals do not have the clean hands that are a necessary condition for moral entitlement.

I will now address the five specific choices or sets of choices that may be made by the rivals of a seller that is trying to contrive an oligopolistic price. First, it is conceivable (though I suspect, extraordinarily unlikely) that such a rival would make otherwise-ex ante-unprofitable moves that were rendered ex ante profitable by their increasing the profits the rival could make by taking advantage of reciprocatory offers from contrived-oligopolistic-pricing initiators that are trying to secure the rival's cooperation. Any such moves that such a rival would make would violate the liberal moral rights of the moves' victims because such moves would be motivated by specific anticompetitive intent.

Second, such a rival would have to choose whether to inform the buyers from whom the contrivance-initiator was trying to secure a COM and, more tellingly, the government that the initiator was attempting to secure COMs (had made a contrived-oligopolistic communication). My argument for the conclusion that liberalism imposes positive duties on the members of a liberal-moral-rights-based society to provide positive assistance to their fellows only when special conditions are fulfilled that will rarely if ever be fulfilled in the circumstances now under consideration would favor the conclusion that the rival would have no such positive reporting-duties even if its making any such report would not create a risk that the contriver(s) might retaliate against it for doing so.

Third, the rival must decide whether to cooperate with the contrivance-initiator's contrived-oligopolistic pricing—that is, (A) when the rival is operating in an individualized-pricing context, whether to beat the contriver's contrived-oligopolistic-price-containing offer with an offer that would be inherently profitable for it to make (with an offer that would be profitable if making it would not subject the rival to retaliation or forfeit an opportunity to profit from the contrivance-initiator's reciprocation) and (B) when the rival is operating in an across-the-board-pricing context, whether to respond to the contrivance-initiator's COM-containing price or the contrivance-initiators' COM-containing prices with prices that would enable the initiator(s) to profit from its (their) contrivance and that presumably would be less profitable for the rival to charge than the price it would find most profitable to charge if the initiator(s) would not retaliate against its non-cooperation. When the contrivance is being practiced in an ARDEPPS in which individualized prices are being charged, the argument for liberalism's not imposing positive duties on moral-rights bearers to help others implies that in the relevant circumstances the contrivance-initiator's rival has no liberal moral duty to benefit the contriver's customer by beating the contrivance-initiator's contrived-oligopolistic-price-containing offer, regardless of whether the rival has reason to believe that the initiator will retaliate against the rival's non-cooperation but certainly if the rival has been threatened with retaliation or has reason to believe that it might be targeted for retaliation should it not cooperate so long as the rival did not abstain from beating the initiator's offer to profit from the initiator's promised reciprocation (see below). When the contrivance is being practiced in an ARDEPPS in which across-the-board prices are being charged, the relevant analysis is certainly more complicated, and the appropriate conclusion may be contestable. The correct liberal conclusion still seems to me to be that the rival has no liberal moral obligation to prevent the contrivance-initiator's conduct from imposing an equivalent-dollar loss on the initiator's actual and possible customers. I also think that the initiator's rival has no liberal moral obligation to respond to the initiator's across-the-board-price contrivance by charging a price that prevents the initiator from profiting from its contrivance when such a response would elicit a retaliatory or non-retaliatory reaction from the initiator that would leave the rival worse-off than it would have been absent the contrivance My disposition is to think that the liberal moral duty of an across-the-board pricer that is a rival of one or more contrivance-initiators is to respond to the initiator's/initiators' contrived-oligopolistic price(s) with the price that would yield the rival the smallest possible gain from the contrivance, though it has no liberal moral obligation to respond with a price that it should predict will leave it worse-off than it would have been had no contrivance been practiced where the relevant gains and losses are those the rival should predict, taking account of the estimates it should make of the probability distributions of the retaliatory and non-retaliatory reactions the contrivers would have to the various response-prices the rival could charge. Of course, I recognize that it will almost certainly not be possible to apply this test of liberal permissibility.

Fourth, in individualized-pricing situations, the rival must decide whether to verbally accept the initiator's promise of reciprocation and/or to take advantage of the initiator's reciprocitory acts. I have no doubt that liberalism implies that a rival's accepting any such offer of reciprocation or taking advantage of any such reciprocitory act would violate the liberal moral rights of its own customers and would also render its related cooperation with the contriver violative of the liberal moral rights of the contriver's customers. Once more, these conclusions reflect the fact that such rival-conduct would be motivated by specific anticompetitive intent.

Fifth, I also think that liberalism would condemn an individualized-pricing rival of a contrived-oligopolistic pricer from profiting from the contriver's liberal-moral-rights-violating contrivance by raising its prices to customers to take advantage of the fact that the contriver's securing of COMs from its own customers increased the contextual marginal costs the contriver would have to incur to match relevant offers the rival in question might make. This possibility will be salient when the contriver is privately-second-placed to supply a customer of the rival in question or would have been that buyer's privately-second-placed supplier absent the contrivance. Once more, I recognize that it rarely will be possible to prove that a contriver-rival has increased its price to one of its own customers self-consciously to take advantage of the fact that the contriver's contrivance raised the CMC the contriver would have to incur to charge various relevant prices to the possible buyers of the relevant rival's product.

The Liberal-Moral-Rights-Violativeness of the Choices Involved in Seller-Practiced Natural-Oligopolistic Pricing

I will focus first on natural-oligopolistic pricing in individualized-pricing contexts and then comment on natural-oligopolistic pricing in across-the-board-pricing contexts. In individualized-pricing contexts, it will be convenient to address separately (1) the choices that may be made by sellers that are trying to secure NOMs from buyers the sellers are privately-best-placed to supply and (2) the responses that the rivals of such privately-best-placed sellers can make to the latter's charging natural-oligopolistic prices.

Individualized pricers can make up to five categories of choices to secure NOMs. First, they can make a variety of otherwise-ex ante-unprofitable choices to put themselves in a position to practice natural-oligopolistic pricing by increasing their OCAs and/or decreasing the costs they must incur to change initial bids. All such choices are liberal-moral-rights-violative because all are motivated by specific anticompetitive intent in that their perpetrators' perception that they were ex ante at least normally profitable was critically affected by a belief that they would reduce the absolute attractiveness of the most-attractive rival offers against which the perpetrators would have to compete (and because the chooser[s] cannot morally justify the profits the choices yield them or the losses the choices impose on their "victims" because all such choices are presumptively economically inefficient and because the equivalent-dollar losses all such choices impose on their victims exceed the equivalent-dollar gains they confer on their chooser[s]).

Second, a privately-best-placed individualized pricer who is trying to secure NOMs may choose to inform its rivals that they will not find it profitable to beat its NOM-containing offer because the relevant buyer will give the natural-oligopolistic pricer an opportunity to beat any initially-superior offer they might make, and it will take advantage of that opportunity because doing so will be inherently profitable. In many situations, the natural-oligopolistic pricer will not have to communicate this information explicitly to its rivals because they will be aware of the relevant facts. However, if any such communication is made, the choice to make it will be liberal-moral-rights-violative because any such choice will have been made with specific anticompetitive intent and, for reasons I have already addressed, all choices that are so motivated are on that account liberal-moral-rights-violative.

Third, a privately-best-placed individualized pricer who is trying to secure NOMs will have to charge the relevant buyers natural-oligopolistic prices. I recognize that the following conclusion will certainly be contested and may be contestable. Admittedly, (1) the seller had to charge its prospective customer a price, (2) the act of setting a natural-oligopolistic price does not communicate the price-setter's intention to do anything inherently unprofitable to reward its rivals' cooperation and/or to punish its rivals' non-cooperation, and (3) at least if the seller did not do anything inherently unprofitable to render it unprofitable for its rivals to beat its NOM-containing offer, its rivals' choosing not to beat its NOM-containing offer reflects attributes of the competitive situation whose existence are not the natural-oligopolistic pricer's fault—indeed, its rivals' not beating its NOM-containing offer cannot be attributed to its charging the relevant buyer(s) a natural-oligopolistic price (obviously, they would not have beaten its better, HNOP-containing offer either). Nevertheless, I am disposed to conclude that the intentional charging of an NOM-containing individualized price is in itself liberal-moral-rights-violative because it leaves the buyers charged such NOMs worse-off than they would have been had their privately-best-placed supplier not operated at all (and its absence had not resulted in the entry of another firm that would have also obtained at least as high an NOM from the buyers in question) and because the natural-oligopolistic pricer's operation deters these buyers' privately-second-placed suppliers from making (HNOP-containing) offers to them that would have been more attractive than the natural-oligopolistic pricer's NOM-containing offer (assuming, of course, that the firms that would have been their privately-best-placed suppliers in the absence of the natural-oligopolistic pricer would not have charged them NOMs). At least in combination with the facts that (1) no moral argument can be made for the natural-oligopolistic pricer's securing an NOM, (2) natural-oligopolistic pricing would in any event impose equivalent-dollar losses on the directly-affected buyers that if anything will exceed the equivalent-dollar gains it confers on the natural-oligopolistic pricer, and (3) natural-oligopolistic pricing will almost always be economically inefficient, the fact that the operation of the natural-oligopolistic pricer leaves the buyers it charges natural-oligopolistic prices worse-off than they would have been in its absence does seem to me to warrant the conclusion that the charging of individualized natural-oligopolistic prices is liberal-moral-rights-violative.

Fourth, a seller that is practicing natural-oligopolistic pricing may sometimes have to lower its initial price if a rival does beat its initial offer (either mistakenly or in the ex ante reasonable expectation that it can persuade the relevant buyer to forego the opportunity to secure a still-better rebid from the natural-oligopolistic pricer to deter the natural-oligopolistic pricer in question and the buyer's other suppliers from charging the buyer natural-oligopolistic prices in the future). I am struggling, but I cannot justicize the conclusion that a natural-oligopolistic pricer's making an inherently-profitable rebid to retain a sale it would otherwise lose to a rival that beat its initial offer violates the liberal moral rights of that rival. However, although I recognize that some may find this claim bizarre, if an individualized pricer's efforts to secure an NOM are deemed to violate the liberal moral rights of any buyer from which it secures an NOM, it may follow that such a pricer's conduct also violates the moral rights of any rival that attempted unsuccessfully to secure a relevant buyer's patronage (is morally obligated to compensate any such rival for the costs it incurred when attempting to secure the buyer's patronage).

The rivals of an individualized-pricing seller that is attempting to secure NOMs from its customers face two categories of related choices. First, the rivals of such a natural-oligopolistic pricer must decide whether to report or not to report the natural-oligopolistic pricer's natural-oligopolistic pricing to the natural-oligopolistic pricer's customers (when decisions to report the natural-oligopolistic pricing to the buyer being charged NOMs could benefit the reporter by reducing the natural-oligopolistic pricer's goodwill or by leading the buyers to patronize the reporter [to forego the opportunity to solicit rebids from the natural-oligopolistic price]), to the antitrust-law-enforcement authorities (if natural-oligopolistic pricing is prohibited), and/or to relevant legislative (regulatory) authorities to persuade them to prohibit such pricing. For the same reasons that I concluded that contrived-oligopolistic-pricer rivals have no liberal moral duty to report contrived-oligopolistic pricing, I believe that natural-oligopolistic-pricer rivals have no liberal moral duty to report natural-oligopolistic pricing.

Second, each rival of an individualized-pricing natural-oligopolistic pricer must choose whether or not to beat the natural-oligopolistic pricer's initial offer and, if it chooses to beat that offer, presumably to attempt to convince the relevant buyer to accept its offer in order to deter the relevant natural-oligopolistic pricer and other suppliers that might otherwise charge it natural-oligopolistic prices in the future from doing so. I believe that no natural-oligopolistic-pricer rival has a liberal moral duty to beat the natural-oligopolistic pricer's natural-oligopolistic-individualized-price-containing offers, much less to do so and to try to persuade relevant buyers to accept its initially-more-attractive offers (though, as I indicated previously, a rival of a natural-oligopolistic pricer that made such efforts but lost the relevant sale to a natural-oligopolistic pricer that rebid to beat the non-cooperator's offer might have a liberal moral right to recover the loss the natural-oligopolistic pricer's rebidding caused it to incur).

I turn now to natural-oligopolistic pricing in across-the-board-pricing situations. To save space, I will restrict the following analysis to two acts that are unique to or different in across-the-board-pricing situations. First, in addition to the other otherwise-unprofitable choices that prospective across-the-board pricers (like individualized pricers) can make to enable themselves to secure OMs naturally by increasing their OCAs, across-the-board pricers can also put themselves in a position to obtain OMs naturally by making and implementing price-announcements "prematurely" in the sense that the dates of the price-announcement and related announced-price-implementation choices were earlier than the dates the firms would otherwise find profitable to enable the firms to progressively jointly lock themselves into prices that are higher than those they would find profitable to charge if their respective rivals had not made price-announcement/implementation choices that rendered it unprofitable for those rivals to charge lower prices. It should be no surprise that any such "premature" price-announcement/implementation choices are liberal-moral-rights-violative—in particular, violate the liberal moral rights of those buyers on whom they impose equivalent-dollar losses by causing them to be charged higher prices.

Second, I need to address the possible liberal-moral-rights-violativeness of a choice by an across-the-board pricer that made no otherwise-unprofitable choice to increase its ability to profit by charging natural-oligopolistic prices to profit by charging a higher price than it would have found (most) profitable to charge had one or more of its rivals not charged natural-oligopolistic prices. Although I recognize that some will find the following conclusion incorrect at best and disqualifying at worst, I do think that, assuming ad arguendo that the practice of natural-oligopolistic pricing is liberal-moral-rights-violative, it would be liberal-moral-rights-violative of affected buyers' rights for a rival of one or more across-the-board-pricing natural-oligopolistic pricers knowingly to profit from the latter firm's or firms' liberal-moral-rights-violative conduct by charging a higher price to its own customers than it would have charged absent its rivals' natural-oligopolistic pricing.

All the other conclusions I reached about the liberal-moral-rights-violativeness of the various natural-oligopolistic-pricing-related choices that individualized pricers may make apply mutatis mutandis when the natural-oligopolistic pricers and their rivals are setting across-the-board prices.

9.1.2.2 The Seller-Practiced Contrived-Oligopolistic-Pricing-Related and Natural-Oligopolistic-Pricing-Related Moral Obligations of the Government of a Liberal-Moral-Rights-Based Society

Section 9.2.2 stated that liberalism imposes a variety of constraints on the choices that a liberal-moral-rights-based society's government can make to deter liberal-moral-rights-violating conduct and give the victims of such conduct an appropriate opportunity to obtain legal redress from those who have violated their liberal moral rights. Some of those constraints relate to the methods such governments are permitted to use to obtain relevant evidence (e.g., such governments are not permitted to coerce confessions or introduce coerced confessions into evidence); some relate to the probability of wrongdoing that must be established to secure a verdict against a defendant (a "preponderance of evidence" standard that must be met in civil trials and a "proof beyond a reasonable doubt" standard that must be met in criminal trials); some relate to liberalism's requirement that moral-rights bearers be treated as ends not as means—that one cannot justicize imposing "costs" (a total of civil fines, criminal fines, prison sentences, and non-custodial restrictions) on convicted wrongdoers that are more onerous than the wrongfulness of the wrongdoers' conduct by arguing that doing so reduces the allocative cost the State must generate to deter wrongdoing to any relevant extent: punishment must fit the crime); and in societies whose knowledge-base, human capital, and natural resources are sufficiently limited to make this possibility salient, some relate to the fundamental moral obligation of the governments of liberal-moral-rights-based societies to maximize the extent to which the liberal-moral-rights-related interests of the moral-rights bearers for whom they are responsible are secured (in such societies, liberalism may permit, indeed may morally obligate, governments to forego deterring oligopolistic-pricing-related conduct that is liberal-moral-rights-violative or to forego providing victims of such conduct with otherwise-required opportunities to secure legal redress if, given the resource-constraints they face, in order to secure these liberal-moral-rights-related interests to any given extent, they would have to forego securing weightier liberal-moral-rights-related interests).

However, the government of a liberal-moral-rights-based society is obligated to do everything it can within these constraints to deter liberal-moral-rights-violative natural-oligopolistic-pricing-related conduct and to provide those whose liberal moral rights such conduct violated with an appropriate opportunity to secure legal redress from its perpetrators. These obligations extend to the efforts that any such government must make to educate firms/individuals not to engage in contrived-oligopolistic and natural-oligopolistic pricing and to use criminal and civil law to deter such conduct—by promulgating laws that prohibit such conduct and authorize the imposition of appropriate "costs" on convicted violators, by creating relevant legal rights for such conduct's victims, by carrying out relevant investigations, by providing non-government actors with incentives to provide relevant evidence, by negotiating appropriate settlement/plea deals, by trying cases appropriately diligently and skillfully, etc. Of course, the concrete implications of several of these conclusions will be affected by the difficulty of establishing that a particular price is natural-oligopolistic or contrived-oligopolistic and that a particular actor has engaged in liberal-moral-rights-violative natural-oligopolistic or contrived-oligopolistic pricing.

9.1.3 The Impact of the Decisions Associated With Seller-Practiced Oligopolistic Pricing on the Instantiation of Various Morally-Defensible Conceptions of the Moral Good and the Implications of the Fact That Such Pricing Disserves the Instantiation of Many Such Conceptions of the Moral Good for the Obligations of the Government of a Liberal-Moral-Rights-Based Society

9.1.3.1 The Impact of the Decisions Associated With Seller-Practiced Oligopolistic Pricing on the Instantiation of Various Morally-Defensible Conceptions of the Moral Good

I have six sets of relevant conclusions. First, with one possible but highly-unlikely exception (contriver-practiced offensive price-retaliation against one or more non-cooperators) and one somewhat-more-likely set of possible exceptions whose salience is attributable to the relevant government's failure to adopt economically-efficient PPR-related policies (all choices that result in production-process researchers' securing OMs), all seller-practiced-oligopolistic-pricing-related choices that are liberal-moral-rights-violative also disserve the instantiation of all the morally-defensible conceptions of the moral good discussed in Sect. 9.2.3. Thus, with those possible exceptions, all liberal-moral-rights-violative seller-practice-of-oligopolistic-pricing-related choices disserve the utilitarian conception of the moral good because they decrease economic efficiency and impose equivalent-dollar losses on individuals (primarily, buyers of the oligopolistic-pricing sellers' product[s] and buyers of the products of some of their rivals) for whom the average marginal utility of money over the relevant range is higher than it is for the individuals on whom the choices confer equivalent-dollar gains (primarily, shareholders, creditors, managers, and employees of the oligopolistic pricer[s]). Moreover, with what I take to be the rare exception referenced in note 3 and no other exception, all liberal-moral-rights-violative seller-practice-of-oligopolistic-pricing-related choices will disserve the instantiation of the equal-utility, equal-resource, and various other sorts of non-liberal-equal-opportunity conceptions of the moral good[11] because, with that rare exception, all such choices will impose equivalent-dollar losses on individuals who (as a class) are poorer and confer equivalent-dollar gains on individuals who as a class are richer.[12] Obviously, with the above qualifications, the preceding conclusions also imply that all such choices will disserve the instantiation of mixed conceptions of the moral good in which two or more of the above-referenced pure conceptions of the moral good play a role (unless the utilitarian conception of the moral good plays a role and one or both of the possible exceptions referenced at the beginning of this paragraph is operative and critical).

Second, I suspect that in the overwhelming majority of instances a contriver's offensive retaliation against one or more rivals that have not cooperated with its contrivance will also disserve the instantiation of all the morally-defensible conceptions of the moral good referenced in the preceding paragraph. The only reason to doubt this conclusion is that such retaliation may generate *short-run* distributive effects that are desirable from the perspective of these conceptions of the moral good. However, I suspect that this clearly-relevant reality is more than offset from the perspective of utilitarianism by the moral undesirability of the long-run distributive impact of such offensive retaliation and its economic inefficiency and from the perspective of the various morally-defensible non-utilitarian-egalitarian conceptions of the moral good just referenced by the moral undesirability of the long-run distributive impact of such offensive retaliation.

Third, the possibility that the offensive retaliation that sellers of the right to use the production processes they discovered practice to punish rivals that have not cooperated with their contrivance may be desirable from a utilitarian perspective (at least if one ignores the equivalent-dollar loss it imposes on liberal observers by dis-satisfying their "external preferences") (1) is contingent on its increasing economic efficiency more by increasing the amount of resources devoted to PPR than it decreases economic efficiency by generating allocative transaction costs, intra-ARDEPPS UO-to-UO misallocation, poverty-and-material-inequality-related misallocation, X-inefficiency-related misallocation, tax-related misallocation, and the short-run misallocation that is caused by any defensive retaliation it elicits and therefore (2) will arise only if (but I think rarely even if) the government has not adopted one or more IP policies, tax policies, antitrust policies, and/or possibly environmental policies to prevent the economy from devoting too few resources to PPR execution from the perspective of economic efficiency.

Fourth, many of the non-liberal-moral-rights-violative decisions that one or more sellers' practice of oligopolistic pricing may result in one or more of its or their rivals' making will disserve the instantiation of the utilitarian conception of the moral good by decreasing economic efficiency and conferring equivalent-dollar gains on individuals who, as a class, are richer while imposing equivalent-dollar losses on individuals who, as a class, are poorer and will disserve the instantiation of the equal-utility, equal-resource, and various other equal-opportunity conceptions of the moral good by imposing equivalent-dollar losses on individuals who, as a class, are poorer and conferring equivalent-dollar gains on individuals who, as a class, are richer. The choices in question include choices (1) not to beat COM-containing and NOM-containing offers, (2) not to inform buyers that have been charged COM-containing or NOM-containing prices that they have been charged such prices, (3) not to try to persuade such buyers to reject the offers that oligopolistic-pricing sellers have made them, (4) not to report their rival's or rivals' oligopolistic pricing to antitrust-law-enforcement authorities, (5) not to supply evidence to such authorities or the relevant buyers or to testify in civil and/or criminal cases brought against their oligopolistic-pricing seller-rivals, and (6) not to engage in defensive retaliation against their contriving rival's or rivals' offensive retaliation against their non-cooperation. I suspect that all such negative decisions, which I believe liberalism implies the relevant sellers have a moral right to make, (1) disserve the instantiation of utilitarianism because they are economically inefficient (because they fail to deter the decisionmakers rivals' practice of oligopolistic pricing, which is economically inefficient) and inflict equivalent-dollar losses on individuals who are, as a class, poorer than are the individuals on whom they confer equivalent-dollar gains and (2) disserve the instantiation of the equal-utility, equal-resource, and the various other equal-opportunity variants of egalitarianism because they harm individuals who are, as a class, poorer and benefit individuals who are, as a class, richer.

9.1.3.2 The Ability of the Government of a Liberal-Moral-Rights-Based Society to Serve the Instantiation of the Various Morally-Defensible Conceptions of the Moral Good and to Fulfill Its Liberal Moral Duty to Give Appropriate, Equal Weight to the Morally-Defensible Moral-Good Positions of All Members of and Participants in the Relevant Society by Responding Appropriately to Seller-Practiced Oligopolistic Pricing

I have three points (related sets of points) to make about the ability of the government of a liberal-moral-rights-based society to secure the instantiation of any morally-defensible pure or mixed conception of the moral good and four points (related sets of points) to make about the moral duty of the government of such a society to give appropriate equal weight to its members'/participants' moral-good positions. The first point I want to make about the ability of the government of a liberal-moral-rights-based society to instantiate any morally-defensible conception of the moral good is that its ability to do so is constrained by its basic moral duty to maximize the extent to which liberal-moral-rights-related interests are secured.

The second set of points I want to make about the ability of the government of a liberal-moral-rights-based society to instantiate various morally-defensible conceptions of the moral good relates to the ability of government to instantiate the utilitarian conception of the moral good or any mixed conception of the moral good in which total utility is positively valued. The first member of this second set of points is that the ability of government to instantiate the utilitarian conception of the moral good is enhanced by the fact that (for reasons explained in Sect. 9.1.3.1) all or virtually all exemplars of seller-practiced oligopolistic-pricing-related conduct decrease total utility by decreasing economic efficiency and redistributing income in a way that utilitarianism disfavors. The second member of this set of points is that the ability of government to increase total utility by responding appropriately to seller-practiced oligopolistic pricing is reduced by the allocative costs the government would have to generate to deter in any way seller-practiced-oligopolistic-pricing-related behavior that reduced total utility. I should point out that the relevant "allocative costs" include the allocative transaction-costs that any effort to deter such behavior would generate, the allocative transaction cost of financing any related enforcement-effort, the economic inefficiency that the financing of the relevant government expenditures would generate (associated allocative transaction costs aside), and any economic inefficiency that any attempt to deter such behavior would generate by deterring firms from charging supra-marginal-cost non-oligopolistic prices (whose charging they fear will increase the probability that they will be falsely found to have practiced oligopolistic pricing) whose charging would promote economic efficiency by incentivizing resource allocators to make more-economically-efficient rather than less-economically-efficient QV investments or to execute more-economically-efficient rather than less-economically-efficient PPR projects. The third member of this set of points is that the ability of a government to increase total utility is also affected by the distributive impact of the choices it makes to deter seller-practiced oligopolistic pricing and that, at least to some extent, this distributive impact is within the relevant government's control.

The third set of points I want to make about the ability of the government of a liberal-moral-rights-based society to instantiate various morally-defensible conceptions of the moral good relates to the ability of such a government to instantiate any pure non-utilitarian-egalitarian conception of the moral good or any mixed conception of the moral good in which one or more non-utilitarian notions of equality are positively valued. The first member of this third set of points is that the fact that (for reasons that Sect. 9.1.3.1 explained) all or virtually all exemplars of seller-practiced oligopolistic pricing disserve the instantiation of all non-utilitarian-egalitarian conceptions of the moral good favors the conclusion that government will be able to serve the instantiation of these conceptions of the moral good by deterring seller-practiced oligopolistic pricing. The second member of this third set of points is that the ability of government to instantiate any of these non-utilitarian-egalitarian conceptions of the moral good by responding appropriately to seller-practiced oligopolistic pricing depends in part on the distributive impact of the choices it makes to finance its responses to such conduct and that those choices and hence the distributive impact of its financing efforts are within the government's control.

I will now make four points or sets of related points about the ability of a government of a liberal-moral-rights-based society to fulfill its liberal moral obligation to give appropriate weight to the morally-defensible moral-good positions of all its society's members and participants by responding to seller-practiced oligopolistic pricing. The first three of these sets of points relate to the content of the moral right of the members and participants of a liberal-moral-rights-based society to have equal, appropriate weight given to their moral-good positions.

First, the relevant moral right of a member or participant of a liberal-moral-rights-based society is to have its government's decisions appropriately reflect (obviously, much work remains to be done here) (1) the percentage of its society's members (or members and participants) that subscribe to his or her morally-defensible moral-good positions, (2) the strength of his/her "preferences for" his/her more-preferred morally-defensible conception of the moral good relative to his or her less-preferred morally-defensible conceptions of the moral good, (3) the percentages of the society's members that subscribe to other morally-defensible conceptions of the moral good, and (4) the strength of the members' of each such other group preferences for their respective conceptions of the moral good relative to other morally-defensible conceptions of the moral good.

The second point in this second subset of points is that the moral-good-related moral duties of the government of a liberal-moral-rights-based society relate to the totality of its decisions (more precisely, to the totality of the decisions of all the governmental units of the society in question). Thus, even if a society's government were totally centralized, one could not tell whether the government fulfilled its moral-good-related moral duties by examining only a subset of the decisions it made (say, only the decisions it made related to seller-practiced oligopolistic pricing or the antitrust-policy decisions it made: what an analytic misery).

The third point in this second subset is that liberalism's corollary that the government of a liberal-moral-rights-based society must give equal, appropriate weight to the morally-defensible moral-good positions of all its society's members and participants implies that at least sometimes the relevant government would be behaving unjustly if it fully instantiated the conception of the moral good that has majority support or even the support of some specified supermajority because in some situations conforming to the positions of a majority or supermajority would give insufficient weight to the positions of those who do not agree with them. (I am fully aware of the practical obstacles to operationalizing the preceding two conclusions.)

The fourth and final point in this second subset is that, even if (as I am disposed to conclude) the argument for sellers' having a liberal moral right not to combat their rivals' practice of oligopolistic pricing in various ways implies that laws that require them to combat such conduct would violate their liberal moral rights, that conclusion would not imply the liberal-moral-rights-violativeness of laws that incentivize sellers' combatting their rivals' practice of oligopolistic pricing by rewarding their undercutting, protecting them against contriver-retaliation, enabling them to secure legal redress from retaliating contrivers, compensating them for any unredressed losses such retaliation imposes on them, rewarding them for informing relevant buyers and/or the antitrust-law-enforcement authorities of the oligopolistic pricing of their rivals, and rewarding them for providing evidence to or testifying for such buyers or authorities (though admittedly, such awards would sometimes taint the relevant evidence or testimony).

9.2 Contrived-Oligopolistic, Natural-Oligopolistic, and Non-Oligopolistic (1) Decisions by One or More Sellers (A) Not to Reveal to Prospective Customers Product-Performance-Related Information and Product-Lifetime-Cost-to-Buyer Information That Will Tend to Prevent Buyers From Making Mistaken Product-Purchase or Product-Purchase-Price Decisions by Militating Against the Buyers' Overestimating the Dollar Value of the Relevant Product(s) to Them and/or Underestimating the Lifetime Cost to Them of Buying, Maintaining, and Repairing the Seller's (Sellers') Durable Product(s) and/or (B) Not to Reveal to the Government (Say, to the Legislature or to Regulatory Authorities) Information About the Errors Buyers Are Making About Its (Their) Products and Information About the External Costs Generated by the Production and Consumption of Its (Their) Product(s) When the Information-Provisions Would Be Economically Efficient or Morally Desirable and (2) Decisions by the Government to Respond to the Prospect or Reality of Such Non-Disclosures in Various Ways

This section differs from the other sections of this chapter in that it considers the economic efficiency and moral character of the conduct on which it focuses (seller non-disclosures of "product-[performance/cost-to-buyer]" information and product-related external-cost information) and the economic efficiency and moral character of various possible government responses to the prospect and/or reality of such non-disclosures both when the non-disclosures eventuated from relevant-seller oligopolistic interactions and when it did not. I acknowledge that it might be more appropriate to analyze seller non-disclosures of the above types when they do not result from two or more sellers' oligopolistic interactions in studies of consumer-protection, environmental, or tort-law policy. However, since much of the relevant analysis is the same for oligopolistic-interaction-generated and non-oligopolistic-interaction-generated seller non-disclosures of these types of information, I decided to cover analyses of the referenced non-oligopolistic-interaction-generated seller non-disclosures as well as the referenced oligopolistic-interaction-generated non-disclosures: I ask your indulgence for this "bonus-coverage," which I hope will be illuminating.

When one or more buyers of a single product or a set of homogeneous or heterogeneous products produced by closely-competitive rivals overestimate the dollar value to them of the product(s) in question and/or underestimate the lifetime purchase, maintenance, and repair cost of using the seller's or sellers' durable product(s), it will be in the seller's (sellers' joint) equivalent-dollar interest not to reveal to the buyers information that would enable the buyers to avoid making mistaken product-purchase or product-purchase-price decisions. Similarly, when government officials who are authorized to prevent buyers from making mistakes do not possess information that one or more sellers have that relates to errors that buyers might make about its or their products and when government officials who are authorized to respond to prospective or past external costs of production and consumption to promote the public interest do not possess relevant information about the external costs generated by the production and consumption of one or more sellers' products, it may be in the equivalent-dollar interest of a set of rivals that individually possess such information not to divulge it to the government.

One can certainly think of situations in which the concealment of such information could be effectuated without any seller's engaging in any type of oligopolistic conduct. For example, no oligopolistic conduct would be needed if (1) only one seller possessed the information in question because only one seller produced any relevant good or (2)(A) two or more sellers possessed the relevant information because they produced a relevant product or product variant and (B) none of those sellers would profit from the revelation of the information in question (would find that the revelation of such information would improve its competitive-position array vis-à-vis other producers in its ARDEPPS sufficiently to outweigh the revelation's negative impact on the seller's competitive positions vis-à-vis its more distant competitors) because none produced a product whose dollar value to its buyers was overestimated or whose lifetime dollar cost to its buyers was underestimated by substantially less than were their counterparts for its in-ARDEPPS rivals, none produced a product whose production and consumption generated significantly-lower external costs than did the production and consumption of the products of its in-ARDEPPS rivals, none was significantly-better-placed than its rivals to do product R&D that would discover a product whose competitive-position array would be improved by product-performance-related or product-lifetime-cost-to-buyer disclosures, and none was significantly-better-placed than its rivals to do product-R&D or PPR that would discover a product whose production and consumption or a production process whose use would be less external-cost-generating. However, I suspect that in other situations sellers will not only have to rely on but will be able to rely on their natural-oligopolistic interdependence to keep the information secret. Take, for example, a case in which each member of a set of rivals ranks from best to worst the following situations: (1) It discloses the information and its rivals either stay silent or claim the information is false (a situation that is best for it because the goodwill benefits and government rewards [or favorable treatment] it obtains by making the disclosure exceed the losses the disclosure would otherwise impose on it); (2) the information remains secret; (3) one or more than one of the firm's rivals disclose the information, and the firm confirms or elaborates on the disclosure; and (4) one or more of the firm's rivals reveal the information, and the firm stays silent or claims the information is false. In this case, each seller (say, X1) will decide not to reveal the information because each will realize that each of its rivals X2…n will perceive that, if any of them (say, X2) discloses that information, X1 and their mutual rivals (X3…n) will have the opportunity to react to that disclosure and will find it inherently profitable to react by confirming and perhaps elaborating on the disclosure and that that sequence of acts will leave the initial discloser X2 worse-off than it would have been had no-one revealed the information (will leave each seller in the third situation described above worse-off than it would have been in the second). I suspect that this kind of natural-oligopolistic interdependence accounts for the failure of cigarette companies to reveal what they knew about the dangerousness of smoking, the failure of automobile manufacturers to reveal what they knew about the accident-losses and the environmental-losses generated by driving, and the failure of pharmaceutical companies to reveal negative information that each had about the efficacy and safety of its own and its rivals' products. But there may also be other situations—for example, situations in which one or more members of a set of rivals are better-placed than their rivals to do relevant profitable product R&D and PPR—in which a set of sellers that would find it jointly profitable to conceal the type of information in question will be able to succeed in doing so only by bribing those of their rivals that would otherwise profit from revealing the information not to reveal it (by paying them money or agreeing to compete less aggressively against them) and/or by threatening to retaliate in one or more ways against anyone that disclosures the relevant information—that is, by engaging in contrived-oligopolistic conduct.[13]

9.2.1 The Economic Efficiency of (1) One or More Sellers' Not Disclosing to Buyers Product-Performance Information That Will Help Buyers Not to Overestimate the Dollar Value to Them of the Relevant Product(s) or Information That Will Help Buyers Not to Underestimate the Lifetime Purchase, Maintenance, and Repair Costs of Using a Product or of One or More Sellers' Not Disclosing to the Government the Above Information or Information About the External Costs Generated by the Production and Consumption of the Product(s) in Question, Both When Such Non-Disclosures Were Secured Through Contrived or Natural-Oligopolistic Interactions and When They Were Not, and (2) Various Responses That the Government Could Make to the Prospect or Reality of Such Non-Disclosures

9.2.1.1 The Economic Efficiency of One or More Sellers' Not Disclosing Buyer-Relevant Product-Information to Prospective Buyers or the Government or Not Disclosing to the Government Information That Relates to the External Costs Generated by the Production and Consumption of the Product(s) in Question

I focus first on the economic inefficiency generated by one or more sellers' not disclosing to their prospective customers product-(performance/cost-to-buyer)-related information that would militate against these buyers' continuing to overestimate the dollar value(s) to the buyers of the seller's (sellers') product(s) and/or continuing to underestimate the lifetime cost to the buyers of purchasing, maintaining, and repairing the relevant durable product(s) when the seller(s) could communicate such information at lower allocative cost than the buyers could discover it or the buyers would not discover it regardless of the "profitability" and allocative efficiency of their doing so. If the relevant economy contained no other Pareto imperfections or the other Pareto imperfections the relevant economy contained had no impact on the economic-inefficiency effects of the non-disclosures (i.e., of the non-sovereignty the disclosures could have eliminated), the non-disclosures would cause economic inefficiency in at least seven ways: (1) by generating allocative transaction costs equal to (the private transaction cost the relevant sellers incurred to secure them if they secured them by engaging in contrived-oligopolistic conduct) *times* (the ratio of the allocative transaction costs generated by the relevant seller-efforts to their private counterparts), (2) by generating inter-ARDEPPS UO-to-UO misallocation by causing misinformed buyers to purchase (from the perspective of economic efficiency) too many units of the goods whose negative attributes were undisclosed and too few units of the goods in other ARDEPPSes the buyers would have purchased instead of the former goods because, given the non-disclosure, the percentage by which the relevant misinformed buyers (overestimated the dollar value to them of the non-disclosing sellers or sellers' product[s])/(underestimated the lifetime dollar cost to them of buying, maintaining, and repairing the non-disclosing seller's or sellers' [durable] product[s])[14] exceeded the weighted-average percentage by which the buyers (overestimated the dollar value to them)/(underestimated the lifetime dollar cost to them) of the goods in other ARDEPPSes they would have purchased had they not mistakenly bought the non-disclosing seller's or sellers' product(s), (3) by generating intra-ARDEPPS UO-to-UO misallocation both when the non-disclosure results from contrived-oligopolistic conduct that involves price-retaliation against one or more disclosers (non-cooperators) and when the relevant buyers' non-sovereignty results in one or more of them purchasing one product in the ARDEPPS in question rather than another in circumstances in which the buyer(s) in question would have been better-off had it/they purchased a different product in that ARDEPPS because the magnitude of the relevant errors the buyers in question were making varied critically among the ARDEPPS' relevant products, (4) by generating (UO and PPR)-to-(product-R&D) misallocation, intra-project (product-R&D)-to-(product-R&D) misallocation, and intra-project QV-to-QV misallocation by deflating the incentives of the non-disclosing seller or sellers to discover alternative products that would have desirable attributes whose dollar value to buyers the buyers underestimate, (5) by generating PPR-to-QV misallocation if (as I assume) buyers of the products created by QV investments are (far) more likely than buyers of the right to use the production processes that PPR can discover to make the errors that would be prevented by the revelation of the information whose non-disclosure's inefficiency this section is analyzing, (6) by increasing poverty-related and material-inequality-related misallocation by conferring equivalent-dollar gains on a set of individuals (perpetrator-shareholders/creditors/managers/employees) that contains fewer poor people and fewer people whose income/wealth position (roughly speaking) is lower than average and imposing equivalent-dollar losses on a set of individuals (underinformed buyers) that contains more poor people and more people whose income/wealth position is lower than average, (7) by generating production-optimum-misallocation-related X-in efficiency to the extent that the non-disclosers respond to the increase in their potential profits that the non-disclosures generate by operating more sloppily, (8) by generating tax-law-related misallocative manager/employee substitutions of untaxed more-attractive-working-conditions and untaxed or lower-taxed fringe-benefits for the goods these parties would have bought with the monetary wages they exchanged for the conditions or benefits in question to the extent that the non-disclosers would have shared some of the potential profits the non-disclosers yielded them with these personnel, and/or (9) by raising the allocative cost of the buyers obtaining the relevant information if they obtained it themselves or from another source.

I will now address the way in which the other Pareto imperfections an economy contains will affect the impact of seller non-disclosures of information about their products' performance and lifetime cost to buyers on each of the categories of allocative costs or economic inefficiency the preceding paragraph references. First, in my judgment, the relevant Pareto imperfections will cause (1) the allocative transaction costs generated by sellers' contrived-oligopolistic efforts to deter rivals from disclosing to buyers or the government negative information about their products' performance or lifetime cost to buyers to exceed the private transaction costs sellers incur when contriving such information non-disclosures and (2) the difference between the private transaction costs the buyers would incur to secure the information in question from other sources and the private transaction costs the sellers would have to incur to communicate the relevant information to the buyers to be lower than the associated allocative-cost difference.

Second, although I do not know whether the other sets of Pareto imperfections that can cause inter-ARDEPPS UO-to-UO misallocation (e.g., differences in the [post-tax-prices]/MC ratios and/or differences in the [external-marginal-cost] to [internal-marginal-cost] ratios of products between whose production the non-disclosures cause resources to flow) compound or counteract the non-disclosure-related-buyer-error differences that would cause inter-ARDEPPS UO-to-UO misallocation in an oPp economy or even the relative magnitudes of the relevant "combination" of the former differences and the relevant-buyer-error differences, I can offer some crude and probably-unwise speculations about the cigarette, automobile, and pharmaceutical examples I referenced previously. Thus, I suspect that the tendency of concealment-affected-consumer-error differences to cause buyers to purchase too many cigarettes relative to other goods from the perspective of economic efficiency (1) is compounded by the tendency of the positive differences between the ratios of (the external costs of consumption) to (the internal costs of consumption) ratio for cigarettes and its weighted-average counterpart for the other goods that cigarette-smokers would buy instead of cigarettes if they reduced their consumption of cigarettes (where the external costs that the smoking of cigarettes generates are related to secondary smoke and the costs borne by family members and friends of smoking-caused-cancer victims) to cause individuals to buy too many cigarettes and too few units of other goods from the perspective of economic efficiency and (2) is counteracted by the difference between the (after-tax-price) to (marginal-cost) ratio for cigarettes and the weighted-average (after-tax-price) to (marginal-cost) ratio for the other goods that would be purchased instead of cigarettes if fewer cigarettes were bought to cause individuals to buy too few cigarettes and too many units of other goods from the perspective of economic efficiency. I suspect that the tendency of concealment-affected consumer-error differences (related inter alia to car-buyers' underestimating the accident losses that driving will impose on them and the cost to them of maintaining and repairing cars as well as to errors the relevant buyers make when estimating the dollar value to them and dollar cost to them of the other goods they would purchase if they bought fewer cars and drove less) to induce buyers to purchase too many cars and drive them too much from the perspective of economic efficiency (1) is compounded by the tendency of what I expect is the positive difference between the ratio of (external costs [not internalized by gas-taxes]) to (internal costs) for driving cars and its weighted-average counterpart for the other goods that car-purchasers/drivers would buy instead if they bought fewer cars and drove less to cause such individuals to purchase more cars and drive more and purchase fewer units of other goods than is allocatively efficient and (2) is counteracted by the tendency of what I expect is the positive difference between the ratio of (the after-tax price for cars, gasoline, and car-maintenance-and-repair services) to (the total marginal cost of these "goods") and its weighted-average counterpart for the goods and services that individuals would buy if they purchased fewer cars and drove less to cause them to buy too few cars and drive too little and purchase too many units of other goods from the perspective of economic efficiency. Finally, I suspect that the tendency of buyers (and their physicians) to overestimate the efficacy of pharmaceuticals and underestimate the pharmaceuticals' harmful side-effects (to overvalue pharmaceuticals by a higher percentage than the percentage by which they overvalue the other goods that they would purchase if they bought fewer units of pharmaceuticals) to cause too many units of pharmaceuticals to be bought from the perspective of economic efficiency relative to the number of units that possible pharmaceutical-buyers would purchase of other goods if they bought fewer units of pharmaceuticals will be counteracted by the tendency of what I expect is the positive difference between the ratio of (the after-tax price of pharmaceuticals) to (their marginal cost) and the weighted-average counterpart ratio for the goods that would be bought instead of pharmaceuticals to cause too few units of pharmaceuticals to be purchased relative to the amount of other goods that are purchased from the perspective of economic efficiency.

Third, although I have not done any empirical research into the magnitudes of the relevant parameters or parameter-differences, I see no reason to believe that differences in the (pre-tax-price)/(marginal-cost) ratios of, differences in the sales-tax rates that apply to the different products produced in any ARDEPPS or differences in the ratios of (external marginal production and consumption costs) to (internal marginal production and consumption costs) of the different products produced in any ARDEPPS will reduce the amount of intra-ARDEPPS misallocation that would be caused in their absence by non-disclosure-affected buyer errors and any price-retaliation involved in any contrived-oligopolistic efforts to secure the non-disclosure.

Fourth, although I see no reason to believe that the other Pareto imperfections that any actual economy contains will tend to affect the amount of economic inefficiency that non-disclosures to buyers generate by deflating the profits the relevant sellers can realize by producing new products that would have fewer deficiencies whose cost to buyers buyers underestimate rather than the extant, more-deficient products, I do think that the other Pareto imperfections actual economies contain will reduce the amount of economic inefficiency such non-disclosures generate by deterring sellers from doing product R&D aimed at discovering products whose actual dollar value to their consumers is higher in that their actual value to their consumers is reduced less by their having negative attributes that the relevant buyers do not recognize or undervalue by inflating the profits yielded by such R&D.

Fifth, the other Pareto imperfections any relevant economy contains will increase the amount of PPR-to-QV misallocation that seller-non-disclosures to buyers who otherwise do not possess this information of their products' performance-attributes and lifetime purchase, maintenance, and repair costs by inflating the profits yielded by such allocations of resources because other Pareto imperfections will also collectively inflate the profits yielded by such resource allocations.

Sixth, and finally, the other Pareto imperfections that actual economies contain or would contain at particular relevant distributions of income and wealth will clearly increase the amount of misallocation that seller non-disclosures to buyers of information about the sellers' products' performance-attributes and lifetime purchase, maintenance, and repair costs will generate by increasing poverty and material inequality and by increasing the non-disclosers' potential profits and hence the economic inefficiency they generate by operating sloppily and the economic inefficiency their managers and employees generate by substituting better working-conditions and higher fringe-benefits for the goods they would have purchased with the monetary compensation they forewent to obtain the better working-conditions and larger fringe-benefits in question.

I turn now to the economic inefficiency generated by one or more sellers' not disclosing to the government (1) information about the seller's (sellers') product's (products') performance and lifetime purchase, maintenance, and repair costs whose possession by its or their prospective buyers would prevent the buyers from overestimating its or their dollar value to them or underestimating its or their lifetime cost to them and (2) information about the external costs that are generated by the production and consumption of the seller's product or sellers' products, which the government may be underestimating. The only significant inefficiency-related difference between one or more sellers' failure to disclose to their prospective customers information that would militate against those buyers' making product-purchase and product-purchase-price errors and the seller's and sellers' not disclosing such information and information on the related errors that the relevant buyers might be making to the government is that the failure of the seller or sellers to disclose such information to the government will prevent the government from making TBLE decisions that will prevent the buyers from making economically-inefficient mistakes (say, decisions to provide information to the buyers, to put an error-offsetting tax on the products, or [at the extreme] to ban the production of the products[15]) as opposed to preventing the buyers from making such mistakes directly.

The economic inefficiency of one or more sellers' not disclosing to legislative or regulatory authorities the amount of external costs the production and consumption of its or their products generate obviously depends on how economic efficiently those government institutions would respond to their receipt of the information in question. To simplify, I will assume (1) that the relevant government institutions would respond third-best-allocative-efficiently to such information and (2) that, to respond third-best-allocative-efficiently to such information, they would not have to make decisions that will increase the magnitude of one or more categories of economic inefficiency (to fail to secure larger decreases in other categories of economic inefficiency). On those assumptions, the following 10 sets of economic-efficiency conclusions will be justified:

(1) in an oPp economy whose only Pareto imperfections are the external costs of production and consumption whose disclosure to the legislature's/regulatory authorities' economic efficiency is at issue, the disclosures will increase (decrease) allocative transaction costs by (A) the amount by which the disclosures

increase (decrease) the sum of the private transaction costs generated by the sellers' communication of the relevant information, to the government, the government's efforts to secure the information independently, costs the government's response to the information it possesses, and any retaliatory or reciprocatory behavior that any contrived-oligopolistic conduct the information's divulgence deters *plus* (B) the amount by which the other Pareto imperfections the economy in question contains cause the associated increase (decrease) in allocative transaction costs to exceed the resulting increase (decrease) in the referenced private transaction costs;

(2) (A) in an oPp economy in which the only Pareto imperfections are the external costs of production and consumption that are not being disclosed to the legislature or regulatory authorities that are unaware of them (or underestimate them), the non-disclosure of this external-cost information to the government will generate inter-ARDEPPS UO-to-UO misallocation by causing too many units of the products whose production's and consumption's external-cost-generating proclivities were not disclosed relative to the number of units of the products in other ARDEPPSes that buyers would have bought had they not purchased the additional units of the former products, and (B) although the other Pareto imperfections that actual economies contain (e.g., supra-competitive prices, sales taxes, buyer errors, etc.) could either increase or decrease the amount of inter-ARDEPPS UO-to-UO misallocation that are generated by seller non-disclosures of external-cost information to a government that is underestimating those external costs and it would certainly be TBLE to pay some attention to the possible impact of such other Pareto imperfections, I doubt that (at least across all relevant instances) these other Pareto imperfections (more precisely, the interaction of the differences in the relevant exemplars of each such type of other Pareto imperfection) will have a significant impact on the amount of inter-ARDEPPS UO-to-UO misallocation that seller non-disclosures of such external-cost information to the legislative or regulatory authorities will generate;

(3) (A) in an oPp economy whose only Pareto imperfections are the external costs whose seller non-disclosure to the government's economic efficiency is at issue, the non-disclosures will cause intra-ARDEPPS UO-to-UO misallocation by preventing the authorities from internalizing the external costs to the sellers and derivatively to the buyers to the extent that the non-internalization critically affects the identity of the product variant that is most "profitable" for the buyer to purchase (because the production-*plus*-consumption external costs that different product variants generate differ), and (B) although it will almost certainly be TBLE to devote some resources to considering the impact of the other Pareto imperfections that actual economies contain on the amount of intra-ARDEPPS UO-to-UO misallocation such seller non-disclosures generate, I suspect that acting together these other Pareto imperfections will prevent such non-disclosures from generating intra-ARDEPPS UO-to-UO misallocation in only a small percentage of cases and will not significantly affect the total amount of intra-ARDEPPS UO-to-UO misallocation that all instances of such seller non-disclosures generate;

(4) (A) in an oPp economy whose only Pareto imperfections are the external costs whose seller non-disclosure to the government's economic inefficiency is at issue, such non-disclosures will cause intra-ARDEPPS QV-to-QV misallocation by preventing regulators from eliminating sometimes-critical positive oPp-externality distortions in the profits that would be yielded by resource allocations to the creation and use of a QV investment whose creation and use would generate higher external costs unknown to regulators from the creation and use of a QV investment whose creation and use would generate lower external costs unknown to regulators (regardless of whether the QV investments in question were knowledge-creating) and (B) although it will almost certainly be TBLE to devote some resources to investigating the relevance of the other Pareto imperfections the economy in question contains that can distort the profitability of such resource allocations, I doubt that across all cases those other imperfections will render false the conclusion that the non-disclosure of externality information to regulators who underestimate the relevant externalities will cause additional intra-ARDEPPS QV-to-QV misallocation to be generated;
(5) the arguments that points (4)(A) and (4)(B) made and the conclusions they proffered on the impact of the seller non-disclosures to the government of externalities the government underestimates on intra-ARDEPPS QV-to-QV misallocation are respectively equally-applicable and equally-justified when the issue is the impact of such seller non-disclosures to regulators on intra-ARDEPPS choice-among-known-production-processes and PPR-to-PPR misallocation;
(6) (A) in an oPp economy in which the only Pareto imperfections are the external costs of production and consumption that government regulators will underestimate if the firms that sell the products in question do not disclose these externalities to the government, these seller non-disclosures will prevent the government from preventing resources from being misallocated from PPR execution to QV-investment creation (or vice versa) if PPR is more likely (less likely) to discover production processes whose use reduces the undisclosed external costs than QV investments are to create products whose production and use generates lower undisclosed external costs and (B) since the other Pareto imperfections that actual economies contain (particularly, imperfections in seller price-competition) tend to cause positive distortions in the profits yielded by resource allocations that withdraw resources from PPR and devote them to QV-investment creation, those other imperfections will increase the amount of PPR-to-QV misallocation that the seller non-disclosures in question generate if those non-disclosures would cause PPR-to-QV misallocation in an oPp economy and will decrease the amount of misallocation between QV-investment creation and PPR execution the relevant economy contains if such non-disclosures would cause too many resources to be allocated to PPR and not enough to QV-investment creation in an oPp economy;
(7) (A) in a realistically-Pareto-imperfect economy, the failure of producers to inform a government that underestimates the external costs that the production

and consumption of their products generate of the actual amount of such costs the production and consumption of their products generate can cause either positive or negative oPp externality distortions in the profits yielded by (UO/QV/PPR)-to-UO, (UO/QV/PPR)-to-QV, and (UO/QV/PPR)-to-PPR resource allocations[16] and (B) the impact that the other Pareto imperfections the relevant economy contains will have on the amount of each of these three types of misallocation the relevant economy contains will depend on whether the $(SW[M/MS/T/NS/NM/BS])D(P\pi_{(C+U)\ldots/(C+U)UO/QV/PPR)})$ figure has the same sign as or the opposite sign to the related $(SW[X]D_{(P\pi(C+U)\ldots/(C+U)UO/QV/PPR})$ figure and the relative absolute magnitudes of the two step-wise-distortion figures in question for each of the three referenced categories of resource allocation (where the category of resource allocation in question will be further specified by a UO, QV, or PPR symbol that replaces the ellipsis in the symbol's subscript);

(8) (A) in an oPp economy whose only Pareto imperfections are the external costs whose seller non-disclosure to the government's economic inefficiency is at issue, the seller non-disclosures in question will tend to cause traditional consumption-optimum misallocation to the extent that the amount of consumption externalities the consumption of the product(s) in question generates varies among their potential consumers, and (B) it may not be TBLE even to consider the possibility that the amount of such traditional consumption-optimum misallocation such seller non-disclosures generate will be affected by the other Pareto imperfections actual economies contain;

(9) (A) in an oPp economy whose only Pareto imperfections at any relevant distribution of income and wealth are external costs whose magnitudes are underestimated by the relevant society's government, producer non-disclosures of the amount of externalities generated by the production and consumption of their products would not cause any economic inefficiency by increasing poverty and material inequality even if, as I suspect, such non-disclosures increase poverty and material inequality, but (B) in actual economies in which the incidence of various other types of Pareto imperfections is influenced by their distributions of income and wealth, producer non-disclosures of the relevant external costs to the government will generate economic inefficiency by increasing poverty and material inequality, and

(10) (A) in an economy whose firms tend to operate more sloppily the higher their potential supernormal profit-rate and to share increases in their potential supernormal profits with their managers and employees, non-disclosures to government of external-cost-related information will tend to decrease economic inefficiency by increasing the non-disclosers' potential supernormal profits and hence the production-optimum-related misallocation they generate and the amount of misallocation their managers and employees generate by making economically-inefficient substitutions of better working-conditions and higher fringe-benefits for the goods they would have purchased with the monetary compensation they forewent to obtain the above desiderata.

I readily acknowledge the qualitative character and contestability of all the preceding conclusions. Still, I have no doubt that, everything considered, on my assumption that the government will respond third-best-allocative-efficiently to the information at its disposal, seller-decisions not to disclose to the government information about the external costs the production and consumption of their products generate will reduce economic efficiency.

9.2.1.2 The Ability of the Government of a Liberal-Moral-Rights-Based Society to Increase Economic Efficiency by Responding Appropriately to Firm-Non-Disclosures to Buyers of Product-Value-Related and Product-Cost-to-Buyer-Related Information and of Firm-Non-Disclosures to Government of Information About Their Product's Value and Cost to Buyers and About the External Costs That Are Generated by Their Product's Production and Consumption

I will make five points that relate to the ability of the government of a liberal-moral-rights-based society to increase economic efficiency by promulgating and enforcing antitrust-law prohibitions of sellers' failing to report to buyers or the government information about the sellers' products that will prevent the buyers from misestimating their dollar value and/or dollar cost to the buyers or failing to report to the government either such information or information about the external costs their products' production and consumption generate. First, the allocative cost of government efforts to secure the disclosure of such information include not only the allocative cost generated by any related educational efforts, by the drafting and promulgation of the relevant prohibitions, by the promulgation of the relevant prohibitions, and by any related enforcement-efforts but also the allocative cost of financing any related government-expenditures. Second, despite these allocative costs, I suspect it will be economically efficient for government to devote a substantial amount of resources to deterring sellers from acting oligopolistically to conceal such information from buyers and the government. Third, although contrived-oligopolistic non-disclosures will tend to be more economically inefficient than non-disclosures that result from natural-oligopolistic interdependencies because contrivance is more allocative-transaction-costly and may involve some moves (e.g., acts of retaliation) that would be misallocative even if they generated no allocative transaction costs, it will be economically efficient for governments to prohibit sellers from securing non-disclosures through both subtypes of oligopolistic behavior (1) because these types of non-disclosures are economically inefficient even when they result from natural-oligopolistic interdependence and (2) because prohibiting such non-disclosures when they result from natural-oligopolistic interdependencies as well as when they result from contrivance reduces allocative transaction costs by obviating proof of contrivance. Fourth, a semantic point whose value is open to question: Although it may be economically efficient to educate firms to or impose a legal obligation on firms to disclose this type of information to buyers and governments even when their decision not to disclose it would not result from any type of oligopolistic interaction (e.g., to educate or impose such a legal obligation on a pure monopolist), any such policy would not properly be called an antitrust policy. Fifth and finally, all the liberal constraints on governments of liberal-moral-rights-based societies are equally applicable in this context as in any other.

9.2.2 The Liberal Moral Duty (Liberal Moral Right) of a Seller to Disclose (Not to Disclose) to Prospective Buyers and the Government Information About Its Product's Performance or Lifetime-Cost to Buyers, the Liberal Moral Duty (Liberal Moral Right) of a Seller to Disclose (Not to Disclose) to the Government Information About the External Costs That Its Product's Production and Consumption Generate, and the Related Moral Duties of the Government of a Liberal-Moral-Rights-Based Society

9.2.2.1 The Relevant-Disclosure-Related Moral Duties and Moral Rights of Sellers in a Liberal-Moral-Rights-Based Society

I will discuss six issues or sets of connected issues that relate to the relevant-disclosure moral duties and rights of sellers in a liberal-moral-rights-based society. The first of these issues is whether an individual seller in a liberal-moral-rights-based society that can keep information about its product secret without engaging in contrived-oligopolistic or even natural-oligopolistic conduct has a moral right not to be placed under a legal obligation to disclose to its prospective customers information about its product that it should realize (1) the buyers do not possess (2) that would militate against the buyers' mistakenly purchasing the seller's product or paying too high a price for the seller's product when any errors the relevant buyers might otherwise make are not attributable to any positive act or culpable act the seller committed. As I indicated previously, one might be able to justify the conclusion that liberalism implies that sellers have such a moral right by citing (1) the "definitional" fact that liberalism places a lexically-highest value on moral-rights bearers' not only having a meaningful opportunity to take their lives morally seriously but also seizing that opportunity, (2) the plausible empirical claim that moral-rights bearers are more likely to take their lives morally seriously if they perceive themselves to be the authors of their own lives, and (3) the clearly-contestable empirical claim that the imposition of positive moral (or perhaps a fortiori legal) duties on individuals to provide benefits to others militates against the individual's perceiving himself or herself to be the author of his/her own life (indeed, does so far more than does the imposition of an otherwise-equally-onerous duty on an individual not to commit positive acts that inflict losses on others in otherwise-comparable circumstances). As I also indicated previously, liberalism recognizes that this liberal argument against imposing positive duties to help others is outweighed by liberal arguments for imposing duties to help others under certain conditions relating to (1) the life-of-moral-integrity-preserving character of the help in question and the character and extent of the cost the help-provider would have to incur to supply the help, (2) the possible benefit-provider's culpability for the possible help-recipient's need for help, (3) the (family, friend, lover, or long-term or repeated contract-partner) status-relationship between the possible help-provider and the party that needs help, and (4) any promises the possible help-provider made to provide help either to the specific individual in need of help or more generally. The question is whether, from the perspective of liberalism, the relationship between a seller and a prospective one-time or infrequent customer is in relevant respects sufficiently similar to the relationship between family members, friends, lovers, and participants in long-term contracts or repeated short-term contracts to justify the conclusion that a seller has a moral duty to perform the positive act of disclosing product-performance or product-lifetime-cost-to-buyer information to a prospective customer that that buyer should find valuable despite the general liberal argument against imposing positive moral duties on moral-rights bearers. My tentative, admittedly-contestable conclusion is that liberalism implies that sellers do have a positive moral duty to disclose product-performance and product-lifetime-cost information to buyers that have entered into a long-term-supply contract, that are repeat-customers, or that the seller should believe may become repeat-customers when the seller should believe that the disclosure would benefit a buyer that either would not obtain it itself or could not obtain it without the seller as allocative-cheaply as the seller could communicate it even when the buyer's error would not be attributable to a positive culpable act of the seller but does not imply that sellers have such a duty to one-off buyers. I admit that I would be tempted to reach a different conclusion about a seller's duty to disclose product-performance information (1) to all such one-off buyers if it should have predicted that the mistaken purchase or purchase-price decisions that some of them would make if none had the undisclosed information would leave them worse-off as a group than they would have been had the seller not produced the product in question or (2) to a particular one-off buyer if the seller should have concluded that the mistaken purchase or purchase-price decision that that buyer would make if it did not receive the undisclosed information would leave it worse-off than it would have been had the seller not produced the product in question when the seller of a product should have predicted that, if it did not disclose the relevant product-performance information to the product's prospective buyers, its production and sale of that product (A) would impose a net equivalent-dollar loss on its purchasers despite the fact that its product's availability improved the terms on which they could purchase rival products because the total equivalent-dollar losses that those buyers that made mistaken purchases of the product at the prices they paid for it would exceed the sum of the equivalent-dollar gains other buyers obtained by purchasing the product (despite the fact that some of them overestimated the quality of the product's performance) and the equivalent-dollar gains the production and pricing of its product conferred on these buyers by decreasing the prices charged for rival products and (B) would decrease economic efficiency because the economic-efficiency losses that would be generated by mistaken decisions to purchase the product when the producer was both privately-worse-placed and allocatively-worse-placed to supply the erring buyer exceed the economic-efficiency gains that would be generated by those sales of the product that were economically efficient. I acknowledge that the preceding analysis assumes that in the relevant cases the seller's decision not to create and sell a product variant whose future performance would be overestimated by buyers would result in the creation of a "rival" product variant whose future performance would not be overestimated by buyers. I also acknowledge that, in some cases in which the preceding two conditions for liberal-moral-rights-violativeness are fulfilled, the private cost to the seller of not creating the relevant product variant and selling it without informing its prospective buyers of its product-performance-related attributes—the supernormal profits it would earn by doing so—will exceed the net equivalent-dollar loss its committing these acts will impose on its customers. Still, because the behaviors on which I am now focusing—creating a product variant and producing and selling units of that product variant—are positive acts that inflict net equivalent-dollar losses on their conventional victims, I am tempted to conclude that, under the conditions specified, they and the decision not to disclose product-performance-related information with which they are associated are liberal-moral-rights-violative. This conclusion may be misguided (I could have used a less gentle modifier), but it is consistent with one variant of the general account of liberalism's concrete implications I have offered. (Does such consistency count for or against me?)

The second issue I want to address is: If liberalism implies that a seller does not have a moral obligation to disclose information to a prospective customer when the seller can secure non-disclosure without engaging in oligopolistic conduct and should realize that the information would prevent the buyer from making a mistake when deciding whether to buy or what price to pay for the seller's product, does liberalism imply that the seller has a liberal moral right not to disclose the information to the buyer in question? Although I am uncomfortable with the following answer to this question, it seems to me that my analysis does imply that liberalism does imply that sellers that have no moral duty to disclose such information to a particular prospective customer have a moral right not to disclose the information to the buyer in question. Of course, this conclusion is perfectly consistent with the additional conclusion that, from the perspective of one or more morally-defensible conceptions of the moral good, it would be morally bad for the seller not to disclose such information to relevant buyers under certain conditions (related to the private and allocative cost of the necessary disclosures [inter alia, to whether they could be effectively made through a general notice or whether, to be effectively communicated, they would have to be made much more privately-and-allocatively-expensively individually to buyers the seller identified as being likely to make the mistake the disclosure could prevent]).

I should probably ignore the third set of issues I will consider at this juncture—namely, issues that are related to the possibility that the imposition of a legal obligation on a seller to reveal to some or all of its prospective customers product-performance-related or product-lifetime-cost-related information that the buyers do not possess and to reveal to the government both buyer-error-related information and external-cost-related information the government does not possess may violate the seller's liberal "right against self-incrimination" in situations in which the seller in question has failed to fulfill this legal obligation in the past and its present disclosure of the information in question will reveal its past violations of the law. I am reluctant to address these issues for at least three reasons: (1) the legal right not to have to testify against oneself is complicated and contains many features that are puzzling; (2) I do not know whether this legal right is perceived to derive from a liberal moral right; and (3) I do not know (A) whether there is such a liberal moral right against self-incrimination in criminal cases, (B) whether there is an analogous right in civil cases, (C) whether that right implies that triers-of-fact may not draw an inference of guilt or liability from a defendant's not taking the stand or justifying his or her refusal to answer a particular question on the stand by asserting a right against self-incrimination, etc. Would it be liberal-moral-rights-violative to "require" an alleged law-breaker to testify about his or her guilty or innocence—i.e., to allow triers-of-fact to draw an inference of guilt from a defendant's refusal to answer any such question? In my judgment, the answer to this question turns on whether the imposition of such an obligation on a defendant would undermine the defendant's or other members of the general public's perception that they are the authors of their own lives and in so doing militate against the defendant's and such others' taking their lives morally seriously. I have my doubts. I also think that the conclusion that societies cannot require their members and participants to reveal adverse information (e.g., about their current taxable income) when doing so would reveal the individual's past failure to fulfill his or her information-disclosure obligations is morally unattractive because it allows the individual to profit from his or her past wrong. In any event, I will assume that individuals cannot establish their liberal moral right not to disclose information to prospective customers and government regulators when they have previously violated a legal obligation to disclose that information to relevant parties by arguing that the imposition of such a legal obligation would violate their liberal moral right not to testify against themselves. I suspect that few will disagree with this conclusion, but if some have doubts, those doubts may be alleviated by the inclusion of a provision in the legal-obligation-creating law precluding a private plaintiff or the State from using the information disclosed to prove previous violations or to discover other evidence that proves previous violations (although I recognize the difficulty of enforcing a legal prohibition of the State's using some information to obtain other information).

The members of the fourth set of issues I want to discuss all relate to sellers' engaging in contrived-oligopolistic conduct to deter their rivals from disclosing product-performance or product-lifetime-cost information to prospective buyers or such information and/or external-cost-related information to the legislature or some other component of the government. For the same reasons that I reached these conclusions about contrived-oligopolistic pricing, I think that (1) it is liberal-moral-rights-violative for a seller to try to deter a rival from disclosing information to prospective customers or the government by threatening to retaliate against the rival if it made the disclosures in question, by retaliating against the rival for making such disclosures, by promising to reward the rival for not making the relevant disclosures, and/or by rewarding the rival for not making the relevant disclosure, (2) that it is not liberal-moral-rights-violative for a potential-discloser target of a threat of retaliation to succumb to such a threat, (3) that it is liberal-moral-rights-violative for a potential discloser that has been offered a reward for not disclosing the information on which this section is focusing to accept such a reward when it can reject the reward without opening itself up to retaliation, and (4) that it is not liberal-moral-rights-violative for a potential discloser to respond to a threat or act of retaliation by making or carrying out a threat of defensive retaliation.

The fifth pair of issues I want to address at this juncture is (1) whether liberalism implies that the members of a liberal-moral-rights-based society have a moral duty when acting in their political capacities to commit positive acts that will contribute to their government's securing the liberal moral rights of the members of their society and (2) whether any such set of positive duties includes duties to report the product-performance-related, product-lifetime-cost-to-buyer, and external-cost-related information on whose disclosure this section is focusing to the government and to report their rivals' contrived-oligopolistic attempts to deter them from reporting such information to prospective buyers and the government. My disposition is to conclude that liberalism does not impose such positive obligations even when the potential discloser should not believe that disclosing this information might make it the target of retaliation for which it could not obtain redress from the retaliator and/or compensation from the government.

The sixth and final set of issues I want to address is whether one can justify the conclusion that sellers have a liberal moral right not to disclose product-performance-related, product-lifetime-cost-to-buyer, or external-cost-related information to the government because they have general property (commercial-property) rights or IP-related rights to such information or because the imposition of any such reporting-duties on companies would sacrifice the national-security-related moral rights of all members of and participants in the society in question. I find all these contentions not only incorrect but frivolous.[17]

9.2.2.2 The Relevant-Disclosure-Related Moral Duties of the Government of a Liberal-Moral-Rights-Based Society

I will restrict myself to making seven points or sets of related points. First, when trying to induce sellers to supply product-performance-related or product-lifetime-cost-to-buyer information to their prospective customers or to the government and when trying to induce sellers to disclose external-cost-related information to the government, the government of any liberal-moral-rights-based society is constrained both by any moral right sellers have not to disclose such information to such entities as well as by various civil/criminal-process-related moral rights sellers possess, the constraint that the total "costs" imposed on a convicted wrongdoer must fit the seriousness of the wrongdoing, and such a government's basic moral duty to maximize the extent to which the moral-rights-related interests of those for whom it is responsible are secured.

Second, in circumstances in which sellers in a liberal-moral-rights-based society have a moral right not to disclose product-performance-related, product-lifetime-cost-to-buyer-related, or product-generated-external-cost-related information, the government of a liberal-moral-rights-based society would still have a moral obligation to elicit such information from sellers by paying them for supplying it if doing so would instantiate a morally-defensible conception of the moral good that the government had a moral duty to instantiate because of its society's citizens' morally-defensible positions on the moral good.

Third, in circumstances in which (1) sellers in a liberal-moral-rights-based society do not have a moral right to keep to themselves product-performance-related, product-lifetime-cost-to-buyer-related, or product-generated-external-cost-related information that would be of value to prospective customers or the government, (2) the conventional victims of such non-disclosures do not have a moral right to the disclosures in question, but (3) sellers do not have a moral duty to disclose the information, the government of a liberal-moral-rights-based society would once again have a moral duty to elicit that information in any way that is not liberal-moral-rights-violative that would promote the instantiation of a pure or mixed conception of the moral good it was morally obligated to instantiate because doing so would protect the moral right of its society's members and participants to have their government's decisions correspond appropriately to their moral-good positions.

Fourth, in circumstances in which sellers in a liberal-moral-rights-based society have a moral duty to disclose product-performance-related, product-lifetime-cost-to-buyer-related, or product-generated-external-cost-related information to prospective customers and/or to their society's governments, the government of any such society has a moral obligation to maximize the securing of the moral rights of those parties who have a moral right that the disclosures be made, subject to the constraints and general obligation referenced in the first point in this list.

Fifth, since it is liberal-moral-rights-violative for one or more sellers to engage in contrived-oligopolistic conduct to induce one or more rivals not to disclose product-performance-related, product-lifetime-cost-to-buyer-related, or product-generated-external-cost-related information to prospective buyers or the government, the government of a liberal-moral-rights-based society has a moral obligation to deter such contrived-oligopolistic conduct to the greatest extent it can without violating the constraints and obligation referenced in the first point in this list.

Sixth, if two or more sellers' relying on their natural-oligopolistic interdependence to keep to themselves information about product-attributes or product-related external costs of production and consumption would violate the liberal moral rights of the buyers or external-cost bearers that would or could gain from the disclosure of the information, the government of a liberal-moral-rights-based society would have a moral obligation to deter such non-disclosures to the greatest extent it could without violating the constraints referenced in the first point in this list. The government of a liberal-moral-rights-based society would also have a moral obligation to deter such non-disclosures and (when relevant) respond appropriately to any information it obtained if its doing so would result in its fulfilling its moral obligation to instantiate a morally-defensible pure or mixed conception of the moral good that corresponds appropriately to its citizens' morally-defensible moral-good positions, again within the constraints imposed by its basic moral duty to maximize the extent to which the moral-rights-related interests of those for whom it is responsible are secured.

Seventh, if one concludes that in particular circumstances sellers have a liberal moral duty to disclose product-performance-related, product-lifetime-cost-to-buyer-related, or product-generated-external-cost-related information to their customers or the government, in those circumstances, the government of a liberal-moral-rights-based society has a moral obligation to enable the following victims of any seller-violation of that duty to obtain legal redress: (1) customers of the non-disclosing seller that can establish that, more likely than not, the non-disclosure imposed an equivalent-dollar loss on them and possibly (2) parties that can establish that, more likely than not, they were victims of the external costs whose generation would have been prevented had the external-cost-related information been disclosed to the government and the government had responded appropriately to the information's disclosure.

9.2.3 The Impact on the Instantiation of Various Morally-Defensible Conceptions of the Moral Good of Seller Non-Disclosures of Product-Performance-Related or Product-Lifetime-Cost-to-Buyer-Related Information to Prospective Buyers of the Relevant Product Who Might Otherwise Make Product-Purchase or Product-Purchase-Price Mistakes and/or to the Government, the Impact on Various Morally-Defensible Conceptions of the Moral Good of Seller Non-Disclosures to the Government of Information Related to the External Costs Generated by the Production and Consumption of Their Products, and the Implications of the Preceding Conclusions for the "Moral Desirability" of the Various Responses That the Government of a Liberal-Moral-Rights-Based Society Could Make to Such Seller Non-Disclosures

9.2.3.1 The Impact of the Referenced Seller Non-Disclosures on the Instantiation of the Various Morally-Defensible Conceptions of the Moral Good

The class of individuals on whom seller non-disclosures of product-performance-related and product-lifetime-cost-to-buyer-related information confer equivalent-dollar gains (non-disclosing-seller shareholders, creditors, managers, and employees) contains fewer poor individuals than does the class of individuals (primarily, misinformed buyers but also the shareholders, creditors, managers, and employees of the sellers to whom the misinformed buyers would have transferred their patronage had they received the undisclosed information) on whom such non-disclosures impose equivalent-dollar losses. The winners from such non-disclosures also tend to be better-off than the losers. Although these claims are more contestable, I think that (1) the set of individuals on whom seller non-disclosures of external-cost-related information confers equivalent-dollar gains (non-disclosing-seller shareholders, creditors, managers, employees, and customers) also tends to include fewer poor people than does the set of individuals on whom such non-disclosures impose equivalent-dollar losses (the victims of the sellers' pollution and accidents who cannot obtain any or full [after legal fees are deducted] compensation for their losses) and (2) the relevant class of winners is on the average wealthier than the relevant set of losers. I also suspect that, over the long run, the class of losers from any retaliation or reciprocation the contrivance of such non-disclosures involves contains more poor people than does the class of winners and that the winners from such contrivance tend to be richer than the contrivance's losers. Finally, as Sect. 9.2.1.1 argued, such non-disclosures will be economically inefficient, particularly if they are secured by contrivance.

If these conclusions are correct, they imply that these non-disclosures and any oligopolistic conduct that secures them (1) will disserve the utilitarian conception of the moral good when they are economically inefficient by reducing economic efficiency and imposing equivalent-dollar losses on individuals for whom the marginal utility of money over the relevant range is higher than is the marginal utility of money over the relevant range for those individuals on whom the conduct in question will confer equivalent-dollar gains and (2) will disserve the equal-utility, equal-resource, and various other equal-opportunity conceptions of the moral good by conferring equivalent-dollar gains on individuals who are as a class richer and imposing equivalent-dollar losses on individuals who are as a class poorer.

9.2.3.2 The Moral-Good-Related "Moral Desirability" of Various Responses that the Government of a Liberal-Moral-Rights-Based Society Could Make to the Seller Non-Disclosures on Which This Section Is Focusing and to any Seller-Practiced Contrived-Oligopolistic Conduct That Secures These Disclosures

"Moral Desirability" is enquoted in the title of Sect. 9.2.3.2 because I am using this expression to cover both the "moral desirability" of securing justice (protecting moral rights) and the "moral desirability" of instantiating a morally-defensible conception of the moral good when that goal can be achieved without violating the applicable conception of justice. Five points or sets of related points are salient.

First, it will not be "morally desirable" for the government of any moral-rights-based society (be it liberal-moral-rights-based or committed to instantiating a non-liberal conception of justice) to instantiate any morally-defensible conception of the moral good through any policy or choice that is moral-rights-violative.

Second, a related, admittedly-contestable point that applies in all policy contexts. I am disposed to conclude that, when determining whether a decision by a government of a liberal-moral-rights-based society to induce sellers to disclose to buyers and/or the government product-performance-related, product-lifetime-cost-to-buyer-related, or product-generated-external-cost-related information that pertains to one or more of the seller's products that the sellers do not have a liberal moral right to keep to themselves by collecting and using evidence in ways that would violate the prima facie liberal moral rights of the sellers, by reducing the probability of wrongdoing that must be established for the seller to be found liable or guilty to levels that would otherwise violate the sellers' prima facie liberal moral rights, and/or by imposing "costs" on sellers that have been found liable or guilty that are more substantial than the sellers' wrongdoing, the analysis should not take into account any contribution that such decisions would make to the government's making choices that give appropriate, equal weight to the morally-defensible moral-good positions of the relevant society's members and participants.

Third, within the just-referenced set of constraints, the governments of a liberal-moral-rights-based society would have a moral duty to induce sellers to disclose to buyers and/or to it product-performance-related, product-lifetime-cost-to-buyer-related, and product-generated-external-cost-related information whenever its doing so would enable those governments better to instantiate a pure or mixed conception of the moral good that their basic obligation to treat each of its society's members with appropriate, equal respect and concern implies it is morally obligated to instantiate.

Fourth, in my judgment, it would be morally desirable from the perspective of all the morally-defensible conceptions of the moral good this study considers for the governments of liberal-moral-rights-based societies to devote a considerable amount of resources to inducing sellers to disclose to buyers and/or to the governments information that relates to their products' performance-attributes, the lifetime cost of buying, maintaining, and repairing, their products, and the externalities generated by their products' production and consumption in ways that do not violate the relevant sellers' prima facie liberal moral rights.

Fifth, although the fourth point obviously reflects my conclusions about the allocative efficiency and distributive consequences of (1) the non-disclosures in question, (2) the policies that government will have to devise and implement to induce sellers to supply the types of information on whose non-disclosure this section is focusing, and (3) the distributive consequences of the public financing of these policies (which are to some extent within the control of the government), I am confident that the policy conclusions articulated in the fourth point are correct.

9.3 (Contrived-Oligopolistic Conduct)/(Natural-Oligopolistic Interdependencies) That Can Reduce Equilibrium Investment in the ARDEPPS in Which (It Is Practiced)/(They Are Operative)[18]

Here is the contrived-oligopolistic scenario. Assume that each member of a set of two or more firms could make a QV or PPR investment in an ARDEPPS that would increase that ARDEPPS' equilibrium investment, increase the investor's profits, but decrease the total profits of all investors in the ARDEPPS in question because it would increase the profits of the firm that made it by less than it would reduce the profits of the other members of set of the investors in question. Assume as well that once one member of this group has made such an investment, it would not be inherently profitable for any other member of the group to make an investment in the ARDEPPS in question. In this situation, each of the members of this group would find it profitable to make an investment that was against the group's joint equivalent-dollar interest if nothing were done to alter this state of affairs. In this situation, one or more members of this group might find it profitable to deter the making of an investment by (1) promising not to make an investment if no-one else invested, (2) threatening to retaliate against any member that made an additional investment in the ARDEPPS in question, and possibly (though I suspect rarely) (3) promising to reward at least some members of the group for not investing. Such conduct would be "oligopolistic" because each's perception that its decision not to invest was ex ante profitable was critically affected by its belief that its rivals' responses would be affected by their respective perceptions that, if the rival responded by not investing, it and their mutual rivals would react by continuing to abstain from investing and possibly by rewarding some abstainers whereas, if the rival responded by making an investment, it (and perhaps its other rivals) would react by retaliating against the investing rival.

Here is the natural-oligopolistic scenario. Assume that (1) each member of a set of two or more firms established in an ARDEPPS would find it profitable to add an investment to the ARDEPPS' total if its investment would not induce any rival to make an investment the rival would not otherwise have made, (2) each of the firms just referenced would not find it profitable to make an investment that would increase the ARDEPPS' equilibrium investment if doing so would make it profitable for a rival to make an investment in the ARDEPPS in question by precluding that rival from deterring the former firm from making an investment by not making an investment (given that *ex hypothesis* the former firm had already made an additional investment in the ARDEPPS in question), and (3) each of the firms in question would not find it profitable to make an investment because it would know that its doing so would induce a rival to make an investment the rival would not otherwise have made for the reason explained in Item (2) in this list. In this situation, each prospective investor's decision not to invest would be oligopolistic in my sense because each investor's perception that its decision not to invest was ex ante profitable was critically affected by the prospective investor's perception that its rivals' responses would be critically affected by their belief that it would react to their decisions to invest by investing itself. In this situation, each prospective investor's decision not to invest would be *natural*-oligopolistic because its rivals' perception of the way it would react to their investing was not created by any anticompetitive offer or threat it made—was generated solely by each rival's perception that its respective rivals would have the opportunity to react to its investment and would find it inherently profitable to react to any investment it made by making an investment the rival would not otherwise have found profitable to make.

(Contrived-oligopolistic conduct)/(natural-oligopolistic interdependencies) can lower equilibrium QV or PPR investment in a wide variety or situations. However, there is one special set of circumstances in which such oligopolistic conduct or interdependence may do so that will be of particular interest to lawyers—circumstances in which (1) the deterring QV investment in question would have created a product whose production and consumption would be less-external-cost-generative than extant products or the deterred PPR would have discovered a production process whose use would generate lower external costs than were generated by the use of extant production processes, (2) the investments in question would be profitable if the purchasers of any product created by the investment or the users of any production process discovered by the investment were liable for the external costs the production of their products generated, were liable for any external costs generated by the consumption of their products, or had the relevant consumption-externalities internalized to them by buyers that were liable for generating them and took full account of these liability costs when making their purchasing-decisions, and (3) the operative tort law and products-liability law do not internalize the external costs in question to the relevant producers because (I am simplifying) (A) these bodies of law make producers liable only for costs they imposed on others negligently, (B) producer decisions not to do accident-and-pollution-loss-reducing product or production-process research are never assessed for negligence, (C) independent research-firms cannot profitably do the relevant research (because knowledge obtained by producing a product critically increases the profitability of doing the relevant research), and (4) once the less-accident-and-pollution-loss-generative product (production process) was discovered, it would be negligent to produce the "less-safe" product variant or to use the "less-safe" production process because the reduction in external costs that the shift to the "safer" product variant or production process would generate would exceed the burden of shifting to producing the "safer" product variant or using the "safer" production process (the sum of any extra production costs of other sorts one would have to incur to produce the "safer" product variant and any positive difference between the dollar values of the "less-safe" product variant and "safer" product variant to relevant buyers or the extra production costs of other sorts one would have to incur to use the "safer" production processes). In such a situation, an investment that would lead to the discovery of the "safer" product variant or production process would be unprofitable for the producers of the extant less- "safe" product variants taken as a whole: The investment would reduce their profits by the sum of its private cost, any increase in other costs the producers would have to incur to produce the safer product variant or to use the safer production process, and any positive difference between the dollar value to relevant buyers of the less- "safe" and "safer" product variants (if I assume for simplicity and neutrally that no relevant choice would affect the amount of buyer surplus generated by the sale of the relevant product variants). In these circumstances, although it might be profitable for one producer (among many) to make a relevant investment if it could prevent its rivals from investing and could obtain fully-protective IP rights in the product variant or production process it would discover, any such investment and any rival investment made in response would be against the collective interest of all sellers in the ARDEPPS in question. In these circumstances, it might be profitable for the sellers in the ARDEPPS in question to deter each other from making such an investment by threatening to retaliate against any investor or (conceivably) by compensating one or more firms for not investing. Moreover, if any investor that made such an investment could not obtain IP rights in its discovery or if two or more sellers could profit by making such investments once one of them made such an investment because each investor could make a similarly-profitable investment that would yield it IP rights, the sellers might be able to rely on their natural-oligopolistic interdependence to deter any of them from making any such investment.

I should not close this section without acknowledging that sellers can also reduce equilibrium investment in an ARDEPPS in which they are operating by consummating horizontal mergers and acquisitions to prevent the participants from waging investment competition against each other, by consummating conglomerate mergers and acquisitions with an effective potential competitor, and/or by participating in joint ventures that reduce the investment competition the parents wage against each other in the joint venture's ARDEPPS by giving each parent a stake in the joint venture and sometimes by including in the joint-venture agreement a clause prohibiting the parents from investing in the joint venture's ARDEPPS (and sometimes in each other's ARDEPPSes) and the joint venture from investing in the parents' ARDEPPSes. These "non-oligopolistic" methods of reducing equilibrium investment in an ARDEPPS in which a perpetrator has an interest will be discussed respectively in Chapters 11, 12, and 15.

9.3.1 The Economic Efficiency of Sellers' (Engaging in Contrived-Oligopolistic Conduct)/(Taking Advantage of Natural-Oligopolistic Interdependencies) to Reduce Equilibrium Investment in the ARDEPPS in Which (It Occurs)/(They Are Operative) and the Economic Efficiency of Various Responses Government Could Make to the Prospect and Reality of Such Contrivance or the Effect of Such Interdependencies

9.3.1.1 The Economic Efficiency of the (Contrived-Oligopolistic Conduct)/(Natural-Oligopolistic Interdependencies) That Reduce Equilibrium Investment in the ARDEPPS in Which (It Takes Place)/(They Are Operative)

I will start by analyzing the economic efficiency of such contrived-oligopolistic conduct. Thirteen points or sets of related points are salient. First, when the relevant ARDEPPS' investments are QV investments, such contrived-oligopolistic conduct will, if successful, increase economic efficiency by reducing equilibrium QV investment in the ARDEPPS in which it is practiced—that is, will increase economic efficiency by decreasing (UO-production and PPR-execution) to (QV-investment creation) misallocation. Second, when the relevant ARDEPPS' investments are investments in PPR, such contrived-oligopolistic conduct will, if successful, decrease economic efficiency by decreasing equilibrium PPR in the ARDEPPS in which it is practiced. Third, such conduct will decrease economic efficiency by generating allocative transaction costs (which, in my judgment, will exceed the private transaction cost of engaging in it). Fourth, if such contrived-oligopolistic seller-conduct is not successful and the contriver(s) retaliate against the non-cooperator, the retaliation such unsuccessful conduct entails will cause economic inefficiency both by generating intra-ARDEPPS UO-to-UO (in the standard case in which the retaliation takes the form of retaliatory pricing and the retaliator makes the sale) and by generating allocative transaction costs (for reasons of self-preservation and reader-preservation, I am ignoring any impact that such retaliation will have on economic efficiency by affecting the retaliator's reputation for carrying out its threats of retaliation and hence the amount of strategic conduct in which it engages in the future and the extent to which its rivals cooperate with its future contrivance). Fifth, I do not know whether such conduct will increase or decrease inter-ARDEPPS UO-to-UO misallocation if one ignores its tendency to lead to offensive and defensive retaliation or inter-ARDEPPS QV-to-QV misallocation. Sixth, I believe that such conduct will decrease economic efficiency by increasing poverty and material inequality by conferring equivalent-dollar gains on the shareholders, creditors, managers, and employees of its perpetrators and imposing equivalent-dollar losses on buyers of the goods produced in the ARDEPPS in question and buyers who would have purchased the ARDEPPS' goods if the conduct had not raised the prices charged for them and reduced the diversity of products and speed of delivery supplied by the ARDEPPS' sellers. Seventh, to the extent that contrivance-secured reductions in equilibrium investment in an ARDEPPS increase/decrease the concentration of the seller-side of the ARDEPPS in question, such contrivance will on this account decrease/increase economic efficiency by increasing/decreasing the expenditures the ARDEPPS' sellers make on political parties/campaigns/candidates and on government-decisionmaking-process participation: In my contestable judgment, investment-reducing contrivance will tend to increase the concentration of the seller-side of the ARDEPPS in which it is practiced (because it is more likely to be practiced by a single large firm to deter a smaller firm from investing than it is to be practiced by two large firms to deter each other from investing) and will on that account tend to decrease economic efficiency by increasing the above-referenced expenditures the ARDEPPS' sellers make. Eighth, seller efforts to contrive investment-reductions will also tend to decrease economic efficiency by increasing the extent to which the relevant sellers engage in contrived-oligopolistic pricing, which is clearly economically inefficient when the goods in question are not production processes. Ninth, seller efforts to contrive investment-restrictions will tend to decrease economic inefficiency because the sellers that contrive such reductions tend to engage in otherwise-unprofitable and partially on the account economically-inefficient conduct to increase their ability to contrive investment-reductions. Tenth, if the amount of production-optimum-misallocation-generating X-inefficiency sellers generate by operating sloppily increases with the supernormal profit-rate they could realize if they did not operate sloppily, seller-contrived investment-restrictions will decrease economic efficiency by increasing the sellers' potential supernormal profit-rate and hence the amount of production-optimum-related misallocation they generate. Eleventh, if sellers share some of any potential supernormal profits they could realize with their managers and employees, seller-contrived investments-restrictions will increase the amount of economic inefficiency their managers and employees generate by making economically-inefficient substitutions of untaxed better working-conditions or lower-taxed fringe-benefits for higher-taxed monetary compensation by increasing the relevant sellers' potential supernormal profit-rate, the relevant managers' and employees' potential monetary compensation and the tax-rate that applies to the relevant personnel's potential (fully-taxable) marginal monetary compensation. Twelfth, although I recognize that this conclusion is contestable, I am disposed to think that, even when practiced in economies that devote too many resources to QV-investment creation from the perspective of economic efficiency, seller efforts to contrive QV-investment reductions will decrease economic efficiency in most cases in which they are successful and do not entail any offensive retaliation against non-cooperators and defensive retaliation by non-cooperators and will be even more likely to decrease economic efficiency when they are unsuccessful and/or do involve such offensive and defensive retaliation.

Thirteenth, it is clear that, in actual contemporary economies (which devote too few resources to PPR from the perspective of economic efficiency), seller efforts to contrive PPR reductions will decrease economic efficiency regardless of whether they are successful or entail offensive and defensive retaliation in part because too few resources are devoted to PPR from the perspective of economic efficiency in all contemporary economies but for a host of other reasons as well.

I turn now to the economic efficiency of the natural variant of this category of oligopolistic conduct. The analysis of the economic efficiency of natural-oligopolistic-interdependence-generated investment-reductions differs from the analysis of contrived-oligopolistic-conduct-secured investment-reductions for three reasons: (1) The relevant natural-oligopolistic interdependencies will cause investment-reductions if and only if they generate critical natural-oligopolistic investment-disincentives; (2) investment-reductions that are generated by natural-oligopolistic interdependencies will usually not come about through an allocative-transaction-costly process (indeed, transaction costs will be generated only in what I take to be the unusual case in which one or more of the prospective investors would not understand the relevant facts if a rival did not explain them); and (3) natural-oligopolistic-interdependence-generated investment-restrictions never involve acts of retaliation (which generate intra-ARDEPPS UO-to-UO misallocation and allocative transaction costs and can either increase or decrease economic efficiency by increasing the incidence of future strategic behavior). However, although for all these reasons, natural-oligopolistic-interdependency-generated reductions in investment will be less economically inefficient than contrivance that generates investment-reductions, the fact that investment-reductions that result from natural-oligopolistic interdependencies will cause economic inefficiency in all the other ways in which contrived investment-reductions cause economic inefficiency leads me to conclude that, taken as a class, natural-oligopolistic-interdependency-generated investment-reductions are economically inefficient not only when the deterred investments are investments in PPR but also when the deterred investments are QV investments (though I acknowledge that the QV-investment-reduction-related conclusion is more contestable, given that contemporary economies devote too many resources to QV-investment creation from the perspective of economic efficiency).

9.3.1.2 The Economic Efficiency of the Various Responses That the Government Could Make to the Prospect or Reality of (Natural-Oligopolistic/Contrived-Oligopolistic)-Secured Investment-Reductions

I will restrict myself to making six points. First, for reasons that Sect. 9.3.1.1 articulated, I believe that the overwhelming majority of contrived-oligopolistic reductions in QV investment, a substantial majority of the QV-investment reductions that are generated by natural-oligopolistic interdependencies, and all reductions in PPR investment that are generated by contrived-oligopolistic conduct or caused by natural-oligopolistic interdependencies decrease economic efficiency. Second, and obviously, if one could identify those contrivance-generated QV-investment/PPR-investment reductions or natural-oligopolistic-interdependencies-generated QV-investment/PPR-investment reductions whose generation was economically efficient without incurring allocative costs that exceed the economic-efficiency gains that allowing such economically-efficient investment-reductions would yield, it would be ex ante economically efficient for the government to identify and allow such economically-efficient investment-reductions. Third, the allocative cost of determining the impact that oligopolistically-secured investment-reductions have on economic efficiency not only directly but by virtue of the choices that firms make to put themselves in a position to secure negative investment-decisions, the choices firms make at the time of the investment reduction to secure it, and the future choices the investment reduction causes to be made includes not only the allocative cost of the antitrust-law-enforcement authorities' and the courts' resolving these issues (which includes the allocative cost generated by government officials but also the allocative costs generated by the participation of defendants, non-defendant witness, and jurors) but also the allocative cost of financing the associated government expenditures. Fourth, I suspect, that it will not be TBLE for the government of a liberal-moral-rights-based society to attempt to identify and permit those oligopolistically-generated QV-investment/PPR-investment reductions that are economically efficient—that it will be TBLE for the government of such a society to prohibit all oligopolistically-generated investment-reductions and to enforce that prohibition when it would be TBLE to do so. Fifth, it will often be extremely-allocative-costly or impossible to prove that a defendant has contrived an investment-reduction or that the decisions of two or more potential investors in a particular ARDEPPS not to make an investment in that ARDEPPS manifested their facing natural-oligopolistic investment-disincentives. Nevertheless, sixth, I think it will often be TBLE for the government of a liberal-moral-rights-based society to devote resources to the identification of contrived-oligopolistic and possibly natural-oligopolistic investment-restrictions, to the prosecution of oligopolistic-investment-reduction cases, and to the punishment of firms that have reduced investment oligopolistically.

9.3.2 The Liberal-Moral-Rights-Violativeness of the Otherwise-Unprofitable Choices Firms Make to Increase the Profits They Will Realize by Contriving Investment-Reductions, of the Choices Firms Make (Given Their Positions at the Time in Question) to Contrive Investment-Reductions, of the Otherwise-Unprofitable Decisions Firms Make to Create Situations in Which They and Their Rivals Will Face Critical Natural-Oligopolistic Investment-Disincentives, of the Negative Investment-Decisions That Firms That Face Critical Natural-Oligopolistic Investment-Disincentives Make, and of the Decisions That Firms That Face Critical Natural-Oligopolistic Investment-Disincentives Make to Insure That Rivals That Also Face Critical Natural-Oligopolistic Investment-Disincentives Do Not Invest

9.3.2.1 The Liberal-Moral-Rights-Violativeness of the Choices Referenced in the Heading of Sect. 9.3.2

I will focus first on seller-practiced contrived-oligopolistic investment-preventing conduct that does not involve the communication of any threat or act of retaliation —that is, contrived-oligopolistic conduct of this type in which two or more contrivers prevent themselves from creating an investment by agreeing not to invest and/or possibly by bribing one or more of the potential investors not to invest.[19] Although one might separate the participants in this variant of contrived-oligopolistic investment-preventing conduct into two groups—the participants that made the relevant offers and paid any relevant bribes (the offerors or promisors) and the participants that accepted the relevant offers and any bribes that were paid (the offerees or promisees), there is no liberal moral point to doing so: If it is liberal-moral-rights-violative to make the offers and pay the bribes, it is liberal-moral-rights-violative to accept the offers and bribes; if it is not liberal-moral-rights-violative to make the offers or pay the bribes, it is not liberal-moral-rights-violative to accept them. (I acknowledge that one difference might be salient: It might be liberal-moral-rights-violative for an offeree not to report the offers to the authorities, but I do not think that liberalism imposes such a duty.)

In my judgment, the conclusion that participation in this variant of contrived-oligopolistic investment-preventing conduct is liberal-moral-rights-violative is justified by the following facts: (1) Such conduct involves positive acts (the making of an agreement and possibly the payment and acceptance of one or more bribes); (2) such conduct inflicts an equivalent-dollar loss on its conventional victims (the prospective buyers of the product or service or production process the prevented investment would have created, the buyers of the other products in the relevant ARDEPPS who paid higher prices for them because the prevented investment was not made, and those individuals who would have bought one or more of the other products in the ARDEPPS at the lower prices that would have been charged for them had the prevented investment been made but did not buy those products at the higher prices that were charged for them in the absence of the prevented investment); and (3) at least as relevantly, each participant's participation in such conduct results in its operation's leaving the buyers just referenced worse-off than those buyers would have been had that participant not operated in the ARDEPPS at all by reducing the absolute attractiveness of the offers the referenced buyers received from other sellers in the ARDEPPS (at least if the participant's failure to enter the relevant ARDEPPS would have resulted in another firm's making an investment in that ARDEPPS that would not have cooperated with the investment-preventing contrivance in question); and (4) (I suspect in virtually all cases) the dollar cost to the contrivers of preventing (avoiding inflicting) this loss on the just-referenced buyers by making the investment(s) whose creation/execution their contrivance prevented—the joint dollar-loss that the prevented investment(s) would have impose on the contrivers—will be lower than the equivalent-dollar loss the prevention of that investment imposed on the referenced buyers.

I acknowledge that Item (4) in this list ignores complications that may arise respectively when (1) the number of firms that would find it profitable to make at least one investment absent contrivance exceeds the number of prevented investments and (2) the prevented investments are QV investments. The complication that may arise when the number of firms that would find it individually profitable to make at least one investment absent contrivance exceeds the number of prevented investments (assuming for simplicity that all the relevant investments are the same size) is that—although *ex hypothesis* the prevented investments taken as a group would impose a collective equivalent-dollar loss on all those involved in the contrivance—the fact that (contrivance aside) the individual prevented investments would be individually profitable for the firms that made them eliminates the possibility that the equivalent-dollar cost to an individual firm of preventing relevant buyers' losses by making an investment would exceed the equivalent-dollar gain its making the investment would confer on the relevant buyers (strengthens the Hand-formula-related case for concluding that the decision not to invest was culpable [was negligent]). Admittedly, one could attack this argument by maintaining that the type of contrivance now under consideration is not likely to be a one-off phenomenon—is likely to persist through time so that over the long haul (in a situation in which equilibrium investment increases through time) each participant in the contrivance would in this situation sometimes be a firm that would otherwise have invested and sometimes be a firm that would otherwise not have invested and hence would over the long haul lose from its decision to not cooperate with the contrivance if its non-cooperation would cause the contrivance not to be practiced through time. The complication that may arise when the prevented investments are QV investments relates to the possibility that, contrary to my judgment, everything considered, contrived reductions in QV investment increase economic efficiency—that is, generate net equivalent-dollar gains for individuals other than the contrivers and the actual and deterred buyers of the products produced in the ARDEPPS in question that exceed the difference between the equivalent-dollar losses it imposes on those buyers and the equivalent-dollar gains it confers on the contrivers. The question is: If the contrivers were aware ex ante of the fact that their contrivance would yield a net equivalent-dollar gain on individuals affected by its "general-equilibrium impacts"—i.e., on individuals not affected because they are the contrivers or are actual or potential buyers in the ARDEPPS of practice—that exceed the net equivalent-dollar loss the contrivance would impose on the contrivers and those buyers, does their awareness of this reality render their otherwise-liberal-moral-rights-violative conduct non-liberal-moral-rights-violative? Although this conclusion makes me uncomfortable, my account of liberalism may imply that sellers' engaging in contrivance that is designed to reduce their ARDEPPS' equilibrium-QV-investment quantity without making or carrying out any threat of retaliation may not be liberal-moral-rights-violative if the perpetrators know ex ante that their conduct was ex ante economically efficient. I take some comfort from the arguments that favor the conclusion that contrivance to reduce QV investment is probably economically inefficient in the vast majority of instances in which it is practiced as well as from the possibility that many if not most sellers that contrive QV-investment restrictions whose contrivance is economically efficient will not realize this fact—may still deserve to be assessed to have behaved illiberally because they committed acts that manifested their willingness to treat others disrespectfully and to show inappropriately little concern for the welfare of others on whom they thought their conduct would impose equivalent-dollar losses. I acknowledge the contestability of the preceding sentence's claim that conduct that was illiberally-motivated (given the actor's inaccurate factual assumptions or lack of concern for some of the morally-relevant effects of their conduct) that would not have been illiberally-motivated had the actor possessed the information the actor would have obtained had it done the research liberalism obligates it to do (the research into its investment-choice options and the morally-relevant consequences of the various investment-decisions it could make that its initial knowledge [including its understanding of its research-abilities] should have led it to conclude liberalism would imply it was obligated to do if it would respond in the way that liberalism implies it is morally obligate to respond to any information the research discovers) is liberal-moral-rights-violative. Of course, one must still resolve the associated damages-issue. In my judgment, an actor that made an illiberally-motivated decision that would not have been liberal-moral-rights-violative had the actor possessed the information it would have possessed had it done the research that liberalism implies the actor had an obligation to do into the range of decision-options it had and the consequences of each of those options (a research-obligation whose operationalization depends on whether the loss the potential injurer could avoid was a "mere-utility" loss or a life-of-moral-integrity-imperiling loss) is obligated to compensate the relevant ARDEPPS' buyers for the "dignity" loss its choice imposed on them but not for the loss it imposed on them by reducing equilibrium investment in the ARDEPPS in question.

Before proceeding to the case in which the contrivance involves threats and perhaps acts of retaliation, I should discuss the classes of individuals whose liberal moral rights are violated by conduct that contrived investment-reductions without making threats of retaliation to potential non-cooperators or carrying out any such threats. The first such class contains the buyers of the products produced by the relevant ARDEPPS and the possible buyers of that ARDEPPS' products that were deterred from purchasing its products by the reduction in its equilibrium investment and attendant increase in its products' prices: These individuals are victims of both the offerors and the offerees. The second such class contains the offerees. They are victims of the offerors, who have treated the offerees with disrespect by soliciting their participation in liberal-moral-rights-violative conduct. Such victims have suffered a dignity loss and may also sustain material losses if their receipt of this offer becomes known and its revelation damages their reputations (because observers suspect them of being complicit). In my judgment, this dignity claim is not available to offerees who accepted the offeror's offer. The third class is a class of *possibly*-morally-entitled victims of such offerors and accepting offerees—those individuals on whom the contrivance's "general-equilibrium" effects impose equivalent-dollar losses. This group would include, for example, potential suppliers of other products that the buyers of the relevant ARDEPPS' products might buy on which the contrivance imposes equivalent-dollar losses by decreasing the demand that the ARDEPPS' customers have for these non-ARDEPPS suppliers' products by increasing the prices the ARDEPPS' buyers must pay for the ARDEPPS' products. I included and italicized the word "possibly" in the sentence before last because I am not sure that these buyers' liberal moral rights are violated by the relevant contrivers' liberal-moral-rights-violative conduct. I have little constructive to say about this issue. The common law contains a doctrine (what used to be called the "proximate cause" doctrine and is now called the "scope of liability" doctrine) that addresses the connection that must exist between a wrongful act and a loss for the culpable actor to be legally responsible for a loss for which the culpable act was a cause-in-fact. However, neither the way in which those doctrines have been applied nor the scholarly literature on them[20] provides much insight into the associated moral-responsibility issue. My efforts to get help from philosophically-knowledgeable academic lawyers and philosophers have been no more successful. Is there any moral relevance to the fact that a liberal-moral-rights violator is not legally entitled to obtain compensation from actors that have obtained equivalent-dollar gains from the general-equilibrium consequences of its liberal-moral-rights-violative act (e.g., from sellers that realize profits on the extra sales they make to individuals who would otherwise have patronized a seller in the ARDEPPS in which the wrongful investment-preventing conduct took place had that conduct not deterred them from doing so by preventing some products from being created and raising the prices of the ARDEPPS' other products) perhaps because a person should not profit from his or her wrong (though the appositeness of this question is certainly contestable)? I am discomfited by the paucity of my thoughts on this issue, but I will proceed not only in this section but throughout this study on the assumption that liberal-moral-rights-violative conduct does not violate the liberal moral rights of those on whom it inflicts losses "indirectly" via its "general-equilibrium" effects.

I turn next to seller-practiced contrived-oligopolistic investment-preventing conduct that does involve threats and perhaps acts of retaliation. The question is: In the current context, is it liberal-moral-rights-violative to threaten a rival with retaliation against its non-cooperation or to threaten and then retaliate against a non-cooperating rival? Threats and acts of retaliation that are motivated by self-interest seem to me to be disrespectful of their target and hence liberal-moral-rights-violative. The facts that such threats and acts could correctly be characterized as coercive or extortive is consistent with this conclusion. The fact that an exemplar of seller-practiced contrived-oligopolistic investment-reducing conduct involves threats and perhaps acts of retaliation is relevant in three ways or related sets of ways: (1) The threats and acts of retaliation in question violate the liberal moral rights of their target (in that they are coercive and extortive) and entitle the target to obtain compensation (A) for any material loss any act of retaliation imposed on it, (B) for any losses it had to incur to retaliate defensively against any offensive retaliation the contriver(s) practiced in reaction to its non-cooperation, (C) for the private transaction costs (including opportunity costs) it had to incur to defend itself if it succumbed to the threat and was subjected on that account to investigation and litigation, (D) for any loss of goodwill it suffered because potential buyers or potential suppliers perceived it to be a willing participant in the contrivance or disapproved of its succumbing to the threat, and (E) for the dignity loss the threat and offensive retaliation imposed on it (for the disrespect the target experienced); (2) the threat of retaliation strengthens what I take to be the independently-persuasive conclusion that the target of any such threat has no liberal moral duty to report the contrivance-effort to the authorities (or to the relevant ARDEPPS' buyers); and (3) if the target of the threat does not cooperate, is subjected to offensive retaliation, and reacts to that retaliation by engaging in defensive retaliation, its defensive retaliation is not liberal-moral-rights-violative.

I turn now to the liberal-moral-rights-violativeness of sellers' not making a QV investment or not executing a PPR project because they realize that their QV-investment/PPR decisions are natural-oligopolistically interdependent. From the perspective of liberalism, the natural-oligopolistic interdependencies that result in an ARDEPPS' equilibrium QV-investment/PPR being lower than it otherwise would be are different from the contrived-oligopolistic conduct that can generate such outcomes in at least three related sets of respects: Unlike the contrived-oligopolistic conduct that can generate reductions in equilibrium investment in the ARDEPPS in which it is perpetrated, the natural-oligopolistic interdependencies that can produce such an outcome (1) do not involve any seller's committing any positive act (involve nothing more than two or more firms' not making investments each would find unprofitable everything considered for reasons that have nothing to do with any of the firms' in question reacting inherently-unprofitably to decisions its rivals would otherwise find profitable [at least if no relevant firm engaged in previous conduct that was critically motivated by a desire to be in a position in which it and its rivals would confront each other with critical natural-oligopolistic investment-disincentives]), relatedly (2) do not involve any firm's making a threat of offensive retaliation (which is disrespectful of its target, fails to manifest appropriate concern for its target's "welfare," and is allocative-transaction-costly), committing any offensively-retaliatory act (which act disrespects its target, fails to manifest appropriate concern for its target's "welfare," is allocative-transaction-costly, and is intra-ARDEPPS-UO-to-UO-misallocation-generative), or engaging in defensive retaliation (which is allocative-transaction-costly and intra-ARDEPPS-UO-to-UO-misallocation-generative), and (3) do not involve any firm's making any promises to reward (say, to reciprocate to) a rival's cooperation ([A] whose communication is allocative-transaction-costly and [B] whose fulfillment by abstaining from price competition [i] is disrespectful of the buyers directly involved, [ii] manifests inappropriately-little concern for those buyers' "welfare," [iii] may be allocative-transaction-costly [if it involves the payment of money or the identification of those of the cooperator's customers the promisor is second-placed to supply], [iv] will tend to offset the economic-efficiency gains the broader conduct generates when that broader conduct involves QV-investment decisions by lowering the ARDEPPS' equilibrium-QV-investment quantity to the extent that the price-increases that the reward's "payment" generates increase the relevant ARDEPPS' equilibrium-QV-investment quantity though it will tend to reduce the economic-efficiency losses the broader conduct generates when that broader conduct involves PPR decisions by lowering the ARDEPPS' equilibrium-PPR quantity to the extent that the price-increases the reward's payment generates increase the ARDEPPS' equilibrium-PPR quantity), and (v) will tend to cause economic inefficiency by increasing poverty and material inequality and, as a result of its increasing the cooperators' potential profits, by increasing the production-optimum-related misallocation they generate by operating sloppily and the misallocation the cooperators' managers and employees generate by substituting lower-taxed or untaxed more-attractive working-conditions and fringe-benefits for the goods they would have purchased with the higher-taxed monetary compensation they exchanged for the working-conditions and fringe-benefits in question. and (4) do not involve any firm's acceptance of any such promise of reward (which [A] would be disrespectful of the buyers involved, [B] would manifest inappropriately-little concern for those buyers' "welfare" when the reward takes the form of abstentions from price competition, and [C] would tend to have the same negative effect on [UO and PPR]-to-QV misallocation when the relevant investments are QV investments and the same positive effect on [UO and QV]-to-PPR misallocation when the relevant investments are in PPR as the offer of an abstinence-from-price-competition reward would have). In the current context, the most important of these differences is the first: The fact that the reductions in investment that result from natural-oligopolistic interdependencies do not involve any positive acts strongly favors the conclusion that decisions not to invest for this reason are not liberal-moral-rights-violative. This conclusion is "in one sense" reinforced by the fact that natural-oligopolistic-interdependence-motivated conduct does not involve threats and acts of offensive retaliation or promises of reward or the fulfillment or acceptance of such promises, all of which are independently liberal-moral-rights-violative as well as by the fact that the natural-oligopolistic-interdependencies-secured reductions in investment are less misallocative than are contrived-oligopolistic-secured reductions in investment.

I turn next to decisions by firms that face critical natural-oligopolistic investment-disincentives and whose relevant rivals also face such critical natural-oligopolistic investment-disincentives to inform rivals whom it fears might not understand the situation they face that their investment will be unprofitable because it will render profitable and therefore induce the informing-firm or some mutual rival to make an investment in the ARDEPPS in question that the informing firm or a mutual rival would not otherwise have made because the induced investment would not otherwise have been profitable. Once more, I am struggling. The choice in question is a positive act, but I cannot bring myself to conclude that it is liberal-moral-rights-violative for a firm to inform a rival that the rival's decision to invest will elicit a not-immoral response that will render the informed rival's decision to invest unprofitable.

I turn finally to the behaviors in which a firm engages that it would not have perceived to be at least normally profitable ex ante had it not believed that the relevant conduct would or might increase its future profits by increasing the profits it will be able to realize by contriving investment-reductions or by creating situations in which it and its rivals will confront each other with natural-oligopolistic investment-disincentives that deter them from making one or more investments that would have increased equilibrium investment in the ARDEPPS in which the conduct would be perpetrated. In my judgment, all conduct that is critically motivated by any such belief is liberal-moral-rights-violative because it manifests the perpetrator's specific anticompetitive intent.

9.3.2.2 The Moral Duties That the Government of a Liberal-Moral-Rights-Based Society Has to Respond in Various Ways to the Choices Referenced in the Heading of Sect. 9.3.2

I will focus first on the moral duties that such a government has to deter contrived-oligopolistic investment-reducing conduct, then on the moral duties that such a government has that relate to firms' deciding not to invest because of the natural-oligopolistic interdependence of their investment-decisions, and finally on the moral duties that such a government has that relate to firms' making choices that are critically motivated by their desire to put themselves in a position to profit from contrived-oligopolistic and natural-oligopolistic investment-reductions. Subject to the constraints imposed by liberalism's implications (1) for the different probabilities of guilt that must be established respectively in civil and criminal cases for a decision of liability or guilt to be just, (2) for the relationship between the sum of the "costs" that are imposed on a "convicted" wrongdoer and the seriousness of the wrongdoing, (3) for the methods that governments may use to secure (A) evidence of wrongdoing or (B) civil settlements or plea bargains, and (4) for the basic duty of governments to maximize the extent to which the liberal-moral-rights-related interests of those for whom they are responsible are secured, the government of a liberal-moral-rights-based society that does not need to save resources when dealing with this type of contrived-oligopolistic conduct to enable it to secure weightier moral-rights-related interests is morally obligated to do everything it can to deter contrived-oligopolistic investment-reductions, regardless of whether the investments in question are QV investments or PPR investments and to enable the following sets of actors to secure legal redress from the contrivers in question—non-cooperating sellers that are recipients of contrived-oligopolistic threats and/or promises and victims of conduct-associated retaliation, buyers on whom the relevant contrived-oligopolistic-conduct-associated acts of reciprocation impose equivalent-dollar losses, and buyers who would have benefited from the contrivance-deterred investments. This conclusion implicitly assumes that contrivance that is designed to reduce either equilibrium QV investment or equilibrium PPR in the ARDEPPS in which it is practiced is liberal-moral-rights-violative even when the resulting reduction in an ARDEPPS' equilibrium QV investment is economically efficient. I have two justifications for this implicit assumption. First, as Sect. 9.3.1.1 argues, contrivance that reduces equilibrium QV investment in the ARDEPPS in which it is practiced by deterring one or more potential investors' investments is almost always economically inefficient all tolled (especially if one takes account of the independent economic inefficiency of the otherwise-unprofitable choices firms make to increase their ability to contrive decisions not to make investments in relevant ARDEPPSes). Second, even if a firm's knowledge that its efforts to contrive reductions in its ARDEPPS' equilibrium QV investment will increase economic efficiency would render such contrivance liberal-moral-rights-non-violative, (1) most firms that attempt to contrive negative investment-decisions will not realize ex ante that their behavior is economically efficient even in what I take to be the relatively-small percentage of cases in which it will be, and (2) choices to contrive reductions in an ARDEPPS' equilibrium QV investment by deterring firms from making inherently-profitable investments in that ARDEPPS will be liberal-moral-rights-violative if the contriver(s) do not believe ex ante that their conduct is economically efficient even if it is ex ante economically efficient and their knowledge of this fact would be exonerating. (I am being realistic about the likely popular awareness and acceptance of my argument for the conclusion that contemporary economies devote too many resources to QV-investment creation from the perspective of economic efficiency.) I should perhaps add that variants of this type of contrivance that involve the communication or communication and carrying out of threats of retaliation might be liberal-moral-rights-violative even if the contrivance would not be absent such actions.

But what of the duties that the government of a liberal-moral-rights-based society has in relation to firm-decisions not to make investments when those decisions reflect solely the firms" natural-oligopolistic interdependencies? At least when no relevant potential investor committed any preceding act that was critically motivated by its desire to create a situation in which it and its rivals would confront each other with critical natural-oligopolistic investment-disincentives, the decreases in an ARDEPPS' equilibrium investment that result from its sellers' facing natural-oligopolistic investment-disincentives come about without any seller's committing a positive act and, perhaps equally importantly, without any seller's communicating or carrying out a threat of retaliation or a promise of (inherently-unprofitable) reciprocation. For these reasons, the decisions of two or more firms not to invest that are made profitable for each such firm by a natural-oligopolistic interdependence that they did not create by engaging in conduct that was motivated by specific anticompetitive intent do not violate the liberal moral rights of the buyers on whom the decisions impose equivalent-dollar losses. Therefore, the government of a liberal-moral-rights-based society would have no buyer-related duty to require a firm that would otherwise be deterred from making an investment by the natural-oligopolistic investment-disincentive it "innocently" faced to make that investment: Indeed, it seems to me that liberalism might imply that any such government order would violate the liberal moral rights of the firm—that is, of its shareholders/creditors/managers/employees. Admittedly, if a government decision to secure the execution of what would otherwise be a natural-oligopolistic-investment-disincentive-deterred PPR investment by subsidizing its execution would instantiate a pure or mixed conception of the moral good whose instantiation would give appropriate weight to the society's members' and participants' moral-good positions (e.g.,would increase total utility and serve the instantiation of the equal-utility, equal-resource, and equal-other-opportunity conceptions of the moral good) better than any other liberal-moral-rights-non-violative policy could do, the government of a liberal-moral-rights-based society would have a moral duty to induce the execution of such PPR investments by subsidizing them to fulfill its moral duty to give each of its society's members' and participants' moral-good positions appropriate, equal weight. However, this possibility is far-fetched (a word I like to use because it is one of the small number of English words that could be Yiddish).

I turn finally to the moral duties of the government of a liberal-moral-rights-based society that relate to a firm's making one or more choices that are critically motivated by its belief that the choices would or might increase the profits it will be able to realize by contriving investment-reductions or would or might increase its profits by creating a situation in which it and one or more relevant rivals would confront each other with critical (investment-deterring) natural-oligopolistic investment-disincentives. Because such choices are liberal-moral-rights-violative, the government of a liberal-moral-rights-based society would have to do everything it could to deter them and give their victims appropriate opportunities to secure legal redress within the constraints that liberalism imposes on such governments. I am aware of the difficulty and allocative cost of identifying choices that were critically motivated by their perpetrator's desire to secure investment-reductions oligopolistically. A final observation: Even if decisions not to make investments for natural-oligopolistic reasons would not otherwise be liberal-moral-rights-violative, those decisions would be liberal-moral-rights-violative if the relevant natural-oligopolistic investment-disincentives were created by perpetrator-choices that were motivated by specific anticompetitive intent (the poisonous tree would poison its fruit).

9.3.3 The Effect on the Instantiation of Various Morally-Defensible Conceptions of the Moral Good of Contrived-Oligopolistic Conduct or Natural-Oligopolistic Interdependencies That Reduce Equilibrium Investment in the Relevant ARDEPPS and of Conduct That Is Critically Motivated by Its Perpetrator's Desire to Be Able to Profit From Such Investment-Reductions and the Moral Desirability of the Government's of a Liberal-Moral-Rights-Based Society's Instantiating Such Conceptions of the Moral Good by Responding Appropriately to the Reality or Prospect of Such Contrived-Oligopolistic or Natural-Oligopolistic Investment-Reductions and to Conduct That Was Critically Motivated by Its Perpetrator's Desire to Secure Such Investment-Reductions

9.3.3.1 The Effect on the Instantiation of Various Conceptions of the Moral Good of (Contrived-Oligopolistic Conduct)/(Natural-Oligopolistic Interdependencies) That (Are Designed to Secure)/(Result in) Reductions in Equilibrium Investment in the Relevant ARDEPPS and of Conduct That Is Critically Motivated by Its Perpetrator's Desire to Profit From Such Investment-Reductions

I will proceed on the following two premises:

(1) contrived-oligopolistic conduct that is perpetrated to reduce and does reduce equilibrium QV or PPR in the ARDEPPS in which it is practiced, the operation of natural-oligopolistic interdependencies that reduce equilibrium QV or PPR in the ARDEPPS in which they are operative, and conduct that is critically motivated by its perpetrator's desire to profit from oligopolistically-secured investment-reductions have undesirable distributive impacts from the perspectives both of utilitarianism and of the other morally-defensible egalitarian conceptions of the moral good I have distinguished (because all such conduct increases poverty and material inequality), and

(2) in actual, otherwise-Pareto-imperfect economies, the practice of contrived-oligopolistic conduct that is perpetrated to reduce and does reduce equilibrium investment in the ARDEPPS in which it is practiced, the operation of natural-oligopolistic interdependencies that have the effect of reducing equilibrium investment in the ARDEPPS in which they are operative, and conduct that is rendered ex ante profitable by its tendency to enable its perpetrator to secure oligopolistic investment-reductions will always decrease economic

efficiency when investment in the relevant ARDEPPS is investment in PPR and will usually (probably almost always decrease economic efficiency when investment in the relevant ARDEPPS is QV investment.

These premises imply the following moral-good-related conclusions:

(1) because all contrived-oligopolistic conduct that is perpetrated to reduce and does reduce an ARDEPPS' equilibrium quantity of QV investment or PPR investment, all decisions not to invest that are generated by the operation of natural-oligopolistic investment-interdependencies, and all conduct that is critically motivated by its perpetrator's desire to increase its ability to profit by securing investment-reductions oligopolistically increase poverty and material inequality, all such conduct disserves the instantiation of the equal-utility, equal-resource, and various other equal-opportunity conceptions of the moral good,
(2) because all contrived-oligopolistic conduct that is perpetrated to reduce and does reduce an ARDEPPS' equilibrium-PPR quantity, all decisions not to engage in PPR that are motivated by natural-oligopolistic investment-disincentives, and all conduct that is motivated by its perpetrator's desire to create a situation that reduces equilibrium PPR in the ARDEPPS of practice by creating a situation in which the perpetrator and its rivals confront each other with critical natural-oligopolistic investment-disincentives not only generate a distributive impact that disserves the instantiation of the utilitarian conception of the moral good but decrease economic efficiency, all such conduct disserves the instantiation of the utilitarian conception of the moral good,
(3) because the overwhelming majority of exemplars of contrived-oligopolistic conduct that is perpetrated to reduce and does reduce equilibrium QV investment in the ARDEPPS of practice, the overwhelming majority of decisions not to make a QV investment that are motivated by the natural-oligopolistic QV-investment disincentives that reduce the profitability of the investments in question, and the overwhelming majority of decisions that firms make that are critically motivated by their desire to secure QV-investment reductions oligopolistically not only generate a distributive impact that disserves the instantiation of the utilitarian conception of the moral good but also decrease economic efficiency, the overwhelming majority of exemplars of such conduct disserves the instantiation of the utilitarian conception of the moral good, and
(4) because it is possible that a few exemplars of conduct that reduces equilibrium QV investment in the ARDEPPS of practice will increase economic efficiency it is possible that some economically-efficient exemplars of contrived-oligopolistic conduct that secures QV-investment reductions, of decisions not to make QV investments that are critically motivated by natural-oligopolistic investment-disincentives, and of decisions that are critically motivated by their perpetrator's desire to earn profits by reducing equilibrium QV investment in the ARDEPPS to which the decisions directly relate will

serve the instantiation of the utilitarian conception of the moral good, even though those exemplars will have distributive impacts that disserve the instantiation of the utilitarian conception of the moral good.

9.3.3.2 The Ability of the Government of a Liberal-Moral-Rights-Based Society to Instantiate One or More Morally-Defensible Conceptions the Moral Good by Deterring Firms From Contriving Decisions Not to Invest, by Inducing Firms to Make Investments That Were Rendered Unprofitable by Natural-Oligopolistic Investment-Disincentives, and by Deterring Firms From Making Decisions That Are Critically Motivated by the Perpetrator's Desire to Profit by Reducing Equilibrium Investment in the ARDEPPS of Practice Oligopolistically

I will restrict myself to making five points or sets of related points. First, Sect. 9.3.3.1's conclusions that the overwhelming majority or all decisions to contrive investment-reductions, not to invest because of natural-oligopolistic interdependencies, and to make otherwise-unprofitable decisions to increase the profits the perpetrator can realize by securing investment-reductions oligopolistically disserve the instantiation of the utilitarian and various non-utilitarian-egalitarian conceptions of the moral good favor the conclusion that the government of a liberal-moral-rights-based society might be able to serve the instantiation of those conceptions of the moral good or some mixed conception of the moral good in which the just-referenced pure conceptions play a role by preventing such conduct or decisions.

Second, and obviously, the liberal-moral-rights constraints that apply generally to the governments of liberal-moral-rights-based societies apply equally to their responses to the prospect and reality of the just-referenced categories of conduct.

Third, in the current context, the relevant set of constraints might be deemed to include those created by the liberal moral right of a firm (i.e., of the individuals connected to the firm who would suffer equivalent-dollar losses if the firm were required to make an unprofitable investment) not to be forced to make an investment that was rendered unprofitable by a natural-oligopolistic investment-disincentive that it did not act culpably to create. However, I see no reason to conclude that such firms would have a liberal moral right not to make an investment that would otherwise have been rendered unprofitable by natural-oligopolistic investment-disincentives if the government subsidized the investment sufficiently to render it profitable.

Fourth, to determine the subsidy that would be optimal to pay investors for making investments that would otherwise be rendered unprofitable by natural-oligopolistic investment-disincentives, the government would have to determine the number of such investments it would be morally good to elicit from such investors (given the allocative cost and distributive consequences of the government's doing and financing the appropriate research and financing and paying the required subsidies) and the subsidy it would have to pay to elicit that number of investments.

Fifth, and relatedly, the allocative cost and distributive consequences of the government's doing and financing what would otherwise be the appropriate research and financing and paying what would otherwise be the appropriate subsidy might render it ex ante morally bad from the perspective of one, more than one, or all morally-defensible pure or mixed conceptions of the moral good for the government to induce or even consider inducing investments to be made that would otherwise be rendered unprofitable by the natural-oligopolistic investment-disincentives their possible creators./executors faced in relation to them.

9.4 Contrived-Oligopolistic Conduct That Is Designed to Induce Its Participants to Place Their Investments in Product-Space Locations That Increase the Profits They Realize From a Given Total Quantity of Investment

I will begin negatively. This section is not concerned with conduct in which a seller seeks to induce a rival to make an investment that is less competitive with the seller's investments or to substitute for an investment that is more competitive with the seller's investments an investment that is less competitive with the seller's investments when the seller-conduct in question does not increase economic efficiency. Seller-efforts to induce rivals to substitute investments that are less competitive with the seller's investments for investments that are or would be more competitive with the seller's investments when the sought-after investment-location shift will decrease economic efficiency will be analyzed in Chap. 10 as predatory conduct. Positively, this section is concerned with seller-efforts to contrive "substitutions" of investments that are less duplicative and collectively more economically efficient for investments that are more duplicative and collectively less economically efficient. Firms can contrive such investment "substitutions" by entering into formal contracts that specify the investments they will respectively make and not make, by promising each other to make only specified investments without the intention of creating legally-enforceable obligations to fulfill their promises, and/or by communicating to each other "instructions" about the investments each of them may and may not make and threatening to retaliate against non-cooperators (and carrying out these threats). This section focuses on these contrivance-possibilities. Firms can also secure the creation of a set of investments of given size that are collectively more economically efficient as well as being collectively more profitable for all sellers in their ARDEPPS by combining (through mergers and/or acquisitions) or by establishing an investment joint venture through an agreement that explicitly prohibits the parents from investing in the relevant ARDEPPS or relies on each parent's partial ownership of the joint venture to deter each parent from making investments in the joint venture's ARDEPPS that are collectively less allocatively efficient (and more to the point from the perspective of the participants are against the joint interest of all parents). Chapters 11 and 12 will address the merger-and-acquisition possibility, and Chap. 15 will address the joint-venture possibility.

From this study's policy-perspective, it is important to distinguish (1) decisions firms make to alter the product-space locations of their rivals and their own investments when the relocations increase economic efficiency from (2) decisions designed to induce rivals to change the locations of the rivals' investments to make them less competitive with those of the perpetrator when the relocation will not increase economic efficiency. From a legal perspective, it is important to distinguish the first set of decisions from the second because the fact that the first set of decisions would increase economic efficiency not only in the actual world but in an oPp economy implies that the first set of decisions (unlike the second set) do not violate the "specific anticompetitive intent" test of illegality I articulated in that the first set of decisions (unlike the second) do not increase the perpetrator's profits by reducing the absolute attractiveness of the best offers against which it must compete *in a way that would render the conduct profitable though economically inefficient in an oPp economy.*

I will illustrate the possibility with which this section is concerned with two examples. In each, I will begin by explaining how a pure monopolist in an ARDEPPS in which potential competition was not effective would locate the investments it made in the relevant ARDEPPS, next explain why the investment-location decisions that would be made by two (or more) firms (if two or more firms were operating in the relevant ARDEPPS) would be different from and less jointly-profitable (and less-oPp-economically-efficient) than the investment-location decisions the pure monopolist would make, then explain the various ways in which multiple firms in a given ARDEPPS could overcome this "problem," and finally analyze the economic efficiency, liberal-moral-rights-violativeness, and moral-good impact of such efforts and the ability of the government of a liberal-moral-rights-based society to increase economic efficiency, secure liberal-moral-rights-related interests, and instantiate various conceptions of the moral good by responding appropriately to efforts by firms to control their respective investment-locations for this reason.

In the first example, (1) only one firm is in a position to build one or more laundromats in a section of a particular town that contains no such businesses, (2) the residents who would want to patronize a laundromat are located linearly and homogeneously between First Street and Forty-Ninth Street and have identical, positive linear dollar-preferences for laundromat-proximity, (3) no economies of scale can be secured by building one laundromat with twice the capacity rather than two laundromats each of which has half the capacity of its larger alternative, (4) the cost of constructing and operating a laundromat does not depend on where it is located between First Street and Forty-Ninth Street, and (5) the laundromat-entrepreneur in question will find it most profitable to construct and operate two (of the smaller) laundromats in the relevant area, regardless of whether they are located next to each other or distant from each other. In this situation, the pure monopolist will find it most-profitable to construct one laundromat on Thirteenth Street and one on Thirty-Seventh Street to minimize the average distance its customers must schlepp their laundry (to maximize the average dollar value of its services to its potential customers and derivatively the profits it can realize by supplying them with laundromat services). Ceteris paribus, this location-decision will also be most-economically-efficient. Now let's assume that two firms are equally-well-placed to create a laundromat in the relevant area, that once a firm has constructed a laundromat it will be prohibitively-costly to change its location, that neither of these two possible investors can construct two laundromats before the other can construct one, that assumptions (2)–(4) of the preceding sentence still obtain, and that an analog to assumption (5) of the preceding sentence still obtains—that two laundromats will be constructed in the relevant ARDEPPS regardless of where they are placed. In this situation, if these two prospective investors cannot prevent this outcome by engaging in contrived-oligopolistic conduct, the first to build a laundromat will locate it in the middle of Twenty-Fifth Street (to prevent its rival from picking a location more to the middle of the relevant geographic area that would give it a competitive advantage in relation to more than half of the relevant prospective customers), and the second would locate next door. These location-decisions would reduce the profits the two investors realize below the profits they would have earned had they located respectively at Thirteenth and Thirty-Seventh Streets by reducing the total dollar value of their laundromats' services to their prospective customers by increasing their laundromats' average distance from their prospective customers. (I recognize that I am ignoring relevant buyer-surplus-related issues.) These location-decisions would also generate economic inefficiency. To prevent themselves from making location-decisions that are jointly unprofitable, the two prospective QV investors could agree in advance to locate their laundromats respectively on Thirteenth and Thirty-Seventh Street or one or both could prevent the other from taking advantage of its jointly-optimal location-decision by threatening to retaliate against the other's doing so.

The second example focuses on the research-project decisions that a set of product-researchers or production-process researchers might make. Assume initially that (1) each potential researcher can execute only one research project, (2) each of 5 particular research-projects has a 50% probability of making at some point in time the sought-after discovery, (3) each of these 5 projects will be successful if and only if the other 4 would be successful, (4) if these 5 projects are successful, one will yield the discovery just sufficiently before the others for its owner to be able to obtain IP protection for its discovery, (5) (for simplicity) no allocative benefits are generated by the advancement of the time of discovery generated by the actual (first) discovery yielded by the member of this set of projects that succeeds first, (6) each of 4 other R&D projects that is different both from the first five just referenced and from each other has an 8 percent probability of succeeding when none of the other 8 projects would succeed, (7) all 9 of the R&D projects in question have the same private (and allocative) cost, (8) given that the private and allocative cost of each project and the private and allocative value of the discovery —where the private value is affected by an IP regime that gives the (first) discoverer substantial IP protection, it would be most-jointly-profitable and oPp-economically-efficient for the prospective researchers "combined" for one of the first 5 similar projects and all 4 of the 4 dis-similar projects to be executed. Now assume that 5 firms are equally-well-placed to execute any of the 9 R&D projects just described, that each of these firms can execute only one of these projects ex ante profitably, and that no other firm is in a position to execute any of these projects (or any other relevant project) ex ante profitably. If these 5 firms do not engage in contrived-oligopolistic conduct to prevent this outcome, all 5 will choose to execute one of the 5 projects that has a 10% chance of making the discovery (first) whereas executing one of the other 4 projects would give it only an 8 percent chance of making the discovery. Once again, the firms in question will have to engage in contrived-oligopolistic conduct to prevent the investment-choices they would otherwise make from generating a reduction in their joint profits (and associated intra-ARDEPPS QV-to-QV or PPR-to-PPR misallocation)—to prevent themselves from executing collectively all 5 of the projects of given private cost and given allocative cost that individually and collectively have a 50% probability of yielding the discovery (at essentially the same time) rather than executing one of those projects and the 4 other projects each of which has an 8 percent probability of succeeding when none of the first 5 would succeed and collectively have a 32% probability of success—that is, rather than executing 5 projects that would create an 82% probability of the discovery's being made and would have the same private and allocative cost as the 5 projects for which they would be substituted that would collectively create a 50 percent probability of the discovery's being made.

9.4.1 The Economic Efficiency of the Contrivance in Which Prospective Investors Might Engage to Increase Their Collective Profits by Reducing the Economically-Inefficient-Duplicativeness but Not the Quantity of Their Investments in an ARDEPPS and the Economic Efficiency of Government's Responding to Such Contrivance in Various Ways

9.4.1.1 The Economic Efficiency of Sellers' Contriving Reductions in the Economically-Inefficient-Duplicativness of Their Investments That Increase the Profits of All Investors in the Relevant ARDEPPS and the Collective Economic Efficiency of Their Investments

Ceteris paribus, the facts that (1) such contrivance results in the substitution of a collectively more-economically-efficient set of investments of given total magnitude for a collectively less-economically-efficient set of investments of that total magnitude and (2) the associated increase in profits exceeds the private transaction cost of arranging (and enforcing) the coordination in question favors the conclusion that the contrivance is economically efficient. I admit that not all the ceteris will or may not be paribus. More specifically, I acknowledge that the conclusion that this type of contrivance is economically efficient is disfavored by the facts that (1) the private transaction costs it generates are lower than their allocative counterparts, (2) any retaliation the contrivance involves will be misallocative, (3) the increase the contrivance yields in the contrivers' potential profits will yield misallocation to the extent that it causes them to operate more sloppily and increases the amount of misallocation their managers and employees generate by making economically-inefficient substitutions of untaxed or lower-taxed better working-conditions and fringe-benefits for the goods they would have purchased with the monetary compensation they exchanged for the just-referenced desiderata (if the contrivers would share some of the associated increase in their potential profits with their personnel), and (4) the profits the contrivance yields the contrivers will tend to cause economic inefficiency by increasing material inequality. However, I doubt that these effects will critically affect the economic efficiency of all exemplars (indeed, of any significant number of exemplars) of this type of contrivance. I also acknowledge that particular exemplars of this type of contrivance could be economically inefficient if the sale of the products/(production processes) it would cause to be created/discovered would generate less buyer surplus than the sale of the products/(production process) it would cause not to be created/discovered would have generated or if the (production and consumption)/use of the products/(production processes) it would cause to be created/discovered were more-external-cost-prone than the (production and consumption)/use of the products/(production processes) it would cause not be created/discovered would have been. However, I see no reason to believe that there will be any such tendencies (indeed, the sale of the less-duplicative set of products the contrivance would cause to be created will tend to yield more buyer surplus) and doubt that any such differences will critically affect the profitability of this type of contrivance in more than a trivial number of instances. Everything considered, I therefore conclude not only that, taken as a class, the exemplars of this type of contrivance will increase economic efficiency but that few if any exemplars of this type of contrivance will decrease economic efficiency. Indeed, to anticipate the conclusions of the next subsection, I doubt that it will be TBLE for antitrust-policy-implementation authorities to consider the possibility that any exemplar of such contrivance will be economically inefficient.

9.4.1.2 The Economic Efficiency of the Government of a Liberal-Moral-Rights-Based Society's Permitting This Type of Contrivance

I suspect that it will be TBLE for the government of any liberal-moral-rights-based society to determine the truth-values of firms' claims that their contrivance was designed to substitute a more-economically-efficient set of investments of a given total quantity for a less-economically-efficient set of investments of that total quantity. I doubt that it will ever be TBLE for a government of a liberal-moral-rights-based society to consider prohibiting particular exemplars of contrivance of this kind. In my judgment, even if some exemplars of this type of contrivance decrease economic efficiency, the allocative cost of identifying these outliers with various relevant degrees of accuracy and of actually prohibiting them render any attempt to do so third-best-allocatively-inefficient. In my judgment, then, the TBLE way for such governments to respond to this possibility is to investigate firms' claims that they are engaging in contrivance for this purpose and to permit all exemplars of such contrivance.

9.4.2 The Liberal-Moral-Rights-Violativeness of Exemplars of This Type of Contrivance and the Moral Obligation of the Government of a Liberal-Moral-Rights-Based Society to Respond to Such Contrivance in Various Ways

9.4.2.1 The Liberal-Moral-Rights-Violativeness of Exemplars of This Type of Contrivance

In my judgment, with one exception, this type of seller-contrivance is not liberal-moral-rights-violative. Exception aside, this conclusion is warranted by the facts that (1) this contrivance is economically efficient, (2) its perpetrators would have every reason to conclude that they are on that account morally entitled to obtain the profits it yields them, (3) this type of contrivance does not tend to impose a net equivalent-dollar loss on the actual and potential buyers of the products produced in the ARDEPPS in which it is perpetrated (indeed, I suspect that in most instances these buyers will benefit from the investment-location changes it elicits), and (4) no individual contriver's conduct will (except for the exception) impose an equivalent-dollar loss on any of its rivals (indeed, all members of the relevant set of contrivers will probably benefit from the contrivance).

What is the related exception? If the contrivance involves the communication of threats of retaliation to one or more potential participants and the carrying out of such threats against one or more non-cooperators, those threats and acts of retaliation violate the liberal moral rights of their addressees/targets, which have no moral duty to participate in this arrangement. Indeed, I think that this last conclusion would be justified even if the non-cooperator had contracted to or given a non-contractually-binding promise to cooperate: I do not think that threats or acts of retaliation can be justicized as legitimate self-help. However, I suspect that this type of contrivance rarely involves threats or acts of retaliation.

9.4.2.2 The Responses That the Government of a Liberal-Moral-Rights-Based Society Is Obligated to Make to This Type of Contrivance

The government of a liberal-moral-rights-based society is morally obligated to deter any threats/acts of retaliation that are communicated/carried out by participants in this type of contrivance and to give the targets of such conduct appropriate opportunities to secure legal redress. With that exception, such governments are if anything morally obligated to allow firms to engage in such contrivance, perhaps because they have a moral right to do so and in some instances because, given the contribution such conduct makes to the instantiation of the utilitarian conception of the moral good, such governments' obligation to give equal, appropriate weight to each of the society's members moral-good positions will impose a moral duty on them to do so when the society's members' moral-good positions warrant this conclusion.

9.4.3 The Impact That This Type of Contrivance Has on the Instantiation of Various Morally-Defensible Conceptions of the Moral Good and the Moral "Goodness" of Various Responses That Government Could Make to Such Conduct

This section assumes that the type of contrivance on which it focuses involves no threats or acts of retaliation.

9.4.3.1 The Impact of This Type of Contrivance on the Instantiation of the Various Morally-Defensible Conceptions of the Moral Good I Have Identified

On the assumption articulated in the preceding sentence, exemplars of this type of contrivance will almost always increase total utility because they will virtually always significantly increase economic efficiency and will impose a significant equivalent-dollar loss on few if any individuals so that, even if the few losers—for example, those buyers of the relevant ARDEPPS' products that realize less consumer surplus from purchasing the products the contrivance cause to be produced than they would have realized from purchasing the products whose creation and production the contrivance deters and possibly some suppliers of inputs (including suppliers of labor) that are more useful for the creation and use of the investments the contrivance causes to be made than for the creation and use of the investments the contrivance deters—are as a class poorer than are the shareholders/creditors/managers/employees of the contrivers and the buyers and relevant input-suppliers who gain from the investment-substitution the contrivance effectuates, the contrivance will almost certainly serve the instantiation of the utilitarian conception of the moral good.

Admittedly, there may be some tendency for this type of contrivance to disserve the instantiation of the equal-utility, equal-resource, and other types of equal-opportunity conceptions of the moral good because (1) the average equivalent-dollar gain that this type of contrivance will yield the shareholders/creditors/managers/employees of the contrives exceeds the average equivalent-dollar gain this type of contrivance will yield the contrivers' customers and (2) as classes, the shareholders/creditors/managers/employees of the contrivers will be materially-better-off than the customers of the contrivers. However, this conclusion is somewhat undercut by the fact that contrivance of this type that relates to the product-space locations of QV investments will tend to benefit the relevant

ARDEPPS' buyers by increasing the buyer surplus they obtain by rendering the ARDEPPS' products less duplicative.

If I had to guess, I would guess that most members of liberal-moral-rights-based societies subscribe to a mixed conception of the moral good in which utilitarianism and one or more non-utilitarian-egalitarian norms play a role and that this type of contrivance would serve the instantiation of the various mixed conceptions of the moral good to which most members of liberal-moral-rights-based societies subscribe.

9.4.3.2 The Impact That the Various Responses That the Government of any Liberal-Moral-Rights-Based Society Could Make to This Type of Contrivance Would Have on the Moral Good

I will restrict myself to three comments. First, because all or virtually all exemplars of this type of contrivance will increase total utility, government decisions to allow this type of contrivance will virtually always increase total utility. Second, although a significant number of exemplars of this type of contrivance may disserve the instantiation of the various morally-defensible non-utilitarian-egalitarian conceptions of the moral good, I suspect that government would have to take great care to control the direct distributive impact of any effort it made to prohibit and deter this type of contrivance for such efforts to serve the instantiation of these non-utilitarian-egalitarian conceptions of the moral good. Third, I suspect that this type of contrivance will be likely to serve the instantiation of any mixed conception of the moral good that values the total utility of all creatures whose utility counts and that it is extremely unlikely that governments will be able to serve the instantiation of such mixed conceptions of the moral good by prohibiting and deterring those exemplars of such contrivance that disserve such mixed conceptions' instantiation (given the allocative and utilitarian cost of any such government-efforts).

9.5 Buyer-Practiced Contrived-Oligopolistic Purchasing

Two or more buyers can try to lower the prices they must pay for a good and/or to improve other terms of their purchasing arrangements by consummating a merger or acquisition, by creating a purchasing joint venture, or by agreeing to bargain together (agreeing not to pay more than a specified price for a particular good [and/or not to accept particular other disadvantaging terms of trade]), and one or more buyers can try to improve their purchasing terms by informing one or more other buyers that buyer(s) that pay more than a specified price for a particular good and/or accept particular non-price disadvantaging terms of trade will not be allowed to participate in the deals the initiator(s) strike and/or will be subjected to retaliation. The relevant mergers and acquisitions will be analyzed in Chaps. 11, 12, and 14, and the relevant joint ventures will be analyzed in Chap. 15. This section focuses on the contrived-oligopolistic conduct in which firms can engage to improve the deals they can make as buyers.

The section will proceed on a contested assumption about the effects of such contrived-oligopolistic purchasing on the marginal kost of the relevant good to the purchasers (recall: I incorporate a lower-case "k" into the expression "marginal kost" and an upper-case "K" into the symbol "MK" when the referent is the cost of buying something) and hence on the prices the purchasers charge for the goods they sell (when the purchasers are manufacturers and the good involved is an input that the manufacturers use to produce final products or when the purchasers are distributive outlets and the good in question is a final product they resell). The standard analysis of such contrived-oligopolistic pricing (by economists and U.S. academic lawyers and judges who are conversant with economics) assumes that—although such contrived-oligopolistic purchasing will reduce the average kost to the contrivers of the good in question—it will increase the marginal kost to the purchasers of the marginal and many intra-marginal units of the relevant good and hence the prices they charge final consumers. This assumption reflects these scholars' and judges' belief that, when acting together, the contrivers face an upward-sloping supply curve and do not engage in individualized bargaining with their potential suppliers—that is, offer all potential suppliers the same per-unit price for the good in question. Under these conditions, (1) the contrivers in question will face a marginal-kost (MK) curve that exceeds the average-kost (AK) curve they face, (2) the contrivance will increase the marginal kost to the contrivers of the marginal and many intra-marginal units of the good in question, and (3) the contrived-oligopolistic purchasing will increase the marginal cost to the contrivers of producing the good or services they produce or distributing the goods they resell and hence the price they charge for the goods they sell. By way of contrast, this section assumes that (1) when acting together, the contrivers deal separately with their individual possible suppliers, (2) those suppliers possess some economic power, (3) both when acting separately and when acting together as contrivers, the buyers strike deals with their supplier in which they are charged a constant per-unit price for each successive unit of the supplier's good they purchase, and (4) the contrivance enables the purchasers to secure from each possible supplier a lower per-unit price for each unit they purchase than the individual purchasers could otherwise have secured. Under these conditions, (1) the contrivance will reduce not only the AK but also the MK of the good to the contrivers, and (2) the contrivance will therefore reduce both the marginal cost to the contrivers of producing their respective products/services and the prices the contrivers charge final consumers of the products they sell.

9.5.1 The Economic Efficiency of Contrived-Oligopolistic Purchasing and of the Various Responses That Government Could Make to Such Conduct

9.5.1.1 The Economic Efficiency of Contrived-Oligopolistic Purchasing

On the assumption that successful contrived-oligopolistic purchasing reduces the prices that ultimate consumers pay for the goods that manufacturers produce with inputs they contrived to buy more cheaply and for the goods that distributors contrived to buy more cheaply, contrived-oligopolistic purchasing (1) will tend to increase economic efficiency (A) indirectly by decreasing poverty and material inequality and (B) by reducing the amount of economic inefficiency generated by economically-inefficient allocations of resources to QV-investment creation when the good whose price the contrivance reduces is created by a QV investment, (2) will tend to decrease economic efficiency (A) by generating intra-ARDEPPPS UO-to-UO misallocation if the contrivers retaliate against one or more non-cooperators and (B) by increasing the amount of economic inefficiency generated by economically-inefficient decisions not to allocate additional resources to PPR execution when the good whose price the contrivance reduces is a production process, (3) can either increase economic efficiency by decreasing allocative transaction costs or decrease economic efficiency by increasing allocative transactions (depending on whether any allocative-transaction-cost savings it generates by enabling the contrivers to take advantage of allocative economies of scale in purchasing exceed or are exceeded by the sum of the allocative transaction cost of communicating the associated promises and threats, of securing the associated agreement, and of carrying out any related retaliation against non-cooperators), (4) will tend to increase economic efficiency to the extent that, acting together, the contrivers do a more-economically-efficient job of identifying the suppliers that are privately and allocatively best-placed to supply them, (5) will tend to increase the economic inefficiency that producers generate because their potential ability to realize supernormal profits leads them to operate sloppily to the extent that the contrived-oligopolistic purchasing increases the joint profits of the buyers and sellers it directly affects by yielding real purchasing efficiencies, (6) will tend to increase the amount of economic inefficiency that the managers and employees of the contrivers and their suppliers generate by making economically-inefficient substitutions of untaxed or lower-taxed better working-conditions and higher fringe-benefits for the goods they would have purchased with the higher-taxed monetary compensation they forego to obtain the working-conditions and fringe-benefits in question to the extent that their employers share with them the potential supernormal profits their employers could realize because the contrived-oligopolistic purchasing increases the joint profits of the buyers and sellers it directly involves by generating real purchasing efficiencies, and (7) can either increase or decrease economic efficiency all tolled by decreasing equilibrium QV investment or equilibrium PPR in the suppliers' ARDEPPS and increasing equilibrium QV investment or equilibrium PPR in the contrivers' ARDEPPS, regardless of whether the relevant ARDEPPS' investments are QV investments or investments in PPR, given that the contrived-purchasing will increase equilibrium investment in the contrivers' ARDEPPS and decrease equilibrium investment in their suppliers' ARDEPPS. Because, in my judgment, the vast majority of contrived-oligopolistic purchasing (1) reduces the prices that final consumers pay and on that account increases economic efficiency by reducing poverty and material inequality, (2) does not involve the making and carrying out of threats of retaliation against non-cooperators, and (3) enables its participants to take advantage of allocative-transaction-cost-related economies of scale in purchasing and to do a more-economically-efficient job of identifying the suppliers that are privately and allocatively best placed to supply them, I believe that almost all contrived-oligopolistic purchasing increases economic efficiency. The sole possible exception is contrived-oligopolistic purchasing that involves the making and carrying out of threats of retaliation against non-cooperators.

9.5.1.2 The Economic Efficiency of the Various Contrived-Oligopolistic-Purchasing Policies That the Government of a Liberal-Moral-Rights-Based Society Could Adopt

I will limit myself to three observations. First, because I believe that virtually all exemplars of contrived-oligopolistic pricing that do not involve the making and carrying out of threats of retaliation against non-cooperators are economically efficient and that it will not be TBLE for antitrust-policy implementers to try to identify the few if any exemplars of such contrived-oligopolistic purchasing that are economically inefficient and to prove that they are economically inefficient, I believe that it will be TBLE for government to allow all exemplars of contrived-oligopolistic purchasing that do not involve the making and carrying out of threats of retaliation against non-cooperators. Second, because I think that it is economically inefficient for contrived-oligopolistic purchasers to make and carry out threats of retaliation against non-cooperators even when the non-cooperation decreases economic efficiency by weakening the contrivance, I think it would be TBLE for contrived-oligopolistic-purchaser retaliation to be prohibited, investigated, and prosecuted and for victims of such retaliation to be given an appropriate opportunity to obtain legal redress. Third, the second point has little practical significance in liberal-moral-rights-based societies because the government of any such society has a moral obligation to deter contrived-oligopolistic-purchaser retaliation against non-cooperators and to give victims of such retaliation an appropriate opportunity to obtain legal redress to the extent that the government can do so by making decisions that do not sacrifice weightier liberal-moral-rights-related interests.

9.5.2 The Liberal-Moral-Rights-Violativeness of Contrived-Oligopolistic Purchasing and the Contrived-Oligopolistic-Purchasing-Related Moral Duties of the Government of a Liberal-Moral-Rights-Based Society

9.5.2.1 The Liberal Moral-Rights-Violativeness of Contrived-Oligopolistic Purchasing

I focus initially on contrived-oligopolistic purchasing that involves no acts of retaliation against any fellow-buyer non-cooperator. I will start by reviewing my analysis of the liberal-moral-rights-violativeness of seller-practiced contrived-oligopolistic pricing. I concluded that such seller-pricing violated the liberal moral rights of the buyers that were charged COMs because in moral essence it was equivalent to theft: It imposed an equivalent-dollar loss on the buyers in question (who were presumably morally entitled to the dollars they lost) and conferred equivalent-dollar gains on the sellers to which they were not morally entitled (which they had done nothing to morally deserve). I also pointed out that (1) the equivalent-dollar losses that seller-practiced contrived-oligopolistic pricing imposed on the buyers charged contrived-oligopolistic prices exceed the equivalent-dollar gain such pricing confers on its practitioners and (2) the practice is economically inefficient, at least when the good in question is not a production process or the right to use a production process and usually even when it is. But I indicated that I did not really think that these two points were morally critical in the context of seller-practiced contrived-oligopolistic pricing.

Does this analysis have any bearing on the liberal-moral-rights-violativeness of buyer-practiced contrived-oligopolistic purchasing? Assume ad arguendo that the relevant seller/sellers could morally justify its/their charging the prices it/they would be able to obtain if the buyers did not exercise buying power—that the extra profits the prices it/they would be able to obtain if their customer(s) did not possess buyer power would constitute just rewards for its/their having made BCA-generating choices for which it/they deserve credit. On this assumption, would not contrived-oligopolistic purchasing (or, for that matter, the exercise of buying power by an individual buyer that deserves no moral credit for possessing such power) also impose an equivalent-dollar loss on seller(s) that are morally entitled to the profits the exercise of buyer power would remove and confer an equivalent-dollar gain on morally-undeserving buyer(s)? Would not the exercise of individual or contrived-oligopolistic-conduct-secured buyer power constitute the moral equivalent of theft? In fact, what if the seller/sellers in question did not morally deserve the extra profits that the exercise of buyer power would remove from them—if those profits would have resulted from their own practice of contrived-oligopolistic pricing or their taking advantage of their rivals' charging their customers supra-conventional-marginal-cost prices (in individualized-pricing contexts because their rivals would have to incur CMCs to charge the relevant seller's customers prices equal to the rivals' respective conventional marginal costs and, in across-the-board-pricing situations, because their rivals find it profitable to charge the rivals' own customers supra-conventional-marginal-cost prices and find it prohibitively expensive to engage in price discrimination). Even if the exercise of buyer power would deprive the seller(s) in question of profits to which it/they had no moral claim and would confer equivalent-dollar gains on buyer(s) with buyer power to which it/they are morally entitled, does the buyer (do the buyers) have a liberal moral right to engage in such self-help or is its/their morally-appropriate course of action to petition their government to promulgate and implement legislation that would deter their supplier(s) from charging liberal-moral-rights-violating prices and/or to secure for them a meaningful opportunity to obtain legal redress from the relevant seller(s)?

I have not tried to distinguish contrived-oligopolistic purchasing (or the single-firm exercise of buyer power) from contrived-oligopolistic seller-pricing by pointing out (1) that the exercise of buyer power confers equivalent-dollar gains on the relevant buyer(s) that exceed the equivalent-dollar losses it imposes on the relevant seller(s) whereas sellers' practice of contrived-oligopolistic pricing confers equivalent-dollar gains on the sellers that are lower than the equivalent-dollar losses it imposes on the relevant buyers or (2) that the exercise of buyer power almost always increases economic efficiency whereas sellers' practice of contrived-oligopolistic pricing almost always decreases economic efficiency because it does not seem to me (for reasons I cannot satisfactorily articulate) that in this context these differences matter. I am not trying to conceal the fact that I am struggling. Help would be appreciated.

To finish with a conclusion about which I feel more confident: In my judgment, regardless of whether contrived-oligopolistic purchasing violates the liberal moral-rights of the seller(s) engaged in the relevant negotiations, any threat or act of retaliation directed at a non-cooperating buyer violates that buyer's liberal moral rights. If the non-cooperator never agreed to cooperate, attempts to coerce it into cooperating violate its liberal moral interests in being shown appropriate respect and concern. And if the non-cooperator originally agreed to cooperate and then changed its mind, each retaliator's efforts to engage in self-help would be illiberal even if the agreement were not liberal-moral-rights-violative.

9.5.2.2 The Contrived-Oligopolistic-Purchasing-Related Moral Duties of the Government of a Liberal-Moral-Rights-Based Society

My belief that any threat/act of retaliation that buyers that are practicing contrived-oligopolistic purchasing direct at any potential/actual non-cooperating buyer violate the targeted buyer's liberal moral rights implies that the government of any liberal-moral-rights-based society is morally obligated to do everything it can (subject to the standard liberal constraints and the difficulties of discovering the relevant probative evidence) to deter such threats and acts of retaliation and to provide any target of such conduct with an appropriate opportunity to obtain legal redress. If contrived-oligopolistic purchasing (or an individual firm's exercise of buyer power) violates the liberal moral rights of each seller that is subjected to the buyer power, the government of a liberal-moral-rights-based society would have the same moral obligation to deter the exercise of buyer power and to give the sellers in question an appropriate opportunity to obtain legal redress. Otherwise, the contrived-oligopolistic-purchasing duties of the government of a liberal-moral-rights-based society depend on whether such contrivance is liberal-moral-rights-violative.

9.5.3 The Impact of Contrived-Oligopolistic Purchasing on the Instantiation of Various Morally-Defensible Conceptions of the Moral Good and the Implications of any Such Moral-Good-Related Conclusions for the Moral Desirability of Various Responses That the Government of a Liberal-Moral-Rights-Based Society Could Make to Contrived-Oligopolistic Purchasing

9.5.3.1 The Impact of Contrived-Oligopolistic Purchasing on the Instantiation of Various Morally-Defensible Conceptions of the Moral Good

Contrived-oligopolistic purchasing will (1) inflict equivalent-dollar losses on the sellers it involves (i.e., on their shareholders, creditors, managers, and employees), though these losses will be reduced in the long run when the price-reductions lower their ARDEPPS' equilibrium- investment quantity, (2) will confer equivalent-dollar gains on the contrived-oligopolistic purchasers (i.e., on their shareholders, creditors, managers, and employees), and (3) on my assumptions, will confer equivalent-dollar gains on the customers of the contrived-oligopolistic purchasers.[21] On the plausible assumptions that (1) the shareholders, creditors, managers, and employees of the relevant sellers are not collectively different in any relevant respect from their counterparts for the contrived-oligopolistic purchasers and (2) the other general-equilibrium distributive effects of purchasing-contrivance can be ignored, I suspect that the class of winners from contrived-oligopolistic purchasing will contain more poor people than the class of the practice's losers and that the average income and wealth of the class of winners from the practice will be lower than the average income and wealth of the practice's losers. Moreover, as I indicated in Sect. 9.5.1.1, all instances of contrived-oligopolistic purchasing that involve the purchase of a good that is created by a QV investment and many instances of contrived-oligopolistic pricing that involve a production process or the right to use a production process increase economic efficiency. These conclusions imply that (1) with the possible exception of some cases in which the good in question is a production process, (2) with the rare exception of instances in which the good involved is a luxury good whose consumers are wealthier than the average member of the relevant society or an input used to produce such a luxury good, and (3) with the rare exception of cases in which the shareholders, creditors, managers, and employees of the producer of the good or input involved are significantly poorer than their counterparts for the contrived-oligopolistic purchasers, contrived-oligopolistic purchasing will increase total utility (will be desirable from the perspective of the utilitarian conception of the moral good). The preceding distributive conclusions also imply that, with the exception of a few cases in which conditions (2) and/or (3) in the preceding sentence are fulfilled, contrived-oligopolistic purchasing will also serve the instantiation of the equal-utility, equal-resource, or various other sorts of equal-opportunity conceptions of the moral good as well as the instantiation of the various mixed conceptions of the moral good in which two or more pure egalitarian conceptions of the moral good and no other consideration play a role.

9.5.3.2 The Moral-Good-Related Moral Desirability of the Government of a Liberal-Moral-Rights-Based Society's Responding in Various Ways to Contrived-Oligopolistic Purchasing

If contrived-oligopolistic purchasing does not violate the liberal moral rights of the sellers of the goods involved, Sect. 9.5.3.1's conclusions imply that with the rare exceptions that that subsection referenced, it would be morally desirable from the perspective of all the conceptions of the moral good I have identified for the government of a liberal-moral-rights-based society to permit contrived-oligopolistic purchasing that involves no threats or acts of retaliation that target one or more non-cooperators. In fact, the difficulty and allocative cost of identifying the exceptions in question may render it desirable from a utilitarian perspective to ignore these possibilities. I should add that, with the important qualification with which this paragraph begins, the moral duty of the government of a liberal-moral-rights-based society to give equal weight to all its members' moral-good positions may entail a moral duty to permit contrived-oligopolistic purchasing.

9.6 Conclusion

The good news is not only that this chapter is now complete but that it contains both economic-efficiency and moral analyses on which the next seven chapters can rely. I hope that these chapters will be better for them. I know that they will be shorter on their account.

Notes

1. The assumption that, to outbid a rival that has beaten its initial NOM-containing offer, a natural-oligopolistic pricer will have to charge its HNOP is wrong for two reasons. First, it ignores the fact that, in individualized-pricing situations, ceteris paribus, if the natural-oligopolistic pricer's initial price contains a non-trivial NOM, its closest rival may well beat its initial offer with a price that exceeds the rival's OMCs—that is, with an offer that the natural-oligopolistic pricer can beat with a price that exceeds the natural-oligopolistic pricer's HNOP. (An equivalent, more-complex-to-express point will apply in across-the-board-pricing situations.)

Second, it ignores the possibility that the relevant buyer(s) may make errors that affect the price that the natural-oligopolistic pricer can obtain from them. In fact, to simplify and because I do not think that error-margins are sufficiently large sufficiently often and are sufficiently identifiable by antitrust-law-enforcement authorities and triers-of-fact to make it TBLE or third-best morally desirable to consider them, the text will ignore error-margins except when analyzing sellers' inducing buyers to make errors, sellers' failing to provide buyers with information that will militate against the buyers making errors, or sellers' failing to provide the government with information that it can pass on to buyers or use to prevent buyer errors.

2. The text's analysis assumes that the contriver will make the sale at its retaliatory price and ignores many of the costs that the contriver will have to incur to offer a retaliatory price—ignores, for example, the costs that making the retaliatory offer imposes on the contriver (1) by inducing its other customers to intensify their bargaining, (2) by causing its other customers to delay their purchases, (3) by costing the contriver the goodwill of buyers that were charged higher, non-retaliatory prices, (4) by providing the buyers that received the retaliatorily-low price with an incentive to engage in arbitrage, (5) by reducing the actual/perceived dollar value of the contriver's product to buyers who (place a positive dollar value on being perceived to be purchasing high-priced goods)/(believe that the price of a good is positively correlated with its material quality), and (6) by generating law-related costs. If the target of the retaliation is given the opportunity to rebid and chooses to (just) beat the contriver's retaliatory offer, the dollar-loss the retaliation will impose on its target will equal the number of dollars by which the retaliatory offer beat the target's HNOP-containing offer, and the dollar-loss the retaliation will impose on the retaliating contriver will equal the private transaction cost of identifying the target's customer and communicating its offer to that buyer *plus* the sum of all the retaliation-costs previously listed.
3. I wrote "almost always" because one can imagine a case in which the owners, creditors, managers, and employees of the oligopolistic pricers—i.e., the main beneficiaries of the contrivance—are poorer than the conventional victims of the contrivance—the buyers of the relevant ARDEPPS' products. Think, for example, of a situation in which the product whose pricing is oligopolistic is a multi-million-dollar yacht designed for family-use as opposed to commercial use.
4. In the literature, these types of economic inefficiency are denominated "X-inefficiency." To the extent that a firm that has a higher potential supernormal profit-rate has higher private costs (generates X-inefficiency) because it uses more resources to perform given functions than it would if its potential profit-rate were lower, the allocative inefficiency associated with its incurring higher private costs will be higher than the extra private costs in question if as I believe the private benefits the extra resources would have yielded the alternative employers from whose use they were withdrawn will be lower than the allocative benefits the resources would have generated in their sacrificed uses. And to the extent that a firm that has a higher potential profit-rate has higher

costs because it incurs higher costs to compensate given managers and employees (offers them better compensation-packages), the associated economic-efficiency loss will equal not the higher "labor" costs the firm incurs on this account but the economic inefficiency the "more generous" wage-package causes by raising the tax-rate that applies to the marginal taxable income of its managers and employees and hence the amount of misallocation they generate by accepting lower monetary wages in exchange for more-attractive working-conditions and fringe-benefits that are either not taxed or taxed at a lower rate than their monetary compensation—that is, the economic inefficiency the higher compensation generates by inducing its managers and employees to make economically-inefficient substitutions of better working-conditions and fringe-benefits for the goods and services they would have bought (put crudely) with the extra monetary wages their employer would have been intrinsically indifferent to substituting for the better working-conditions and fringe-benefits in question.

5. The expression "beyond a reasonable doubt" is ambiguous when used in the current context because it is unclear whether the instruction that a trier-of-fact find a defendant guilty only if he or she finds the defendant "guilty beyond a reasonable doubt" is a "quantitative" instruction, a "qualitative" instruction, or a mixed "quantitative/qualitative" instruction—whether it instructs the trier-of-fact to find the defendant guilty only if he or she believes that the (quantitative) probability of guilt exceeds some number, only if the trier-of-fact can give no defensible reason for doubting the defendant's guilt (a qualitative standard), or only if some mixture of these two standards is satisfied.
6. Unfortunately from a policy perspective, U.S. antitrust law's and E.U. competition law's coverages of seller-practiced oligopolistic pricing is not so comprehensive. Thus, (1) the U.S. Sherman Act does not cover seller-practiced natural-oligopolistic pricing because that practice does not involve "a contract, combination or conspiracy in restraint of trade," monopolization, or an attempt to monopolize in the specific-anticompetitive-intent sense in which I believe it is correct as a matter of U.S. law to interpret these words or expressions in the relevant legal context, (2) although Article 101 of the 2009 Treaty of Lisbon does cover seller-practiced natural-oligopolistic pricing as a concerted practice and does cover seller-practiced contrived-oligopolistic pricing when it involves an agreement between undertakings when its object is to prevent or restrict competition and/or its effect is to prevent or restrict competition, Article 101 does not cover seller-practiced contrived-oligopolistic pricing whose initiator seeks to secure cooperation exclusively by threatening to retaliate against non-cooperators, and (3) although Article 102 of the 2009 Treaty of Lisbon does cover (A) seller-practiced contrived-oligopolistic pricing as an exclusionary abuse of a dominant position if it is practiced by a dominant firm (or, by a legally-dubious interpretation, if it is practiced by a set of rivals that are collectively dominant) and (B) does cover both seller-practiced contrived-oligopolistic pricing and seller-practiced natural-oligopolistic pricing if (i) the practitioner(s) is (are) dominant (or belong to a set of collectively-dominant

rivals), (ii) the conduct in question results in the relevant seller's or sellers' committing an exploitative abuse of its (their) dominant position(s) (on my view, by realizing seller surplus that constitutes an exploitatively-high percentage of the sum of the seller surplus and buyer surplus a relevant set of its/their transactions generates), and (iii) Article 102 is correctly interpreted as a matter of law to promulgate an exploitative-abuse as well as an exclusionary-abuse test of illegality, Article 102 (C) does not cover either seller-practiced contrived-oligopolistic pricing or seller-practiced natural-oligopolistic pricing if the seller-practitioner(s) do not occupy a dominant (collectively-dominant) position and (D) does not cover seller-practiced natural-oligopolistic pricing even if the seller-practitioner(s) in question is (are) dominant (belong to a set of collectively-dominant rivals) if the practice does not result in its practitioner's or practitioners' exploitatively abusing its (their) dominant position(s). See Sherman Act, 26 Stat. 209 (1890) (codified as amended at 15 U.S.C. Sections 1–11) at Sections 1 and 2, Treaty of Lisbon Amending the Treaty of European Union and the Treaty of Establishing the European Community, 2007 OJ C306 p.1 (December 13, 2007) at Articles 101(1) and 102, Markovits (2014) at pp. 75–78, 99–121, and 128–139, and Chap. 17 infra.

7. For more detailed critiques of these evidence-proposals, see Markovits (2014) at pp. 387–460.
8. Unexplained price-relationships could also reflect differences in the extent to which the relevant producer was engaging in predatory pricing at different times in the same region or at the same time in different regions. Obviously, however, defendants would not find it advantageous to explain the relevant price-relationship in this way since predatory pricing is illegal.
9. I am assuming for simplicity that the alleged oligopolistic pricer will not be civilly sued or prosecuted for engaging in oligopolistic pricing if it has not done so.
10. Obviously, the tax-policy point will not be salient if the relevant tax-policy is not likely to be adopted. See Markovits (2020), pp. 6, 66–67, 77–79, 237–248, and 302–305.
11. The text has not analyzed whether the conduct on which this paragraph is focusing disserves the libertarian conception of the moral good because, for reasons that Sect. 9.2.2 explained, I do not think that the libertarian conception of distributive justice is morally defensible. For those who disagree, the relevant issue would be whether liberal-moral-rights-violative seller-practiced-oligopolistic-pricing-related choices increase or decrease the difference between (1) the amount of resources measured by their allocative value that individuals have at their disposal (because they can purchase them or have received them through a non-monetary gift or bequest) and (2) the sum of the amount by which these individuals' labor and saving/investment decisions increased the allocative value of what has been produced and the allocative value of what they can purchase with the money they received and the allocative value of the material desiderata they received through gift and bequest. Obviously, the analysis of this issue would be exceedingly complex (would have to take

appropriate account of all the parameters that can cause the referenced differences and how they interact to cause or not cause such differences). I see no reason to believe that oligopolistic-pricing-related choices would either increase or decrease these differences. The rest of Sect. 9.1.3 will also ignore the impact of non-government and government choices on this libertarian conception of the distributive-justice-related moral good.

12. The text's point does not depend on how the egalitarian norms it lists operationalize the inequality on which they focus—for example, on whether equal-utility egalitarianism measures inequality by the mean deviation of the utility distribution, the variance of the utility distribution, some other measure of the dispersion of the utility distribution, or, for that matter, some attribute of the distribution of the ratios of individuals' utility to the average utility of all individuals.
13. This section does not address the natural-oligopolistic interdependence or contrived-oligopolistic conduct that enables sellers to restrict the product R&D they do to discover products that do not have the negative attributes of their current products that buyers underestimate, the product R&D they do to discover products whose production and consumption are less accident-and-pollution-loss-prone, or the PPR they do to discover production processes whose use is less accident-and-pollution-loss-prone. Section 9.3 addresses these possibilities.
14. Obviously, when buyers may both overestimate the dollar value of a durable good to them and underestimate the dollar cost to them of purchasing, maintaining, and repairing a durable product, the relevant percentage-figures will have to reflect both types of errors.
15. Obviously, ceteris paribus, it would be economically efficient to ban products for this type of buyer-error-related reason only if the economic inefficiency generated by mistaken buyer purchases exceeded the economic-efficiency gains that were generated by economically-efficient sales to buyers who were making the relevant mistakes (who should have bought the product even though they overestimated the buyer surplus they would obtain by doing so).
16. If two or more sellers were involved in the non-disclosure, each of them would withdraw the resources it used to produce its product(s) exclusively from the production of the other non-discoverers' products, and the ratio of external to internal marginal costs were the same for each of the non-disclosers over the relevant ranges of outputs (where the external costs in question include both external costs of production and external costs of consumption), the non-internalization of the relevant externalities would not distort the profits each non-disclosing seller would realize by producing units of its product (e.g., if there were no external costs of consumption, would leave undistorted the marginal cost to each such producer of producing the relevant successive units of its product: the non-internalization of the external costs the other non-discloser's production would have generated would inflate each's marginal

costs by precisely the same number of dollars as the non-internalization of its own external costs of production deflated its marginal costs).

17. For discussions of these and various other dubious arguments against imposing legal obligations on polluters to provide pollution-information to government, see Wagner (2004).
18. It is important to distinguish sellers' relying on contrivance or their natural-oligopolistic interdependence to prevent an investment from being made that would increase a relevant ARDEPPS' equilibrium investment from a seller's not making an investment that would increase an ARDEPPS' equilibrium investment because it was deterred from making the investment by a *monopolistic* investment-disincentive—that is, by the fact that the investment in question would reduce its other projects' profit-yields by more than those projects' profit-yields would have been reduced by any rival investments the investment in question would deter (usually because the investment in question would not deter a rival investment). A seller's decision not to make an investment because of a monopolistic investment-disincentive is morally distinguishable from a seller's decision to deter a rival from investing by engaging in contrivance or to rely on natural-oligopolistic interdependencies to deter a rival investment because a seller does not have a moral duty to compete against itself and a decision not to invest because of monopolistic investment-disincentives was not motivated by specific anticompetitive intent in that the seller's perception that the decision not to invest was ex ante profitable was not critically affected by its belief that the decision would reduce the absolute attractiveness of the best rival-offers against which it would have to compete.
19. The contriver(s) whose cooperation will most likely have to be secured by the payment of a bribe are potential competitors, given that potential competitors have no pre-existing investments in the relevant ARDEPPS whose profit-yields will be increased by the reduction in the relevant ARDEPPS' equilibrium-QV-investment quantity. Admittedly, potential competitors may also be deterred from entering exclusively by threats of retaliation, particularly if the potential competitor is established in one or more other ARDEPPSes in which one or more of the other contrivers are operating.
20. For a detailed account and critique of an article that describes and analyzes the economic efficiency of the "scope of liability" doctrine, see Markovits (2020) pp. 60–64, assessing Shavell (1980).
21. I recognize that, like all its predecessors, this distributive-impact analysis is far from complete.

References

Clayton Act, 38 Stat. 730 (1914) (codified as amended at 15 U.S.C Sections 12-27).

Federal Trade Commission Act, 38 Stat. 717 (1914) (codified as amended at 15 U.S.C Sections 41-45).

Markovits, R. (2014). *Economics and the interpretation and application of U.S. and E.U. antitrust law* Vol. I *Basic concepts and the economics-based legal analysis of oligopolstic and predatory conduct*. Springer.

Markovits, R. (2020). *Welfare economics and second-best-theory: A distortion-analysis protocol for economic-efficiency prediction*. Springer.

Shavell, S. (1980). An analysis of causation and the scope of liability in the law of torts. *Journal of Legal Studies, 9*, 463–516.

Sherman Act 26 Stat. 209 (1890) (codified as amended at 15 U.S.C Sections 1-11).

Treaty of Lisbon Amending the Treaty on European Union and the Treaty Establishing the European Community. 2007 OJ C *306* (p. 1) (December 13, 2007).

United State Department of Justice and Federal Trade Commission, Horizontal Merger Guidelines (August 19, 2010).

Wagner, W. (2004). Commons ignorance: The failure of environmental law to produce needed information on health and the environment. *Duke Law Journal, 53*, 1619–1745.

Predatory Conduct 10

This chapter focuses on "predatory conduct." "Predatory conduct" is conduct perpetrated by one or more actors whose ex ante perception of its ex ante profitability was "critically affected" by its/their belief that it would or might reduce the absolute attractiveness of the best offers against which it/they would have to compete by driving a rival out, by inducing an established rival to sell out to the predator(s) at a distressed price, by deterring a potential competitor from entering the predator's/predators' ARDEPPS or an established rival from expanding the amount of investment it made in the relevant ARDEPPS, or by inducing non-economic-efficiency-increasing changes in the product-space location(s) of extant or planned rival investment(s) in the relevant ARDEPPS. This chapter has 11 sections: 10 focus on a particular type of predatory conduct, and one on a type of conduct alleged to be predatory that I think rarely is predatory (systems rivalry).

To avoid uninstructive repetition, I have organized this chapter differently from Chap. 9. Section 10.1 focuses exclusively on (1) the economic efficiency of the 10 variants of uncontestably-predatory predatory conduct and the economic efficiency of the type of conduct (systems rivalry) whose predatory character is contestable and (2) the ability of the government of a liberal-moral-rights-based society to increase economic efficiency by deterring each of these types of conduct (without violating relevant defendants' [investigative-treatment/legal-proof/legal-sanction]-related liberal moral rights). Section 10.2 focuses on the liberal-moral-rights-violativeness of predatory conduct (of all types) and non-predatory systems rivalry and the moral duties of the government of a liberal-moral-rights-based society to deter predatory conduct and provide its victims with appropriate opportunities to obtain legal redress. Section 10.3 focuses on the impact of predatory conduct of each type and non-predatory systems rivalry on the instantiation of the utilitarian and non-utilitarian-egalitarian conceptions of the moral good I have distinguished and on the moral desirability from the perspective of each such conception of the moral good of the government of a liberal-moral-rights-based society's attempting to deter each such type of conduct in various ways.

R. S. Markovits, *Welfare Economics and Antitrust Policy - Vol. I*,
https://doi.org/10.1007/978-3-030-79812-3_10

10.1 The Economic Inefficiency of Predatory Conduct and of Allegedly-Predatory Systems Rivalry and the Ability of the Government of a Liberal-Moral-Rights-Based Society to Increase Economic Efficiency by Deterring Predatory Conduct Without Violating Defendants' (Investigative-Treatment/Legal-Proof/Legal-Sanctions)-Related Liberal Moral Rights

10.1.1 The Economic Efficiency of Predatory Pricing and of Government's Trying to Deter Predatory Pricing

One or more firms are correctly said to have threatened a target with predatory pricing or to have charged predatory prices to a target's prospective customers if the perpetrator(s) would not have found the threat or prices ex ante profitable had it/they not believed that those prices would or might increase its/their profits by driving a rival out, inducing an established rival to sell its business to it/them for a distressed price, deterring a (potential/established) competitor from making an additional investment in the ARDEPPS in question, and/or inducing a competitor to make a non-economically-efficient change in the location of its planned or extant investment to one that was less competitive with the perpetrator's (perpetrators') project(s) when the perpetrator-conduct in question's yielding it/them profits in these ways would render its/their conduct profitable even though it would be economically inefficient in an oPp economy. Although many Industrial Organization economists believe that predatory pricing is rarely if ever practiced,[1] my analysis of the practice's potential profitability makes me suspect that predatory pricing is profitable sufficiently often in individualized-pricing situations to be practiced quite often in such situations.[2]

Before proceeding to analyze the economic inefficiency of predatory pricing or the ability of government to increase economic efficiency by deterring such conduct, I want to explain why I believe that sellers that set individualized prices will often find it profitable to practice predatory pricing. To simplify, I will assume (1) that the predation in question aims to induce its target to withdraw an investment (as opposed to deterring its target from making an investment or inducing its target to change the location of its extant or planned investment) and (2) that the predator will not be able to induce its target to sell its investment to the predator for a distressed price. I will first analyze the determinants of the dollar-loss a predator must inflict on a target to induce it to withdraw a particular investment, then analyze the determinants of the cost to the predator of inflicting various dollar-losses on its target by charging predatory individualized prices to buyers the target was privately-best-placed to supply (which I will sometimes denominate "the target's customers"), and finally analyze the determinants of the dollar-benefits to the predator of inducing a target to withdraw an investment.

The dollar-loss that a predator must inflict on a target to induce it to withdraw a particular investment depends on (1) the profits the investment would yield the target absent predation, (2) (A) the profits that the target's withdrawal of the relevant investment would cause it to lose on the target's other investments by encouraging not only the predator in question but others to attack it and/or (B) the profits that the target's refusal to withdraw the target investment and any defensive retaliation the target practices against the predator would enable the target to preserve on the target's other investments by deterring the predator in question and other firms from targeting it with predation (and perhaps retaliation), and (3) the cost the target would have to incur to finance short-term losses (whether the target has retained earnings and/or is well-placed to finance such losses through the debt or equity market).

The determinants of the dollar-cost to the predator of inflicting various amounts of dollar-losses on its target by charging buyers the target is privately-best-placed to supply predatory prices include: (1) the private transaction cost the predator must incur to identify the buyers to which it will be cost-effective to offer predatory prices, (2) the private transaction cost the predator must incur to calculate the prices it must charge these buyers to inflict dollar-losses on the target (see below) and the private transaction cost the predator must incur to make offers to these buyers when the predator would not otherwise have bid for their patronage, (3) the losses that a practitioner of individualized predatory pricing would have to incur to inflict any given amount of direct harm on a target by making sales to buyers its target was privately-best-placed to supply—if I assume for simplicity that the target is charging its HNOPs to the relevant buyers, that the relevant buyers are making no mistakes, that each relevant buyer will purchase just one unit of the good in question, that the predator's predatory offer must be at least one cent superior to its target's HNOP-containing offer, and that the relevant buyer will accept the predator's predatory offer, the dollar-loss that the predator will impose on the target by taking one unit of sales from it will equal the target's OCA on the sale, and the dollar-loss that the predator will incur to take each sale from its target will equal one cent *plus* the amount by which the predator is worse-than-privately-second-placed[3] to make the sale in question *plus* any amount above one cent by which the predator chooses to beat the offer of its target so that the relevant (underspecified) determinant is the frequency with which the predator is given amounts worse-than-privately-second-placed to steal buyers in relation to which its target enjoys various OCAs,[4] (4) any certainty-equivalent law-related costs the predator should expect to incur to engage in the relevant predatory pricing, (5) the certainty-equivalent losses the predator should anticipate incurring because of the possibility that the target may retaliate defensively to the predator's predatory price, (6) any losses the predation imposes on the predator because the buyer charged the predatory price engages in arbitrage, and (7) any losses the predation imposes on the predator because its own customers discover that it charged another buyer a lower price than it charged them—because that discovery reduces the predator's goodwill and/or causes the "discoverers" to intensify their bargaining—Markovits (2014a, pp. 504–505).

It is useful to distinguish 5 sets of determinants of the private benefits that individualized predatory pricing that targets a particular rival can confer on its practitioner. The members of the first set relate to the impact that individualized predatory pricing that drives out a single target would confer on its practitioner by increasing its HNOPs if the target's investment would not be replaced and the exit of the target would not cause any rival to change the location of an investment: (1) (the number of sales the predator and target were uniquely-privately-equal-best-placed to make) *times* (the average amount by which in those instances they were privately-better-placed to supply the relevant buyers than were those buyers' pre-predation privately-third-placed suppliers), (2) (the number of sales that the predator was uniquely-privately-best-placed to make and the target was uniquely-privately-second-placed to make) *times* (the average amount by which in those instances the target was privately-better-placed to make the sale in question than were the relevant buyers' respective pre-predation privately-third-placed suppliers), and (3) (the number of sales the target was privately-best-placed to make and the predator was uniquely-privately-second-placed to make) *times* (the average amount by which in those instances the predator was privately-better-placed than the relevant buyers' pre-predation privately-third-placed supplier[s]).

The members of the second set of determinants relate to the impact of individualized predatory pricing that targets one rival of the predator on the predator's NOMs. These determinants relate to the possibility that any predation-generated increase in the predator's (HNOP−MC) differences will critically affect its ability to obtain OMs naturally by increasing an (HNOP−MC) gap that, pre-predation, was lower than the cost the predator would have had to incur to change an initial price to one that, post-predation, was higher than those costs.

The members of the third set of determinants relate to the possibility that the predation might increase the profits the predator could realize by practicing individualized contrived-oligopolistic pricing in the ARDEPPS in which the predation is being practiced. I will be brief: except when the target is what antitrust-enforcement authorities call a "maverick"—that is, is a firm that was disposed not to cooperate with contrived-oligopolistic pricing, I do not think that predation will tend to increase the profits the predator can make by engaging in contrived-oligopolistic pricing in the ARDEPPS in which the predation is being practiced because, by increasing its OCAs and NOMs, predatory pricing will increase the safe profits the predator must put at risk to try to obtain COMs.

The members of the fourth set of determinants relate to the possibility that the predation might increase the profits that the predator can realize by engaging in strategic (contrived-oligopolistic and predatory) conduct in other ARDEPPSes. A predatory effort might increase the predator's ability to profit from strategic behavior elsewhere by "improving" its reputation for engaging in strategic conduct —by making its threats of retaliation and promises of reciprocation more credible and by enabling it to communicate the threats and promises that contrived-oligopolistic conduct entails simply by charging one or more contrived-oligopolistic prices. However, it is important to emphasize that such reputational effects are a double-edged sword: To the extent that a firm has such a reputation and/or has been convicted of predation, that fact may decrease the profitability of its engaging in strategic behavior in both the ARDEPPS of practice and elsewhere by increasing the likelihood that any future strategic behavior in which it engages will result in victims' and antitrust-law-enforcement authorities' bringing related civil and criminal suits against it as well as (in practice) the probability that it will lose the cases that are brought against it. Still, if one concludes that all tolled the reputational effects of a seller's engaging in predation increase the profitability of its engaging in strategic conduct in the future in any of the ARDEPPSes in which it will be operating, the magnitude of any related gains will depend on the frequency with which such behavior would have been close to profitable or profitable for the prospective perpetrator absent its engaging in the relevant predatory conduct, which will depend on the magnitudes of all the factors I am now identifying.

The fifth set of determinants relates to the extent to which the private benefits of such predation will be reduced by any tendency it may have to critically increase the profitability of an established rival's or potential competitor's making an investment in the ARDEPPS in question. The relevant determinants in this set are: (1) How close are such established and potential competitors to being effective potential investors pre-predation, (2) would and to what extent would predatory pricing deter such rival investments by raising the operative retaliation barriers to investment, (3) how long would it take any rival investment the predatory pricing would induce to be operative, (4) to what extent would any such individual rival investment be less competitive with the predator's projects than was/were the target's investment(s), and (5) could and if so to what extent could the predator decrease the reduction in the profit-yield of predation that its tendency to induce rival investments generates by making one or more investments itself to deter one or more rival investments?

In my judgment, the preceding analyses warrant at least the following 3 conclusions: (1) Some sellers that charge individualized prices will find it profitable to engage in predatory pricing; (2) a seller that sets individualized prices need not be the dominant firm in or have a high share of the sales made in a relevant ARDEPPS to find predatory pricing profitable; and (3) the fact that a prospective predatory pricer that sets individualized prices operates in an ARDEPPS whose potential competition is effective (or faces an established rival that would respond to its predation by adding to the ARDEPPS' QV-investment quantity if nothing were done to deter it from doing so) does not imply the ex ante unprofitability of its engaging in predatory pricing.

10.1.1.1 The Economic Efficiency of Predatory Pricing

Charging individualized predatory prices will or may affect economic efficiency in at least 12 ways:

(1) it will decrease economic efficiency by the allocative transaction costs the predator generates to determine the amount of harm it must inflict on its target to drive it out;

(2) it will decrease economic efficiency by the allocative transaction costs the predator generates to identify the customers of its rival to which it is cost-effective for it to make predatory offers and to make offers to these buyers (if it would not otherwise have done so);
(3) if the predatory pricing leads to buyers' accepting the predator's offers and makes it profitable for the relevant buyer to resell the good it purchased to a buyer the predator would otherwise have supplied directly (because the predator was their privately-best-placed supplier), it will decrease economic efficiency by the allocative transaction costs that the predator's efforts to prevent such arbitrage generates *plus* any allocative transaction costs the buyer that received the predatory price generates to identify and negotiate with its arbitrage partner *plus* any extra allocative delivery costs that are generated when the arbitrage takes place because the circuitous delivery of the good from the predator to the arbitrage-seller and from the arbitrage-seller to the arbitrage-buyer is more allocative-costly than the direct delivery of the good from the predator to the arbitrage-buyer would have been (for mechanical-transaction-cost, delivery-time, and good-perishability reasons);
(4) if the predatory pricing leads to the target's making a second offer to the buyer that received the predatory offer, it will decrease economic efficiency by the allocative transaction costs generated by the target's making and the buyers' considering the target's second offer;
(5) if the predatory pricing leads to the predator's supplying one or more buyers its target was privately-best-placed to supply and/or leads to the target's engaging in defensive retaliation that results in its making one or more sales to the buyers the predator was privately-best-placed to supply, the predatory pricing will tend to decrease economic efficiency on those accounts by generating intra-ARDEPPS UO-to-UO misallocation;
(6) if the good the predatory pricer produces is a good that is created by a QV investment and the predatory pricing decreases (increases) equilibrium QV investment in the ARDEPPS in which the predatory pricing is practiced (see below for the relevant possibilities), the predatory pricing will tend to increase (decrease) economic efficiency on that account by decreasing (increasing) (UO-producing and PPR-executing) to (QV-creating) resource misallocation;
(7) if the good to which the predatory pricing related is a production process and the predatory pricing decreases (increases) equilibrium PPR in the ARDEPPS in which the predation is practiced, it will increase (decrease) economic efficiency on that account by increasing (decreasing) the amount of economic inefficiency generated by failures to execute economically-efficient resource allocations from (UO-producing and QV-investment-creating resource-uses) to (PPR-executing resource-uses);
(8) if the predatory pricing concentrates the seller-side of the ARDEPPS in which it is practiced, it may on that account yield economic inefficiency by enabling the ARDEPPS' sellers better to overcome the public-good-type problem that would otherwise prevent them from securing economically-inefficient government decisions that were in their collective interest by making expenditures

on political parties/campaigns/candidates and on government-decisionmaking-process participation;

(9) unless the ARDEPPS in which the predatory pricing is practiced produces goods that are complements to leisure, the practice of predatory pricing will tend to decrease economic efficiency by generating price-increases that increase the amount of economic inefficiency generated by economically-inefficient allocations of time to (leisure-production and do-it-yourself-labor performance) from (market-labor performance);

(10) to the extent that (A) the compensation-costs that a firm incurs to compensate given individual employees and managers increase with the supernormal profit-rate it could otherwise realize, (B) increases in the taxable "compensation" a given employee or manager receives increase the tax-rate applied to the recipient's marginal and possibly some intra-marginal taxable compensation, and (C) some components of the "compensation" individuals receive—namely, those that relate to the attractiveness of a firm's work-environment and/or one or more "fringe-benefits"—are not taxed or are taxed at a lower effective rate than are monetary payments, predatory pricing will increase the amount of economic inefficiency that the employees and managers of the predatory pricer and its non-targeted-rivals generate by making economically-inefficient substitutions of untaxed or lower-taxed attractive working-conditions and fringe-benefits (including the future purchases they can make by exercising stock-options) for the goods and services they would have bought with the monetary wages they "exchanged" for the superior working-conditions and fringe-benefits they received by increasing the supernormal profit-rates the predator and its non-targeted rivals could obtain if they did not respond by improving the compensation packages they provide their employees and managers;

(11) if, as some believe, the amount by which the private costs that a firm incurs because "it operates sloppily" as opposed to because the monetary compensation, working-conditions, and fringe-benefits it provides given workers and managers increase with the supernormal profit-rate it could realize if it did not respond to any increase in this profit-rate by operating sloppily and/or providing its workers and managers with higher "compensation," predatory pricing will decrease economic efficiency by the allocative costs generated by the sloppiness induced by the extra supernormal profits it would enable the predator and the predator's non-targeted rivals to obtain;[5] and

(12) if as I believe (see below) predatory pricing will tend to increase poverty and material inequality, it will tend to decrease economic efficiency on those accounts.

As the preceding list indicates, two issues it references need to be discussed. The first is whether the practice of predatory pricing in any ARDEPPS will increase or decrease equilibrium QV investment or equilibrium PPR in that ARDEPPS. The answer to this question depends on (1) the relative heights of the (Π_D + R) barriers the target faced on its withdrawn investment and the (Π_D + R) barriers that would face the potential entrants into and established-firm potential investment-expanders in the ARDEPPS in question, (2) whether the predation would confront non-predator potential investors in the ARDEPPS of practice with retaliation barriers to investment, (3) whether potential competition was effective and, if not, on whether the established firm that was privately-best-placed to replace the target's investment or to increase the ARDEPPS' investment-quantity above its pre-predation total would face higher or lower investment-disincentives or incentives than the target faced on the investments in question, and (4) whether the prices that would be charged in the ARDEPPS if the target's investment were replaced by an investment (of the same size) by another investor would be higher or lower than they would have been had the target survived (the prices will tend to be higher/lower if the investor that made the replacement-investment was more/less able than the target to time its price-announcements to increase the relevant ARDEPPS' HNOP array and was more/less willing and able than the target to cooperate with the ARDEPPS' sellers' practice of contrived-oligopolistic pricing). I suspect that the practice of predatory pricing in a given ARDEPPS will sometimes decrease and sometimes increase its equilibrium investment quantity and am unable to justify (even to myself) any generalizations about this impact of such predation.

Before proceeding, I want to make one related point. For 4 reasons, one cannot prove that predatory pricing will always decrease equilibrium investment in the ARDEPPS in which it is practiced by arguing that if it did not do so it would not have been profitable: (1) any "replacement" investment might not be operational for some time, (2) any "replacement" investment may be less competitive with the predator's projects than was the target's investment, (3) the predator may find it profitable to make a "replacement" investment, and (4) predatory pricing might be practiced mistakenly.

The second issue is the impact of predatory pricing on poverty and material inequality. Obviously, the following comments do not take account of many distributive effects that a general-equilibrium analysis would address. The simplified analysis I will execute focuses on the facts that successful predatory pricing will (1) confer dollar-gains on the shareholders, creditors, managers, and employees of the predator and its non-targeted in-ARDEPPS rivals, (2) impose dollar-losses on the shareholders, creditors, managers, and employees of the predator's target, and (3) impose dollar-losses on the customers of the predator, the target, and the predator's other in-ARDEPPS rivals. I see no reason why the wealth/income positions of the shareholders, creditors, managers, and employees of the predator and the predator's non-target in-ARDEPPS rivals should be different from the wealth/income positions of their target-counterparts. However, because I suspect that the consumers of the relevant ARDEPPS' products will tend to be poorer than any of the relevant stockholder/creditor/employee/manager sets of individuals, I suspect that predatory pricing will increase the incidence of poverty and the extent of material inequality in the society in which it is practiced.

What do the preceding observations imply for the economic efficiency of predatory pricing? Although I acknowledge that the predatory pricing of goods created by QV investments may increase economic efficiency in a small percentage of the cases in which it decreases equilibrium QV investment in the ARDEPPS in which it is practiced and that the predatory pricing of production processes may increase economic efficiency in a small percentage of the cases in which it increases equilibrium PPR in the PPR-ARDEPPS in which it is practiced, with those rare exceptions (that would themselves be eliminated if government implemented appropriate tax/IP/antitrust/environmental policies), predatory pricing will decrease economic efficiency whenever it is practiced.

10.1.1.2 The Economic Efficiency of the Government's Trying to Deter Predatory Pricing (in Ways That are Not Liberal-Moral-Rights-Violative)

I will assume at this juncture that predatory pricing always decreases economic efficiency. On that assumption, it will in my judgment be economically efficient for the government to educate the general public and actual and prospective business-persons about the immorality of predatory pricing, to pass laws that declare such pricing illegal, to authorize courts to impose civil and criminal fines and custodial and non-custodial non-monetary sentences on predatory pricers that do not exceed liberal limits, to urge courts to impose such "legal-sanctions" on predatory pricers, and to give targets of predatory pricing appropriate opportunities to obtain legal redress from the predators that have targeted them.[6] The question remains: What steps will it be economically efficient for a government to take to implement such policies? I suspect that it will be economically efficient for a government to devote a significant amount of resources to "educating" the prospective and actual employees and managers of firms to dissuade them from engaging in such conduct. The difficult issues relate to the amount of resources that will be allocatively efficient for government to devote to collecting evidence of predatory pricing. The issue is complicated to resolve for the same reason that its oligopolistic-pricing counterpart was difficult to resolve: (1) some types of evidence that scholars and officials claim is probative of predatory pricing and (allocatively) cheap to collect is neither probative nor allocatively cheap to collect, and (2) the evidence that is actually probative is often either unavailable or too allocative-costly to obtain from the perspective of economic efficiency. I will now address each of these points in turn.

Some scholars—Baumol (1979), pp. 4–6 and Joskow and Klevorick (1979), p. 255—have argued that one can establish economic-efficiently at least a substantial likelihood that predatory pricing was practiced in response to a rival's investment by proving that the seller(s) in question responded to a new entry or an established-rival investment by making a substantial price-cut that they reversed within 5 years (Baumol) or two years (Joskow and Klevorick) after the new investment was withdrawn.[7] Some versions of this claim limit it to sellers that were dominant, and Joskow and Klevorick qualified their proposal by allowing firms that it would otherwise "condemn" to exonerate themselves by demonstrating that their post-exit price-increase could be attributed to an increase in the firm's lowest legitimate price (say HNOP or [HNOP + NOM]) that had nothing to do with the withdrawal of the recent investment. Unfortunately, these facts are not so probative as Baumol and Joskow and Klevorick suppose: The addition of an investment to an ARDEPPS would lead to a reduction in the prices of existing products in the ARDEPPS even if their sellers did not engage in predatory or retaliatory pricing (would reduce these products' HNOPs or [HNOP + NOM]s), and the exit of a recent investment (or, indeed, of any investment) would lead to an increase in the prices of the other products in the ARDEPPS even if their producers had not engaged in predatory or retaliatory pricing—would increase the lowest legitimate prices (the HNOPs or, under current U.S. law, the [HNOP + NOM]s) of the other products in the ARDEPPS. Moreover, even if it were possible and not allocative-costly to determine the prices that were being charged for an ARDEPPS' products at the relevant points in time, it would be impossible to apply the variant of this proposal that limited its application to "dominant firms" non-arbitrarily or at a low allocative cost because, as we have seen, there is no non-arbitrary way to define a firm's "dominance" and, even if there were, it would be highly-allocative-costly to determine whether a given firm was "dominant," given the metric for dominance that was deemed appropriate.[8]

Another scholar—Williamson (1977)—has claimed that one can prove that a dominant firm has practiced predatory pricing in response to entry by establishing that a dominant firm increased its output (by more than 10%) within 12–18 months of the entry's occurrence. I find such evidence less probative than Williamson claims since the output-increases in question may well be attributable to decreases in HNOPs or increases in ARDEPPS demand. I should add that Williamson's restriction of this claim to "dominant firms" is problematic for the reasons discussed in Note 7 of this chapter.

Other scholars—Areeda and Turner (1978) Vol. 3. 711a and Williamson (1977) —have argued that in all cases (not just when investments have been recently added to an ARDEPPS) one can prove allocative-efficiently that predatory pricing has or has not been practiced by comparing the alleged predator's price(s) with various costs it incurred. Thus, (1) Areeda and Turner have claimed that (A) a price above "full cost" (i.e., average total cost) should be irrebuttably presumed to be non-predatory, (B) a price above average variable cost but below average total cost should be rebuttably presumed to be non-predatory (a presumption that can be overridden by evidence of predatory intent or evidence that the price was inherently unprofitable [presumably was below average marginal cost over the relevant range, which could be the case if marginal cost exceeded average variable cost)]), and (C) a price lower than average variable cost should be irrebuttably presumed to be predatory, and (2) (contra Areeda and Turner) Williamson proposed that prices that do not cover average total cost be deemed predatory—Williamson (1977, pp. 296 and 333–334). In addition, virtually everyone seems to agree that prices below marginal cost should be irrebuttably presumed to be predatory (or illegally retaliatory). I think that all these claims are incorrect: (1) Prices above average total cost will be predatory if they are lower than the seller's lowest legitimate price (HNOP or [HNOP + NOM]) and are being charged for predatory reasons; (2) prices between average variable cost and average total cost are too often predatory (because they are lower than the seller's HNOP or [(HNOP + NOM)] and manifest the seller's predatory intent) for any even-rebuttable presumption that they are non-predatory to be warranted; (3) prices that fall below average variable cost are in my judgment too likely to be non-predatory (A) because they exceed marginal cost and are non-predatory or (B) because they fall below conventional and overall marginal cost but manifest promotional pricing, learning-by-doing pricing, defensive retaliation, or seller mistakes for it to be permissible to irrebuttably presume them to be predatory; (4) for the same reasons, prices that are below average total costs are too likely to be non-predatory for any irrebuttable presumption that they are predatory to be warranted; and (5) prices that are below marginal cost also should not be irrebuttably presumed to be predatory—a seller should be allowed to exonerate itself by proving that the low prices it charged were (A) rendered legitimately conventionally profitable by the profits they would enable the firm to earn in the future (i) by making repeat sales to the buyers whom the low prices induced to purchase the product in question, (ii) by making future sales of the product in question to other buyers to whom the buyers in question recommend the product or who observed its high-quality performance for the induced buyers, (iii) by making sales of the relevant product's complements or of other products in the relevant product's product-line, (iv) by making sales of other unrelated products it produced to buyers who were positively impressed by the performance of the extra units sold of the good in question and revised upward on that account their estimates of the quality of the firm's other products, (v) by reducing the cost the firm in question had to incur in the future by enabling it to "learn by doing," and (vi) by deterring future retaliation and predation that would target it (when the low prices were defensively retaliatory), (B) rendered privately-desirable overall though not conventionally profitable because they were partially motivated by spite (by a preference for inflicting losses on the rival they harmed),[9] and/or (C) mistaken. I should add that, even if such price–cost-related evidence were more probative than I believe, the allocative cost of collecting it might render it allocatively inefficient to use.

The U.S. Supreme Court has claimed that one can prove that a firm has practiced predatory pricing by establishing that it charged different prices in different geographic markets—see Utah Pie Co. v. Continental Baking Co. (1967), though the court more recently pointedly refused to endorse this position—see Brooke Group Ltd. v. Brown and Williamson Tobacco Coop. (1993, pp. 220–222)—and various U.S. Courts of Appeal have implicitly questioned this claim—see A.A. Poultry Farms, Inc. v. Rose Acre Farm, Inc. (1989, p. 1404). In fact, for the same reason that evidence of inter-regional price differences has little or no probative value when the issue is whether the seller that is charging the different prices contemporaneously in different regions is practicing oligopolistic pricing, such evidence has little or no probative value when the issue is whether the price-setter is engaging in predatory pricing—namely, such price differences are far more likely to manifest the fact that the seller's HNOPs (or HNOP + NOM sums) differ from region to region than to manifest the fact that the seller is charging predatory prices in one region but not in the other or is making larger, predatory price-cuts in one region than in the other.

In short, it will not be allocatively efficient for a government to try to prove predatory pricing by using any of the kinds of evidence (in isolation) whose use for this purpose other scholars or U.S. courts have claimed would be economically efficient. Since predatory prices are prices that are below the seller's lowest legitimate price (its HNOP) that have been charged for predatory reasons while oligopolistic prices are prices that are above the seller's highest legitimate price (its HNOP) that have been charged for oligopolistic reasons, it should be no surprise that the 5 types of evidence that Chap. 9 argues can establish that a firm has engaged in oligopolistic pricing and may be able to be used economic-efficiently for this purpose can also be used sometimes economic-efficiently to prove that a seller has engaged in predatory pricing. I will now review these 5 types of evidence and comment on any differences in the subtypes of these types of evidence that can be used to prove predatory *versus* oligopolistic pricing and any differences in the probability that it will be possible and economically efficient for a government to use each such type of evidence to prove predatory *versus* oligopolistic pricing.

The first such type of evidence is eyewitness testimony, audio and/or audio/visual recordings, or perpetrator admissions. Because the targets of predatory pricing are far more likely to be aware of the character of the conduct that is imposing dollar-losses on them than are the buyers that are being charged oligopolistic prices, eyewitness testimony is more likely to be available in predatory-pricing cases than in oligopolistic-pricing cases. In fact, it will often be allocatively efficient for government to elicit target-testimony by giving the targets of predatory pricing a legal right to obtain legal redress, by helping them with their cases, or perhaps by paying them monetary rewards for relevant information. On the other hand, audio recordings of and non-recorded admissions of guilt may be less available in predatory-pricing cases than in oligopolistic-pricing cases because the statements that may appear to be self-incriminating often turn out to be ambiguous. Thus, as U.S. Court of Appeals Judge Frank Easterbrook (an economically-sophisticated former Professor of Law at the University of Chicago) once noted in A.A. Poultry Farms, Inc. v. Rose Acre Farms, Inc. (1989, p. 1402), defendant's statement to the plaintiff—"We are going to run you out of the egg business. Your days are numbered."—is as consistent with the defendant's intention to engage in intense legitimate competition as with its intending to practice predatory pricing.

The second type of evidence that can be used to prove predatory pricing is evidence on (1) the actual price charged by a seller and (2) its lowest legitimate price —that is, evidence that the seller charged one or more prices that were lower than its/their lowest legitimate counterpart(s). Since a seller's lowest legitimate price equals its highest legitimate price (HLP), it should be no surprise that Chap. 9's explanation of the difficulty and allocative cost of estimating with requisite accuracy a seller's LLP for the purpose of determining whether its actual price was oligopolistic applies equally when the issue is the difficulty and allocative cost of estimating with requisite accuracy a seller's HLP for the purpose of determining whether its actual price was predatory. In fact, because I think that a seller's LLP is more likely to be affected than its HLP by the promotional-pricing benefits, possibly by the learning-by-doing benefits, by the defensive-retaliation benefits, and possibly by the spite-indulgence benefits that price-cuts can generate, I suspect that it is even less likely to be allocatively efficient for government to try to collect and use this type of evidence to prove predatory pricing than to prove oligopolistic pricing, though I acknowledge that the relevant difference can be reduced by imposing the "burden of proof" on these exonerating possibilities on the defendants—that is, by imposing on the defendants not only the burden of persuasion on these issues but also the burden of discovering the relevant evidence and the burden of paying for such evidence's discovery. (Although I suspect that sellers charge unprofitably-high prices by mistake more often than they charge unprofitably-low prices by mistake [i.e., that seller-mistake is more often "relevant" in oligopolistic-pricing cases than in predatory-pricing cases], I have no empirical justification for this claim and therefore am taking no position on whether this possibility makes it more or less likely that it will be allocatively efficient for the government to collect the type of evidence now under discussion in predatory-pricing cases than in oligopolistic-pricing cases. In any event, it will clearly be allocatively efficient to place the "burden of proof" in all 3 senses on any seller-mistake issue on the defendants in both predatory-pricing and oligopolistic-pricing cases.)

The third type of evidence that can be used to prove predatory pricing is evidence on the prices charged for the relevant product(s) in two different regions and/or at two different times and evidence on the relevant seller's LLPs in the two regions or at the two times—that is, evidence that provides a basis for determining whether the relationship between the prices the seller charged in the two regions at the same time or at the two times in one region matches the relationship between the seller's LLPs in the two regions or at the two times. Three conclusions are justified: (1) The argument that it is more likely that government will be able to increase allocative efficiency by using this type of comparative evidence than the second type of evidence just discussed to establish the requisite probability that oligopolistic pricing has been practiced applies equally forcefully when the conduct at issue is alleged predatory pricing; (2) even if firms never had promotional, learning-by-doing, or defensive-retaliation incentives to reduce their prices, it would possibly not often be allocatively efficient for government to try to use this type of comparative evidence to prove either oligopolistic pricing or predatory pricing; and (3) because promotional, learning-by-doing, and/or defensive-retaliation incentives are more likely to be operative when sellers are charging suspiciously-low prices than when sellers are charging suspiciously-high prices and because the magnitudes of these incentives often vary from place to place and time to time, the fact that these incentives will sometimes be operative probably undercuts the allocative efficiency of using this type of evidence to prove predatory pricing more than it does the allocative efficiency of using this type of evidence to prove oligopolistic pricing.

The fourth category of evidence that a government might find allocatively efficient to use to prove predatory pricing is behavioral evidence other than recorded or reported threats or admissions of guilt or evidence of prices charged the alleged target's customers. Examples of such additional types of behavioral evidence include (1) evidence that the alleged predator had made an offer to buy out the target, particularly if the offer was at a distressed price (a price that was lower than the value the target's business would have if it were not a target for predation), (2) evidence that the alleged predator had tried to induce potential capital-suppliers, other-input suppliers, and customers of the alleged target not to deal with the alleged target by threatening to stop dealing with them if they dealt with the alleged target, by offering to make deals with them on terms that were otherwise-unprofitable for the alleged predator, or to pay them money if they stopped dealing with the alleged target, (3) evidence that the alleged predator had directed other types of predatory moves (predatory advertizing or unfair competition) at the alleged target, (4) evidence that the alleged target had made moves that could be defensively retaliatory against the alleged predator, (5) evidence that the alleged predator or one or more of its managers or employees had engaged in predation or other types of strategic behavior in the past, were committing other such acts currently, or were planning to engage in strategic behavior in the future, and (6) evidence that the alleged target had lost customers to the alleged predator and that these outcomes could not be explained by contemporaneous changes in the target's competitive position in relation to these buyers. I suspect that when such evidence is available its collection and use will be both probative and allocatively efficient.

The fifth type of evidence that may be allocatively efficient for a government to use to prove predatory pricing is conventionally called "structural evidence" because it is understood to refer to structural features of the "market" in which predatory pricing has allegedly been practiced that favor the conclusion that the alleged predator would find the alleged predatory pricing ex ante profitable. Obviously, Chap. 6's demonstration that market definitions are inherently arbitrary not just at their peripheries but comprehensively and this chapter's account of the non-market-aggregated parameters that determine the profitability of an individualized pricer's charging a particular rival's customers predatory prices imply that it will not be feasible or allocatively efficient for a government to try to prove predatory pricing by defining the market in which the alleged predation was practiced, identifying the market-structure attributes that affect the profitability of predatory pricing, and collecting evidence on the allegedly-relevant market-aggregated structural parameters that establishes that predatory pricing would be profitable for the alleged predator. However, this conclusion is perfectly compatible with the claim that it might be allocatively efficient for a government to include in its evidence in a predatory-pricing case data on non-market-aggregated parameters that establish that the alleged predatory pricing would have been ex ante profitable for the alleged predator, though given what I hope is the fact that companies usually do not engage in conduct that is illegal, liberal-moral-rights-violative, and moral-good-disserving when it would be profitable for them to do so, this type of "background" evidence will primarily be relevant negatively to counteract any attempt by a defendant to establish its innocence by establishing that it would have found the alleged conduct ex ante unprofitable than positively to establish that the defendant had engaged in predatory pricing (though I do think such evidence does have some corroborative value if other evidence supports a guilty verdict).

A summary is in order. Although I do not think that it will often be possible much less allocatively efficient for a government to try to establish a predatory-pricing defendant's guilt by proving that its actual prices to one or more customers of a particular rival or its actual across-the-board price (in the rare instances in which the allegation is that the defendant charged predatory across-the-board prices) was/were lower than its lowest legitimate price(s) to these buyers, I do think that it will be allocatively efficient for government to try to prove that a suspect has practiced predatory pricing by eliciting probative information from the suspect's alleged target—namely, evidence about threats the suspect made, about buyout-offers it made that contained distressed prices, about customers the alleged target lost that the target was best-placed to supply at the time of the lost sale(s), and about the alleged target's "practice" of defensive retaliation. I also think that it will sometimes be allocatively efficient for government to use inter-regional and inter-temporal comparative evidence to prove predatory pricing and to support cases built primarily on the various kinds of evidence just referenced with evidence that establishes that the alleged predatory pricing would have been ex ante profitable for the defendant, that the defendant had engaged in strategic conduct in the past in the ARDEPPS in which the predatory pricing was alleged to have been practiced and/or in other ARDEPPSes, and that the defendant had plans to engage in strategic conduct in the future. Unfortunately, I cannot be more precise.

10.1.2 The Economic Efficiency of Predatory Investments and the Economic Efficiency of Government's Trying to Deter Predatory Investments in Various Ways That Are Not Liberal-Moral-Rights-Violative

If I assume that advertizing that is predatory should not be said to constitute an investment, 3 categories of investment decisions are predatory: (1) decisions to create a QV investment or execute a PPR investment that the investor would not have perceived to be ex ante profitable but for its belief that it had a monopolistic investment-incentive to make the investment in question, (2) decisions to invest in a known, higher-average-total-cost production process that the investor perceived to be ex ante profitable because (A) the marginal-cost curve it would face if it used the known, higher-average-total-cost production process was lower than the marginal-cost curve it would face if it used the known, lower-average-total-cost production process, and (B) the use of the known production process that was associated with a lower marginal-cost curve would yield the investor benefits by inducing one or more extant rivals to exit, by deterring one or more potential investors in the relevant ARDEPPS from investing in it, by inducing one or more investors in the ARDEPPS in question to relocate its/their investment(s) to locations that made its/their investment(s) less competitive with the predator's projects when the investment location shift was not economically efficient, and/or by inducing one or more potential investors in the relevant ARDEPPS to make an investment in that ARDEPPS that was less competitive with the predator's projects than the investment the potential investor(s) in question would otherwise have chosen to make when the investment-shift was not economically efficient, and (3) decisions to execute an otherwise-unprofitable PPR project (or to make an otherwise-unprofitable substitution of one PPR project for another) when the decisions were rendered profitable by the fact that the chosen PPR project would discover a production process whose use would generate lower marginal costs and as a result drive a rival of the investor out, deter an actual or potential rival of the investor from making a QV investment in the relevant area of product-space, or induce a rival-investor in that area of product-space to make an investment that was less competitive with the PPR investor's QV investments in the relevant area of product-space than the investment the induced investor would otherwise have made would have been when the investment-shift was not economically efficient.

10.1.2.1 The Economic Efficiency of Predatory Investments

I will first address the economic efficiency of predatory QV investments, predatory investments in PPR, and predatory investments in known production processes. I will begin by analyzing the economic efficiency of 3 categories of predatory QV investments and predatory investments in PPR, the last of which has 4 subcategories. For expositional reasons, I will assume that the individual predatory investments whose economic efficiency is at issue have been made (are not prospective predatory investments). This subsection will conclude by analyzing the economic efficiency of predatory choices among known production processes.

I will start by explaining why the fact that a firm has a monopolistic investment-incentive to make a particular QV investment or investment in PPR implies that, on that account, the profits the investment in question will yield are inflated. I will then explain why the fact that the potential investor whose investment a predatory investment deters had a monopolistic investment-incentive to make the deterred investment deflates the profits the predatory investment yielded by inflating dollar-for-dollar the private cost of the predatory investment. I will finally analyze the implications of the preceding two conclusions for (1) the monopolistic-investment-incentive-related distortion in the profits yielded by any predatory investment that deterred a firm that is an established rival of the predator in the ARDEPPS in which the predatory investment was made from renewing an existing QV investment (say, a distributive outlet) in that ARDEPPS or from making an additional investment in that ARDEPPS or (B) a potential competitor of the predator from making an investment in the ARDEPPS in which the predatory investment would be made and (2) the economic efficiency of predatory investments that deterred (A) an established rival of the predator from renewing or making an equally-large investment in the ARDEPPS in question or (B) a potential competitor of the predator from making an equally-large investment in the ARDEPPS in which the predatory investment was made.

First, regardless of whether the investment in question was predatory, the fact that a potential investor had a monopolistic investment-incentive to make an investment implies that, on that account, the investment's profits were inflated. Thus, to the extent that an investor had a monopolist investment-incentive to make a particular investment because the investment it made (could make) would be less competitive with its other investments in the relevant ARDEPPS than the rival investment its investment did/would deter, the profits the investment yielded/(would have yielded) the investor on this account will tend to inflate the investment's profit-yield dollar-for-dollar because this private gain has no economic-efficiency counterpart: the fact that an investor's investment is less competitive with (say, less duplicative of) its other projects than the rival investment it would deter would have been has no bearing on the relative economic efficiency of the investment in question and the investment it would/did deter—the fact that the predatory investment would be less competitive with (say less duplicative of) the predator's other projects than the deterred investment would have been does not imply that the use of the predator's investment yielded a larger economic-efficiency gain on that account than the use of the deterred investment would have yielded because the fact that the predatory investment was less competitive with (say, less duplicative of) the predator's other projects than the deterred investment would have been implies that the predatory investment was more competitive with (say, more duplicative of) the investments of other firms in the relevant ARDEPPS than the deterred investment would have been. And again, to the extent that an investor had a monopolistic investment-incentive to make a particular investment because that investment (1) would induce its established rivals to make non-retaliatory responses (say, price-reductions) that lower its profits by less than the non-retaliatory responses its rivals would have made to the investment the investment in question deterred and/or (2) had less of a tendency than the investment it deterred would have to reduce the extent of contrived-oligopolistic pricing in the ARDEPPS in question (e.g., because the investment it deterred would have been made by a new entrant), those realities would tend to be associated with an inflation in the profits the relevant investment yielded the investor that exceeded the private gains the investment yielded the investor on these accounts because the extra price-reductions the investment in question deterred will have increased economic efficiency at the same time that they imposed a loss on the investor in question.

Second, it is important to consider the implications for the monopolistic-investment-incentive-related distortion in the profits yielded by a predatory investment of the possibility that the investor whose investment the predatory investment deterred may have had a monopolistic investment-incentive to make that investment. Since, for reasons just discussed, any monopolistic investment-incentive any such deterred investor faced on its deterred investment would be associated with an inflation in the profits that deterred investment would have yielded the deterred investor that was at least as large as the monopolistic investment-incentive it faced and since, in essence, the predatory investor bid away from the deterred investor the resources the deterred investor would have used to execute its deterred investment, any such inflation in the profits the deterred investment would have yielded the deterred investor will show up as an inflation in the private cost to the predatory investor of its predatory investment.

I turn third and finally to the implications of the conclusions of the preceding two paragraphs for the monopolistic-investment-incentive-related distortion in the profits yielded by a predatory investment and for the economic efficiency of predatory investments. I will analyze these issues on the following assumptions or "analytic realities": (1) Taken together, the other Pareto imperfections the relevant economy contains (all the Pareto imperfections other than those that lie behind the relevant investor's or investors' having any monopolistic investment-incentive to make its/their respective relevant investment) will yield the same distortion in the private benefits the relevant investments would confer on the investors that could make them (an assumption that is made more plausible by the fact that the predatory investment and the investment it would deter are located in the same ARDEPPS); (2) when the deterred investment would have been made by a rival of the predator that was established in the ARDEPPS in which the predatory investment would be made, the deterred investor might have no monopolistic investment-incentive to make the deterred investment or, if it did have a monopolistic investment-incentive to make the deterred investment, that incentive might be larger than, equal to, or lower than the monopolistic investment-incentive the predator had to make the predatory investment; and (3) when the deterred investment would have been made by a firm that was a potential competitor of the predator in the ARDEPPS in which the predatory investment would be made, the deterred investor (potential entrant) would have no monopolistic investment-disincentive to make the deterred investment (which is admittedly an "analytic reality" rather than an "assumption").

Two additional preliminary points need to be made. First, assumption (1) in the preceding list implies that, if one ignores the economic-efficiency implications of the fact that the predator faced monopolistic investment-incentives and of any monopolistic investment-incentives the investor whose investment the predatory investment deterred had to make the deterred investment and assumes for simplicity that the creation and use of the predatory and deterred investment would "consume" the same resources, the predatory investment will be (economically efficient)/(economically inefficient) if it is more/less profitable than the investment it deters (monopolistic investment-incentives aside). The second additional point I want to make at this juncture is more complicated to explain and is somewhat more contestable. It derives in part from (1) the fact that any monopolistic incentive a firm has to make an investment (including any predatory investment) because its investment will be less competitive with its other investments in the relevant ARDEPPS than the rival investment the investment in question will deter would have been will (across all exemplars) inflate the profits yielded by the investment in question dollar-for-dollar by the profit-yield in question and (2) the fact that any monopolistic incentive a firm has to make an investment (including any predatory investment) because its investment will induce its established rivals to reduce for non-oligopolistic-pricing-related reasons their prices by less than they would reduce their prices in response to the rival investment the investment in question would deter and/or will reduce the contrived-oligopolistic margins the investor obtains by less than they would be reduced by the rival investment the investment in question would deter will inflate the profits the investment yields by more than the associated monopolistic investment-incentive because these price-effects will (virtually always) decrease economic efficiency. If it is third-best-allocatively-efficient to assume that the ratio of the monopolistic investment-incentives that, respectively, the predator and any deterred investor that had a monopolistic investment-incentive to make its deterred investment, respectively, had on these two accounts is the same, the preceding two "facts" would justify the conclusion that, controlling for any differences in the profits that would be yielded by the predatory investment and the investment it deterred, the "substitution" of the predatory investment for the investment it deterred would reduce/increase economic efficiency if the predator had a higher/lower monopolistic investment-incentive to make its investment than the investor whose investment the predatory investment deterred had to make its deterred investment.

I should now be able to assess the economic efficiency of predatory investments. Three "categories of predatory investments" (enquoted because the expression is something of a misnomer) (one of which has 4 subcategories) need to be distinguished for this purpose.

The first contains predatory investments that deterred new entries. Such predatory investments are economically inefficient for two reasons: (1) monopolistic-investments-incentive effects aside, they are less profitable than the new entries they deterred because, monopolistic investment-incentives aside, by definition, predatory investments are unprofitable whereas the new entries they deterred were inherently profitable, and (2) the profits of this category of predatory investments (indeed, of all predatory investments) are inflated by the monopolistic investment-incentives the predator had to make them whereas the prospective profits that would have been yielded by the new entries the predatory investment deterred would not have been inflated by monopolistic investment-incentives because deterred potential entrants have no monopolistic investment-incentive to make their respective deterred entry-investments.

The second category of predatory investments contains predatory investments that deterred an investment expansion that an established rival of the predator would otherwise have made in the ARDEPPS in which the predatory investment is located that the deterred predator-rival has no monopolistic investment-incentive to make. (I assume that any established rival whose investment a predatory investment deterred would never have had a monopolistic investment-*dis*incentive to make the relevant deterred investment since any such deterred investment would have deterred the predatory investment, which presumably would have reduced the relevant predatory-investor rival's other projects' profit-yields by at least as much as the rival's own deterred investment would have reduced those profits.) The exemplars of this second category of predatory investments will be economically inefficient for the same two reasons that predatory investments that deterred new entries will be economically inefficient.

The third category of predatory investments contains predatory investments that deterred an investment expansion that an established rival of the predator would otherwise have executed in the ARDEPPS in which the predatory investment is located that the rival in question had a monopolistic investment-incentive to make.

I analyze this third category of predatory investments on the simplifying assumption (which I have been making throughout this study) that any investment that is made yields the investor more profits overall than any investment the executed investment deterred would have yielded the deterred investor. Even on this (I hope plausible) simplifying assumption, 4 subcategories of this "category of predatory investment" need to be distinguished.

The first subcategory contains any predatory investment that deterred an established-rival (predatory) investment (1) that was inherently-less-profitable than the predatory investment whose economic efficiency I am analyzing, (2) that the deterred investor had a higher monopolistic investment-incentive to make than the predator whose predatory investment's economic efficiency is at issue had to make its predatory investment, and (3) that was less profitable overall than the predatory investment whose economic efficiency is at issue because the amount by which the deterred investment was inherently less profitable than the predatory investment that was made exceeded the amount by which the deterred investor's relevant monopolistic investment-incentives exceeded the monopolistic investment-incentives of the investor that made the predatory investment whose economic efficiency is at issue. My assumptions and conclusions imply that this subcategory of predatory investments will be economically inefficient both because they are less-inherently-profitable than the investments they respectively deter and because the investors that made them had lower monopolistic investment-incentives to make them than the (prospective predatory) investors whose investments the relevant predatory investments deterred had to make their deterred (predatory) investments.

The second subcategory contains any predatory investment that deterred a (predatory) rival investment (1) that was inherently-equally-unprofitable as the predatory investment whose economic efficiency is at issue, (2) that the deterred investor had a lower monopolistic investment-incentive to make than the predator whose predatory investment's economic efficiency is at issue had to make its predatory investment, and (3) that would have been profitable overall had the predator whose investment's economic efficiency is at issue not bid for the resources the deterred investor would have used to execute its investment because the lower monopolistic investment-incentive the deterred rival had to make its deterred investment exceeded the loss that that investment would otherwise have imposed on it under those conditions. My assumptions and conclusions imply that predatory investments in this category are economically inefficient because the economic inefficiency any investment in this category generates by virtue of the facts that give the firm that makes it the higher monopolistic investment-incentive it had to make it exceed the economic inefficiency that the investment it deterred would have generated by virtue of the facts that gave that deterred investor the lower monopolistic investment-incentive it had to make its deterred investment.

The third subcategory contains any predatory investment that deterred an established-rival (predatory) investment (1) that was more-inherently-unprofitable than the predatory investment whose economic efficiency is at issue, (2) that the deterred investor had a higher monopolistic investment-incentive to make than the predatory investor whose investment's economic efficiency is at issue had to make its predatory investment, but (3) that the deterred investor did not make because the amount by which the monopolistic investment-incentive it had to make its deterred investment exceeded the monopolistic investment-incentive the firm that made the predatory-investment whose economic efficiency is at issue had to make that investment was lower than the amount by which the loss the deterred investment would have yielded the deterred investor (monopolistic investment-incentives aside) exceeded the loss the predatory investment whose economic efficiency is at issue would have imposed on its maker (monopolistic investment-incentives aside). The exemplars of this subcategory of predatory investment are economically efficient because the investment each such investment deters (for which each such predatory investment might be said to have been substituted) was more unprofitable (monopolistic investment-incentives aside) and would have yielded more of the profit-inflating profits I denominate monopolistic investment-incentives. I hasten to add that, although this conclusion complicates the analysis of the economic efficiency of any individual predatory investment, it does not call into question the economic efficiency of prohibiting all predatory investments since in the scenario just described both the predatory investment whose economic efficiency I have been analyzing and the predatory investment that the deterring predatory investment deterred would have reduced economic efficiency relative to the situation that would obtain if neither investment had been made.

The fourth subcategory contains any predatory investment that deterred an established-rival (predatory) investment (1) that was less-inherently-unprofitable than the predatory investment whose economic efficiency is at issue, (2) that the deterred investor had a lower monopolistic investment-incentive to make than the predatory investor whose investment's economic efficiency is at issue had to make its predatory investment, but (3) that the deterred investor did not make because the amount by which the monopolistic investment-incentive it had to make the deterred investment was lower than the monopolistic investment-incentive the predator whose investment's economic efficiency is at issue had to make its investment was larger than the amount by which the loss the deterred investor's deterred investment would have imposed on it (monopolistic investment-incentives aside) was higher the amount by which the loss the deterred investment would have imposed on the deterred investor (monopolistic investment-incentives aside). Unfortunately, I cannot generate any a priori conclusions or any empirically-grounded predictions that are worth expressing about whether the substitution of a predatory investment for the investment it would deter would increase or decrease economic efficiency in this category of situations. Once more, however, I can say that in this subcategory of situations economic efficiency would be higher if neither the predatory investment that was made nor the predatory investment that that predatory investment deterred had been made.

I turn next to the economic efficiency of any predatory choice among known production processes—that is, to bring the following discussion under the coverage of this subsection, of any predatory investment in the production facility, machines, worker-selection protocol, and worker-training regime that would result in the firm's using one known production process rather than another known production process. Such an investment would be predatory if the firm that made it believed ex ante (1) that it would be unprofitable if it would not reduce the attractiveness of the best offers against which it would have to compete because the production process selected would raise the sum of the fixed and variable costs the investor would have to incur to produce the unit-output of its product it would find profitable to produce using its most-profitable rejected production process by more than its substitution of the selected production process for its most-profitable alternative would increase its profits by lowering the marginal cost of its producing successive units of its product if its use of the selected production process would not drive one or more rivals out by worsening its (their) array(s) of competitive positions and/or deter one or more rival investments by worsening the prospective array(s) of competitive positions of the deterred investor(s) (by lowering the predator's marginal costs) and (2) that the production-process choice (related investment) the firm made was at least normally profitable because, by reducing its marginal costs, it would reduce the absolute attractiveness of the best offers against which the firm would have to compete in one or more of the ways just referenced. Admittedly, such predatory investments can have mixed economic-efficiency effects: (1) will decrease economic efficiency by increasing the total allocative cost the predator would generate when producing the unit-output it would produce if it made a non-predatory production-process choice (in my judgment, by more than it will increase the total private cost to the predator of producing those units of output), (2) will tend to decrease economic efficiency by concentrating the seller-side of the ARDEPPS in question and thereby increasing the expenditures its sellers will make on political parties/campaigns/candidates and on government-decisionmaking-process participation, (3) can either increase or decrease economic efficiency by increasing or decreasing poverty (depending on whether it decreases prices more by lowering marginal costs than it increases them by increasing "seller-concentration" and [perhaps] decreasing equilibrium investment in the ARDEPPS of practice), (4) if the relevant ARDEPPS' investments are QV investments, can either increase economic efficiency by reducing the ARDEPPS' equilibrium-QV-investment quantity or decrease economic efficiency by increasing the ARDEPPS' equilibrium-QV-investment quantity (where the predation's net impact on that equilibrium-QV-investment quantity depends on the relevant extents to which the predation reduces price-competition at relevant ARDEPPS-QV-investment quantities and the extent to which it decreases QV-investment competition in the ARDEPPPS of practice), and (5) in what I take to be the empirically-less-significant cases in which investments in the ARDEPPS of practice are investments in PPR, can either increase economic efficiency by increasing equilibrium PPR (in what I take to be the unlikely situation in which the predation increases equilibrium PPR more by decreasing price-competition than it decreases PPR by decreasing investment-competition) or decrease economic efficiency by reducing the equilibrium-PPR quantity (because the relevant effect of its decreasing price-competition is smaller than the relevant effect of its decreasing investment-competition). Perhaps I should not speculate, but I suspect that in the vast majority of cases predatory choices to use known, marginal-cost-reducing production processes will decrease economic efficiency.

I turn finally to the economic efficiency of predatory choices by firms that both do PPR and produce the good to whose production their PPR relates (1) to execute an otherwise-unprofitable PPR project that is rendered profitable by the facts that the use of the production process it discovers (A) will reduce the marginal costs the producer-researcher that executes it will incur to produce the product G the discovered production process will be used to produce and (B) in so doing, will drive out one or more producers of products that are rivalrous with G, deter potential QV-investors in the G-ARDEPPS from making an investment in that ARDEPPS, and/or induce potential QV-investors in the G-ARDEPPS to make new QV investments in the G-ARDEPPS that are less-competitive with the G-investment than the investments they otherwise would have made would have been or (2) to substitute a PPR project that is designed to discover a production process whose use involves lower marginal costs for a PPR project that is designed to discover a production process whose use involves higher marginal costs when the substitution in question would be unprofitable but for the fact that the substitution of the production process that would be discovered by the executed PPR project for the production process that would have been discovered by the rejected PPR project would, by reducing the marginal cost of producing G, reduce the absolute attractiveness of the best offers against which the integrated production-process-researcher/producer-of-G would have to compete in its producer-of-G capacity.

I will begin by discussing the economic efficiency of the second type of predatory PPR-choice just referenced. The conclusion that this second type of predatory PPR-choice is economically inefficient is favored by the fact that the relevant choice would be unprofitable but for the selected project's yielding the research-producer more profits by driving its product-G rivals out, deterring QV investments in the G-ARDEPPS, or causing investors in the G-ARDEPPS to create products that are less competitive with G than the products they would otherwise have created would have been. It seems to me that any tendency of this type of predatory PPR-choice to cause the predator's rivals to substitute QV investments that create products that are less competitive with G and the predator's other products in the G-ARDEPPS for QV investments that would have created products that were more competitive with G and the predator's other products in the G-ARDEPPS (or, for that matter, any similar effect in other ARDEPPSes in which the predator is operating) has no bearing on the economic efficiency of this type of predatory PPR-choice (because there is no reason to believe that the relevant changes in QV-investment locations will either increase or decrease economic efficiency). Admittedly, if as I assume virtually all ARDEPPSes in contemporary economies contain too much QV investment from the perspective of economic efficiency, any tendency of exemplars of this type of predatory PPR-choice to decrease/increase equilibrium QV investment in the G-ARDEPPS will increase/decrease economic efficiency directly on that account. However, I do not know whether predatory PPR-decisions of this type that drive out some products in the G-ARDEPPS and deter some potential QV investors in the G-ARDEPPS from making QV investments will tend to decrease or increase equilibrium QV investment in the G-AREPPS all tolled. As I have already indicated, such predatory

PPR-decisions' impact on equilibrium QV investment in the G-ARDEPPS will depend on the extent to which they decrease the intensity of the price-competition that will prevail at relevant ARDEPPS-QV-investment quantities as well as on the extent to which they decrease the intensity of QV-investment competition in the G-ARDEPPS. (Recall: Predation can be profitable even if the investment it deters or eliminates will be replaced when the predator can profit by making additional investments and/or when the predation causes investments to be located differently rather than to be eliminated or deterred.) In any event, predatory PPR-decisions in this category will or may also decrease economic efficiency by increasing poverty and material inequality, by causing the sellers in the G-ARDEPPS to make additional misallocative expenditures on political parties/campaigns/candidates and government-decisionmaking-process participation, by causing the predator and its surviving rivals to operate more sloppily (to generate on that account production-optimum-related misallocation), and by causing the managers and employees of the predator and its surviving rivals to generate more economic inefficiency by substituting better working-conditions and fringe-benefits for the goods they would have purchased with the monetary wages they forewent to secure the just-referenced desiderata (to the extent that the predator and its surviving rivals share some of the profits the predation yields them with their managers and employees). All tolled, I am confident that predatory PPR-decisions in this category will decrease economic inefficiency.

The last subcategory of predatory investment-decisions whose economic efficiency I will analyze is predatory PPR decisions to execute a PPR project that is designed to discover a production process whose use will reduce its employer's marginal costs when the production-process researcher in question is not substituting the predatory PPR project in question for an alternative PPR project it would itself execute. Three subsubcategories of such predatory PPR projects need to be distinguished.

The first contains predatory PPR projects that will deter another firm from executing a non-predatory PPR project. A decision to execute a predatory PPR project that deters another firm from executing a non-predatory PPR project will almost certainly reduce economic efficiency: (1) the fact that the deterred non-predatory PPR project was inherently profitable while (by definition) the predatory PPR project was inherently unprofitable and (2) "the fact that" the predatory PPR project will, by "virtue" of its predatory character, generate effects that on balance reduce economic efficiency both favor the economic inefficiency of decisions to execute predatory PPR projects whose execution will deter the execution of a non-predatory PPR project by another firm.

The second subsubcategory of predatory PPR projects that the relevant researcher does not substitute for an alternative PPR project it would otherwise have executed contains predatory PPR projects that deter another firm from executing a different predatory PPR project. The economic efficiency of such a predatory PPR project is harder to predict even if one accepts as being TBLE my standard assumption that when one investment is made instead of another the investment that is made is more profitable than the investment that was not made. The difficulty is created by the following "facts": (1) Differences in the profits that would be yielded by two alternative predatory investments can reflect both or either differences in their inherent unprofitability and differences in the profits they would yield the firm that made them by performing their predatory function; (2) the more-profitable predatory PPR investment could be more profitable because (A) it was less inherently unprofitable and yielded its maker more profits by performing its predatory function, (B) it was less-inherently-unprofitable but yielded its maker lower profits by virtue of its performing predatory functions and the inherent-unprofitability advantages of the predatory PPR investment that was made exceeded the predation-generated-profits disadvantage of the predatory PPR investment that was made, or (C) it was more-inherently-unprofitable but yielded its maker higher profits by virtue of its performing predatory functions and its inherent-unprofitability disadvantage was smaller than its predation-generated-profits advantage; and (3) I have no view worth listening to about the relative magnitudes of the following two ratios: (A) the ratio of (the difference between the inherently unprofitability of the two investments) to (the difference in their economic efficiency that is linked to the differences in their inherent unprofitability) and (B) the ratio of (the difference in the profits each of the two investments would yield its maker by virtue of its performing predatory functions) to (the difference in the economic inefficiency the two investments would generate by virtue of their respective performance of predatory functions). Even if it is TBLE to assume that the predatory investment that is made is more profitable overall than the predatory investment that is deterred, I see no way to justify the conclusion that, taken as a class, predatory PPR projects that deter other firms' predatory PPR projects tend to be either economically efficient or economically inefficient. Of course, this conclusion is compatible (1) with the claim that some such executed predatory PPR investments increase economic efficiency and some decrease economic efficiency, (2) with the claim that it will sometimes be TBLE for antitrust-policy-enforcement authorities to determine whether particular predatory investments in this subsubcategory increase or decrease economic efficiency, and (3) with the claim that it will be TBLE for antitrust-policy-enforcement authorities to deter all predatory PPR projects.

The third subsubcategory of predatory PPR projects that are executed by a researcher that would not otherwise itself have executed a different PPR project contains PPR projects that increase equilibrium PPR in the PPR-ARDEPPS in which they are located (because they do not deter the execution of any other PPR project in the ARDEPPS of practice [I am ignoring the possibility that the relevant predatory PPR project may cause other PPR projects to be executed in the ARDEPPS of practice by making scientific or technological discoveries that increase the profitability of other PPR projects in that ARDEPPS]). In an oPp economy, "the facts that" (1) the PPR projects on which I am now focusing are inherently unprofitable and (2) their performance of predatory functions makes them less economically efficient than they would otherwise be would imply that this subsubcategory of predatory PPR projects would decrease economic inefficiency. However, if as I claim the Pareto imperfections that actual economies contain deflate the profits yielded by production-process research in general and perhaps especially by PPR projects that yield marginal-cost-reducing production-process discoveries, it is far from clear that the predatory PPR projects in this subsubcategory tend to decrease economic efficiency. Once more, of course, it may be TBLE for antitrust-policy-enforcement authorities to determine whether individual predatory PPR projects in this subsubcategory or identifiable subsubcategories of predatory PPR projects in this subsubcategory are economically efficient.

10.1.2.2 The Economic Efficiency of a Government's Attempting to Deter Predatory Investments

I will restrict myself to 4 points or sets of related points. First, the economic efficiency of the government's attempting to deter individual predatory investments is favored by the fact that virtually all such investments reduce economic efficiency relative to the situation that would prevail if the predatory investment in question were not made. Second, the economic efficiency of a general policy of deterring predatory investments is also favored by the fact that the existence of the one subcategory of predatory QV or PPR investments whose individual exemplars increase economic efficiency—predatory QV and PPR investments that deterred other predatory QV or PPR investments that would be even more economically inefficient if both investments' economic efficiency were calculated by comparing the state of the world that they would respectively generate with the state of the world that would prevail if neither were made—supports the conclusion that effectively prohibiting all predatory investments would increase economic efficiency if it were allocative-costless to formulate and implement. Third, it will of course be allocative-costly to deter predatory investments so that the economic efficiency of any policy that is designed to deter such investments depends on the relative size of its allocative benefits and allocative costs. Fourth, although I am not optimistic that such evidence will often be available, government will be more able to prove predatory investing by introducing defendant-studies of the profitability of their investment decisions than to prove predatory pricing by introducing defendant-studies of the profitability of their pricing decisions because (I suspect) investment-studies of this kind are more common than pricing-studies.

10.1.3 The Economic Efficiency of Predatory Advertizing and the Economic Efficiency of Government's Trying to Deter Predatory Advertizing

Advertizing is predatory when the advertizer's ex ante perception that it would be at least normally profitable was critically affected by its belief that it would or might increase its profits by inducing an established rival to exit, by deterring an established rival or potential competitor from adding to its ARDEPPS' investment-quantity, by inducing an established rival to relocate an extant investment to a position that rendered that rival's investment less competitive with the predator's project, and/or by inducing an established rival or potential competitor to change the location of a future investment to make that investment less competitive with the predator's projects. Predatory advertizements are designed usually inter alia to reduce the demand curve for their targets' extant or planned products. Such advertizements can achieve this object (1) by improving the predator's product's/products' image(s), (2) by correcting relevant-buyer errors that cause them to undervalue the predator's product(s) or to overestimate the cost of buying, maintaining, and repairing the predator's product(s), (3) by misleading relevant buyers into overvaluing the predator's product(s) or underestimating the cost of buying, maintaining, and repairing them, (4) by undermining the image(s) of its target's product(s), (5) by providing its target's possible customers with accurate information that prevents them from overvaluing the predator's target's product(s) or underestimating the cost of buying, maintaining, and repairing the target's product(s), or (6) by misleading its target's possible customers into undervaluing its target's product(s) or overestimating the cost of buying, maintaining, and repairing its target's product(s). Predatory advertizing that is misleading may be a tort for which the targeted rival of the predator or, possibly, misled buyers can obtain legal redress. Predatory advertizing that is misleading may also violate the consumer-protection laws of the society in which it is practiced. But, for the purposes of this study, the important point is that advertizing can be predatory even if it is not misleading—more specifically, will be predatory regardless of whether it is misleading if the advertizer's ex ante perception that it was at least normally profitable was critically affected by the advertizer's belief that it would or might increase the advertizer's profits in one or more of the ways referenced in the first sentence of this paragraph.

10.1.3.1 The Economic Efficiency of Predatory Advertizing

In an economy whose only Pareto imperfections are the buyer non-sovereignty and buyer non-maximization that predatory advertizements could prevent or generate, predatory advertizing would decrease economic efficiency by the dollar-loss it would impose on the advertizer if it did not yield the advertizer any benefits by generating any effect referenced in the first sentence of the preceding paragraph *minus* any decrease in economic inefficiency that predatory advertizing that prevented buyer errors generated by preventing buyers from making purchasing decisions that were economically inefficient as well as personally disadvantageous *plus* any increase in economic inefficiency that misleading advertizing generated by inducing buyers to make purchasing-decisions that were equally inefficient as well as personally disadvantageous *minus* the number of dollars by which predatory advertizements that enhanced the image(s) of the predatory advertizer's product(s) increased the dollar value that owners of previously-purchased units of the product(s) in question placed on those units[10] *plus* the number of dollars by which predatory advertizements that denigrated the image(s) of the predator's target's product(s) reduced the dollar value that owners of previously-purchased units of the target's product(s) placed on those units[11] *minus/plus* any (economic-efficiency gains)/(economic-efficiency losses) the predatory advertizing generates when the advertized good was created by a QV investment by decreasing/increasing equilibrium

QV investment in the ARDEPPS in question *minus/plus* any (economic-efficiency gains)/(economic-efficiency losses) the predatory advertizing generates when the advertized good is a production process by increasing/decreasing equilibrium PPR in the ARDEPPS in question[12] *plus* the amount of economic inefficiency that the predatory advertizing generates indirectly by increasing poverty and material inequality (roughly speaking, because some of the losses it imposes are suffered by buyers of the predator's products and buyers of the same-ARDEPPS non-targeted-rivals-of-the-predator's products—a set of individuals that contains a higher percentage of poor individuals than do the sets of shareholders/creditors/managers/employees of, respectively, the predator, the predator's non-targeted rivals, and the predator's target) *plus* the amount of economic inefficiency that the predatory advertizing generates by concentrating the seller-side of the predator's ARDEPPS and thereby enabling the sellers it contains to better overcome the public-good-type problem that militates against their spending as much on political parties/campaigns/candidates and government-decisionmaking-process participation as would be in these sellers' joint interest[13] *plus* the amount of economic inefficiency the predatory advertizing generates by increasing its practitioner's potential supernormal profit-rate and thereby the production-optimum-related misallocation it generates by operating sloppily (if such a connection exists) and the amount of misallocation the predator's managers and employees generate by substituting untaxed or lower-taxed better working-conditions and fringe-benefits for the goods they would have purchased with the higher-taxed monetary compensation they forewent to obtain the better working-conditions and fringe-benefits in question.

All tolled, I am confident that predatory advertizements as a class would be economically inefficient both in an oPp economy and in economies that contain a realistic amount of unrelated Pareto imperfections. However, I must admit that some predatory advertizing that conveys accurate information about the predator's product or the products of one or more rivals of the predator may be economically efficient. I wrote "may be" because the economic efficiency of such accurate advertizing is disfavored by the unprofitability of the advertizing and the "fact" that its private cost is lower than its allocative cost: I regret that I have no sense of the relationship between the private benefits that such advertizing yields the relevant producer and distributors by increasing the unit sales of the producer's product and the prices for which units of the producer's product are sold and the economic-efficiency benefits such advertizing generates by preventing buyers from making personally-erroneous purchases that are also misallocative.

10.1.3.2 The Economic Efficiency of Government's Attempting to Deter Predatory Advertizing and to Provide Its Victims With Appropriate Opportunities to Obtain Legal Redress

Once more, I will focus exclusively on the facts that make this subsection's analysis different from its predatory-pricing-focused and predatory-investment-focused counterparts. At least 3 such facts or sets of facts deserve consideration.

The first is the fact that some exemplars of predatory advertizing—namely, those that involve advertizing that misrepresents the attributes of the predator's product(s) or the cost of the predator's product(s) to its buyers and those that misrepresent the attributes of the predator's target's product(s) or the cost of the targets product(s) to buyers—would be illegal and would be prohibited by the government of a liberal-moral-rights-based society of perfect moral integrity even if they were not predatory. The fact that these exemplars of predatory advertizing would be liberal-moral-rights-violative and illegal (would constitute business torts and/or contract-law and consumer-protection-law violations) even if they were not predatory is relevant (1) because they affect the total antitrust-law-generated sanctions that the government of a liberal-moral-rights-based society can impose on a perpetrator of such advertizing without violating the liberal constraint that "the punishment must not be more severe than the misdeed is wrong" both by increasing the wrongfulness of the conduct in question and by leading to non-antitrust-law sanctions being imposed on the perpetrator and (2) because they increase the likelihood that victims of predatory advertizing that contains misrepresentations will publicly allege or prove that the misrepresentations have been made, which will increase the ability of antitrust authorities to increase economic efficiency by deterring predatory advertizing by facilitating their identification of instances of predatory advertizing to the extent that advertizing that contains misrepresentations that relate to the advertizer's product(s) and/or to product(s) of one or more rivals of the advertizer is more likely to be predatory than other sorts of commercial advertizements and by providing evidence that contributes to the authorities' predatory-advertizing case.

The second fact that is relevant in the current context is the fact that the evidence that will have to be provided to prove that advertizing was predatory is not the same as the evidence required to prove predatory pricing or predatory investing. Admittedly, in all three types of predation cases, it will be relevant for the government to prove that the defendant's conduct caused or was designed to cause a rival to exit, deterred an established-rival or potential-competitor investment, and/or induced an established rival to change the location of an existing investment or an established or potential competitor to change the location of a future project to one that was less competitive with the alleged predator's projects. However, the evidence that one would need to establish that a defendant would not have perceived its advertizing to be ex ante profitable had it not believed that the advertizing would or might generate one or more of the just-referenced effects is different from the evidence that would be needed to establish the "inherent unprofitability" of a seller's pricing or investment decision(s). If I am correct in suspecting that the "inherent unprofitability" of many advertizing campaigns is highly uncertain and that advertizers rarely do studies of the profitability of prospective advertizements or advertizing campaigns, the prospects for a government's increasing economic efficiency by proving predatory advertizing may not be good.

The third fact that is relevant in this context is the fact or possibility on which the last two sentences of the immediately-preceding subsection focus: Predatory advertizements that convey accurate information about the predator's product and/or about one or more products that are competitive with the predator's product may be economically efficient. I do not know whether it would be TBLE for antitrust-policy-implementation authorities for which it would be TBLE to try to deter other sorts of predatory conduct to declare lawful either all accurate advertizing or all accurate advertizing that they conclude was economically efficient (that is, to ignore the possibility that such advertizing might be predatory).

10.1.4 The Economic Efficiency of Predatory "Unfair Competition" and the Economic Efficiency of a Government's Trying to Deter Unfair Competition

A firm engages in unfair competition when it makes a choice it would not otherwise have found ex ante profitable that gives it a private competitive advantage over its rivals that has no relative-allocative-efficiency counterpart. Section 10.1.3 referenced some types of "unfair competition"—knowingly, recklessly, or negligently exaggerating the value of one's product, claiming that the cost of buying, maintaining, and repairing one's product is lower than it actually is, disparaging a rival's product, or claiming that the cost of buying, maintaining, and repairing a rival's product is higher than it actually is. Many other kinds of conduct deserve to be said to constitute "unfair competition": inter alia, knowingly, recklessly, or negligently (1) influencing a trade association or consumer-report publisher (or government regulatory-authority) to give a rival's product an undeservedly-low rating or to withhold a seal of approval (perhaps by inducing such actors to use criteria that unjustifiably disadvantage the rival), (2) deterring a potential supplier or customer of a rival from dealing with it by claiming falsely that the rival was a poor credit-risk, would use the prospective supplier's input to produce an inferior product whose poor performance would tarnish the reputation of the supplier's input, was a bad employer, etc., (3) intimidating or harassing a rival's customers, employees, or suppliers, (4) illegitimately obstructing access to the rival's business, (5) bribing the agent of a buyer not to patronize the rival, (6) claiming that the rival would be an unreliable supplier because it was violating another firm's IP rights, (7) bribing target input-suppliers, employees, or distributors to supply inferior services, (8) making otherwise-unprofitable hires of target-employees or target-managers or making otherwise-unprofitable purchases of IP rights or other material inputs to prevent a rival from purchasing them, and (9) agreeing (ideally in negotiations with a national union) to pay some class or classes of workers higher wages than one would have had to pay them when doing so gives the agreer a private competitive advantage because it uses a production process that employs fewer of these workers per unit of output than does the alternative production process used by its disadvantaged rivals.[14] Of course, not all such unfairly-competitive acts are predatory—some might be retaliatory (might be engaged in to deter the target rival from undercutting or undermining the unfair competitor's oligopolistic prices or to enable an advertizer to make more profits by improving relevant buyers' perceptions of its product's relative quality or cost without inducing the disadvantaged rival to exit, to refrain from making an additional investment, or to change the location of an extant or planned investment).

10.1.4.1 The Economic Efficiency of the Different Variants of Predatory Unfair Competition

I will begin by analyzing the economic inefficiency that each of the various types of unfair competition just identified will generate even if it does not produce any of the target-responses whose perpetrator-anticipation, in combination with other facts, would make it predatory and then analyze the economic inefficiency that unfair competition that is predatory generates because it does generate the target-responses whose perpetrator-anticipation (in combination with other facts) render it predatory.

The unfair competition that firms wage by making public pronouncements that lead buyers to overestimate the dollar value of the communicator's product, to underestimate the lifetime cost of buying, maintaining, and repairing the communicator's product, to underestimate the dollar value of one or more products produced by the communicator's rivals, or to overestimate the cost of buying, maintaining, and repairing one or more products produced by the communicator's rivals will decrease economic efficiency by (1) the allocative cost of their communication *plus* (2) the allocative cost their audience generated when listening to them and considering them *plus* (3) the allocative cost of any countering messages their target(s) communicated *plus* (4) the allocative cost that the recipients of the countering messages generated when listening to and considering the countering messages *plus* (5) the intra-ARDEPPS or inter-ARDEPPS UO-to-UO misallocation the original misleading messages generated by causing their audience to make purchasing-decisions that were against the relevant buyers' interests (and were therefore presumptively economically inefficient). The unfair competition that firms wage by inducing trade associations or consumer-report publishers (or government regulatory-authorities) to give a rival's product an undeservedly-low rating or to unjustifiably deny such a product a seal of approval will generate economic efficiency equal to (1) the allocative cost the unfair competitor generated when engaging in the conduct in question *plus* (2) any extra allocative costs the unfair competitor's efforts led the (trade association)/publisher/(government authority) to generate *plus* (3) any allocative costs the unfairly-treated rival generated to try to protect itself *plus* (4) any allocative costs the rival's defensive efforts caused the relevant (trade association)/publisher/(government authority) to generate *plus* (5) any misallocation such unfair competition generated by inducing buyers to make economically-inefficient purchasing-decisions (or, if I ignore the fact that I am currently disregarding the predation's effects on the target's exit/investment decisions, by causing the unfairly-treated product to be banned or to be withdrawn). The unfair competition that firms wage by deterring others from supplying or buying from a rival by misrepresenting the rival's reliability or legal position equals the allocative transaction costs such behavior causes the perpetrator and others to generate *plus* the misallocation such unfair competition generates by deterring transactions that were ex ante profitable for their prospective participants and should therefore be presumed to be ex ante allocatively efficient as a class. The unfair competition that a firm wages by intimidating or harassing a rival's suppliers or customers, by obstructing a rival's place of business, or by bribing a rival's prospective suppliers or customers not to deal with it causes economic inefficiency equal to the allocative transaction costs such conduct generates directly and indirectly *plus* the economic-efficiency gain that would have been generated by the deterred transactions. The unfair competition that a firm wages by inducing a rival's prospective suppliers/employees to provide the rival with inferior goods or services by promising to reward and rewarding their cooperation and/or threatening to retaliate against and actually retaliating against their non-cooperation equals (1) the allocative transaction costs such unfair competition causes all relevant parties to generate *plus* (2) the economic inefficiency generated by the supply of the inferior services *plus* (3) the economic inefficiency generated by any retaliation such unfair competition entails (related-allocative-transaction-cost effects aside). The unfair competition that a firm wages by agreeing to pay higher wages to employees than it need have paid equals (1) the intra-ARDEPPS UO-to-UO misallocation such conduct generates by causing the wage-concession granter's array of (private) competitive positions to be better than its array of relative-allocative-efficiency positions *plus* (2) any choice-among-known-production-processes-generated misallocation the unnecessary wage-concessions generate by inducing the relevant firms to shift to production processes that use less of the category of labor to which the wage-concessions were made *plus* (3) any intra-ARDEPPS PPR-to-PPR misallocation the unnecessary wage-concessions generate by inducing researchers to devote resources to discovering production processes that will use less of the category of labor to which the wage concessions were made *minus* (I suspect) (4) the reduction in labor-negotiation allocative transaction costs that was generated by the unnecessary wage-concession.

I turn now to the impacts that unfair competition that is predatory has on economic efficiency because the conduct achieves its practitioner's predatory objectives. I have already indicated that predatory unfair competition that drives its target out will tend to decrease economic efficiency on that account if it does not alter any other investment decisions because, I believe, across all cases, the fact that the target would have found it profitable to continue to operate absent the predation implies that the relevant investment's continued use would have been economically efficient (a conclusion that is perfectly consistent with the conclusion that the original creation of the target's investment was economically inefficient). If the predatory unfair competition induces established firms to change the product-space location of an extant investment, I assume that (across all cases) it will decrease economic efficiency on that account by the allocative transaction cost of executing the move: I see no reason to believe that the new investment locations will be either more or less allocatively efficient than the original investment locations. If the predatory unfair competition induces the predator's established or potential competitors to locate new investments further away from the predator's projects than they would otherwise have chosen to do, it will on that account across all cases affect economic efficiency only when it causes these actors to alter plans they have already made (in which case it will generate economic inefficiency equal to the allocative transaction cost of making the new plans). If the predatory unfair competition increases equilibrium investment in the ARDEPPS in which it is practiced (because its tendency to increase equilibrium investment by increasing the prices that are charged at relevant investment-quantities outweighs its tendency to decrease equilibrium investment by decreasing investment competition in the ARDEPPS in question), it will decrease economic efficiency on that account when the good involved is created by a QV investment and increase economic efficiency on that account when the good involved is a production process (assuming that the government of the society in question has not independently adopted policies that prevent its economy from devoting too many resources to QV-investment creation and not enough to PPR from the perspective of economic efficiency). If the predatory unfair competition decreases equilibrium investment in the ARDEPPS in which it is practiced, the opposite economic-efficiency conclusions will be justified. I have no view worth considering about whether predatory unfair competition will tend to increase or decrease equilibrium investment in the ARDEPPSes in which it is practiced. By increasing the potential profit-rate its practitioners could realize, predatory pricing may also increase production-optimum-related misallocation by increasing the extent to which its practitioner operates sloppily (if such a connection exists) and the amount of misallocation the predator's managers and employees generate by making misallocative substitutions of untaxed or lower-taxed better working-conditions and fringe-benefits for the goods they would have purchased with the monetary compensation they exchanged for such desiderata (if the predator would have shared some of the profits the predation generated with its mangers and employees).

In my judgment, all acts of unfair competition that are not predatory and virtually all acts of unfair competition that are predatory decrease economic efficiency. I suspect that it will rarely be TBLE to attempt to identify those exemplars of predatory unfair competition that increase economic efficiency (usually because they involve production processes and increase PPR in the ARDEPPSes in which they are, respectively, practiced).

10.1.4.2 The Economic Efficiency of the Government's Trying to Deter Predatory (and Non-Predatory) Unfair Competition

Yet again, I will focus exclusively on the facts that make this subsection's analysis different from its earlier counterparts in this chapter. In this case as well, the most important differences relate to the feasibility of and allocative cost of proving that the various choices that a firm made that might constitute unfair competition were in fact unfairly competitive—that is, (1) to the reality that the facts that are relevant to proving predatory-pricing, predatory-investment, and predatory-advertizing cases are different from the facts that are relevant to proving, respectively, some, most, and all predatory-unfair-competition cases and (2) to the reality that the rival-targets of unfair competition, in some situations the prospective customers of such targets, and prospective buyers of all products produced in the ARDEPPS in question may have non-antitrust-law-based claims for legal redress. The second of these realities makes it more likely that government will be able to increase economic efficiency by deterring predatory unfair competition by making it likely that victims of predatory unfair competition will make public facts that establish that the perpetrators of predatory unfair competition have engaged in unfair competition even if the government does not enable them to obtain legal redress on the ground that the conduct that imposed a dollar-loss on them was an antitrust-law violation. (Of course, to win a predatory-unfair-competition case, the government will have to prove more facts than its victims would have to prove to win related non-antitrust cases—namely, that the defendant's ex ante perception that its unfair competition was ex ante profitable was critically affected by its belief that it would or might yield it benefits in one or more of the ways that successful predatory conduct yields predators benefits.) The first of these realities is relevant because I suspect that it is more feasible and less-allocative-costly for a government to prove without being "voluntarily" supplied with evidence by the predator's victims that a suspect had engaged in predatory unfair competition (1) by knowingly, recklessly, or negligently misrepresenting to prospective buyers the value and/or lifetime-cost of its own product(s) or a target rival's product(s), (2) by telling damaging untruths about its target to prospective suppliers of the target or to buyers that were contemplating entering into long-term relationships with the target, (3) by bribing prospective customers or suppliers of the target not to deal with the target or to supply the target with inferior goods or services or by threatening to retaliate against such suppliers or buyers if they did deal with the target and supply it with sound goods and services, (4) by obstructing the target's premises, (5) by making inherently-unprofitable purchases of raw materials, intermediate products, IP rights, or the services of workers or managers to deny the target the ability to buy/hire them, or (6) by agreeing to pay unnecessarily high-wages to workers in a national or regional or industry-wide union contract to give it a competitive advantage over its target than it is for a government to prove that a defendant's pricing, investing, or advertizing was predatory.

10.1.5 The Economic Inefficiency of Predatory Refusals to Deal and Predatory Efforts to Induce Others Not to Deal and the Economic Efficiency of a Government's Trying to Deter Such Predatory Conduct

Three subcategories of refusals to deal or decisions that cause refusals to deal should be distinguished: (1) decisions by one actor not to deal with one or more other actors, (2) decisions by one actor to induce one or more other actors not to deal with still other actors, and (3) decisions by two or more actors to agree not to deal with other actors. Exemplars of these three categories of refusals-to-deal-related decisions will correctly be said to be predatory if its perpetrator would not have found the decision to be ex ante profitable had the perpetrator not believed that the refusals would increase its profits by driving a rival out, deterring an established or potential competitor from making an investment in the relevant ARDEPPS, or inducing an established or potential competitor to change the product-space location of an extant or future investment in the relevant ARDEPPS.

I should state at the outset that in my judgment (1) the overwhelming majority of individual-firm decisions not to deal with another actor are not predatory, (2) the overwhelming majority of individual-firm decisions to induce one or more others not to deal with still others are not predatory, but (3) a significant percentage of the agreements in which two or more firms promise not to deal with specified others or not to make investments that would put them in a position to deal with specifiable others would accurately be said to be predatory (though some of these decisions that are not predatory and some of those that are predatory could also be said to involve contrived-oligopolistic conduct).

I will now attempt to justify each of these three conclusions. The individual-firm decisions not to deal with one or more other firms that are suspected of being predatory are decisions not to deal with actual or potential rivals. In my judgment, few decisions by an individual firm not to deal with (sell to or buy from) an actual or potential rival are predatory. I reach this conclusion for three reasons. First, the overwhelming majority of decisions that are made not to deal with a rival or potential rival are legitimately profitable (are made because the rejected deal was inherently unprofitable). Scholars and antitrust-enforcement officials sometimes argue that the inherent unprofitability of a vertically-integrated concern's decision not to sell to or buy from a rival that is either equally-vertically-integrated as the suspected refuser or competitive with the vertically-integrated suspected refuser at one or more but not all of the "levels" at which the vertically-integrated suspected refuser is operating can be established by proving that the relevant rival was offering the vertically-integrated concern a price for its product that exceeded the shadow price the vertically-integrated concern was charging its downstream division for that product, but that argument fails when the vertically-integrated concern's upstream division's productive capacity is limited and the downstream division earns profits (in its separately-kept set of accounts) by using the input involved or reselling (distributing) the final good involved. Similarly, scholars and antitrust-enforcement officials sometimes argue that the inherent unprofitability of a vertically-integrated concern's refusal to purchase an input from an independent supplier can be proven by showing that the price the independent was offering the vertically-integrated concern was lower than the marginal, average variable, or average total cost the integrated concern would have to incur to supply itself, but that argument is at least somewhat undermined by the fact that the vertically-integrated concern's reliance on the independent supplier might be unprofitable in the long run if it would involve the integrated firm's closing down the division that competed with the independent supplier and it would be costly for the integrated firm to reopen its former division after closing it down in favor of buying from the independent—that is, if its reliance on the independent would result in its having to pay the independent prices in the future that exceed the costs it would have had to incur in the future to supply itself had it not closed its own division down. Second, in at least some cases, the vertically-integrated firm's refusal to deal with a rival will not be predatory because the deal the integrated concern turned down would not have given its actual or potential rival any surplus. Third, in most cases in which the rejected deal would have yielded the refuser's actual or potential rival some conventional surplus, the refusal will not be predatory because the associated profit-loss to the refused party will not actually affect its decision to stay in the relevant business, to make an investment in the relevant ARDEPPS, or to change the product-space location of one or more of its extant investments or of any future investment it would make in the relevant ARDEPPS and the refuser would have known ex ante that its refusal would not cause the refused party to make any such decision. In part, this last conclusion reflects the fact that in many situations the refused party will be able to reduce the long-run loss the refusal imposes on it (1) by vertically integrating into the production of the refused input, final good, or distributive service, (2) by inducing an independent firm to enter into the relevant business by informing it of the investment opportunity, providing it with information that will improve the entry's proficiency, entering into a long-term full-requirements contract with the prospective entrant, and/or subsidizing the relevant entry, or (3) by participating in a joint venture that will produce the refused input, final good, or distributive service.

Although these options might not be viable in a static situation in which the relevant ARDEPPS' equilibrium-investment quantity is stable through time, I suspect that they will frequently be viable in the many situations in which the relevant ARDEPPS' equilibrium-investment quantity increases through time (with the relevant society's population and *per capita* income and wealth).

I will now explain why I believe that most decisions of an individual firm to prevent a trading-partner from dealing with an actual or potential rival of the decider are not predatory. Unfortunately, at least 8 subcategories of such decisions require separate analysis. The first are decisions by a seller of one good to require its customer to purchase the customer's full requirements of a second good from the seller as well. As Sects. 13.1 and 13.2 will explain in some detail, these decisions are rarely if ever predatory because the tying seller's conclusion that such a decision is ex ante profitable is almost always attributable to the seller's conclusion that it will (1) reduce the cost it must incur to control the quality of the complement(s) its customer combines with its product, (2) reduce the cost it must incur to practice meter pricing on the durable product, franchise, or production process it is selling, (3) reduce the amount of transaction surplus it must destroy to remove a given relevant amount of buyer surplus from its customer through supra-marginal-cost pricing by shifting the locus of its supra-marginal-cost pricing from the tying product to a tied product when changes in the tying and tied products' demand curves are highly positively correlated and their relative transaction-surplus-maximizing unit outputs, marginal-cost-curve slopes, and relevant-demand-curve slopes make this pricing-technique profitable, and (4) reduce the amount of transaction surplus it must destroy to remove a relevant amount of buyer surplus by engaging in supra-marginal-cost pricing when selling an input against which substitution is possible (A) by substituting for the supra-marginal-cost pricing of that input a tie-in in which the seller's input is priced at its marginal cost and the buyer is obligated to purchase its full requirements of a second input used to produce the same final product against which substitution is not possible for a price that exceeds that second input's normal market price or (B) by substituting for the supra-marginal-cost pricing of the input against which substitution is possible a tie-in in which that input's price is reduced on condition that the buyer agree to purchase from the seller its full requirements of the input that can be substituted for the seller's input for a price that exceeds that second input's normal market price by a percentage that equals the percentage by which the price of the seller's input in the tie-in exceeds the marginal cost the seller must incur to produce its input.

Before proceeding, I should point out that part of the preceding analysis also applies to the practice that is called "systems rivalry" in the literature. "Systems rivalry" is the expression used to refer to conduct in which a producer of a "primary product" (e.g., a camera, computer-mainframe, or piece of durable equipment) engages to prevent its customers from purchasing complements of its primary product (film and developing services when the primary product is a camera, peripherals when the primary product is a computer-mainframe, and repair-and-maintenance services when the primary product is a durable machine) from suppliers it does not want them to patronize (i.e., by sellers' trying to induce their customers [in essence] to refuse to deal with various potential suppliers). Sometimes, a seller tries to achieve this objective by requiring buyers of its primary product to purchase their full requirements of the relevant complements from it or from one or more other complement-suppliers it designates, but sellers are often deterred from proceeding in this straightforward way by the (legally-mistaken) view of courts and antitrust-enforcement agencies that their use of such tie-ins would violate extant antitrust law—R. Markovits (2014b, pp. 694–722). Often sellers try to achieve this objective (1) by not revealing to potential complement-suppliers attributes of the seller's new product they would have to know to develop compatible complements or (2) by not revealing to particular independent service-organizations (ISOs) information about the seller's machine that the independents need to know to maintain and repair the machine, by not selling to the ISOs replacement-parts and repair-equipment the ISOs need to maintain and repair the machines, and/or by obligating independent manufacturers of those replacement-parts and repair-equipment that supply these goods to the primary-good producer not to supply them to any ISO unless the primary-good producer explicitly authorizes their supply to the ISO in question.

For two reasons, I think that systems rivalry is never predatory. The first, more-straightforward reason is that practitioners of systems rivalry will almost always find it ex ante profitable for one or two of the following legitimating reasons: (1) It reduces the cost to them of practicing meter pricing on the primary good when the dollar value to any buyer of the primary good increases with the quantity of complements it combines with the primary good (the amount of film and developing services it combines with the camera, the number of peripherals it combines with the mainframe, or the amount of maintenance-and-repair services it combines with [the intensity of its use of] the durable product) by enabling it to use the complement as an ersatz meter, and (2) it reduces the cost to them of controlling the quality of the complements its customers combine with the primary product. The second reason I think systems rivalry is not predatory is more contestable: I think it is perfectly legitimate for the primary-product producer to prevent potential entrants into the primary-product-production business from reducing the barriers to entry they face by supplying complements to the primary-product producer's customers—namely, from learning the names and addresses of the primary-product producer's customers, by learning things about the primary product by producing complements for it or maintaining and repairing it, and by taking advantage of the opportunity to establish friendly relations with the primary-product producer's customers and impress them with their reliability. I think it is legitimate for a primary-product producer to prevent prospective new entrants from securing these advantages: Our legal system recognizes that firms have a property right in their customer-lists (in part to provide them with incentives to increase economic efficiency by identifying buyers they are best-placed to supply and enabling those buyers to make the most-economically-efficient purchases they could make); our legal system also recognizes that firms have property rights in information about their products to which the firms are not given IP rights, once more to encourage firms to develop better products. In any event, even if there were cases in which the relevant perpetrator did not believe that its practice of systems rivalry was rendered ex ante profitable by its reducing the cost of practicing meter pricing and controlling the quality of the complements its customers combine with its primary product, I would not find the practice predatory if the perpetrator's perception that its systems rivalry was ex ante profitable was critically affected by its belief that the systems rivalry would or might deter entry or make entry less effective by preventing possible complement-suppliers that are also potential entrants (or are established rivals whose survival was problematic) from obtaining the advantages previously referenced by supplying complements to buyers of the systems-rivalry practitioner's primary product because in an oPp economy it would be ex ante economically efficient for the primary-product producer to deny relevant complement-producers access to its customers when the primary-product producer would find it ex ante profitable to do so.

The second subcategory of individual-firm decisions that are designed to deter a trading-partner from dealing with one or more other firms are decisions to include in reciprocity agreements clauses that legally obligate one of the participants to purchase its full requirements of a particular good from the other participant or from someone else that the other participant specifies. Such decisions are not predatory because the party that is inducing its contract partner to agree to purchase its full requirements of a particular good from it or someone it specifies almost always finds it ex ante legitimately profitable to do so because this decision lowers the cost it must incur to control the quality of an input its trading partner is using to produce a good it is supplying to the "restrictor" in question.

The third subcategory of decisions that firms make that, in effect, induce a trading-partner not to deal with some firms are decisions to include clauses in reciprocal-trading agreements that legally obligate the other participant to supply its total output of a particular good to the other party to the agreement (not to sell any of its output to anyone else). Decisions to include such clauses in reciprocal-trading agreements are not predatory because the actor that includes them finds it ex ante profitable to do so because their inclusion (1) reduces the cost it must incur to practice meter-pricing (when the restrictor is supplying a durable machine, production process, or product or franchise idea and the restriction obligates the restricted party to supply the restrictor with its total output of the good in question at a price that is lower than the price the restricted party would otherwise have obtained for it [where the reduced price functions as a meter-rate for using the durable machine, production process, or product-idea]), (2) reduce the amount of transaction surplus the restricting party must destroy to eliminate a relevant amount of the restricted party's overall-deal surplus by non-marginal-cost pricing by reducing the price the restricting party charges for the good it is supplying the restricted party in exchange for the restricted party's agreement to supply the restricting party with the restricted party's total output of a good it produces for less than it would otherwise have changed for this good when the demands for the two goods are highly positively correlated and their relative transaction-surplus-maximizing outputs, marginal-cost-curve slopes, and relevant-demand-curve slopes make this arrangement profitable, (3) reduces the amount of transaction surplus a restricting party that produces an input against which substitution is possible must destroy to eliminate a relevant amount of the restricted party's overall-deal surplus by engaging in non-marginal-cost pricing by substituting for the supra-marginal-cost-pricing of its input a clause that legally obligates the buyer of its input to supply it with the buyer's total output of the good the input-buyer uses the input to produce for a lower price than the input-buyer/(final-good producer) would otherwise charge for its product.

The fourth subcategory of decisions that firms make that, in effect, induce a trading-partner not to deal with some firms are decisions by sellers to impose full-requirements obligations on their customers outside of tie-ins or reciprocity agreements. I suspect that the vast majority of such decisions are not predatory because I believe that the vast majority of them are made by firms that perceived them to be ex ante profitable because the full-requirements legal obligations (1) reduce the private "mechanical" transaction cost the buyer and seller must incur to buy and sell the good involved, (2) reduce the sum of the risk costs the buyer and seller incur, (3) enable the buyer and seller to increase the transaction surplus their transactions generate with each other by making it profitable for them to adjust their operations in their joint interest, and (4) put the relevant seller and/or buyer in a more-secure financial position that enables it or them to make profitable investments. I acknowledge, however, that in a few instances a seller may find it profitable to engage in predation by inducing buyers to enter into full-requirements contracts that prevent them from patronizing an actual competitor the seller wants to drive out or prevent them from purchasing a good that would be created by a new investment in the ARDEPPS in question whose execution by an expanding established rival or potential competitor the predator is seeking to prevent. For this conduct to succeed, the relevant seller must reduce the volume of sales not "locked up" that the relevant actual or potential competitor was or would otherwise be well-placed to make below the volume the rival-firm in question must make to break even despite the fact that it would be against the relevant buyers' collective interest to allow this to happen (see below) and the "frozen-out" rivals must not be able to reduce the loss the conduct in question did or would impose on them sufficiently to make it profitable for them to remain in business, to invest, or not to shift their actual or planned investment's location by vertically integrating forward into buying/using their own products, subsidizing, encouraging, or taking advantage of an independent relevant new entry, or participating in a relevant joint venture.

I need to comment on (1) why such predatory induced refusals to deal are against the collective interest of the buyers whose agreeing to full-requirements contracts precludes them from dealing with the predator's rivals and (2) why such buyers may enter into the full-requirements contracts in question despite this fact—indeed, may have to be paid only a pittance to secure their agreement to the full-requirements provisions in question. To start, a set of full-requirements contracts that induce the exit or relocation of the participating seller's rivals, deter those rivals from making investments in the relevant ARDEPPS, and/or induce those rivals to locate their new investments further away in product-space from the predatory seller's projects will harm the customers of the predatory seller by worsening the best offers they receive from any actual or potential competitor of that seller. In fact, in almost all situations, the equivalent-dollar losses that predatory buyer-refusal-inducing behavior imposes on the buyers that have agreed to the full-requirements clauses in question will exceed the equivalent-dollar gains that those clauses confer on the predator that has induced the relevant buyers to accept them. The reason that sellers may find it profitable to engage in this type of predation despite the fact referenced in the last sentence is that, from the perspective of each of the buyers in question, not locking itself in to a full-requirements contract creates a kind of public good (benefits all buyers that have not locked themselves in) by preventing the exit of alternative suppliers, causing other firms to make additional investments in the ARDEPPS in question, and/or preventing suppliers from relocating their extant and future investments. Because no individual buyer can secure any of these benefits by not locking itself in if enough other buyers have locked themselves in for the predatory seller's rivals to exit, not make additional investments, and/or not change their extant and future investments' locations, a seller that can convince individual buyers that it will induce enough of their fellow-buyers to lock themselves in to enable it to achieve its predatory objectives will be able to secure the requisite amount of agreements for a pittance: The buyers will be tyrannized by their small decisions since each, acting on its own, will be correct in concluding that it was giving up nothing to lock itself in. Although—in part for the above reasons—I do recognize that some medium-term and long-term full-requirements provisions that are not part of tie-in or reciprocity agreements are predatory, I still think that only a small percentage of such agreements are predatory —that most are inherently profitable and that most of the possible targets of such predation will be able to protect themselves by vertically integrating, encouraging/subsidizing/(taking advantage of) independent entry, or participating in joint ventures.

The fifth subcategory of individual-firm decisions that prevent trading-partners from dealing with others contains decisions by producers to require their independent distributors to agree to single-brand exclusive-dealership agreements (dealership-agreements that place the distributor under a legal obligation not to sell any product other than the producer's products [or at least not to sell any product that is a competitor of a producer-product]). I think that few single-brand restrictions in dealership agreements are predatory because such clauses can generate legitimate profits in a variety of legitimate ways and are usually profitable for these reasons: namely, (1) by reducing the risk cost the producer bears in relation to variations in the amount of its products that will be sold, (2) by making it profitable for the producer to train the distributor (e.g., to make it profitable for the producer to give potentially-jointly-profitable advice to the distributor about sales-techniques, promotional displays, media-advertizing, shelf-space choices) by preventing the dealer from using this advice to sell products that are rivalrous with one or more of the producer's products, (3) by preventing the distributor from advertizing, promoting, making efforts to sell, and actually selling products that are rivalrous with one or more of the producer's products when those distributor activities are against the joint interest of the producer and distributor (a situation that may arise when the per-unit price the seller is charging the distributor for a good exceeds the marginal cost the producer must incur to supply the distributor with that product), and relatedly, (4) by making it profitable for the producer to make jointly-profitable decisions about the prices it charges the distributor for its product(s) and the resale prices the distributor is permitted to charge for the product(s) of the manufacturer that might not be jointly-profitable for them if the distributor were also selling products produced by rivals of the manufacturer. Once more, I acknowledge that a producer may sometimes engage in predation by imposing single-brand restrictions in the distributorship contracts it enters into with one or (probably) far more than one of its distributors.[15] However, for the same reasons that I doubt that a significant percentage of refusals to deal and full-requirements restrictions in sales contracts with other sorts of buyers (that are not part of tying or reciprocal-trading agreements) is predatory, I doubt that a significant percentage of single-brand exclusive dealerships is predatory.

The sixth subcategory of decisions that an individual firm may make to induce a trading-partner not to deal with specified other actors contains decisions by manufacturers to limit their individual dealers to selling the manufacturer's goods to buyers in certain geographic territories or to buyers in specified non-geographic categories—that is, to require its independent distributors not to deal with various sets of prospective customers. Even if these vertical territorial restraints and other sorts of vertical customer-allocation clauses deter the restricted distributors from making investments that would put them in a good position to make sales to the buyers whose patronage they are being required to refuse to supply, they would never be predatory because the manufacturer that included such vertical restrains in its dealership agreements (or adopted a policy of not renewing the franchises of dealers that supplied buyers with whom they had been instructed not to deal) would almost always have found such restraints to be ex ante profitable for legitimate reasons—because they enabled the manufacturer to increase the total profits that it and its independent distributors realize combined (and hence the profits it could obtain inter alia by charging its independent distributors lump-sum franchise fees in addition to the per-unit prices they must pay for the manufacturer's goods) (1) by inducing the distributors to place advertizements that are "organizationally-profitable" (i.e., that increases the total profits of the manufacturer and its independent distributors), to provide "organizationally-profitable" promotional-displays, to make organizationally-profitable salesmanship efforts, to make organizationally-profitable shelf-space-allocation decisions, to provide organizationally-profitable warrantee services and maintenance-and-repair services more generally by reducing the extent to which such efforts would yield sales to other distributors of the manufacturer's products, (2) by deterring them from making organizational-unprofitable expenditures on advertizing, promotional displays, salesmanship, and maintenance-and-repair services that are organizationally-unprofitable because they take sales away from other distributors of the manufacturer's goods, (3) by inducing individual independent distributors to inform the manufacturer of uses of its products, of better ways to make use of its products, and of particular advertizements, promotional displays, and sales-techniques by guaranteeing them that this information will not be used against them by other distributors of the manufacturer's products, (4) by enabling the manufacturer to prevent its independent distributors from reducing the organization's profits by engaging in price-competition against each other (by charging prices for the manufacturer's goods that are lower than the prices the relevant buyers would have been willing to pay for them)—to see why it is legitimate for a manufacturer to prevent such intra-brand competition, note that it would be perfectly legitimate for a manufacturer that was vertically integrated forward into distribution to instruct its distribution-employees not to compete against each other and that there is no reason why a firm that chose to use independent distributors should be prohibited from instructing them to behave in the way it could order its own employees to behave, and (5) by enabling the manufacturer to prevent its independent distributors from charging low prices that reduce the organization's profits because some buyers mistakenly believe that the material quality of the relevant category of good is privately correlated with its price, because some buyers want to buy high-priced goods because doing so convinces others that the buyers are wealthy or have other attributes that purchasers of high-priced goods of the type in question possess, or because some franchisees find it profitable to offer low price-quality combinations that appeal most to local patrons but are dispreferred by travelers who find it impossible or significantly costly to determine ex ante the quality of the goods and services than an individual franchisee is supplying and therefore place a significant positive value on the franchisor's making certain that all its franchisees supply goods and services of an advertized (higher) quality.

One further point needs to be made about vertical territorial and other sorts of vertical customer-allocation restraints. In rare cases, two or more manufacturers may impose such restraints on their respective independent distributors to implement their horizontal-market-division agreement, and, in even rarer cases, two or more distributors may induce their manufacturer-suppliers to impose such vertical restraints on them to enable the distributors to implement the distributors' horizontal market-division. However, although such arrangements manifest their perpetrators' specific anti-competitive intent, I do not think it is instructive to characterize them as "predatory."[16] In any event, this kind of predatory conduct really belongs in the third large category of predatory conduct—refusals to deal.

The seventh subcategory of decisions that an individual firm can make to prevent a "trading-partner" from dealing with others are decisions to include in employment contracts provisions that impose a legal obligation on the employee not to work for a competitor of the employer and not to reveal to (in practice, not to sell to) a rival of the employer information the employer provides the employee in question. Employment contracts that include such provisions also contain clauses that prohibit the employee from going into competition with the employer on their own—that is, from competing for the patronage of the employer's actual or possible customers. A decision to include such provisions in employment contracts will be predatory if the restricted employee would otherwise have made an investment that enabled it to compete with its employer and the employer would not have found it profitable to include such a clause in its contract if it would not have prevented the employee from competing with the employer independent of its having worked for the employer. However, I suspect that the ex ante employer-perceived profitability of few such employment-contract restrictions is critically affected by their preventing such competition[17]—that the vast majority of such clauses are perceived to be ex ante profitable by those who include in their employment contracts because the employer believes that they will make it profitable for the employer to provide the employee with training and experiences that increase the employee's productivity when it would not be profitable for the employer to do so if the employee could "defect" to a competitor, sell its knowledge to a competitor, or go into competition with the employer. Before proceeding, I want to indicate that I have included decisions to put clauses in employment contracts restricting the ability of the employee to deal with others into the category of refusals to deal to which one firm induces another actor to agree because in employment situations the employee-participant in the contract is almost always fungible—has no special attributes that give it power in the relevant negotiation.

The eighth subcategory of decisions that an individual firm or actor can make to prevent a "trading-partner" from dealing with others are decisions to include in contracts for the sale of a business or professional practice a clause prohibiting the seller from entering into competition with the buyer. Again, such provisions could be predatory, but I suspect that the vast majority of decisions to include such clauses in such contracts are not predatory—are perceived ex ante to be profitable for the seller that includes them in its contract of sale because they enable the seller to sell his or her customer/client-list and goodwill, which often constitute a high percentage of the value of the business/(professional practice) being sold, by prohibiting the seller from lowering the value of the customer-list or goodwill by going into competition with the buyer.

I turn finally to decisions that two or more firms or actors can make to deter each of them from dealing with the other's or others' customers or one of them from dealing with the other's customers. I will distinguish three subsubcategories of this subcategory of refusal-to-deal-related conduct.

I have already identified the first—contrived-oligopolistic behavior in which two or more firms divide up customers by agreeing not to make investments that would enable them to compete for the patronage of particular sets of buyers. Such horizontal-market-division agreements are prohibited by the antitrust laws of virtually all societies that have such laws.

The second subsubcategory of this third subcategory of refusal-to-deal-related conduct includes decisions by two or more individuals who are forming a partnership to include in their partnership-agreement a clause prohibiting each of them from working for a competitor of the former partnership if it dissolves, from competing on his or her own for the patronage of actual or prospective customers of the partnership after it dissolves, or from selling information obtained from other partners to competitors of the partnership. I suspect that most such clauses in partnership agreements are not predatory—were perceived by each of the partners to be ex ante profitable because the clause in question would increase the legitimate profits the partnership would yield by inducing each partner to convey valuable information to his or her fellows and to provide the other partners with valuable learning experiences when it would not have been individually profitable for the "educating" partner to do so if the partner whose knowledge or skills were enhanced could use them to compete against the remaining (original) partner(s) or put them at the disposal of others that would use them to compete against the remaining (original) partner(s). Of course, some such partnership-agreement clauses may be predatory—may not have been rendered ex ante profitable for the above reason, may have been included to prevent partners who would otherwise have competed against each other from doing so.[18] However, I suspect that only a tiny percentage of such partnership-agreement clauses are predatory.

The third subsubcategory of decisions that the individual members of a set of two or more firms make to induce others to refuse certain deals are decisions by joint-venture parents to include in their joint-venture agreements provisions that prohibit the parents from making investments that would enable them to compete for each other's customers or for the customers of the joint venture and provisions that prohibits joint ventures from making investments that would enable them to compete for the parents' customers. I am certain that some decisions of these sorts are predatory—are made by firms that would not have found the relevant provisions ex ante profitable had they not believed that the provisions would reduce the absolute attractiveness of the offers against which they would have to compete by preventing fellow-parents that would otherwise have competed against them from doing so. However, I am also certain that many decisions to include such provisions in joint-venture agreements are not predatory—are made by firms that found the provisions ex ante profitable because the provisions enabled the parents to increase the normal-accounting-calculated profits yielded by the joint venture by supplying it with information and personnel that increased its proficiency when the parent in question would not have found it profitable to do so if the other joint-venture parent or the joint venture could use that information and the better-trained personnel the parent's contribution enabled the joint venture to "possess" to compete against it.

10.1.5.1 The Economic Efficiency of Predatory Individual-Firm Refusals to Deal, Predatory Efforts by Individual Firms to Deter Others from Dealing With Third Parties, and Predatory Decisions by Two or More Firms to Refuse to Deal

I focus first on the economic efficiency of the rare decisions of a vertically-integrated firm to refuse to deal with a rival that are predatory. The fact that the refused deals would have been inherently profitable for the refusing and refused firms taken together implies that, across all instances, their refusal would decrease economic efficiency even if it had no relevant further consequences. If the refusal resulted in the exit of the refused company (say, in its not renewing its plant when the plant depreciated or in its selling its plant to a firm that would use it to produce goods in another ARDEPPS), the impact that the predation will have on that account will depend on whether the exit of the target increases, decreases, or leaves unchanged the equilibrium-investment quantity in the relevant ARDEPPS. If I make the assumption (which I assume will usually be accurate) that the refused party produces a good created by a QV investment rather than a production process, the predation will increase/decrease/(have no effect on) economic efficiency by altering the relevant ARDEPPS' equilibrium-QV-investment quantity if it decreases/increases/(has no effect on) the relevant ARDEPPS' equilibrium-QV-investment quantity. If by increasing the potential supernormal profit-rate the refusing company could earn, the predatory refusal to deal causes that firm to operate more sloppily, the predatory refusal to deal will increase departure-from-production-optimum misallocation. If the firm that engages in the predatory refusal to deal shares some of the resulting increase in its potential profits with its managers and employees, the predatory refusal to deal will decrease economic efficiency by increasing the amount of misallocation these individuals generate by substituting untaxed or lower-taxed better working-conditions and fringe-benefits for the goods they would otherwise have purchased with the monetary compensation they forego to secure the improved working-conditions and larger fringe-benefits in question. If the predatory refusal to deal increases the concentration of the seller-side of the ARDEPPS of practice, it will tend to increase economic inefficiency by increasing the amount of misallocative expenditures the sellers in the ARDEPPS of practice make on political parties/campaigns/candidates and government-decisionmaking-process participation. Such predatory refusals to deal will also tend to increase economic inefficiency by increasing poverty and material inequality. I am confident that such predatory refusals to deal will decrease economic efficiency all tolled.

The preceding analysis applies mutatis mutandis to the rare exemplars of single-brand exclusive dealerships that are predatory. In my contestable judgment, the fact that predatory single-brand exclusive dealerships increase economic efficiency in some ways affects their overall economic efficiency but does not critically affect their overall economic inefficiency.

For the same reasons, predatory competition-prohibiting provisions in partnership-agreements, (business/professional-practice)-sale agreements, or joint-venture agreements will be economically inefficient all tolled even though those provisions will generate some allocative benefits. Decisions to use vertical-territorial-restraint-imposing clauses to implement manufacturer or retailer horizontal market-divisions will decrease economic efficiency for the same reasons that contrived-oligopolistic pricing reduces economic efficiency.

I have not yet addressed non-predatory refusal-to-deal-related categories of conduct. The economic efficiency of (1) the various functional categories of (non-predatory) tie-ins and reciprocity agreements in which one participant accepts a legal obligation either (A) to purchase its full requirements of some product from the other participant or someone the other participant nominates or (B) to supply its total output of some good to the other participant and (2) vertical territorial restraints or vertical customer-allocation clauses of other sorts will be analyzed in detail in Sects. 13.2 and 13.3. However, I do think that it would be appropriate for me to consider the economic efficiency of these categories of refusal-to-deal-related conduct more briefly at this juncture and to discuss now more thoroughly the economic efficiency of various other categories of non-predatory refusal-to-deal-related conduct.

Before proceeding, I should admit at the outset that the analyses that follow will ignore the fact that—to the extent that the non-predatory refusals to deal or refusal-to-deal-inducing conduct on which they separately focus increase the profits the perpetrators realize on the investment with which the conduct is connected and thereby increase equilibrium investment in the ARDEPPSes in which the conduct takes place—it will decrease economic efficiency on that account when the ARDEPPS' investments are QV investments and increase economic efficiency when the ARDEPPS' investments are investments in PPR. I am ignoring this complication not only to shorten the exposition but also because, when all members of a set of rivals engage in a relevant category of non-predatory refusals to deal or refusal-to-deal-inducing conduct, all of their doing so may not increase the profits that each of them realizes on its investments in the relevant ARDEPPS.

To start, even in an economy that is as highly-Pareto-imperfect as are contemporary economies, it seems to me appropriate to assume that across all cases firms' refusals to deal with actual or potential competitors that are not predatory because the refused deals were inherently unprofitable are economically efficient, and, although the following conclusion is certainly contestable, I also expect that it will not be TBLE for government to investigate whether individual refusals to deal in this category were rendered economically inefficient by the Pareto imperfections the relevant economy contains and to act to deter such economically-inefficient non-predatory refusals to deal. I also think that the non-predatory refusals to deal that result from a seller's (1) including in a tying agreement a clause that legally obligates the buyer to purchase from the seller or another firm the seller designates its full requirements of a tied good that is a complement to the tying good or

(2) engaging in systems rivalry to induce its customers to purchase from it a complement to its primary product are economically efficient because (A) seller efforts to control the quality of the complements that better combine with their "primary goods" through tie-ins or systems rivalry will tend to be economically efficient when they are profitable and (B) (i) sellers will use full-requirements tie-ins or practice systems rivalry to secure such control only when that is the most profitable way for them to do so, (ii) the technique that a seller finds most profitable to use to achieve such complement-control will tend to be the technique that is most economically efficient for the seller to use for this purpose, and (iii) systems rivalry will itself almost always be economically efficient when it is profitable. The preceding arguments imply that, when a firm X that is purchasing a final good or an input from a trading-partner Y finds it profitable to control the quality of the inputs that its trading-partner Y incorporates into or uses to produce the relevant final good or input it is supplying by using a reciprocal-trading agreement that legally obligates Y to purchase its full requirements of the relevant input from X or a firm X designates, X's use of this technique will be economically efficient (more accurately, it will be TBLE to assume that its use of this technique is economically efficient).

It is less clear whether a firm's non-predatory use of a full-requirements-clause-containing tying agreement or a total-output-supply-clause-containing reciprocity agreement to implement a meter-pricing pricing-technique when selling a durable product or the right to use an idea (including to operate a branded franchise) will increase or decrease economic efficiency. On the one hand, if the relevant seller would engage in meter pricing even if it could not use such a tie-in or reciprocity agreement to implement that pricing technique, the fact that the seller found it most profitable to use the tie-in clause or reciprocity clause in question to implement its meter pricing creates a strong presumption that these methods of implementing meter pricing are more economically efficient than the alternative methods the seller would use in their stead. On the other hand, if the relevant seller would not engage in meter pricing at all if it could not use a tie-in clause or reciprocity-agreement clause to implement this technique, the economic efficiency of such refusal-to-deal-inducing clauses will depend on the economic efficiency of the seller's practicing meter pricing by using such a clause as opposed to its pricing its product in some other way, and it is not clear whether meter pricing is more or less economically efficient than the pricing-technique that would be substituted for it—presumably, the outright sale of the machine, right to use the idea or production process, or right to operate the franchise in question. Sellers find it profitable to substitute meter pricing for the outright sale of their machine, idea, production process, or franchise when the benefits the shift to meter pricing confers on the seller (1) by reducing the loss it sustains because it underestimates the frequency with which the relevant buyer will use its product, (2) by reducing the loss the seller sustains because the buyer underestimates the frequency with which the buyer will use the seller's product, (3) by reducing the "loss" it sustains because the relevant transaction imposes risk costs on both the seller and the buyer related to their not knowing how frequently the buyer will use the seller's product (where the buyer's risk costs are salient to the seller because they affect the lump-sum fee the buyer will be willing to pay the seller for the right to purchase its product or the right to make an individual use of its product at a specified per-unit price) by shifting some of the relevant risk from the buyer to the seller (that will usually be a larger, more-diverse firm with more retained earnings and that will usually on these accounts be less risk-averse than the buyer and may be in a position in which the shift to meter pricing places less risk on it than it removes from the buyer [as will be the case when the seller is a franchisor that is concerned solely with the total sales made by all its franchisees and the buyer is a franchisee that is concerned not only with fluctuations in the chain's total sales but with its share of the chain's total sales]), and (4) by reducing the buyer's incentive to engage in arbitrage *exceed* the costs the shift to meter pricing imposes on the seller (1) by increasing the private transaction costs it incurs (when the extra cost of drafting, negotiating, and enforcing the meter-pricing agreement exceed the cost-savings the shift enables the seller to secure by reducing its need to devote resources to discovering the buyer's [different buyers'] future quantity demand[s] and to persuading buyers that they were pessimistic about the frequency with which they would use the seller's product), (2) by reducing the total transaction surplus the relevant transaction generates by deterring the buyer from making demand-increasing expenditures that would be in the joint interest of the buyer and seller (by raising the cost to the buyer of marginal and extra-marginal uses of the seller's product above the cost of such uses to the seller and/or causing the seller to incur costs to prevent this result), and (3) in the relatively-rare instances in which the buyer is larger, more diversified, and better-heeled than the seller, by increasing the sum of the buyer's and seller's risk costs. Because inter alia (1) the first two (seller-pessimism-and-buyer-pessimism-related) benefits have no allocative counterparts (if one considers the associated allocative-transaction-cost ramifications separately) and (2) I assume both (A) that the shift to meter pricing will normally increase private transaction costs and (B) that the allocative-transaction-cost effects are likely to exceed their private-transaction-cost counterparts, I am unable to reach any conclusion about whether shifts from meter pricing to pure-lump-sum pricing that would have been unprofitable had the seller been able to implement its meter pricing by including appropriate clauses in a tying agreement or reciprocity agreement should be assumed to decrease or increase economic efficiency.

I am also uncertain about the economic efficiency of non-predatory refusal-to-deal-inducing full-requirements clauses in tying agreements and total-output-supply clauses in reciprocity agreements that the producer of a final good enters into to reduce the amount of transaction surplus its non-marginal-cost pricing destroys (its supra-marginal-cost pricing destroys by preventing sales of the tying product that would have yielded an increase in transaction surplus or its submarginal-cost buying destroys by inducing purchases of the "tied product" in a reciprocity agreement that reduce transaction surplus). In the one direction, these clauses tend to reduce economic efficiency by increasing the private and a fortiori the allocation transactions costs the relevant producer generates to sell its product. In the other direction, these clauses tend to increase economic efficiency by reducing the amount of transaction surplus the seller's non-marginal-cost per-unit pricing destroys by deterring demand-increasing expenditures that would have increased transaction surplus and/or inducing demand-increasing expenditures that decrease transaction surplus.

Next, I think that non-predatory refusal-to-deal-inducing clauses in the tying agreements and reciprocity agreements entered into by firms that produce inputs against which substitution is possible are economically efficient because I think that (1) such clauses will be more economically efficient than the other techniques that the input manufacturer would use to prevent substitutions against its input when the input manufacturer finds such clauses more profitable to use than these other techniques and (2) it will be economically efficient for an input manufacturer to use such clauses to prevent the substitutions against its input that would result from its charging a supra-marginal-cost price for the input in an independent transaction when the input manufacturer finds it profitable to do so—that the amount by which the use of such clauses will increase economic efficiency by preventing choice-among-known-production-process-generated misallocation will exceed the amount by which the use of such clauses will decrease economic efficiency by increasing the allocative transaction costs the input manufacturer's pricing causes to be generated.

I turn finally to the economic efficiency of the non-predatory, non-horizontal-price-fix-implementing refusal-to-deal-inducing decisions of producers to contractually forbid their independent distributors from reselling the producer's products to various classes of buyers defined by their geographic location or some other characteristic. If producers that were legally prohibited from inducing their independent distributors from accepting such vertical territorial restraints or other sorts of customer-allocation provisions would respond to this prohibition by vertically integrating forward into distribution, the fact that the relevant producers found it more profitable to use constrained independent distributors to distribute their products than to distribute their products themselves would justify the conclusion that these vertical restraints increased economic efficiency in the circumstances in question. I also think that such vertical restraints will increase economic efficiency when the producers that employ them would not respond to their prohibition by integrating forward into distribution: (1) The fact that such vertical restraints induce the restrained distributors to do various things that are in the joint interest of the producer and its independent distributors combined—in particular, to make demand-increasing expenditures on media-advertizing, promotional-displays, and salesmanship, to perform maintenance-and-repair services, and to convey information to the manufacturer about uses to which the manufacturer's products can be put, the best way to employ the manufacturer's product, and the sales-techniques, promotional displays, and media advertizing that will increase the relevant "organization's" profits—implies that they will increase economic efficiency on those accounts, and (2) the fact that such vertical restraints will prevent the producer's independent distributors from engaging in intra-brand competition that would increase allocative transaction costs (by increasing the number of bids made for given buyers' patronage), generate intra-brand UO-to-UO misallocation by causing sales to be made by worse-than-best-placed distributors, and (by driving down the prices of the producer's products) increase economic efficiency by reducing equilibrium QV investment if the product in question were created by QV investments, by reducing leisure/do-it-yourself-labor/market-labor misallocation, and by reducing poverty and material inequality is of little import because producers that are prohibited from preventing their independent distributors from engaging in intra-brand competition by getting them to agree to vertical territorial restraints and other sorts of customer-allocation clauses (and/or to resale-price-maintenance clauses) will respond to such prohibitions by lowering the lump-sum (franchise) fees they charge their independent distributors and raising the per-unit prices they charge these distributors for their products to levels that make it unprofitable for any distributor to engage in intra-brand price-competition that would result in final buyers being charged prices that were lower than the prices they would have been willing to pay for the producer's products.

10.1.5.2 The Economic Efficiency of a Government's Trying to Deter in Various Ways Predatory Decisions to Refuse to Deal and Predatory Decisions to Induce Others to Refuse to Deal

Once more, it will be allocatively efficient for a government (1) to make such predatory decisions illegal, (2) to make some efforts to persuade through "education" possible perpetrators of this kind of predation not to engage in such conduct, (3) to authorize the imposition of the highest sum of damage-awards, civil fines, criminal fines, prison sentences, and non-custodial restrictions on individuals and firms convicted of engaging in this kind of predation that can be imposed on them without exceeding the amount that fits the seriousness of their wrongdoing and without incurring criminal-sentence-implementation allocative costs for any increase in such sentences that exceed the allocative benefits the sentence-increases generate, (4) to help victims of such predation with their suits to obtain legal redress, and (5) to secure plea bargains and make sentencing recommendations that are allocatively efficient. Once more, the more difficult issue relates to the allocative costs that will be allocatively efficient for the government to incur to collect the evidence that is probative of the various kinds of refusal-to-deal-related predatory conduct I have distinguished. To be honest, unless the government can obtain relevant, credible eyewitness testimony, e-mails, firm-meeting minutes, confessions, etc., I suspect it will rarely be possible much less allocatively efficient for the government to establish the requisite probability (1) that a vertical firm's refusal to deal with a rival was predatory or (2) that provisions in employment contracts, partnership agreements, (business/professional-practice)-sale agreements, or joint-venture agreements that prohibit one or more participants from competing against other participants are predatory.

I will close this section by commenting on the ability of a government to increase economic efficiency without violating liberal moral rights by deterring non-predatory refusals to deal or refusal-to-deal-inducing conduct. In brief, I do not think that a government will be able to increase economic efficiency by deterring such conduct without violating liberal moral rights because (1) most exemplars of most categories of such non-predatory conduct are economically efficient and (2) although some exemplars of some categories of such conduct will be economically inefficient, (A) there is no reason to believe that, taken as class, the exemplars of any of these latter subcategories of such conduct reduce economic efficiency, (B) it would almost certainly be ex ante economically inefficient to try to identify those exemplars of such conduct that are economically inefficient even if those exemplars could be deterred at no allocative cost, and (C) from the perspective of economic efficiency, it would probably be prohibitively-allocative-costly to deter those exemplars of such conduct that one could prove were economically inefficient.

10.1.6 The Economic Efficiency of Predatory Participation in Government-Decisionmaking Processes and Predatory Government-Election Participation and the Economic Efficiency of Government's Trying to Deter Such Predatory Conduct in Various Ways

A firm's or individual's participation in a legislative, administrative, or adjudicative decisionmaking process is predatory if ex ante the actor in question would not have found that participation ex ante desirable (I wrote "desirable" because an individual may find such participation desirable for non-monetary reasons) had the actor not believed that the participation would yield it, him, or her benefits to which it, he, or she was not morally entitled by driving a rival out, deterring a rival investment, or causing a rival to change the location of an extant or future investment. Efforts by a firm to secure the promulgation of legislation, administrative regulations, executive orders, or judicial decisions or holdings that restrict the number of entries that can be made into a particular business, require new entrants to pay entrance-fees (e.g., fees for taxi medallions), promulgate unjustifiable safety, other-product-performance-related, or environmental standards, or promulgate unjustifiable IP laws can all be predatory as can a firm's or individual's efforts (1) to have an actual competitor's license be legally-incorrectly revoked, a potential competitor's license-application to be legally-incorrectly rejected, or an actual competitor's product to be legally-incorrectly deemed unsafe in an administrative hearing or (2) to have an actual or potential competitor's application for a patent to be legally-incorrectly denied, an actual competitor's conduct to be legally-incorrectly deemed a patent infringement, or an actual or potential competitor's conduct to be legally-incorrectly found to be tortious or violative of a land-use or environmental regulation in an administrative hearing or trial.

A firm's or individual's participation in electoral-processes can also be predatory. More specifically, a firm's or individual's oral or written support of, in-kind contributions of other sorts to, and monetary contributions to a particular political party, campaign, or candidate will deserve to be called predatory if the relevant actor's ex ante perception that its support-decision was desirable was critically affected by its belief that the political party, campaign, or candidate it was supporting would or might increase the likelihood that the government (the candidate[s] himself, herself, or themselves or the administrative officials or judges he, she, or they would appoint) would make legally and/or morally unjustified decisions that yield the firm or individual in question predatory benefits.

I should add that the preceding two paragraphs, respectively, made reference to "justifiable IP rights" and "unjustifiable decisions" in part because IP-right holders might have a moral right to prevent others from violating the IP rights to which they might be morally entitled if individuals are morally responsible for their abilities and choices. This point is similar to my argument that systems rivalry should not be deemed predatory if the firm that engaged in it would not have found it ex ante profitable but for its belief that it would or might deter the entry of or reduce the post-entry competitiveness of a potential competitor by giving the potential competitor access to the perpetrator's customer-list, customers, and product because the systems-rivalry perpetrator has a morally-justifiable property right to not help others obtain access to the information in question.

10.1.6.1 The Economic Efficiency of Predatory Participation in Government-Decisionmaking Processes and Predatory Participation in Government Electoral-Processes

Before proceeding, I need to address a second-best-theory-related issue whose resolution will affect whether individual (i.e., single) efforts to induce the government to make decisions that yield the perpetrator predatory benefits, all such efforts to influence government, government decisions that deter a single such effort, and government decisions that reduce the incidence of such efforts will increase or decrease economic efficiency. The complication that needs to be considered is that —even if a single effort to induce government to make choices that yield the perpetrator predatory benefits that the perpetrator would not have found ex ante profitable had it not believed that it would or might yield it such predatory benefits would decrease economic efficiency in a society in which no other such efforts were made—taken together, the multiple efforts of this kind that are currently made in the societies with which this study is concerned do not decrease economic efficiency because they counteract each other and, relatedly, government decisions that deter an individual effort of this kind or reduce the incidence of such efforts will not tend to increase economic efficiency on these accounts or at least will increase economic efficiency only to the extent that the allocative cost of the relevant government efforts exceeds the allocative transaction costs that the deterred predatory conduct would have generated both directly and indirectly. This second-best-type argument is an analogue to John Kenneth Galbraith's argument in his study The Theory of Countervailing Power—Galbraith (1951). In my judgment, the separate efforts of firms and individuals to induce government to make decisions that generate the various outcomes that other categories of predatory conduct generate do not counteract each other when the relevant issue is their impact on economic efficiency. In other words, in my judgment, the larger the number of such non-government-actor efforts, the greater the resulting economic inefficiency, and the greater the extent to which the government deters such efforts (or prevents them from being successful), the smaller the amount of resulting economic inefficiency (if one ignores the allocative cost of the government's deterrence efforts). In any event, the analyses that follow will proceed on these assumptions.

Predatory participation in government-decisionmaking processes will reduce economic efficiency by the sum of the allocative transaction costs the perpetrator's efforts generate directly, the allocative transaction costs the perpetrator's target(s) generate when responding to the perpetrator's efforts, and the allocative transaction costs the relevant government decisionmaker(s) generate(s) when considering the predator's "submissions" and the predator's target's or targets' responses. Predatory participation in government-decisionmaking processes will also affect economic efficiency by affecting the economic efficiency of the decisions that government makes when the predatory efforts are successful. I am disposed to conclude that successful predatory efforts to get tariffs raised tend to cause economic inefficiency by generating intra-ARDEPPS UO-to-UO misallocation by reducing the sales of the imported good on which the tariff is levied (though it would almost certainly be TBLE to consider the relevance of [1] any difference in the externalities that would have been generated by the production, respectively, of the foreign goods on which the tariffs are levied and the domestic goods that are purchased instead of those foreign goods, [2] the impacts the tariffs have on the incidence of poverty and material inequality in both the country that is imposing the tariffs and the country on whose goods the tariffs are imposed, and [3] the impacts that the tariffs have on the amount of misallocation the government imposing the tariff and other affected governments generate when financing their operations [or eliminating expenditures to avoid having to finance them]). I am also disposed to think that any time that a firm's predatory participation in government product-standard, environmental, and land-use-policy decisionmaking processes enables it to induce government to promulgate product-attribute standards, environmental policies, and land-use regulations that generate the kinds of effects that make predation of all kinds beneficial to its perpetrators or to apply those laws or regulations in incorrect ways will tend on that account to cause intra-ARDEPPS UO-to-UO misallocation to the extent that it shifts sales from the target to the perpetrator and intra-ARDEPPS QV-to-QV misallocation or intra-ARDEPPS PPR-to-PPR misallocation if the predator replaces a prevented QV investment or PPR project with one of its own (which was presumably less profitable than the deterred investment of its rival). I also believe that any time that a firm's predatory participation in the government's IP-policy-promulgation-or-application decisionmaking processes results in the government's promulgating IP laws that have predatory effects or applying the laws it has promulgated incorrectly in ways that have predatory effects, its conduct will cause intra-ARDEPPS QV-to-QV misallocation or intra-ARDEPPS PPR-to-PPR misallocation when the predator replaces the deterred investment with one of its own. Moreover, if the predatory-behavior-induced government IP-law-related decisions reduce equilibrium PPR in the ARDEPPSes to which they relate, they will tend to cause misallocation on that account if the government has not independently promulgated and applied other policies to eliminate its society's tendency to devote too few resources to PPR from the perspective of economic efficiency. I acknowledge that, if the government has not adopted other policies to prevent the society's devoting too many resources to QV-investment creation from the perspective of economic efficiency, any tendency of a firm's predatory efforts to affect the government's IP-related decisions to reduce equilibrium QV investment in the ARDEPPSes to which those decisions apply will tend to increase economic efficiency on that account. Predatory participation in government-decisionmaking processes also, by increasing the predator's potential profits, increase the amount of production-optimum-related misallocation the predator generates by operating sloppily and the amount of misallocation the predator's managers and employees generate by making misallocative substitutions of better working-conditions and additional fringe-benefits for the goods they would have purchased with the monetary compensation they forewent to get better working-conditions and more fringe-benefits. Predatory efforts to induce government to raise its license-fees or (say) taxi-medallion prices will tend to increase economic efficiency by reducing the amount of revenue it must raise in other ways to finance its operations and by obviating its making various spending-cuts. All tolled, I think that predatory participation in government-decisionmaking processes will virtually always decrease economic efficiency.

With one possible qualification, the preceding analyses also apply to attempts by a firm to induce a government to make decisions that will benefit it by generating the same kinds of effects that are generated by other kinds of predatory conduct in which the firm can engage by supporting in various ways political parties, campaigns, and candidates that the firm believes will promulgate legislation, administrative regulations, executive orders, and/or judicial decisions and doctrines that generate these effects and/or will apply "the law" incorrectly to generate these effects. The only possible qualification is that the party or candidate that the firm believes will benefit it in these ways may be less likely than its (his or her) alternative to decrease economic efficiency in other ways. However, I suspect that in general parties and candidates that are more likely to help one supporter by making economically-inefficient decisions are also more likely to make economically-inefficient decisions to benefit other supporters.

10.1.6.2 The Ability of Government to Increase Economic Efficiency Without Violating any Liberal Moral Right by Deterring Firms From Participating Predatorily in Government-Decisionmaking Processes and in Government Electoral-Processes

I have assumed so far and will continue to assume that the efforts of the governments on which this study focuses to increase economic efficiency by deterring the various categories of business conduct that antitrust laws could cover are constrained by the liberal moral rights of the members of their societies. The liberal moral rights that constrain government efforts to deter all kinds of conduct that antitrust law could cover relate to the methods that government employs to obtain evidence (torture and even milder forms of coercion are forbidden as is entrapment [which engenders offenses in addition to producing evidence of their commission]), the probability of guilt that the government must establish to win a criminal case and the probability of non-criminal-law violation that a private party or the government must establish to win a civil case, and the norm that limits the total sanctions that may be imposed on a wrongdoer who or that has lost a civil or criminal case to a quantum that does not exceed the amount that "matches" the seriousness of the relevant wrongdoing. When the antitrust-offense at issue is predatory participation in a government-decisionmaking process or a government electoral-process, another liberal-moral-right constraint *may be* operative—a constraint that is related to the moral right of each (competent and trustworthy) member of a liberal-moral-rights-based society to participate in its government's electoral and decisionmaking processes. I have italicized "may be" in the preceding sentence because I do not think that liberalism recognizes that actors have a moral-right-related interest in participating in government electoral or decision-making processes with predatory intent. This conclusion must be clarified in two ways. First, the fact that at the time that an actor chose to support a particular political party or candidate he, she, or it realized that that party's or candidate's electoral success would increase the probability that the government would make decisions that would yield the actor benefits by driving one or more of its rivals out, deterring one or more of its rivals from making investments in its ARDEPPS, and/or inducing one or more of its rivals to change the product-space location of one or more of their extant or future investments and the fact that, at the time that an actor chose to participate in a government electoral or decisionmaking process to increase the probability that a particular piece of legislation, executive order, administrative rule, judicial doctrine, or administrative or judicial case-resolution would be promulgated or made, it realized that the government decision it was trying to secure would yield it benefits in one or more of the ways listed above are not sufficient conditions for the choice's being predatory because its choice would not be predatory if the chooser could establish that it was motivated by "the public interest" and that it acted in the good-faith belief that the government decisions it was hoping to elicit were consistent with liberalism and instantiated a morally-defensible conception of the moral good. Second, it may be that an actor has a liberal moral right to communicate to electors information about political parties and candidates that it believes in good faith to be accurate and relevant to the moral desirability of their electoral success and to communicate to government decisionmakers information that it believes in good faith to be accurate and relevant to the moral desirability or the legal correctness of the choices the communicator is trying to influence even if the communicator's motive is predatory (though, I suspect, in such cases the communicator would have a liberal moral duty to reveal its parochial interest in the matter at issue). To be frank, I am not sure whether—if actors have any such liberal participation-right—they have it (1) because they have on their own account a liberal moral right to participate in this way or (2) because others have a liberal moral right (rights-related interest) to the information that information-providers are providing (as well as to the communicator's informing them of any facts that bear on the communicator's credibility in the relevant context). Although some of the problems of using these normative criteria may be reduced by placing the various burdens of proof on the associated factual issues on the "defendant," I recognize not only the difficulty of determining motive, accuracy, good faith, and possibly relevance in such cases but also the danger to liberal values of authorizing courts to resolve such issues in litigative contexts. In any event, this section will proceed on the assumption that no member of a liberal-moral-rights-based society has a moral right to induce its government to make morally-unjustifiable decisions that will drive one or more of its rivals out, deter one or more of its rivals from making an investment in its ARDEPPS, or induce one or more of its rivals to change the location of an extant or future investment to one that will reduce the extent to which the rival is competitive with the actor when the sought-after investment-location shift would be economically inefficient.

On that assumption and the further assumption that predatory participation in government electoral and decisionmaking processes always reduce economic efficiency, the only differences between the analysis of the economic efficiency of a government's expending resources to deter such predatory conduct and the analysis of the economic efficiency of a government's expending resources to deter other types of economically-inefficient antitrust-policy-coverable conduct relate to differences in the evidence that a government must present to win the various subcategories of predation cases. I see no reason to believe that government will be more likely or less likely to win predatory government-(electoral/decisionmaking-process)-participation cases than other kinds of predation cases by using eyewitness testimony, audio recordings, e-mails, firm-meeting minutes, boasts, confessions, etc. The ability of an antitrust-enforcement authority to increase economic efficiency by using the other kinds of evidence that would establish the predatory character of a defendant's participation in a government electoral or decisionmaking process will depend on the allocative cost the government would have to incur to establish with the requisite degree of certainty that (1) the tariff for which a firm argued (A) is allocatively inefficient or morally undesirable and (B) would/did generate outcomes that did/will yield the "arguer" predatory benefits, (2) the quantitative entry-limitations or individual license-application rejections for which a firm argued (A) were/are allocatively inefficient or morally undesirable and (B) did/would yield the "arguer" predatory benefits, (3) the high license-fee (taxi-medallion price) for which the firm argued (A) was/will be allocatively inefficient or morally undesirable and (B) did/will generate effects that yield the "arguer" predatory benefits, (4) the product-safety/other-product-qualiy/environmental-protection/land-use standards or related individual-case resolutions for which the firm argued (A) was/will be allocatively inefficient or morally undesirable and (B) did/will yield the "arguer" predatory benefits, (5) the IP-law provisions or their application to particular IP cases for which a firm argued (A) was/will be allocatively inefficient or morally undesirable and (B) did/will yield the "arguer" predatory benefits, and undoubtedly most problematically (6) a particular political party or political candidate a firm supported did/will increase the amount of benefits the firm will obtain by causing government to make allocatively-inefficient or morally-undesirable decisions that yield the firm benefits by producing the kinds of effects that other forms of predation generate.

I have no expertise in the absolute allocative cost an antitrust-enforcement authority will have to generate (perhaps with the help of other government personnel) to establish the facts it must establish to win a predatory government electoral or decisionmaking process-participation case or the relative magnitude of these costs and their counterparts for the other categories of predatory-conduct cases previously discussed. Of course, the relevant question for current purposes is the frequency with which an antitrust-enforcement authority will be able to establish the facts it must prove to win predatory participation in government electoral or decisionmaking process-participation cases at an allocative cost that is lower than the allocative benefits winning such cases will generate. Unfortunately, I also have no expertise that bears on this issue.

10.2 The Liberal-Moral-Rights-Violativeness of the Different Variants of Predatory Conduct and the Moral Obligation of the Government of a Liberal-Moral-Rights-Based Society to Deter the Different Variants of Such Conduct and to Provide the Victims of Such Conduct With an Appropriate Opportunity to Obtain Legal Redress

10.2.1 The Liberal-Moral-Rights-Violativeness of the Different Variants of Predatory Conduct

With one possible exception, all variants of predatory conduct violate the liberal moral rights of their target, of the customers of their target, and of all other buyers in the ARDEPPS in question on whom such conduct imposes equivalent-dollar losses (by eliminating the target and by raising the prices that the predator and its remaining rivals charge for their products). Predatory conduct fails to treat these victims with appropriate respect or to manifest appropriate concern for their welfare because no moral justification can be supplied for the predator's obtaining gains at these parties' expense. The only possible exception is predatory participation in government electoral or decisionmaking processes by predators that or who disclose their parochial interest in engaging in the relevant participation and participate solely by communicating information to relevant decisionmakers that they in good faith believe to be accurate and relevant, certainly when the decision the relevant information favors is morally defensible from one or more defensible normative perspectives but conceivably even when that decision is not morally defensible from any normative perspective. The last part of the immediately-preceding sentence may be justified because the opposite conclusion would disrespect the information's recipients by manifesting a concern that their receipt of accurate information might lead them to make or support a morally-indefensible decision.

10.2.2 The Duties of the Government of a Liberal-Moral-Rights-Based Society to Deter Predatory Participation in Government-(Electoral and Decisionmaking Processes) and to Provide the Victims of Such Conduct With an Appropriate Opportunity to Obtain Legal Redress

Assuming that the relevant society's resources suffice to enable its government to secure all its members' liberal moral rights, the government of a liberal-moral-rights-based society should do everything in its power to deter predation of all kinds (with the possible exception of some exemplars of predatory government electoral and decisionmaking-process participation) without violating the standard liberal constraints on its acting to achieve any objective. I am uncertain whether the preceding conclusion should be adjusted to take account of the possibility that the prospect of being sued/prosecuted for predation and possibly being erroneously convicted of predation might deter firms from engaging in non-predatory conduct in which they have a moral right to engage when the non-predatory conduct in question might make the enforcement authorities, private plaintiffs, and/or triers-of-fact suspect or conclude that the firms had acted predatorily.

10.3 The Impact of Predatory Conduct on the Instantiation of Various Morally-Defensible Conceptions of the Moral Good and the Ability of the Government of a Liberal-Moral-Rights-Based Society to Secure the Instantiation of Such Conceptions of the Moral Good by Deterring Predatory Conduct

Except in the rare instances in which (put crudely) the owners, creditors, managers, and employees of the predator and its non-targeted in-ARDEPPS rivals are poorer than their counterparts for the targets of the predation and the buyers of the relevant ARDEPPS' products, all categories of predatory conduct will tend to increase the incidence of poverty and material inequality in the society in which the predation is practiced. Moreover, except in a small percentage of the cases in which the predation (1)(A) takes place in an ARDEPPS whose sellers' products are created by QV investments, (B) takes place in a society whose government has not adopted policies to prevent it from devoting too many resources to QV-investment creation from the perspective of economic efficiency, and (C) decreases equilibrium QV investment in the ARDEPPSes in which it is practiced or (2) (A) takes place in an ARDEPPS whose products are discovered production processes, (B) takes place in a society whose government has not adopted policies to prevent it from devoting too few resources to the execution of PPR projects from the perspective of economic efficiency, and (C) increases equilibrium PPR in the ARDEPPS in which it is practiced, predation will always reduce economic efficiency.

Taken together, the conclusions articulated in the preceding two sentences imply that, except in very rare instances, predation will reduce total utility (disserve the instantiation of the utilitarian conception of the moral good) (1) almost always by decreasing economic efficiency and redistributing income undesirably from a utilitarian perspective but occasionally (2) by redistributing income sufficiently undesirably from a utilitarian perspective for this effect to outweigh its increasing economic efficiency or (3) by decreasing economic efficiency sufficiently for this effect to outweigh its redistributing income desirably from a utilitarian perspective.

Moreover, the first sentence of this section implies that, with rare exceptions, predatory conduct will disserve the instantiation of the equal-utility, equal-resource, and various other types of equal-opportunity conceptions of the moral good by increasing material inequality.

10.3.1 The Ability of the Government of a Liberal-Moral-Rights-Based Society to Increase the Extent to Which Various Morally-Defensible Conceptions of the Moral Good Are Instantiated Without Violating Liberal Moral Rights by Deterring Predation and Providing Its Victims With an Appropriate Opportunity to Obtain Legal Redress

The government of any liberal-moral-rights-based society whose resource-limitations are not critical in this regard has a moral duty to deter predation in all ways that do not violate liberal moral rights in other ways and to provide the victims of predation with an appropriate opportunity to obtain legal redress.

This chapter has established (1) that, with limited exceptions, predatory conduct of all kinds is economically inefficient, liberal-moral-rights-violative, and undesirable from the perspective of all the morally-defensible non-liberal egalitarian conceptions of the moral good this study considers and (2) that it will only sometimes be possible for government to increase economic efficiency, secure liberal-moral-rights-related interests, and/or instantiate those various morally-defensible conceptions of the moral good by prohibiting such conduct, prosecuting suspected perpetrators of such conduct, penalizing those convicted of such conduct, and enabling victims of such conduct to obtain legal redress from its perpetrators. These conclusions parallel their Chap. 9 oligopolistic-conduct counterparts.

I want not just to describe the world but to improve it. What is to be done? I fear that the following proposal will appear to reflect and may in fact reflect the Pollyannish hopes and aspirations of a naïve researcher/educator. But I do think that the incidence of undesirable oligopolistic and predatory conduct might be reduced if undergraduate and graduate economics, business, and finance programs included in their required curricula courses that deal with ethical theory in general and business ethics in particular—courses that require students to write papers on the moral desirability of business choices and government economic-policy decisions. In fact, I think that government should try to secure this outcome by conditioning its financial support of institutions of higher learning (not only the grants it gives to their researchers but the tax write-offs it permits their donors to take) on those institutions' including satisfactory courses of this kind in their relevant curricula and enforcing this requirement by inspecting the courses that are taught and certifying their acceptability.

Notes

1. Economists and legal academics who are conversant with economics make at least 4 arguments to justify this conclusion: (1) the argument that predatory pricing will rarely or never be profitable because the direct cost of predatory price-cutting will always be prohibitive (Easterbrook 1981)—an argument I reject because it assumes incorrectly and in some instances implicitly that the predatory price-cut will be across-the-board, that predation can be profitable only for firms with large market shares, that all products in a given "market" are equally competitive, that any rival investment that is made to replace the exited investment will be as competitive with the predator's investments as the target's investment(s) was/were, and that the only way that predation will benefit the predator is to do so directly by driving out the target; (2) the argument that predatory pricing will never or rarely be practiced because it will almost always be less profitable than buying the target (McGee 1958)—an argument I reject because the choice between predatory pricing and buying the target is not an either/or choice and because in many situations the antitrust-law-generated legal costs of the buy-out will be higher than their predatory-pricing counterparts (given the difficulty of proving the predatory character of prices); (3) the very clever argument that predatory pricing will never be profitable because the predatory threat will never be credible in a finite game of complete and perfect information (Selten 1978)—an argument I reject primarily because the relevant players perceive the relevant game not to be finite (but also because I suspect that the relevant players are not so clever as the argument's author); and (4) the argument that predatory pricing will be practiced only by firms with monopoly power when "conditions of entry" are difficult ("barriers to entry are high") (Joskow and Klevorick 1979)—an argument I reject inter alia because (A) a firm without monopoly power may find it profitable to drive out a rival whose operations significantly reduces its BCAs, (B) there is not much of a correlation between the "condition of entry" or "the height of the barriers to entry" and the effectiveness of potential competition, (C) the conclusion ignores the fact that the profitability of predation may also depend on the ability of established rivals to make profitable additional investments in the ARDEPPS in question, (D) the conclusion ignores the fact that predation may also be profitable if any replacement-investment that is made is less competitive with the predator's

project(s) than the target's investment(s) was/were, and (E) the conclusion ignores the fact that a predator may be able to increase the profitability of predatory pricing by replacing the target's investment with an investment of its own. For more detailed discussions of these arguments and my responses to them, see R. Markovits (2014a, pp. 517–530).

I should add that there is an "unrecognized" and unjustified exception to my claims that Industrial Organization economists believe that predatory pricing is rarely if ever practiced: IO economists do believe that (either in all cases or when "barriers to entry" are "moderate to substantial") established firms that confront an "effective potential competitor" (a potential competitor that will enter if nothing is done to prevent its doing so) will respond to this reality by charging lower prices than they would otherwise find profitable and possible to charge (by engaging in what is called "limit pricing") and that this tactic will succeed in deterring entry (Bain 1956; Gaskins 1971). The economists who subscribe to this limit-pricing "theory" do not recognize that it contradicts their claim that sellers rarely if ever practice predatory pricing—more specifically, do not recognize that, if limit pricing were practiced, it would be a variant of predatory pricing. This exception to the IO consensus that predatory pricing is rarely if ever practiced is "unjustified." I believe this to be the case because (1) the standard arguments for the deterrent value of limit pricing are not persuasive, (2) except in rare circumstances—namely, when (A) the relevant established firm fears that the revelation of the profit-potential of the ARDEPPS will induce new investments to be made that will raise the ARDEPPS' investment-quantity above its equilibrium-investment quantity, (B) a relevant individual established firm realizes that it will not be able to compete successfully against the more proficient firms that will invest if the profit-potential of the relevant ARDEPPS is revealed, or (C) (for some reason I cannot imagine) limit pricing that causes the established firms to sacrifice an absolute X% profit-rate will cause the relevant potential entrant to reduce its predicted post-entry-profit-rate estimate by more than absolute X%, limit pricing will be less profitable than allowing entry to occur, and (3) even if limit pricing were more profitable than allowing entry to occur, it would usually be less profitable for the established firms than making one or more (limit) investments that would deter entry. For more detailed discussions, see R. Markovits (2014a, pp. 517–518) and R. Markovits (2014b pp. 221–232).

2. I wrote "suspect" because, like the IO economists I am criticizing, I am basing my conclusion on theoretical analyses of the profitability of predatory pricing rather than on direct evidence of the practice of predatory pricing. For my theoretical analyses, see. R. Markovits (2014a, pp. 503–517) and the text of this study that immediately follows the paragraph to which this footnote is attached.
3. The amount by which the predator is worse-than-privately-second-placed to supply a buyer its target is privately-best-placed to supply equals the amount by which the predator's basic competitive disadvantage (BCD) in relation to the

relevant buyer exceeds the BCD of the buyer's privately-second-placed supplier *plus* the amount by which the contextual marginal costs the predator would have to incur to match the target's HNOP-containing offer (usually because the predator's matching offer would be discriminatory) exceeds the CMCs that the buyer's privately-second-placed supplier would have to incur to match the HNOP-containing offer of the predator's targets.

4. To be somewhat more precise, for individualized predatory pricing to be most cost-effective, the predator should (1) determine the dollar-loss it must inflict on its target to drive it out, (2) rank each of its target's customers by the (dollar-loss inflicted) to (dollar-loss incurred) ratio associated with the predator's stealing that customer, and (3) proceed to "steal" customers in this list in the order of their (dollar-loss-inflicted)-to-(dollar-loss-incurred)-ratio ranking until the requisite dollar-loss has been inflicted. The relevant determinants are those that affect the above ratios. The preceding analysis assumes that the target will not retain the buyers the predator is charging predatory prices by revising its initial offers to them or that any such ability the target has will not critically affect the predator's calculations (which is not likely).
5. For an analysis of the relationship between this point and the "X-inefficiency" claim to which it is related (i.e., for a critique of the relevant aspects of the X-inefficiency literature), see footnote 4 of Chap. 9.
6. The government of a liberal-moral-rights-based society has a moral duty to provide victims of predation with an appropriate opportunity to obtain legal redress even when its doing so is not economically efficient.
7. In some passages, Joskow and Klevorick limit this claim to post-entry price-cuts to below-average-total-cost prices that cannot be attributed to the presence of "substantial excess production capacity" that was not created to deter entry—see Joskow and Klevorick (1979, pp. 252–254).
8. Thus, if a firm's "dominance" is defined in terms of its market share, the determination of a firm's dominance would be rendered arbitrary by the inevitable arbitrariness of market definitions. And if a firm's "dominance" is defined in terms of its securing supra-competitive outcomes, the determination of its dominance (1) would be rendered arbitrary by the inevitable arbitrariness of the choice of the metrics one uses to define (A) the supra-competitiveness of a firm's price, (B) the supra-competitiveness of a firm's profits, and (C) the overall supra-competitiveness of a firm's outcomes as a function of the supra-competitiveness of its prices and profits and (2) would be rendered highly-allocative-costly by the allocative cost of determining prices, marginal costs, investment, and actual and normal rates-of-return. For more detail, see Chap. 7 supra.
9. The "spite" possibility requires further analysis. I will address 3 matters. First, I want to point out that conduct that is motivated by spite may or may not confer on the price-cutter the benefits that predatory price-cutting confers on predatory pricers because price-cutters whose price-cutting is motivated by a desire to inflict harm on the target for the sake of doing so may find it desirable to do so even when it is not "monetarily" profitable to do so—even when the price they

charge does not benefit them in the ways that predatory pricing benefits its practitioners or does not do so sufficiently to be rendered monetarily profitable. Second, I want to raise a definitional question: Should conduct committed by actors that realized or should have realized that its ex ante profitability was critically raised by those of its effects that normally render conduct "predatory" be classified as "predatory" if its perpetrator would have engaged in the conduct even if it believed that it would have been monetarily unprofitable? Third, I want to address the liberal moral status of spite-motivated conduct: Does conduct that is motivated by a desire to inflict losses on another violate the basic liberal moral duty to treat other moral-rights bearers with equal, appropriate respect and to show appropriate concern for their welfare? I suspect that, to conclude that a particular exemplar of spite-motivated conduct did not violate the liberal moral rights of its target, one must find (1) that the "spite-indulger" (say, "avenger") did appropriate research into the moral character of its target's conduct, (2) that the "avenger" concluded that its target had violated the liberal moral rights (preferably) of the "avenger," (less preferably) of one or more intimates of the "avenger," or (least preferably) of one or more "strangers" to the "avenger," and (3) that it was morally acceptable for the avenger to engage in this type of self-help as opposed to (A) denouncing the perceived wrongdoer, (B) (when possible) going to law or encouraging and possibly helping its relevant intimates or relevant strangers to go to law, or (C) (when possible) bringing the matter to the government's attention and urging and helping it to take legal action. We are entering deep and turbulent waters that I may not be well-placed to navigate. My somewhat-conservative disposition and legal training incline me to conclude that, although it would be morally desirable for individuals to denounce liberal-moral-rights violators and encourage others to do so, to sue them if one was their victim, to encourage and help other victims to sue them, and to petition and help the government to act against them, other avenging acts are liberal-moral-rights-violative. (I am ignoring the argument that when the seller is not a self-owned/self-managed company an individual manager's or employee's engaging in conventionally-unprofitable predatory pricing to satisfy his or her desire to inflict losses on the target would violate his or her liberal moral obligation to the company's shareholders and possibly to its creditors unless the CEO or other relevant officer of the company was informed of the actor's intentions and authorized the actor to proceed as part of the actor's wage-package.)

10. Although I question these assumptions' accuracy, the text assumes that owners of goods really do secure a one-equivalent-dollar gain for each dollar by which a product-image-enhancing advertizement increases their valuation of a product they own and that product-image advertizing does not generate equivalent-dollar losses by making the relevant society's members and participants more image-conscious.
11. Although I question these assumptions' accuracy, the text assumes that owners of goods really do secure a one-equivalent-dollar loss for each dollar by which a product-image-denigrating advertizement decreases their valuation of a

product they own and that such advertizements do not affect economic efficiency by influencing the extent to which the relevant society's members and participants are image-conscious.

12. Three points need to be noted. First, the text's conclusions about the economic efficiency of the various possible effects that predatory advertizing can have on equilibrium QV investment or equilibrium PPR in any ARDEPPS in which it is practiced assumes that the government of the relevant society has not adopted other policies to prevent its economy's allocating too many resources to QV-investment creation and too few to PPR execution from the perspective of economic efficiency. Second, the impact of predatory advertizing on equilibrium investment in any ARDEPPS in which it is practice is uncertain. Third, I suspect that the percentage of predatory-advertizing conduct that involves goods created by QV investments as opposed to production processes is far higher than the percentage of the resources devoted to QV-investment creation and PPR execution that is devoted to QV-investment creation. This last claim reflects the fact that images are less-important components of production processes than of QV-investment-created goods (at least when the production process' environmental soundness is not an issue) and my belief that buyers of production processes are better-informed and less misleadable than buyers of the goods created by QV investments.
13. I acknowledge that the text is assuming that on balance the decisions that the sellers in any ARDEPPS succeed in getting a government to make (because they are in the sellers' parochial interests) will be economically inefficient.
14. In the literature, some of these methods of unfair competition are denominated "conduct that is designed to 'raise rivals' costs.'" I should acknowledge that some exemplars of at least two other categories of predatory conduct I distinguish—predatory participation in government-decisionmaking processes and predatory refusals to deal—could also be placed in the "predatory unfair competition" category.
15. The conditions that must be satisfied for single-brand exclusive dealerships to secure predatory objectives must also be satisfied for full-requirements tie-ins or refusals to deal to secure such objectives.
16. For more detailed explanations of the functions that vertical territorial restraints, other sorts of vertical customer-allocation clauses, and single-brand exclusive dealerships can perform, see R. Markovits (2014b, pp. 339–344) and Sects. 13.3 and 13.5 infra.
17. I should add that it might be more descriptive to denominate those employment-contracts that contain provisions that deserve to be called "predatory" "agreements not to compete," though that designation might not accurately reflect the legitimacy of the rest of the agreement in question.
18. It might be more descriptive to denominate those partnership-agreements that contain provisions that deserve to be called "predatory" "agreements not to compete," though that designation might not accurately reflect the legitimacy of the rest of the agreement in question. I should add that decisions by one partner to place such restrictions on one or more other partners when the restricting

partner was not similarly restricted would belong in the second subcategory of refusal-to-deal-related decisions I have distinguished. The analysis of the predatoriness of such unidirectional restrictions is the same as the analysis of the reciprocal restrictions analyzed in the text.

References

A. A. Poultry Farms, Inc. v. Rose Acre Farms, Inc., 881 F. 2d 1396 (7th Cir. 1989).

Areeda, P & Turner, D. (1978). Antitrust Law. Little Brown.

Bain, J. S. (1956). *Barriers to new competition*. Harvard University Press.

Baumol, W. (1979). Quasi-permanence of price reductions: A policy for prevention of predatory pricing. *Yale Law Journal, 89*, 1–26.

Brooke Group Ltd. v. Brown and Williamson Tobacco Corp., 509 U.S. 209 (1993).

Easterbrook, F. (1981). Predatory strategies and counterstrategies. *University of Chicago Law Review, 48*, 263–337.

Galbraith, J. K. (1951). *The theory of countervailing power*. Harvard University Press.

Gaskins, D. (1971). Dynamic limit pricing: Optimal limit pricing under threat of entry. *Journal of Economic Theory, 3*, 306–322.

Joskow, P., & Klevorick, A. (1979). A framework for analyzing predatory pricing policy. *Yale Law Journal, 89*, 213–270.

Markovits, R. (2014a). *Economics and the interpretation and application of U.S. and E.U. antitrust law* Vol. I *Basic concepts and economics-based legal analyses of oligopolistic and predatory conduct*. Springer.

Markovits, R. (2014b). *Economics and the interpretation and application of U.S. and E.U. antitrust law* Vol. II *Economics-based legal analyses of mergers, vertical practices, and joint ventures*. Springer.

McGee, J. (1958). Predatory price cutting: The Standard Oil (N.J.) case. *Journal of Law and Economics, 1*, 137–169.

Selten, R. (1978). *The Chain Store Paradox: Theory and Decision, 9*, 127–159.

Utah Pie Co. v. Continental Baking Co., 386 U.S. 685 (1967).

Williamson, O. (1977). Predatory pricing: A strategic and welfare analysis. *Yale Law Journal, 87*, 284–340.

MIX
Papier aus verantwortungsvollen Quellen
Paper from responsible sources
FSC® C105338

If you have any concerns about our products,
you can contact us on
ProductSafety@springernature.com

In case Publisher is established outside the EU,
the EU authorized representative is:
Springer Nature Customer Service Center GmbH
Europaplatz 3, 69115 Heidelberg, Germany

Printed by Libri Plureos GmbH
in Hamburg, Germany